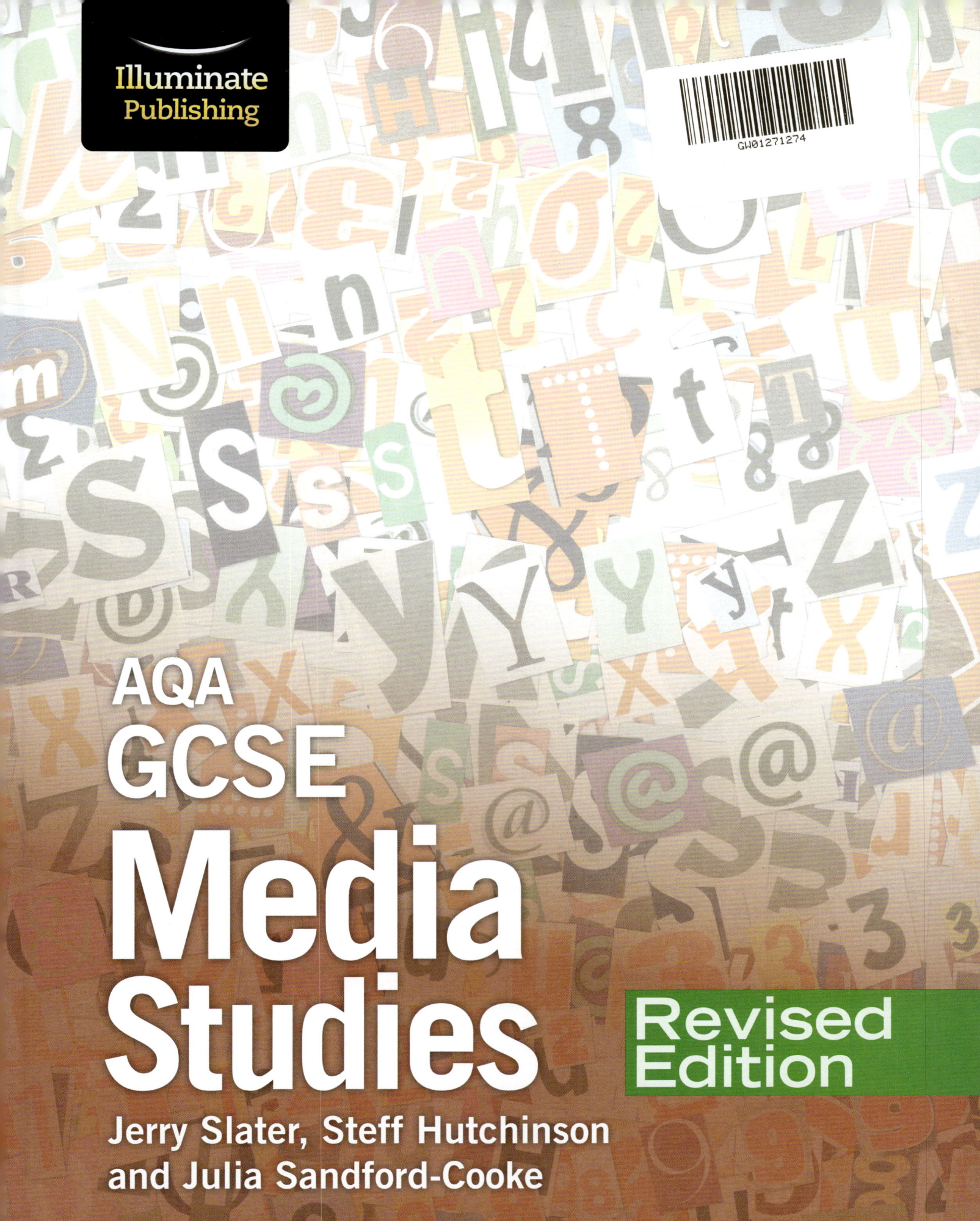

Published in 2022 by Illuminate Publishing Limited, an imprint of Hodder Education, an Hachette UK Company, Carmelite House, 50 Victoria Embankment, London EC4Y 0DZ

Orders: Please visit www.illuminatepublishing.com
or email sales@illuminatepublishing.com

© Jerry Slater, Steff Hutchinson and Julia Sandford-Cooke 2022

The moral rights of the authors have been asserted.

All rights reserved. No part of this book may be reprinted, reproduced or utilised in any form or by any electronic, mechanical, or other means, now known or hereafter invented, including photocopying and recording, or in any information storage and retrieval system, without permission in writing from the publishers.

British Library Cataloguing-in-Publication Data

A catalogue record for this book is available from the British Library

ISBN 978-1-913963-26-2

Printed in Wales by Cambrian Ltd

03.22

The publisher's policy is to use papers that are natural, renewable and recyclable products made from wood grown in sustainable forests. The logging and manufacturing processes are expected to conform to the environmental regulations of the country of origin.

Every effort has been made to contact copyright holders of material produced in this book. Great care has been taken by the authors and publisher to ensure that either formal permission has been granted for the use of copyright material reproduced, or that copyright material has been used under the provision of fair dealing guidelines in the UK – specifically that it has been used sparingly, solely for the purpose of criticism and review, and has been properly acknowledged. If notified, the publisher will be pleased to rectify any errors or omissions at the earliest opportunity.

Editor: Dawn Booth
Design and layout: Kamae Design
Cover design: Nigel Harriss
Cover image: Dinga / Shutterstock

All weblinks are correct at time of going to press. AQA have not approved these external links.

**Acknowledgement**
Many thanks to Shirley Slater for her help in the preparation of this book.

### Approval message from AQA

This textbook has been approved by AQA for use with our qualification. This means that we have checked that it broadly covers the specification and we are satisfied with the overall quality. Full details of our approval process can be found on our website.

We approve textbooks because we know how important it is for teachers and students to have the right resources to support their teaching and learning. However, the publisher is ultimately responsible for the editorial control and quality of this book.

Please note that when teaching the GCSE Media Studies course, you must refer to AQA's specification as your definitive source of information. While this book has been written to match the specification, it cannot provide complete coverage of every aspect of the course.

A wide range of other useful resources can be found on the relevant subject pages of our website: www.aqa.org.uk.

# Contents

## How to use this book — 5
Introduction — 5

## 1 Media Language — 8
How the media communicate meanings — 8
**CASE STUDY:** Front page analysis: the *Daily Mirror* and the *Sun* — 25
Narrative — 29
**CASE STUDY:** Narrative analysis of *Tatler*, including reference to Propp's character types — 33
**CASE STUDY:** Narrative evaluation and analysis of the pre-title sequence of 'The City of Magpies' — 34
Genre — 36
**CASE STUDY:** 'An Unearthly Child' — 44

## 2 Media Representations — 48
The construction of reality — 48
Who do the media represent? — 50
What do the media represent? — 56
Stereotypes — 58
**CASE STUDY:** Advertising and marketing – NHS Blood and Transplant online campaign video 'Represent' featuring Lady Leshurr — 61
Representing values and beliefs — 62
**CASE STUDY:** Marcus Rashford (2023 CSP) — 65
Representations of reality — 67
Focus topic: gender — 72
**CASE STUDY:** Tomb Raider/Lara Croft GO and other video games — 77
Putting representation in context — 79
**CASE STUDY:** The teenager — 80
**CASE STUDY:** *His Dark Materials* and *Doctor Who* — 84

## 3 Media Audiences — 87
Why study audiences? — 87
Defining the audience — 88
Categorising the audience — 89
Psychographics — 92
Who does audience research? — 93
Audience theories — 95
**CASE STUDY:** Newspaper 2023 CSP: the 'Amazon shops' story in *The Times* and the *Daily Mirror* — 103
**CASE STUDY:** The Whovians — 108
**CASE STUDY:** Arctic Monkeys — 108
Reaching the interactive audience — 109

## 4 Media Industries — 110
Introduction — 110
**CASE STUDY:** The UK newspaper industry — 116
**CASE STUDY:** The film industry — 123
**CASE STUDY:** Radio: key events in the development of radio 1967–2021 — 130
**CASE STUDY:** UK television: today's viewing landscape — 135
**CASE STUDY:** Music videos — 140
**CASE STUDY:** Video games — 145

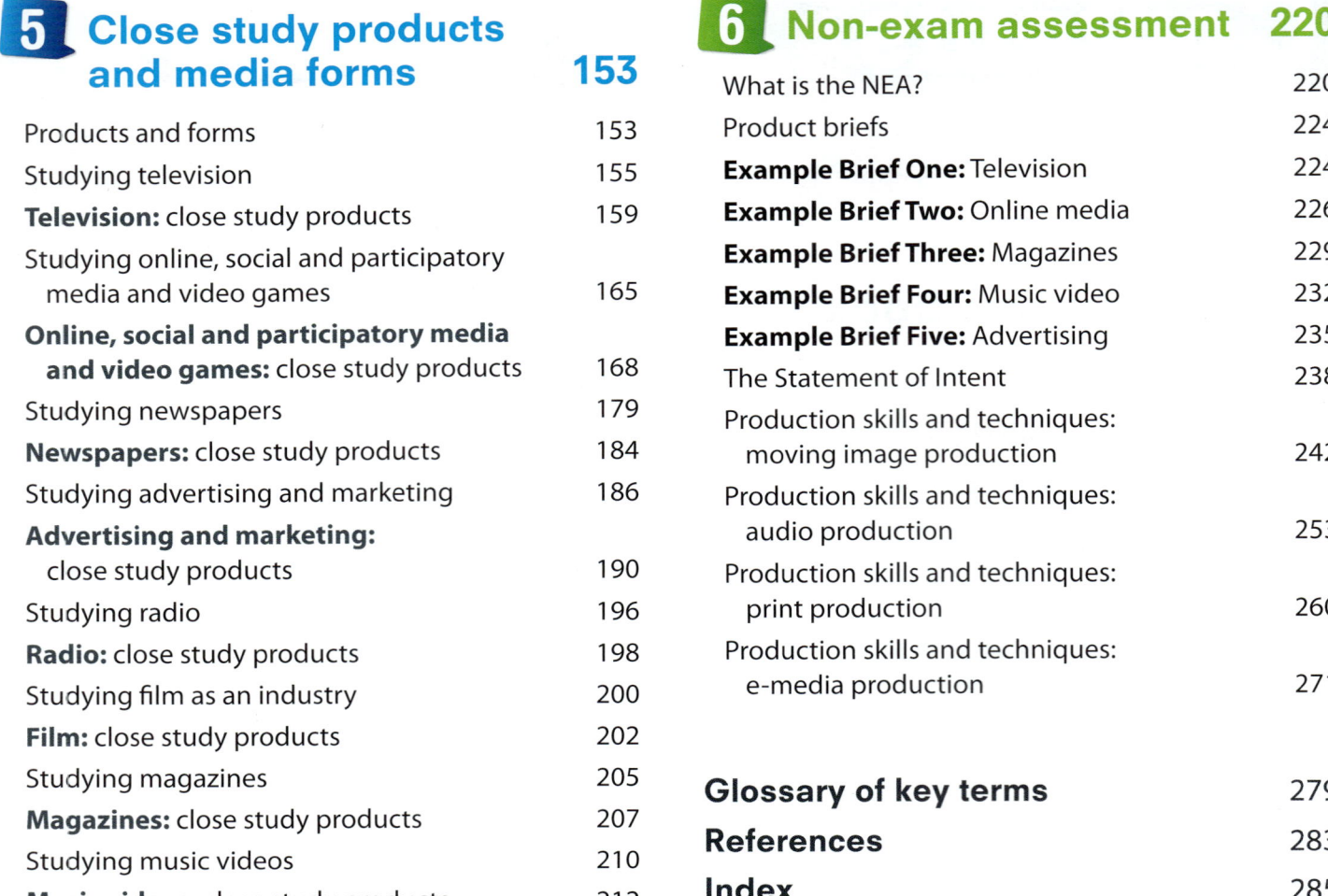

## 5 Close study products and media forms — 153

| | |
|---|---|
| Products and forms | 153 |
| Studying television | 155 |
| **Television:** close study products | 159 |
| Studying online, social and participatory media and video games | 165 |
| **Online, social and participatory media and video games:** close study products | 168 |
| Studying newspapers | 179 |
| **Newspapers:** close study products | 184 |
| Studying advertising and marketing | 186 |
| **Advertising and marketing:** close study products | 190 |
| Studying radio | 196 |
| **Radio:** close study products | 198 |
| Studying film as an industry | 200 |
| **Film:** close study products | 202 |
| Studying magazines | 205 |
| **Magazines:** close study products | 207 |
| Studying music videos | 210 |
| **Music videos:** close study products | 212 |

## 6 Non-exam assessment — 220

| | |
|---|---|
| What is the NEA? | 220 |
| Product briefs | 224 |
| **Example Brief One:** Television | 224 |
| **Example Brief Two:** Online media | 226 |
| **Example Brief Three:** Magazines | 229 |
| **Example Brief Four:** Music video | 232 |
| **Example Brief Five:** Advertising | 235 |
| The Statement of Intent | 238 |
| Production skills and techniques: moving image production | 242 |
| Production skills and techniques: audio production | 253 |
| Production skills and techniques: print production | 260 |
| Production skills and techniques: e-media production | 271 |

| | |
|---|---|
| **Glossary of key terms** | 279 |
| **References** | 283 |
| **Index** | 285 |
| **Acknowledgements** | 287 |

# How to use this book

## Introduction

The media are so important in today's world that it makes a lot of sense to take a course in media studies. It will help you to understand more about yourself as a media user and more about the important role that the media play in society and culture.

You should have a lot of fun and creative satisfaction in planning and making your own media products. You will also gain insights into the power and influence of the media and an ability to analyse media products from different points of view.

This is a textbook, so its most important job is to help you and your teacher make sure that your course leads to GCSE Media Studies success. Just as importantly, though, we hope that this book opens your mind to some new ideas, new interests and new opportunities.

It may be that you discover fascinating areas of the media that are new to you, or perhaps develop a passion for some practical or creative skill. It could be that you get some ideas for future studies, jobs you'd like to do or ideas that you would like to explore in greater depth. We'd like to think that you'll get more out of your course of study and this book than just 'a load of stuff you have to remember'; we hope you enjoy it.

## Getting to know the theoretical framework and CSPs

This book closely follows the AQA specification, as you would expect. It will help you to use the book if you are familiar with the language and structure of the specification. Media studies has been broken down into four major categories, called the theoretical framework. They are:

**Media Language (Chapter 1)**
This chapter explores the ways in which media products make meanings. You will learn how to analyse all sorts of media products such as moving images, print and advertisements. One of the book's main themes is introduced here: the ongoing digital revolution that is transforming the relationship between the media and us.

### Media Representations (Chapter 2)
This chapter looks at who and what get included in media products, how they are shown (or represented) and who gets left out. Stereotypes, values, issues and beliefs are all considered, as well as how you can use the opportunity to represent yourself using social media.

### Media Audiences (Chapter 3)
In this chapter the ways that audiences are categorised and counted are explored, mainly so that media products can be targeted at specific audiences. The many ideas and discussions about the effects that the media may or may not have on audiences are also considered.

### Media Industries (Chapter 4)
Most media products are expensive to make and distribute to their audiences. This means that the great majority of media is produced by very large companies and corporations. This chapter explains the ways in which these giant organisations work in a series of case studies that compare and contrast different sectors of the media.

Early mobile phone? Studying historical contexts can help us understand today's media.

Of course, these four framework areas are very closely linked, and it is difficult to consider them in isolation. To show how they work together, you will study a selection of close study products (CSPs) from a range of different media forms. Some are studies in great depth, that is, in relation to all four of the framework areas. Some are targeted, which means that you only need to study them in relation to one or two of the framework areas. All this is explained in detail at the beginning of Chapter 5, the CSP chapter. You will probably need to hop into Chapter 5 frequently, even before you have worked your way through the first four chapters. Throughout the book, you will find plenty of *links* that will help to show how CSPs and the framework fit together.

All the CSPs for 2023 are discussed in Chapter 5. If you are studying for the exam at a later date, you may find that a few have changed, as the CSPs will be reviewed annually. The specific editions of the two newspaper CSPs will certainly change every year. Any new CSPs will be studied and assessed in exactly the same way, so it is worth familiarising yourself with as many examples as possible.

## Important contexts of the media

This is a third component of the AQA specification. When you study a CSP or a framework area, you will need to think about a least one of the following contexts: historical, political, social and cultural.

To make sure that you get a sense of the historical background, at least a few of the CSPs will always be several decades old. In this book, for example, you will look at an advert from the 1950s and a radio show from the 1960s. The idea is that studying these historical media products helps you, by making comparisons, to understand today's media.

There aren't any separate chapters devoted to these contexts, but they run like a thread through the first five chapters. There are plenty of examples to show how contexts should be brought into your study of the media. You will soon get used to thinking about these.

## Coursework

Chapter 6 deals with coursework, which is called non-exam assessment (NEA). You will find plenty of advice about how to plan and produce you own media product. The weighting of this component is 30%, so you will need to make sure that you are well prepared for this practical element of the course. As this chapter explains, AQA provides a new set of briefs every year. These are the detailed instructions, the designated purpose and the target audience for each one of the range of scenarios. Chapter 6 works through a number of these briefs as examples, but the advice is general. That is, you are shown how to produce a successful media product in different media forms: video, audio, print and web-based.

Create your own media products

## The exam

There is a free downloadable chapter available under the 'Resources and Downloads' tab on the following Illuminate webpage: illuminatepublishing.com/AQA_Media_GCSE_RevEd_ExamChapter.

This chapter will look at the structure of the exam papers, examples of questions and some 'right and wrong' techniques in answering them.

**NB: This exam chapter is not approved by AQA.**

## Help along the way

Throughout the book you will find Quick questions, Tips, Activities and discussion points called Talk about it. If you can follow these up, ideally with others in your media studies class, you will find that the information and skills are much more likely to remain in your head. Your teacher is certain to provide you with more activities and examples, so that soon, we hope, you will be asking your own questions about the media in your life.

Lastly, there is a Glossary (a list) of key terms. Like all subjects, media studies has its own set of specialist words and you will be expected to use this terminology. The key terms in the chapters should give you a confident understanding of this vocabulary and the Glossary will be handy when you need to look anything up or learn the terms and concepts.

The authors of this book wish you good luck, enjoyment and success in your media studies course.

# 1 Media Language

### What's in this chapter?

- As you would expect in a chapter called Media Language, you will be looking at some of the ways in which the media communicates in the same ways as a language.
- This chapter introduces you to many of the key terms and concepts that you'll need when it comes to doing one of the most interesting things in media studies: the practical analysis of media products such as television programmes, video games, newspapers, magazines and advertisements.

## How the media communicate meanings

### The linear model

The introduction to this book gave some idea of what the mass media are and you can now start asking some more questions. For example:

- What do the mass media do?
- How do they do it?

The answer to the first question is fairly straightforward. You can simply say that the mass media communicate to a very large number of people. Then we could add that they usually do this in a short space of time by using a range of technologies. Some are lightning fast such as the internet, live television and radio, while some are relatively slow such as the print media. How is this done? That's media language.

Later in the book you will be looking in more detail at the ways in which different media technologies communicate, but in this chapter the focus is a little different. Here, you will be exploring some basics of communication. If the mass media are all about communication, then they must be able to make meanings and audiences must be able to understand these meanings. But how does this process work? How do we manage to communicate meaningfully with each other?

# 1 Media Language

**Sender » Message » Receiver**

Above is a very basic diagram or **model** of the communication process. If someone speaks to you, they are the sender, what they say to you is the message and you are the receiver.

Just as easily, you could apply this model to a mass media example:

| Sender | Message | Receiver |
|--------|---------|----------|
| BBC | Episode of *EastEnders* | All the viewers of this episode |

In this simple and straightforward model, the sender creates the message and then pushes it towards the receiver (in this case by transmitting it as a television programme). Anyone who has the correct receiving equipment (a television set, a computer, a smartphone) can view this message and become a receiver.

This creates a view of communication in which a message travels along a line. The sender is at the beginning of the line and the receiver is at the end of the line. That's why it is called a **linear model of communication**.

How helpful is this linear model in understanding the mass media?

- It has the advantage of simplicity.
- It can be a useful way to describe important elements of communication.

Also, it does seem to make the senders all-important. They are the ones who plan and create the message and find a way of sending it on its way to the receiver. All the receiver has to do is just watch or read or listen.

As it stands, the linear model doesn't quite capture the **interactive** part of communication. Even when having a chat with a friend, we don't just passively receive messages and then switch roles to actively send messages. A conversation involves both people contributing all the time. Even when you are not speaking you are nodding, frowning, smiling or making noises such as 'Mmm' and 'Uh huh'.

### Key term

**Model**
A model seeks to capture an idea or concept in a simplified form, often as a graphic or diagram.

### Quick question 1.1

In your classroom are you more likely to be a sender or a receiver?

### Activity 1.1

The following list contains six senders, six messages and six receivers. Identify which is which and link them together. For example: Charles Dickens (sender), *Oliver Twist* (message) and Book readers (receiver).

Internet surfers
Charles Dickens
*The Grand Tour*
Book readers
Radio 1
Reach
*Oliver Twist*
Radio listeners
*Nick Grimshaw Show*
Newspaper readers
*Sunday Mirror*
Amazon Prime subscribers
Twitter follower
DMG media
MailOnline
Amazon video
Twitter user
A tweet

Facial expressions and gestures are important signs in interactive communication.

### Key term

**Interactivity**
Two-way communication in which the participants both actively engage in the process.

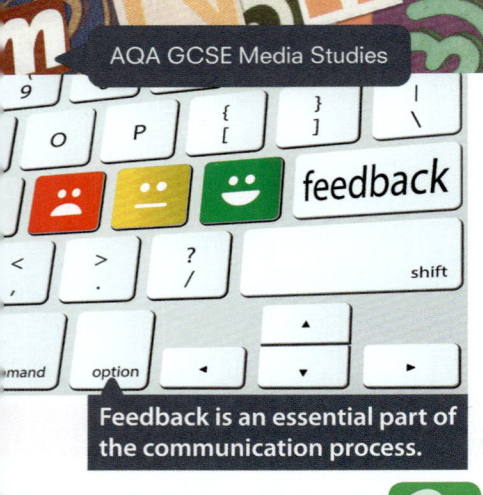

Feedback is an essential part of the communication process.

## Quick question 1.2

Have you ever used social media to give feedback to a media producer?

### Key terms

**Semiotics**
The use and study of signs, sign systems and their meanings. Also known as semiology.

**Conventions**
Established rules or shared understandings are used in media products as 'the way we do things'. Conventions are more likely to be taken for granted than formally stated.

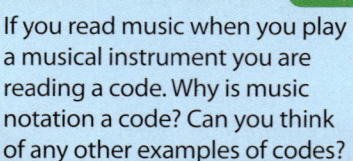

## Quick question 1.3

If you read music when you play a musical instrument you are reading a code. Why is music notation a code? Can you think of any other examples of codes?

The same is true to some extent of mass media communication. Receivers use social media to comment on films, videos, games, television and music. Receivers are often encouraged to provide feedback in which they react to the content of messages to express an opinion or a comment. So, the idea of communication simply going in one direction along a straight line is limited, to say the least.

Another difficulty for the linear model is that it doesn't tell you much about the messages themselves. As media studies students, you want to know all about those messages, not just how they are sent and received but what is in them and, above all, what they mean.

## How are meanings made?

This really is one of the key questions in media studies. It's also quite a difficult question and in order to get to grips with it you need to move beyond the linear model to a rather different approach called **semiotics**.

A starting point is the idea of a **code**. You have probably played about with secret codes at some stage in your lives. In stories (often spy stories) the secret code contains some information that has been put into a form that is inaccessible to everyone, unless they have the specific knowledge that enables them to crack the code. By using a secret code, the sender of the message has made it completely meaningless to anyone except a receiver who has the key to that secret code. Sometimes, clever outsiders are able to crack the codes by working out the patterns and rules in the jumble of letters or numbers or shapes. Secret codes are popular in adventure stories because people have a fascination with the idea of messages with meanings that are locked away and hidden from them.

This familiar idea of the secret code is a useful starting point as you begin to explore semiotics and codes.

A code is a communication system with the following three elements:

- **SIGNS** – anything that expresses a meaning is a sign. This could be a written or spoken word, an image, a sound, a gesture or an item of clothing.

- **RULES** – signs are nearly always used in combination with other signs to create meanings. For example, the words in a sentence are organised together using rules. For a language such as English we call these rules 'grammar'. In media studies the rules are called **conventions**.

- **SHARED UNDERSTANDING** – just like the secret code discussed earlier, a code only works when people share a knowledge and understanding of the rules and signs. Of course, most codes aren't secret at all; all of us use and understand numerous different codes.

The title of this chapter, 'Media Language', suggests that the media create meanings in the same way as languages such as English, German or Chinese do. This is because these languages are codes, each with their signs, rules and shared understanding. The mass media also have many codes that work in a similar way.

Top secret job: women were employed as code breakers during World War II.

At this stage, you are going to take a short diversion away from the media to have a look at the English language as a code.

The signs of English are words (or parts of words) that can be spoken or written. There are over 170,000 English words, but most of us get by with a vocabulary of about 3,000 words. However, we need to know a lot more about these words than just their simple dictionary definitions. Once you are over the age of two, people get a bit bored with you pointing at things and telling them what they are: 'Lorry', 'Tree', 'Cat'. As we get older we need more sophisticated ways of communicating.

Beyond the age of two (or thereabouts) you need to start putting words together to make more complex meanings such as 'I feel sick' and 'I don't like carrots'. You soon learn that words can't be put together randomly ('Carrots don't like I'). A set of rules has to be used that are shared by all speakers of English. These rules are the grammar of the language.

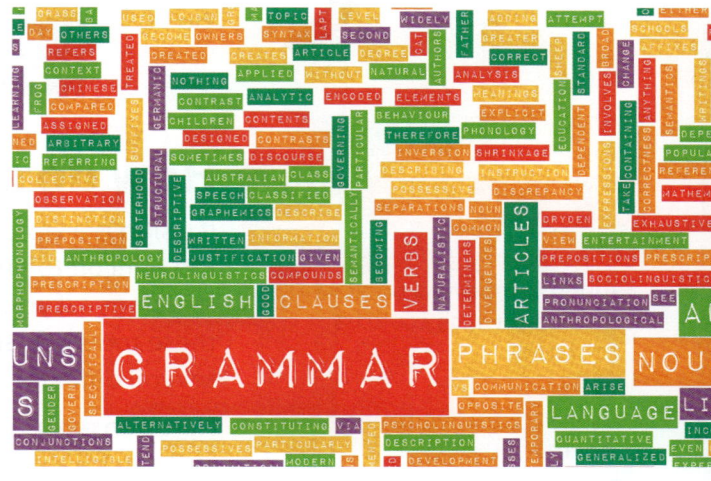

The interesting thing about these rules of grammar is that nobody ever tries to teach them to us as pre-schoolers. They don't have to be formally taught because we just pick them up without thinking about them. When we speak or write, listen or read we are not even aware that we are applying these rules. For many of us we only start to think about the rules of language when we have English language lessons at school or when we try to learn another language and have to work things out, like whether to put adjectives before or after nouns and how to change a verb to the past tense.

Most codes, including media codes, work just like this. We don't really think about the rules, we just use them all the time as we create meanings by putting signs together or by understanding signs used by other people.

Remember the last key element of the code? It is 'shared knowledge and understanding'. The English language is a code that is shared by a lot of people: over 1,500 million including 375 million native speakers (those for whom English is their first language). Within this very large group of people, there are many sub-groups: people who speak different variants of English and people who only speak English in a particular context such as medicine, for example.

**English-speaking countries**

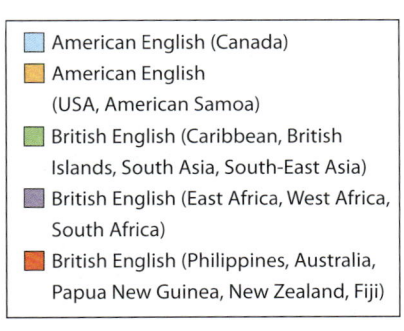

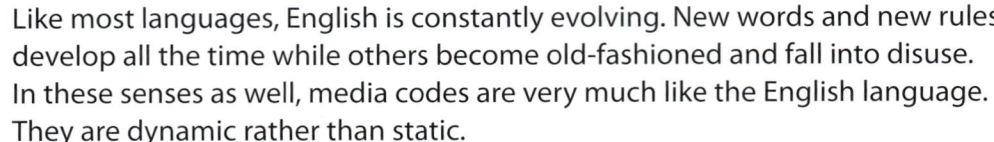

Like most languages, English is constantly evolving. New words and new rules develop all the time while others become old-fashioned and fall into disuse. In these senses as well, media codes are very much like the English language. They are dynamic rather than static.

As media studies students, you will be learning how the codes of media work to create meanings. In some ways, it will be a bit like learning a new language, as we delve into the signs, the rules and our shared knowledge and understandings.

HANGRY – a state of anger caused by lack of food. A recent addition to the ever-changing English language.

**Key terms**

**Ambiguous/Ambiguity**
A sign with several possible meanings which could be confused.

**Context**
Used in two ways in media studies:
1 The immediate surroundings of something, like the other words in a sentence providing a context for each individual word.
2 The wider social, cultural, political or historical circumstances of a media product or process.

## How do signs create meaning?

If a sign is a word and you don't know the meaning of that word, then it isn't too difficult to find out the meaning. You could ask someone, do an online search or – if you were really desperate – look it up in a dictionary. Even with all these tools and solutions to hand we can still make mistakes. Many words have several different meanings. These words are **ambiguous**.

Here's an example. The word 'jars' can mean a number of glass containers or it can be a version of the verb to jar, meaning to send a shock through something. This ambiguity doesn't usually cause problems because of the context of the surrounding words:

- 'Put the jam *jars* in the cupboard.'
- 'She *jars* her elbow every time she plays tennis.'

So, **context** is a very important way of pinning down the meaning of an individual sign, in this case the ambiguous word 'jars'.

Moving from language to other codes, you will find that the meanings of signs are not at all as cut and dried as the meanings of words. A photograph can be very meaningful but you can't look up its meaning in a dictionary.

As users of the mass media, we are active users of many codes and countless signs. As well as written and spoken language, the media communicate with us using still and moving images, colours, sounds, music, fashion, behaviour, facial expressions and so on. How are we able to make sense of all these signs and all the rules that apply to them?

**Tip**

For examples of different cultural codes check out the HSBC Funny Culture adverts on YouTube.

The answer is that you store meanings in your heads. As you grow up you learn the meanings of words and the rules of language. In the same way, you learn the meanings of media codes. The learning curve is very steep at first but you never reach a point where everything is known. You keep on learning what signs and codes mean for the rest of your life.

Just as there are many different human languages, there are many variants of media codes. How do you know which ones to learn? Well, you don't really have to make any decisions, you just pick up the codes that surround you. Different cultures have different codes. If you move between cultures you will observe the codes and gradually begin to pick up the meanings of signs and rules as you begin to unlock new codes.

As media studies students, you have to look at these codes rather differently. Instead of relying on the instant 'meaning grab' that you do as you watch a film or read a magazine, you have to learn how to dissect media products to find out how they work and how they communicate meanings.

## Semiotics

The main toolkit used for dissecting and analysing media products is called semiotics.

As already discussed, the basic unit of communication is the **sign**. Semiotics is an approach to studying these signs and the systems of rules, the **codes**, which link these signs together to create meanings.

A basic principle of semiotics is that a sign always has two components: the **signifier** and the **signified**:

- Signifier: the *form* of the sign – something that can be seen, heard or touched.
- Signified: the *meaning* of the sign – it exists only in your head.

The best way to understand the difference between the signifier and the signified is to look at some examples.

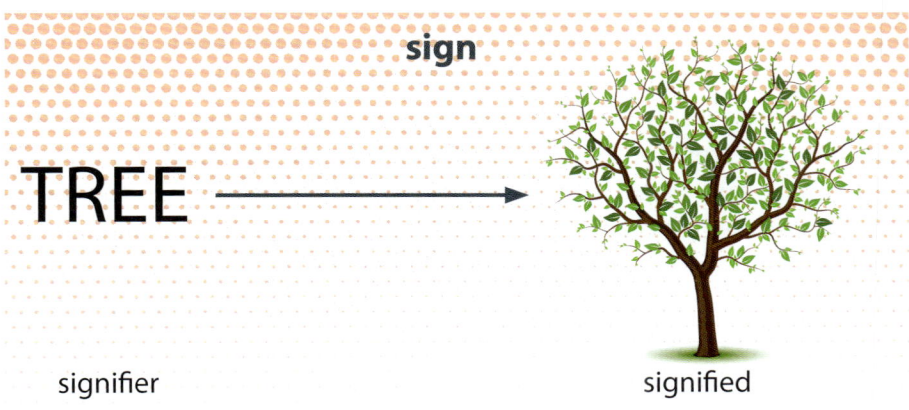

Credit: Chapter Agency Ltd

The 2019 print advert for Halfords features a photomontaged image of a car wheel trim and a medal ribbon. Let's concentrate on that image first. What you see is a signifier: some coloured ink on a page in a very distinctive shape. If you are looking at the image on a screen you see a light pattern in that same distinctive shape. There is something physical to look at but it is not, of course, a real wheel trim and medal ribbon. What you are looking at is a signifier.

As you look at this shape, a very rapid act of interpretation goes on in your head. This is a shape that matches things you have seen before – the individual parts and the overall shape are familiar and recognisable. Now you can attach a meaning to the signifier: it is a service medal incorporating a car wheel. This meaning or 'idea of service medal' is the signified. The meaning is the one we all share … probably. It is possible that a very young child could look at the image and attach a different meaning to it, 'badge' perhaps, but they would be gently corrected by others so that they eventually would attach the widely agreed meaning to the image.

Now look at another element of the ad, the word 'halfords' in lower case letters. Once again, there is something there to look at (the signifier) and, once again, most of you will attach an agreed meaning (the signified).

This time, though, the signified will be restricted to fewer people: those who can read and who also know that Halfords is a British motoring and cycling store.

## Denotation and connotation

These are two ways in which signs create meaning. Returning to the service medal example, it is easy to attach an agreed signified to the image of the ribbon because the whole image clearly matches the overall shape of a service medal, and the ribbon part is a photographic image of a real medal ribbon. It is the most obvious and straightforward meaning for the ribbon. This is **denotation**. The phrase 'medal ribbon' is also a signifier that denotes that same object.

However, if we look again at the image, but this time in the context of the advertisement as a whole, it is clear that the image has other meanings. The words 'We're proud to have signed the Government's Armed Forces Covenant, supporting career opportunities for service leavers' plus the word 'halfords' tell us the context is an advertisement for Halfords stores. The combined image of the medal ribbon and wheel trim stands for experienced service personnel and also represents an idea that Halfords is proud to employ them and the experiences they've had in the services are useful when helping customers in Halford stores. These messages are not so obvious or so straightforward. These meanings 'by association' are called **connotations**.

The image of a service medal has other connotations such as heroism, gallantry, leadership and being able to support others. These are welcome meanings for a store that provides repair services, but it is clear from the words 'supporting career opportunities' that you are being invited to **interpret the image in a particular way**. This is an example of how the context of a sign helps to reduce its ambiguity.

### Key terms

**Denotation**
The straightforward, obvious or literal meaning of a sign. For a word it would be a dictionary definition of that word.
A photo of you simply denotes you. A denotation has no hidden, subtle or underlying meanings.

**Connotation**
Meaning by association. As you grow up, in your culture you learn that many signs have meanings that are not obvious or direct. For example, the word pig can connote greed or dirtiness or arrogance, among many other connotations. Signs often have different connotations for different groups of people.

# 1 Media Language

## Activity 1.2

Practise your skills of identifying denotation and connotation by completing the following chart for the remaining four images.

| Image | Denotes | Connotes | Could be used in an advert for |
|---|---|---|---|
| (red rose) | A flower, a red rose | Romance | Expensive chocolates |
| (rhinoceros) | A wild animal, a rhinoceros | Power, strength, longevity, freedom | A 4 × 4 vehicle |
| (leaf with water droplet) | | | |
| (bowler hat and briefcase with umbrella) | | | |
| (diamond) | | | |
| (stream in woodland) | | | |

## Anchorage

Anchorage is a technical term referring to the way in which ambiguous meanings can be tied down. Words are often used to anchor the meanings of images. For example, the picture of people running (right) could be anchored very differently by the use of any one of the three captions that are shown within the photo frame.

Anchorage gives us more **context** so that meanings are clearer.

1 Reality TV show hosts help kick-start new NHS get fit campaign.
2 Struggling to find a partner in your 30s? Visit the run4love website for help and advice.
3 Enjoying a final run in local beauty spot before the building of controversial new housing development begins.

AQA GCSE Media Studies

## Symbols and icons

These are two different types of sign.

**Symbols** are signs that don't look anything like the thing that they stand for. Words are symbols. Whether they are spoken or written, you can't really guess the meaning of a word from what it looks like or what it sounds like. Many other signs are symbolic as well. Their meanings are much more likely to be culturally specific. For example, the signs on the left can mean 'the United States of America' if you are part of the culture that shares this meaning.

The Stars and Stripes and the American Bald Eagle are symbols used to represent the United States of America.

On the other hand, signs that resemble whatever it is they refer to are called **icons**. By the way, don't be confused by the use of the word 'icon' to mean 'very famous' as in 'Brad Pitt is an iconic film star'. In semiotics, the word is used in its more technical sense: a sign that physically resembles its object (the thing it stands for). Shown here are a few familiar examples.

This photo of the Millennium Bridge, London, is an icon of the Millennium Bridge, London.

An iconic representation of singer Ed Sheeran

Road sign containing icon of a car and a quayside or riverbank.

Photographs are icons; if you take a selfie, it's an icon of yourself.

Signs often communicate as both symbol and icon. Looking back to the earlier activity, we said that:

|  | Denotes a flower, a red rose | Connotes romance | Could be used in an advert for expensive chocolates |
|---|---|---|---|

In this case the picture is an icon of the flower and a symbol of romance. In the road sign above, the red triangle is a symbol for 'warning'. As you will know if you have attempted the Driving Theory Test, some parts of the *Highway Code*, such as the meaning of red circles and red triangles, just have to be learned and remembered.

Semiotics differs from the sender–message–receiver approach because it takes the view that the meaning of the message has as much to do with the receiver as the sender or the message. Semiotics tends to refer to messages as **texts** and to receivers as **readers**. Different readers are likely to interpret a text in different ways because the meaning of a text can never be entirely fixed by a sender.

When media producers create a media product, they do their best to ensure that the meanings they want to communicate are clear and unambiguous. However, they cannot *force* their audience to accept their meanings. Some of us may take very different meanings about the product from the ones intended by the producers.

This is not a case of 'wrong meanings and right meanings'. A lot of time is spent discussing 'what things mean', especially those things that are brought to you by the mass media. People read texts differently because of different contexts and different identities; their readings are influenced by factors such as age, gender, ethnicity, class, religion and education.

### Link

For more on intended meanings by producers see Chapter 3, pages 97 and 101.

### Quick question 1.4

Think of a recent disagreement that you have had with someone about the meaning of a media text – an advertisement, maybe, or a music video. What do you think influenced your different interpretations?

## Media codes

Now that you have got to grips with some basic semiotic ideas, you can start to examine and illustrate some of the most important media codes that will be helpful in your analysis of media products.

### Non-verbal codes

Strictly speaking, all codes other than languages are non-verbal, as 'verbal' means 'of language'. However, we usually restrict non-verbal communication (NVC) to human display and behaviour. Sometimes this is called 'body language'.

These are some of the components of NVC:

- **Dress and appearance**, including clothing, hairstyle, body adornment such as makeup, tattoos, and accessories such as handbags, glasses or walking sticks. All of these items carry connotations and all cultures have distinctive codes of dress and appearance. Codes here include the associations between clothing and social class, occupation, occasion, religion, age and gender.

  On the right are two examples of the use of dress and appearance to communicate meanings. As is always the case with a code, a shared knowledge and understanding of 'the rules' is vital – even if the rules are being broken.

- **Facial expression, head movement, gestures**: the face is the most expressive part of the body and even slight adjustment of smiles, frowns and eye narrowing can convey meaning. We often make the mistake of assuming that gestures are universal in their meaning but different cultures have their own codes of meaning.

Clothing can reinforce our differences or our similarities.

### Quick question 1.5

How do different cultures use non-verbal communication in different ways? You may be able to use your own experience of living in a different country or region or of travelling.

### Activity 1.3

Try saying the following sentences using your voice in different ways. How many contrasting meanings can you create?
- 'I loved the party last night.'
- 'Do that again and I'll kill you.'
- 'Let's all do our best to support Tammy; she really deserves it.'
- 'Well that was an interesting class, wasn't it?'

### Key term

**Mise-en-scène**
All the elements chosen by producers to make up the content of images, including codes such as location, lighting, non-verbal communication (NVC), props, accessories, etc. are often referred to as the mise-en-scène.
It is a French term meaning 'put in the scene', which emphasises the idea that elements are included deliberately to communicate specific meanings.

- **Body movement, body closeness**: these codes can be difficult to interpret as they depend so much on the context. 'Getting very close' can be a sign of warmth and friendliness but in a different context it can signal aggression or the unacceptable invasion of another person's personal space.

- **Paralanguage**: as all actors know, 'it ain't what you say, it's the way that you say it'. Paralanguage covers all those ways in which the meaning of a word can be inflected by the use of tone, voice quality, pitch, volume and pace of delivery. Something said in a sarcastic tone can change its meaning completely, but the code only works if the listener recognises sarcasm.

### Activity 1.4

Describe the **mise-en-scène** elements in this still from the Galaxy 'Audrey Hepburn' advertisement (2023 CSP).

## Print codes: design, layout, typography

The pages of newspapers, magazines and print advertisements demonstrate the use of various codes. An important aspect of page design is the number of elements on the page, often referred to as the 'use of whitespace' (even when the page isn't white). On the one hand, a page with few words and/or images will usually communicate a sense of upmarket style or of an important statement. The Halfords' advertisement on page 14 (shown again on the left) does this quite well. On the other hand, a page with lots of elements crammed together can communicate excitement and liveliness, with popular appeal. The magazine cover opposite, for example, suggests that *Inside Soap* is bursting with interesting stories that demand your attention as they jostle together.

Credit: Chapter Agency Ltd

**Quick question 1.6**

Have the designers succeeded in making *Inside Soap* seem exciting and packed with interesting stories? What techniques has the cover designer used?

*Inside Soap* – a busy cover suggesting popular appeal.

Two ways of communicating meaning by the arrangement of signs are **superimposition** and **juxtaposition**. Superimposition can be seen on the *Inside Soap* cover (right) where elements of the design overlay each other. To superimpose is simply to place or lay something on top of something else, usually so most of the two elements can still be seen. The effect of this is to reinforce the connection between the two in the mind of the reader.

Juxtaposition is to place two elements closely together in order to influence the meaning attached to one or both. For example, by juxtaposing a child with a puppy in a mise-en-scène, the puppy's connotations of innocence and playfulness are transferred to the child.

This ad effectively juxtaposes signs to make a powerful point.

AQA GCSE Media Studies

### Key terms

**Masthead**
A publication's name or title in a distinctive form, usually placed at the top of the front or cover page.

**Serif and sans serif**
A serif is a small decorative line added to the letters of certain typefaces, as shown below left. Sans means without, so sans-serif typefaces, as shown below right, don't have these features.

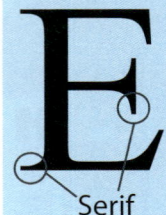 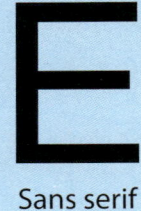

Serif      Sans serif

A comparison of the **mastheads** of the two 2023 newspaper CSPs gives us some idea of the very different identities that *The Times* and the *Daily Mirror* are trying to project. *The Times'* masthead runs right across the top of the front page. The font is a **serif**, as opposed to a **sans-serif**, font all in upper case. Although there are always colour images on the front page of *The Times*, the masthead itself is black on a white background.

Other design codes for print include the use of alignment and angles. Pages that are carefully aligned on a horizontal and vertical grid look more serious and formal, and can certainly have impact, as seen in *GQ* magazine below. Pages with tilted text and images may look more dynamic and have more youth appeal.

There are also colour codes to consider in print design. Black and white imagery suggests timeless, classic qualities and is often used in advertisements for upmarket products. Green has connotations of health and the environment, blue is cool and calm, while red is more passionate and emotional.

These elements of *The Times'* masthead communicate a sense of authority and stability. Serif fonts are associated with tradition and unchanging values; precisely the qualities that the newspaper wants to associate with its brand.

*GQ* magazine uses vertical and horizontal alignment of text around the central photograph to give the magazine a sophisticated, stylish look.

The *Daily Mirror*, however, uses a white sans-serif font on a red background. There is a contrast between two different font sizes with the smaller word 'DAILY' incorporated into the larger word 'Mirror'. One word is all upper case, the other is upper case (the capital M) and lower case. These typographical features help to reinforce the *Daily Mirror*'s brand. Sans-serif fonts are more modern and dynamic. The red background has an association with excitement and with the more popular, broad appeal that the newspaper wants to associate with its brand.

Here are some different types of serif fonts that are available:

Amasis MT Pro    Century Old Style    Bembo    Times New Roman.

Here are some different types of san-serif fonts that are available:

Arial    Helvetica Neue    Futura LT Pro    Myriad Pro.

### Activity 1.5

Collect some other examples of mastheads from newspapers and magazines. How have the typographical features contributed to the brand of the publication?

AQA GCSE Media Studies

# Photographic codes

Photographers use many techniques to add layers of meaning to their subjects. **Lighting**, **composition**, **framing**, **camera position**, **lens type** and **length of exposure** are all under the control of the photographer and all can make a significant difference to the meaning of the image that eventually appears in print.

**Link**

For more on camera angles and shots see pages 243–245.

## Shot types

A photographer decides how much of their field of vision to include within a shot. Standard shot types include:

Extreme close-up (ECU)

Big close-up (BCU)

Close-up (CU)

Medium close-up (MCU)

Mid-shot or medium shot (MS)

Wide angle (WA)

## Composition

In order to make shots more interesting and pleasing to the eye, photographers and camera operators often use the following techniques:

- **Rule of thirds**
  Horizontal and vertical lines create a grid of nine squares in the camera's viewfinder or digital display. Main subjects of interest (for example, the horizon, a building or a person) are aligned with the grid. Inexperienced photographers tend to place points of interest in the centre of the image, but the rule of thirds makes for better images.

Using the rule of thirds grid

- **Use of space**
  Still or moving images of an object in motion are more appealing if space is left in front of the moving object. This is known as leading room. Similarly, shots of people (unless in big close-up) look better if a small amount of space (headroom) is left between the top of the head and the edge of the image.

Headroom — Too much headroom

Leading room

## Diagonals

Diagonal lines give shots a sense of excitement or dynamism. This can be achieved by tilting the camera or by using lines of perspective to create this effect.

Using lines of perspective

Tilting the camera

AQA GCSE Media Studies

In this shot, the photographer has used a shallow depth of field to contrast between the sharp focus of the foreground subject – the footballers – and the out of focus crowd in the background.

The second shot, using a wider-angle lens, has a much greater depth of field so that more is in focus.

## Focus and lighting

The different ways in which this code is used in the two photographs above changes the meanings. In the first, the crowd is blurred and all the attention is on the individual contest between two players. In the second, a wide-angle shot with greater **depth of field**, much more is in focus so that the stadium, the crowd and the players are united by the photographic codes used to create this image.

In the fashion shot below, the subject has been lit from one side, making a strong contrast between light and shadow. The dramatic contrast gives the impression of mystery and intrigue.

These photographic codes also apply to moving image codes. All of the print codes here may be found in websites and social media too.

### Key term

**Depth of field**
In photographic or video terms this is the distance between the nearest and furthest points from the camera that are in focus.

Lighting is used for dramatic effect.

### Activity 1.6

Make a collection of digital still images that demonstrate the use of different photographic codes. How has the use of these codes affected the meaning of each image?

1 Media Language

**CASE STUDY:**

## Front page analysis: the *Daily Mirror* and the *Sun*

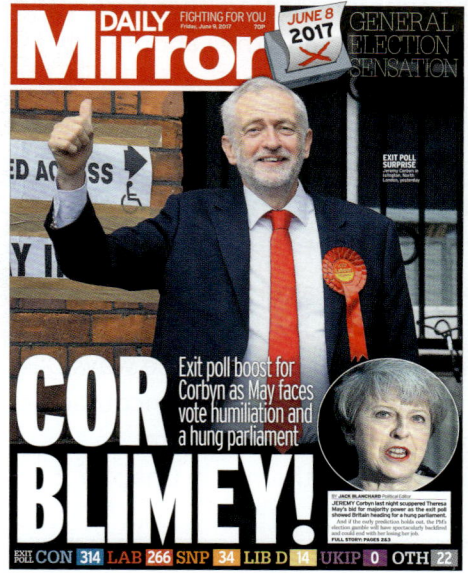
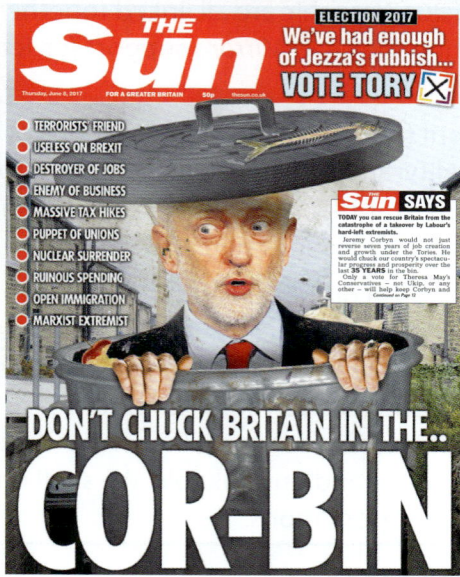

### Tip

Should you wish to look online at these two newspapers they are dated:
- the *Daily Mirror* – 9 June 2017
- the *Sun* – 8 June 2017.

The above two newspaper front pages appeared at the time of the General Election in June 2017. In this election campaign the *Sun* supported the Conservative Party and the *Daily Mirror* supported the Labour Party.

We have already discussed the masthead of the *Daily Mirror*, but what other semiotic codes are at work on this front page?

Let's start with the photograph of Jeremy Corbyn. As the main component of this page, it is the **dominant signifier**. The camera is angled upwards towards Corbyn, so he appears confident and authoritative. His thumbs-up gesture also connotes confidence, as does his facial expression. Corbyn is formally dressed but the open jacket connotes a degree of informality. Red is the brand colour of the Labour Party, so the red tie and, more powerfully, the red rosette symbolise Jeremy Corbyn's allegiance to the party.

The image is **anchored** by a two-part caption. The main part 'Cor Blimey!' is not only a play on Corbyn's name but also an expression of pleased surprise. Further anchorage for Corbyn's confidence is provided by the second caption: 'Exit poll boost for Corbyn as May's election gamble looks in doubt'. This leads us to interpret Corbyn's facial expression as a reaction to this 'boost'.

The second image is of then Prime Minister Theresa May. It is smaller and much less dominant than the photograph of Jeremy Corbyn, connoting him in the ascendency and her in decline. While Corbyn looks directly at the camera and at us, May is looking away. Furthermore, she is looking away from the centre of the page. This gives a slight impression of 'shiftiness' and is a technique often used by newspapers and magazines when they wish to add negative connotations to a photographic image. These negative connotations of the image are anchored by the copy beneath, 'Theresa May suffered an exit poll blow …'.

### Links

See Chapter 4, page 121 and Chapter 5, page 180 for more on the political preferences of newspapers.

### Key term

**Dominant signifier**
On a page or a poster or in a photo containing a number of signifiers grouped together, the dominant signifier is simply the most important (usually the largest) of these signifiers.

> **Activity 1.7**
>
> Attempt an analysis of the front cover of the *Sun* yourself. Try to include all the following terms:
> - sign
> - denotation
> - connotation
> - anchorage.
>
> Also, refer to non-verbal, photographic, design and typographic codes in your analysis.

Both photographs are icons denoting the two party leaders. The background to the Jeremy Corbyn picture is also an icon, denoting a polling station.

To draw together the elements of the one story that dominates the page, the designer has used superimposition so that print, graphic and photographic elements are placed over each other. The masthead, Corbyn's head and the June 8, 2017 graphic are all linked together by superimposition, therefore connoting the *Daily Mirror*'s support for Jeremy Corbyn and the Labour Party in this election.

Sans-serif fonts, with their connotations of simplicity, modernity and informality, are dominant, although serif fonts are used for contrast ('GENERAL ELECTION SENSATION') and for greater legibility in the body text ('Early indications suggested …').

A comparison of the *Sun* and the *Daily Mirror* front pages certainly shows that media products can create very different messages by the selection and omission of elements, and the use of codes and conventions. In these ways, media products often communicate sets of values and beliefs that encourage us to think certain ideas are 'normal and natural' while other ideas are unacceptable and unthinkable. We shall return to these themes in Chapter 2 Media Representations.

## Moving image codes

Film and video makers use many of the codes described above, but also add a few more. Non-verbal codes are used in performances by actors and presenters, and a version of the print codes of design, layout and typography is at work in titling, credits and graphic elements. Production codes in film and video add camera movements to the photographic codes used in creating still images. These include:

- **Pan**: a fixed camera rotated either left or right through 180 degrees.
- **Tilt**: a fixed camera tilted either up or down.
- **Zoom**: a power button on a fixed camera that allows a subject to be brought closer (zoom in) or made more distant (zoom out).
- **Dollying**: the camera is moved in or out to follow the action.
- **Tracking**: the camera is moved from left to right to follow the action.
- **Crane shot**: traditionally a crane but now often a drone lifts the camera above the action, giving a more dramatic perspective.

Some examples of how meaning is created using camerawork include:

- A **crane shot**: often used at the end of an episode or film. The camera is raised above the scene to give the impression that you are leaving the story and the characters behind.
- A **slow zoom** to a big close-up (BCU): puts the viewers in touch with the subject's state of mind. In drama, it is often used to make an emotional connection between the audience and a character.

A crane shot literally involves placing a camera on a crane, often giving the viewer a feeling of power over the characters.

- **Point-of-view shot**: shows us exactly what the subject sees and connects the viewer to the experience of the subject. If the subject is moving, a hand-held camera is often used. The jerky movement of the camera gives authenticity to the scene.

### Activity 1.8

Here are more types of shot used in television and video:
- cutaway
- two shot
- over-the-shoulder shot
- whip pan
- low angle
- fish eye.

Research these shot types and find examples (or create examples to show to the class). Explain how the shot type helps to create meaning in your examples. An excellent resource for this activity can be found on the Media College website, at http://www.mediacollege.com/video/shots/.

This is a point-of-view shot, where the viewer sees what a character sees.

## Digital and post-production codes

Some television and video products present events in real time. The live transmission of sport or live news coverage are examples of real time. Television news often combines live presentations with pre-recorded reports. In these cases, programme makers will use a technique called vision mixing: switching between different camera positions and, if relevant, pre-recorded material. A great deal of video material found on the internet is also in real time; it is unedited and shot with a single camera.

Sky's presentation of live football is a big operation with up to 70 people involved in a live broadcast. A *Radio Times* (2016) behind the scenes feature reported that,

> On the day I looked round there were a total of 25 cameras for the coverage, including those focused on the studio, a new drone camera dubbed 'Batcam' flown from a nearby car park for aerial views and a remote controlled 'kartcam' driving onto the pitch to try to get a new type of shot as the players walk out.

Drama is very rarely in real time. Along with the majority of professionally produced film and video output, editing is used to control the passage of time. Usually, time is compressed. For example, in a television mini-series, the events portrayed may take place over several years, but they have to be compressed into, say, six 55-minute episodes.

The idea is to communicate clearly to the viewers when and where the action is taking place while at the same time making **transitions** between shots and between scenes as smooth as possible. Viewers will be unaware of edits, as their attention is drawn to the story rather than the way it has been put together as a television product. The set of techniques for achieving this effect is called continuity editing. These are rules or conventions that were established in the very early days of Hollywood. They have been refined and developed over more than 100 years.

### Key term

**Transition (editing)**
The joining together of two shots. The most common type of transition is the **cut**: an instant shot change between the two shots. Others are **crossfade** (or **mix** or **dissolve**), in which one shot gradually merges into the next. Digital editing can also achieve many special effect transitions. A **fade in** is a transition between a blank screen (usually black) and a shot. **Fade out** is the same in reverse.

As we have all grown up with these rules, we have come to understand the meanings of editing techniques as they guide us through a sequence of events. A key rule of continuity editing is that we assume events happen in the order in which they are shown. When the intention is to move backwards rather than forwards in time (a flashback), editing gives the viewer strong clues. For example, a scene could end with a slow fade to a blurry white and the next could start with a caption superimposed on the screen, e.g. 'December 1963'. Other flashback techniques include transitions from colour to black and white or to a grainy 'home movie style' sequence. Slow motion can be used to communicate a feeling that 'time stands still' for a character, while time lapse images may show that we are moving forwards rapidly through the seasons.

Continuity editing also links events together by suggesting cause and effect. For example, if you see a shot of someone driving erratically followed by a shot of the same person lying in the back of an ambulance, you 'fill in the gaps' by assuming that the erratic driving has caused the injury. This also demonstrates another feature of editing: **ellipsis**. Time is compressed by leaving out a lot of detail. In this case the car crash and the resulting injuries don't have to be shown, they will exist in the imagination of the viewers.

In other types of moving image production such as music video, reality television and documentary, continuity is not so important and more dynamic styles of editing are often used. These may include **montages** of shots and scenes without the implication of time order or cause and effect. Unlike the smooth transitions of continuity editing, music videos sometimes use edits that are deliberately jarring or unusual.

## Sound

Sound makes a huge contribution to meaning in moving image products. Dialogue, voiceovers and interviews are obviously important, as is music. There are a number of codes and conventions relating to sound in film and video.

It has already been explained that continuity editing tries to 'hide' the editing process from viewers. Sound can be very helpful in smoothing transitions between shots and especially between scenes. The key point here is that sound and video tracks do not have to be cut at the same time. In fact, moving images flow much more smoothly if the audio track runs across cuts in the video track.

| Video track | Black | Fade-up to Shot 1 | Shot 2 | Shot 3 | Shot 4 | Shot 5 |
|---|---|---|---|---|---|---|
| Audio track | Music | Fade-down music | Voiceover narration | | | Music |

> **Key terms**
>
> **Ellipsis**
> In film and video editing, ellipsis is the omission of a period of time. The audience is expected to work out what has happened from the context.
>
> **Montage**
> A technique of putting together fragments of still or moving images and/or sounds from different sources to create a meaningful sequence. Often used to compress time.

### Activity 1.9

Research the following editing terms and find examples to show to the class:
- intercutting
- jump-cut and the 180-degree rule
- crossing the line
- cutting on action
- cutaway.

How do these edit techniques help to create meanings in your examples?

## Types of sound

**Wild sound**: the naturally occurring background noise, e.g. birds, traffic or the hum of machinery, often recorded separately and used in the editing process.

**Diegetic sound**: sound produced from within the action on the screen, e.g. people talking, tyres screeching, a band playing, dogs barking and so on.

**Non-diegetic sound**: 'soundtrack' sound that is added at the editing stage. Music and voiced narration are the most common examples of non-diegetic sound, although various sound effects are sometimes used. As viewers, we hear everything but the people on the screen only hear diegetic sound.

**Heightened sound**: when a piece of diegetic sound is unnaturally amplified, usually for dramatic effect. Typical examples are the cocking of a gun, a key turning in a lock or a droplet falling into water.

A post-production sound desk

### Key term

**Diegesis**
The world of the characters in the story. Information available to any of these characters is diegetic, information only known to the audience is non-diegetic.

# Narrative

All media products, from a simple photograph used in a website to a three-hour-long feature film, tell a story. Narrative is the way that these stories are put together.

The word 'story' may suggest that we are dealing with events that are made-up, but in media studies that isn't the case at all. For media studies students, narratives and story refer to all media products, including advertisements, newspapers and television documentaries. All of these 'tell a story' in a way that is structured as a narrative. Simple statements ('it's hot', 'that's a mountain') are not narratives because a narrative deals with:

- **causality**: why things happen
- **time**: when things happen
- **space**: where things happen.

It isn't just the media that organise events by imposing a narrative structure. We all do it.

- I got up.
- I had a shower.
- I got dressed.
- I ate some toast.
- Just as I was about to leave a letter dropped on the mat.
- I'd just won first prize of £5,000 in a competition.

Imagine these events really happened to you (it would be nice, wouldn't it?). How would you tell your friends about your morning? Which order would you put the events in? Would you try to increase the drama of the event (e.g. by saying, 'You'll never guess what happened to me'). In whatever way you go about it, you will be using the structures and 'rules' of narrative to fashion a story out of the events.

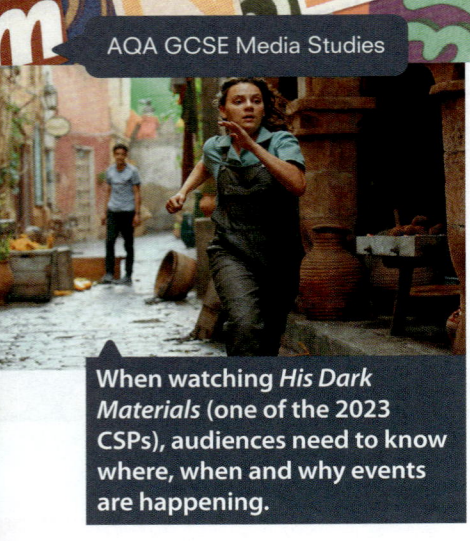

When watching *His Dark Materials* (one of the 2023 CSPs), audiences need to know where, when and why events are happening.

Of course, there are many different ways of telling stories. It would be boring if every story was told in the same way. Even so, there are a number of themes and features of narrative organisation that have become so familiar to us that we can often predict the way that a story is going. Half the fun of being told a story, whether as a television programme, a film or a video game, is guessing what is going to happen next. The events themselves are not the narrative. It's the *telling* of the story by converting it into a media product that makes it into a narrative.

Just like the codes we have already discussed, narratives have their own sets of features, conventions and rules. Here's one simple model of a narrative structure.

> Equilibrium ≫ Disruption ≫ Recognition of disruption ≫ Attempts to restore equilibrium ≫ New equilibrium

This won't make much sense without an explanation of the word 'equilibrium'. Equilibrium is 'a state of balance'. The idea here is that a narrative begins with normality, harmony and balance. Then something happens to disturb this happy state: the disruption. People recognise and attempt to deal with this disruption and, eventually a new but different state of balance is achieved at the end: the new equilibrium.

Here's an example of a story with this narrative structure:

- In a small rural community, villagers live and work in peace and harmony. (**Equilibrium**)
- A gang of villains invades the village forcing them to hand over food and money by using violence. They keep asking for more. (**Disruption**)
- Secretly, the villagers decide that something must be done. They use their last funds to bring seven mercenaries [hired fighters] to protect them. (**Recognition of disruption**)
- The mercenaries confront the villains several times. In a final epic fight they defeat the gang of villains, although most of the mercenaries die as well. (**Attempts to restore equilibrium**)
- Peace and harmony are restored but now the villagers are stronger, more confident and more resourceful. (**New equilibrium**)

## Vladimir Propp and narrative

Vladimir Propp developed his theories of narrative by studying many hundreds of Russian folk tales. He identified underlying patterns and character types found in these tales and his ideas have been widely used in the analysis of media products.

Propp's tales were 'quests' in which a hero sets off on a mission to retrieve something of value or to solve a great mystery. The mission involves obstacles and difficulties that must be overcome to achieve an ultimate goal. Standing between the hero and this goal is the villain. The villain (and any villain's allies or henchmen) must be vanquished before the hero can accomplish the objectives of the mission and triumphantly return home to claim a well-earned reward.

1 Media Language

The 'character types' identified by Propp are:

- **The hero**: the **protagonist** and the main agent of change.
- **The villain**: the opponent who places obstacles in the path of the hero and who must be defeated in a climatic confrontation.
- **The donor**: the hero is given a magical gift by the donor. In modern stories the gift may be more rational than 'magic', for example a secret weapon, a key or a piece of information.
- **The helper**: the hero's trusted sidekick. The hero may have several helpers. Helpers are often hurt or killed to strengthen the hero's motivation.
- **The dispatcher**: the hero is sent off on the mission by the dispatcher. The dispatcher has to overcome the hero's reluctance and objections.
- **The princess**: this is the 'sought for' person who may be the object of a rescue mission and/or the hero's reward for succeeding in the quest. Once again, for modern narratives, we shouldn't see 'the princess' too literally. For example, the character may be male and have nothing to do with royalty.
- **The princess's father**: this character is naturally protective of the princess and this may place him in competition with the hero. Alternatively, the roles of princess's father and dispatcher may combine to send the hero off on a quest.
- **False hero**: other characters often mistake the false hero for the real hero, making the real hero's quest even more difficult.

### Key term

**Protagonist**
The main character in a story. The protagonist is actively opposed by another character: the antagonist.

### Quick question 1.7

Do Lyra, Will or Mrs Coulter from *His Dark Materials* fit any of Propp's character types?

Lyra

Will

Mrs Coulter

Some modern narratives have characters that fit Propp's scheme very well, but it would be a mistake to think that writers and media producers 'learn' these character types and functions and then apply them to their work. It is more likely that Propp's folk tales are representative of the many thousands of stories that contribute to our culture. Writers and audiences share the same cultural context, so it is not surprising that familiar characters and familiar storylines often appear. As will be seen in the later section on genre (pages 36–43), most media products are based on familiar narrative structures and character types but introduce endless 'twists' and variations on these themes to keep audiences interested.

## Confrontation, mystery and action

Narratives always try to keep the audience engaged and interested. Some fail, of course, but there are some tried and trusted methods used to keep us viewing, reading or listening. Narratives are usually driven forwards by confrontation. The contest between hero and villain is an obvious example of this, but there are often broader issues to consider. In most quests, you identify with the hero and boo the villain because they represent ideas that we approve or reject. The hero may be flawed and the villain may have a few redeeming features but in the wider picture they stand for good and evil.

### Quick question 1.8

What does the villain stand for? Draw up your own list of possibilities to contrast with the hero qualities alongside.

Typically, the hero demonstrates at least some of the following qualities:

- self-sacrificing
- honest
- kind
- considerate
- fair
- unselfish
- patriotic
- humane
- devout.

The triumph of the goodie over the baddie confirms the audience's central commitment to these values. We identify with the hero and find pleasure (the 'feel good factor') in a resolution that reinforces our beliefs.

The confrontation between good and evil is not the only opposition driving narratives forward. Narratives set up tension between two ideas. The tensions are explored in the action and character development, with one side usually winning out over the other. These pairs are called **binary opposites**. Examples are:

Wealth vs Poverty

Present vs Past

Family vs Individual

Law vs Natural justice

City vs Country

Masculinity vs Femininity

Education vs Instinct

Age (and experience) vs Youth (and vitality)

The key point is that our culture's value system is reinforced by our exposure to numerous narratives that resolve these oppositions in the same way.

### Activity 1.10

Find your own examples of media products that use these binary oppositions to move the narrative forwards. Can you add any more examples of binary oppositions?

The familiar 'whodunnit' narrative structure of ITV crime drama *Midsomer Murders* has given pleasure to audiences since 1997.

## Enigma and action codes

An enigma is simply a mystery or clue that draws the audience in. For example, if a television crime drama begins with a body floating face downwards in a swimming pool, it immediately stimulates our interest because the following questions are raised:

- Whose body is it?
- How did it get there?
- Was it a murder?
- If murder, who did it and why?
- Will the perpetrator be caught?

These questions are like an itch that we want to scratch; it's hard to tear ourselves away until we know the answers. Naturally, the answers are not going to be revealed anytime soon. The writers of the drama will structure the narrative by revealing the story in tantalising snippets before a 'big reveal', the resolution, ties up all the details at the end. Along the journey there will be clues, red herrings, false trails, dead ends and new mysteries – more enigmas – for the audience to ponder. This process is called plotting the story. As the pieces of the story are revealed, like pieces of a jigsaw, you use your knowledge and experience of crime dramas to fill in the gaps by making educated guesses about the whole picture.

A drama serial or soap opera may end with an enigma (a cliffhanger) in order to persuade the audience to come back for more, such as the classic 'You ain't my muvva' cliffhanger in one of Eastenders' duff-duff moments. Similarly, a news broadcast may contain an enigma in the introduction, for example: 'It was the final of the men's singles at Wimbledon today but who emerged victorious?'

Enigma codes provide plenty of satisfaction and pleasure for an audience in unravelling the mysteries and by trying to out-guess the plot. However, audiences may be disappointed if there is no resolution and may feel that they have been 'left hanging' by a story that hasn't delivered a satisfying sense of closure.

Another way of driving narrative forward is through action codes. Here, tension is built up by a series of signs that suggest something may happen. For example, the hero is alone in a graveyard at night. An owl hoots, a cloud passes in front of the moon, a twig snaps, a strange rustling sound gets louder.

In the following case studies, focus is on the narrative structure of two CSPs from 2023: the cover of *Tatler* magazine and *His Dark Materials*: 'The City of Magpies'. In the first of these, *Tatler* is examined in terms of Propp's narrative theory, while the second looks at the effectiveness of narrative features in grabbing the attention of the audience.

**CASE STUDY:**

## Narrative analysis of *Tatler*, including reference to Propp's character types

This cover deals with wish fulfilment; it suggests that your desires to fantasise about luxuries will be met by the magazine's content. *Tatler* is an aspirational magazine. This means it appeals to readers who aspire to be like the people who feature in the magazine – wealthy, beautiful, attractive and confident. The cover casts the reader in the role of a hero who is invited to undertake a quest. The prize (princess) is self-gratification. You will be able to form a fantasy relationship with the people who inhabit the magazine's world and, however briefly, feel that you have become one of them.

The cover invites readers to explore the contents with 'teasers' or enigmas ('How the social set get married in a crisis'), which can be resolved by exploring within. This dispatches the reader on a quest.

The cover offers tantalising glimpses of the private lives of the wealthy elite and promises the reader a 'key' to joining them. You will be given insider information ('Their habits, codes and mating practices' or 'The workings of the Westminster web' or 'Who to stay in touch with on the continent') in much the same way as Propp's donor supplies magical powers that will assist the hero in overcoming the villain and winning the prize.

The model herself could be your 'helper' as you set off on your quest within the magazine. She is already in the fantasy world that lies behind the superimposed masthead and superimposed copy. She seems to look directly and invitingly at the reader.

If there is a villain of the piece it is in the head of the reader. Only your inhibitions, self-doubts and weaknesses are preventing you from joining the beautiful people within. Overcome these doubts and win the prize!

Media language is used to signal these narrative features. The model's dress connotes wealth, her makeup and hairstyle connote exotic beauty. The use of language positions the reader as fun-loving and sociable, ready to take on the challenge of the quest – 'A costume drama at Longleat' and 'Meet Boris's brother Max'.

### Activity 1.11

Choose another magazine cover and carry out your own narrative analysis using Propp's ideas.

## CASE STUDY:

## Narrative evaluation and analysis of the pre-title sequence of 'The City of Magpies'

This analysis will make more sense if you watch the scene first. We will be referring to the sequence after the 'Previously' montage up to the opening title credits, so from 3 minutes to 6 minutes. Just to refresh your memory, the episode begins with Lyra waking with a start, alone with her daemon Pan. As she tilts her head to look up, an **establishing shot** locates us in a new landscape of trees and rocks near to the stream of light that Lord Asriel created in the 'Previously' montage. The sequence cuts to an extreme long shot of airships flying in formation in front of a forbidding sky, closely followed by further extreme long shots of witches taking off and flying. We hear a female voiceover explaining the witches' prophecy, while seeing Lyra walk through the thick forest, cross-cut with a submarine and the airships approaching the stream of light, with Mrs Coulter on board. Lyra and Pan eventually come to a spot where they can see the 'city in the sky' that was revealed by Lord Asriel in the previous series.

There are a number of 'hooks' in this sequence to grab the attention of the family and teenage **target audience**. The main characters drawn from the audience's own demographic hold out the prospect of interesting and exciting interactions with each other. The different characters offer the audience contrasting spectating positions from which to engage with the action.

The voiceover tells us that 'the witches believe this is the start of a powerful prophecy, one that could destroy all existence, or make it anew'. Dramatic music fills the pause before the final phrase, emphasising the threat to the world, before the voiceover ends the statement on hope. As we are told that 'it is time to prepare, to draw sides,' we see Lyra moving with Pan, and the airships and submarine massing on the other side of the divide between worlds, with Mrs Coulter sitting calmly examining documents. This establishes the conflict between hero and villain. The equilibrium of Lyra's world in the previous series

### Key terms

**Establishing shot**
A type of shot that fulfils the narrative function of locating the action in space. For example, a television news report about UK politics may begin with an establishing shot of the Houses of Parliament.

**Target audience**
Producers of media products always have in mind an intended audience, often defined by age, gender or social class. The product is fashioned to appeal to the specific wants and needs of this group, a process called *targeting* the audience.

The initial equilibrium is disrupted when Lord Asriel severs the connection between child and daemon to create a bridge between worlds.

has been broken by the disruption of the stream of light crossing between worlds. This signals to the audience the start of a quest in which they can expect twists and turns for the hero as she overcomes dangers and challenges in the mission to stay ahead of both her mother and her father, to secure a prized object: her own safety and liberty.

Perhaps, though, the complex set of enigmas in the pre-title sequence could put off potential viewers because it suggests a demanding narrative that will require the full attention of the viewers.

The enigmas set up in the title sequence include:

- What is special about the city in the sky?
- How can Lyra, alone with Pan, stay ahead of the massive airships?
- How can the witches help?
- What are Mrs Coulter's intentions?

Enigma: what is the significance of the city in the sky?

These questions are the puzzles for the audience and they hold many narrative pleasures for the audience as the fundamental conflict between Lyra and Mrs Coulter is played out.

In Propp's terms, we have a hero, a villain and, in the flying witches, a group of helpers. The knife has already been mentioned as a potential magical gift, although we do not yet know the identity of the donor. The machinery of the Magisterium is being pitted against the natural magic of the witches, in binary opposition. The reward (princess) sought by Lyra is not just her own safety, but that of all children in her world.

Binary oppositions: the innocence of Lyra and Pan versus ...

As well as good vs evil, and machine vs nature, other binary oppositions emerge:

- Youth vs Age
- Power vs Innocence
- Humane vs Brutal
- Civilisation vs Wilderness
- Familiar vs Unknown.

Various narrative codes are used to locate the audience in time and place. These include the light stream in the shots of Lyra and the airships, establishing them as being on different sides of the divide between worlds, the different types of weather showing that each group is somewhere new, and the use of both daylight and moonlight to show the passage of time as Lyra and Pan walk.

... the power of Mrs Coulter.

Continuity is provided by the dramatic orchestral non-diegetic soundtrack that links the sequence. In common with many television dramas, the period of balance and harmony is non-existent in this opening sequence. It has become a convention to 'front load' dramas with action and foreboding, so that audiences can be attracted by action codes as well as enigmas. This sequence contains examples of implied 'cause and effect' action. For example, when Mrs Coulter looks at the photographs of Lyra, she gains a new sense of determination in her eyes, implying a threat. This is immediately followed by Pan reminding Lyra that they can't go back. For some viewers, this focus on the **visceral pleasures** of threatened action rather than the **cerebral pleasures** of equilibrium followed by disruption may be a turn-off, but most of the family and teenage target audience expect reassurance from the start that the narrative will be driven by a sense of threat.

### Key terms

**Visceral pleasure**
A type of audience pleasure that is like a physical experience.

**Cerebral pleasure**
Pleasure of the mind rather than the body.

### Link

See Chapter 3, page 100 for more on audience pleasure.

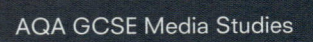

# Genre

A genre is a category or type into which media products are slotted. The best way to demonstrate this idea is with a few examples:

| Media form | Genre examples | Product examples |
| --- | --- | --- |
| Magazines | Celebrity | *OK!* |
| | | *Hello!* |
| | TV listings | *Radio Times* |
| | | *TV Quick* |
| Newspapers | Local | *Manchester Evening News* |
| | | *Daily Gazette* (N E Essex) |
| | Tabloid | *Daily Mirror* |
| | | *Sun* |
| Video games | Platform | Super Mario |
| | | Sonic the Hedgehog |
| | Role-playing games | GTA |
| | | Legend of Zelda |
| Television | Soap opera | *EastEnders* |
| | | *Neighbours* |
| | Game show | *Pointless* |
| | | *The Chase* |
| Radio | Music radio | Kiss Breakfast |
| | | *Steve Wright Show* (R2) |
| | Sport | *Test Match Special* (R5) |
| | | *Alan Brazil Sports Breakfast* (Talksport) |
| Film | Science fiction | *The Martian* |
| | | *Gravity* |
| | Action/adventure | *Kong: Skull Island* |
| | | *Jason Bourne* |
| Social media | Vlog | K.S.I. |
| | Content sharing sites | YouTube |
| | | Pinterest |
| Music video | Performance | Arctic Monkeys – 'I Bet You Look Good on the Dancefloor' |
| | | Kasabian – 'Switchblade Smiles' |
| | Story based | Katy Perry – 'Roar' |
| | | Taylor Swift – 'Love Story' |

## Types of genres

Looking at the chart opposite, you can see that there are several different ways of classifying media products. For example, video games are usually allocated to genres by the nature of the gameplay rather than by the content. Similarly, online and social media genres tend to be grouped by the function or purpose of the site rather than content. Newspapers were traditionally categorised by the size of the paper: broadsheet and tabloid. Even though these distinctions no longer apply, as most newspapers have switched to a tabloid format, we still tend to use the categories broadsheet, mid-market and tabloid as the distinctive genres of the press. Today, these terms refer to the target audience not the size of the paper. Broadsheets or 'quality' newspapers target the professional end of the market and the tabloid or popular press target the mass market.

Film and television products are categorised by the content type, although even in these cases the boundaries between different genres are rarely clear-cut.

## Hybrids and subgenres

A **hybrid** is something with mixed origins, so a hybrid genre is derived from two or more genres to create a new category. Here are some useful examples from film:

| Original genres | Hybrid | Product |
|---|---|---|
| Science fiction<br>Horror | Sci-fi/Horror | *Prometheus* |
| Science fiction<br>Western | Sci-fi/Western | *Westworld* |
| Action and adventure<br>fantasy | Action/Fantasy | *Pirates of the Caribbean* |

Hybrid genres are also found on television. *Strictly Come Dancing* contains elements of light entertainment, reality television and celebrity talent show. Television **docudramas** and, on radio, *The News Quiz* (BBC Radio 4) are self-evidently hybrids. In music video, One Direction's 'History' combines a performance of the song with a visual representation of the song's story.

Hybrids combine elements of the broad categories to make something separate and distinct, while subgenres are specialist groupings within the 'parent' genre.

The relationship between subgenres and a main genre can clearly be seen in the example of music radio. This category has numerous subgenres based on different types of music such as:

- AOR (adult-oriented rock)
- easy listening
- grime
- hip-hop
- folk
- heavy metal.

Some of these subgenres are even further divided. Within the music radio subgenre 'heavy metal' we find, for example:

- death metal
- progressive metal
- thrash metal
- classic metal.

> **Key terms**
>
> **Hybrid**
> A genre that combines two or more pre-existing genres to create a new category.
>
> **Docudrama**
> A genre that combines fiction with real events. Real people and actual events are recreated in a docudrama.

> **Quick question 1.9**
>
> Can you identify any of the subgenres of the other music radio categories: AOR, easy listening, grime, hip-hop and folk?

**Key term**

**Hierarchy**
A system with different levels based on rank, size or importance.

This sort of genre and subgenre **hierarchy** can also be seen in the magazine industry:

CONSUMER MAGAZINES
⬇
Hobby
⬇
Fishing
⬇
Coarse fishing
⬇
Carp fishing

You may suspect that at this level in the hierarchy there could only be one magazine … but you would be wrong, as the selection of carp fishing magazines on this page shows.

**Activity 1.12**

Build up a genre and a subgenre hierarchy in the following areas:
- online and social media
- television.

## Recognising genres

Media products that fall within a particular genre must have recognisable features in common with the other products in the same genre. One of the most important functions of media language is to communicate the membership of genres through shared codes and conventions.

Let's look at two BBC news examples (watch the breakfast news and the evening news on BBC or search for them on the internet).

The following signs help us to identify the television news genre:

- formally dressed presenters
- studio setting
- direct gaze at camera
- backdrop (city skyline, world globe).

A further set of signs enables us to put the television news into different subgenres:

**Breakfast news**

- co-presenters sitting side by side
- warmer colour palette based on reds and yellows
- superimposed digital clock
- relaxed facial expressions
- settee.

**Evening news**

- dark formal clothes
- solo presenter
- presenter standing
- dramatic colour palette, dominated by:
  - red
  - black
  - white
- globe image.

In addition to these, other signifiers of the television news genre include the dramatic music, use of highly polished desks, interviews, filmed reports, etc.

## The appeal of genres

Genres appeal to media audiences and media producers for different but related reasons.

**For audiences:**

- Genres offer the pleasure of familiarity and comfort; you know what to expect.
- Genres help you to select media products for personal use from the huge range available.
- Over time, individuals build up a substantial knowledge and understanding of favourite genres. This makes it very easy for them to find their way around a new product from a familiar genre.

### Activity 1.13

What are the distinctive signs and features that help us identify the television genres in the two photos below?

The audience's knowledge of genre is also essential for navigating the menus of online sites linked to television, radio and video gaming. Netflix, Amazon Prime and Spotify, for example, all invite customers to 'Browse by Genre'.

**For producers:**

Genre products give many advantages to the media industry:

- They are economical to produce. Standard formats and experienced staff help to make efficiency savings.
- Audiences are targeted more easily with genre products.
- There is a lower risk of financial failure with a new product that sticks to a tried and trusted formula.

## Genre pros and cons

Genre products are often criticised for being boring and predictable. But is this fair?

Genre products have to strike a very careful balance between predictability and surprise. The television murder mystery, for example, certainly has some very familiar elements of narrative, character and appearance. However, within these constraints, the best writers, cast and crew can still produce enough variations on the theme to keep audiences wanting more.

### Talk about it

For you, which are the most successful genre products in television, music video, video games or film? Which products in these media forms have become too boring and predictable and why?

However, it is not hard to find examples of this and other genre products that have become tired and stale.

In addition to finding new and interesting variations on a theme, producers also have the option to break genre rules. This is known as subverting genre conventions. The subverting of conventions can be a very effective technique in 'freshening up' a genre. For example, BBC Television News introduced a 'new look' in 2006 by breaking the convention that news presenters always sat behind a desk.

When genres are subverted in this way, the effect can be shocking at first, but remarkably soon the change will either become the 'new normal' or sink without trace.

## Intertextuality

As you know, media products can also be referred to as texts, so **intertextuality** literally means 'between texts'. Texts frequently borrow from or quote from other texts to give shape and colour to meanings. Think, for example, of the sampling of older tracks in popular music or the 'mash up' style of many videos.

Sometimes, intertextual references are a way of paying respect to another text but they can also be used to ridicule or parody the original.

> **Key term**
>
> **Intertextuality**
> A feature of texts (media products) that borrow or quote from other texts.

## Genre in context

You will need to get used to analysing media products in context, especially in their social, cultural, political and historical contexts.

This is why several of your CSPs are over 50 years old. Looking at these examples helps to show how the values, attitudes and beliefs of people in a different time period influenced the use of media language and interpretations of the audiences. It also shows us how much – or how little – the distinctive features of genres have changed over time.

The case study on page 44 looks at the first episode of *Doctor Who*, broadcast in 1963, and considers the ways in which the context of that period influenced the meaning of television sci-fi.

AQA GCSE Media Studies

## 1963

Society in the UK was still dominated by two wars: World War II and the Cold War between the USSR and USA, as well as their respective allies. This American/Russian competition was also seen in the Space Race, which the USSR led in 1963. Valentina Tereshkova became the first female astronaut to fly in space, on 16 June. (It was another 20 years before the Americans put a woman in space.)

CND marches were common in the early 1960s.

Britain was a nuclear power with nuclear weapons and nuclear reactors supplying electricity. The Campaign for Nuclear Disarmament (CND) was at its height, with huge protest marches to London attracting lots of media attention.

In 1963, the country was obsessed with spies and it became public knowledge that Russian spies had infiltrated the intelligence services. A senior government minister, John Profumo, sensationally resigned after his affair with a model, Christine Keeler, who was associated with a Russian spy, was exposed. National security seemed at risk and the prime minister, Harold Macmillan, resigned soon after.

World War II finished in 1945 and by 1963 young people were increasingly disconnected from the wartime values of patriotism, duty and respect. The majority of teenagers in 1963 had been born after the end of World War II and wanted their own culture. This cultural shift was powerfully symbolised by the emergence and phenomenal success of The Beatles.

The 1960's Russian astronaut, Valentina Tereshkova – the first woman in space.

The Beatles created a sensation in British pop music in the 1960s.

The post-war boom contributed to the country's economic success. People felt better off. The labour shortages caused by the war were slowed by a surge of immigration from the late 1940s onwards, with many people arriving from the West Indies, India and Pakistan. By the late 1950s, racial conflicts became more serious, with race riots in many cities stirred up by right wing political groups.

Serious tensions were emerging in the USA, firstly over its involvement in Vietnam and, secondly, over the policies of racial segregation in the southern states. Terrible news images of monks setting themselves on fire in protest against the American presence in Vietnam and increasing confrontations over Civil Rights undermined the moral authority of the USA. 1963 was the year in which Martin Luther King Jr delivered one of the most famous speeches in the history of America. The 'I have a dream' speech included the lines:

> I have a dream that my four little children will one day live in a nation where they will not be judged by the color of their skin but by the content of their character. I have a dream today.

Another event, which took place in Dallas, Texas on the day before transmission of 'An Unearthly Child', massively overshadowed the broadcast of the first *Doctor Who* episode: President John F. Kennedy was assassinated on 22 November 1963.

President John F. Kennedy's motorcade through Dallas, Texas in November 1963.

Civil rights activist Martin Luther King Jr

## CASE STUDY:
## 'An Unearthly Child'

How does the account of 1963 on pages 42–43 help with an analysis of 'An Unearthly Child'?

In the episode, the audience's suspicions are gradually confirmed. There are two aliens hiding in the midst of a familiar community. They are indistinguishable from the humans, at least in appearance. This relates to the widespread anxiety about an 'enemy within', usually in the form of Russian spies. There are also more generalised fears of 'outsiders' and of threats to peace and stability: nuclear weapons, civil unrest, and divisions between young and old.

However, the story soon establishes that these are superior aliens. Susan is clearly much more well informed and more clever than her teachers. The TARDIS (Time And Relative Dimension In Space), a time machine (a well-known convention of science fiction), has many signs of advanced futuristic science and technology. The brightly lit interior, knobs, dials and switches all confirm the expectations of a positive future. When the teachers move from the dark and gloom of the junkyard into the brightly lit interior of the TARDIS it's as if they are entering a better, more enlightened world. This reinforces the audience's hope that science and technology will make a better world for everybody. Notably, by the end of the episode, women are travellers in space and time, in roles that challenge the more **patriarchal** attitudes of the 1950s and that reference the triumphant flight of Valentina Tereshkova.

In the early 1960s, 'experts' such as scientists, engineers and mathematicians were held in high regard. Doctor Who himself certainly has something of the expert about him, but he is not a sympathetically drawn character when he is first introduced. He dresses eccentrically, has long hair in spite of his age and is arrogant and confrontational. He seems to have imprisoned the two Coal Hill teachers, Barbara Wright and Ian Chesterton.

At the end of the episode we are left in some doubt about the Doctor. Does he represent the audience's fears and anxieties about 'the other' or is he an inspirational hope for a better world and brighter future? This contradiction seems perfectly to reflect the uncertain moods of Britain in 1963.

> **Link**
>
> You will find further discussion of *Doctor Who*: 'An Unearthly Child' in Chapter 5, pages 162–165.

> **Key term**
>
> **Patriarchy**
> A system or society in which men are all-powerful and women are excluded from positions of influence or responsibility. Patriarchal attitudes are the views and beliefs that justify this inequality.

# Technological convergence and media language

Digital technology has enabled the **convergence** of previously distinct media forms such as print, radio, television, film and online and social media. All of these can be accessed virtually instantly on personal computers and mobile devices. These developments have had a major impact on media language.

As the content of 'old technologies' shifted to the internet, many of the existing codes and conventions were simply transferred over. For example, as newspapers developed their own webpages, the version on the screen looked very much like the version on the page. Steadily, though, new codes and conventions emerged. Online newspaper content has become interactive, with lots of branching menus and embedded videos. Readers are invited to comment on the stories or participate in polls and surveys.

The television industry is also adapting to changing viewing habits and evolving digital technology. Viewers using smart televisions and mobile devices prefer to select their own content rather than watching the 'bundled' programmes of traditional broadcasters. These traditional programmes have always relied on 'flow': the careful assembly of an evening's viewing and the ongoing demand of soap operas and drama series.

This is especially important for companies that need to attract viewers to their advertising. Many programmes have a little narrative 'hook' to ensure that viewers come back after the advertising break. Self-selected viewing completely rejects flow and threatens advertising. The slots of traditional television scheduling mean little to viewers who choose what they want to watch and when. Many prefer video entertainment in much shorter segments than the traditional half-hour to one-hour programme slots. Conversely, drama fans often prefer to 'binge-watch' a whole series in a couple of sittings.

Advertising, too, is adapting its media language to the internet. Targeted pop-up adverts are based on our internet browsing and social media use. Advertising messages can be 'personalised' so that advertisers give the impression of an individual relationship with browsers.

Social media has also seen the integration of advertising, celebrities and reality television. Among leaders in this field are the Kardashians, whose own celebrity brand is reinforced through the endorsement of other products on Twitter, Instagram and Facebook.

> **Key term**
>
> **Convergence**
> There are two ways in which we use the term convergence in media studies.
> Firstly, it refers to the ways in which media industries converge through takeovers and mergers.
> Secondly, it refers to media forms merging together as a consequence of digital technology.

### Activity 1.14

Choose one of Marcus Rashford's social media homepages or the homepage of marcusrashfordofficial.com
Use your knowledge of media language to:
- Find three examples of the conventions of website/social media design.
- Identify three signs and describe the connotations and denotations of each one.
- Briefly describe the narrative features of your chosen homepage.
- Describe the genre features of your chosen homepage.

Technological developments have put powerful media production tools in the hands of millions of people. Smartphone owners can shoot and edit video or audio blogs and enhance still images. These media products are easily uploaded to the internet, giving the everyday phone user as much potential to communicate with a mass audience as a powerful media organisation. All of this user-generated content and the widespread availability of media technology have had an interesting effect on media language.

Most of you are now well aware of the ability to manipulate images (also known as photoshopping) because most of you do it yourselves. This familiarity means that it is difficult for media industries to impress audiences simply by using high-end technology in the creation of media products. Your consumption of video, for example, is very likely to fill a whole spectrum from shaky, unedited, low-resolution scraps of material uploaded to YouTube, to the most intensely spectacular sequences in blockbuster movies.

The spectrum of technology – from hand-held to big screen blockbuster

Developments such as **high definition (HD) and ultra-high definition (UHD) TV**, **computer-generated imagery (CGI)** and 3D television have all had an influence on television, but they haven't so much raised the bar as extended the range of our viewing expectations. When comparing two products separated by over 50 years, such as *Doctor Who*: 'An Unearthly Child' and *His Dark Materials*: 'The City of Magpies'. It is easy to see the impact that technological developments have had on media language and production values. But we still understand 'An Unearthly Child' perfectly well. What's more, we are accustomed to the use of user-generated content such as grainy mobile phone footage in prime time news broadcasts. In other words, the audience's capacity to decode media language hasn't just moved on as technology moves on, it has expanded. We have to deal with media language that is more diverse, more sophisticated and much more extensive than ever before. Amazingly, our capacity to understand all this media language has kept pace and we have a much deeper understanding, not least because we are creators as well as consumers.

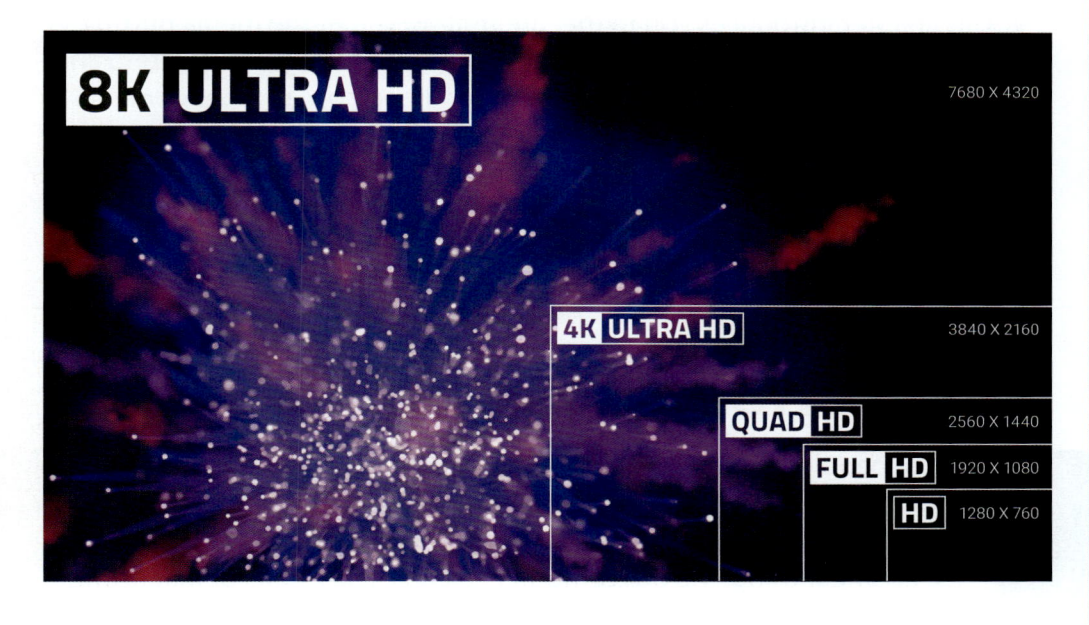

### Key terms

**High definition (HD) and ultra-high definition (UHD) TV**
Standard definition (SD) television is gradually being replaced by HD television (at four times the resolution) and the next generation of UHD and 4K (eight times SD resolution) television sets are available. UHD and 4K TV adds other technologies that increase the clarity, definition and colour range of images. Making programmes in UHD has many implications for media language. The quality of the image is so high that viewers are able to interact with their television sets, for example in sports coverage, by panning and zooming within the images to pick out a particular piece of action. UHD television is much more expensive to produce, so it is likely to be used to create material that can be used many times, for example natural history and science programmes.

**Computer-generated imagery (CGI)**
The use of graphics software to generate still or moving images. CGI is often associated with animation and special effects in blockbuster films but is increasingly being used to enhance conventionally shot sequences in advertising and television.

### Link

For more about CGI see the Galaxy ad, pages 190–191.

### References

Dainty, S. & Kilkelly, D. (2016, 18 February) *EastEnders* Cliffhangers Ranked: The 13 All-time Greatest Duff-Duff Moments, http://www.digitalspy.com/soaps/eastenders/feature/a783903/eastenders-cliffhangers-ranked-the-13-all-time-greatest-duff-duff-moments/.

Kirst, S. (2015, 17 December) The Kardashian's Social Media Influence, Forbes.com, https://www.forbes.com/sites/seamuskirst/2015/12/17/the-kardashians-social-media-influence/?sh=1513797b1f03.

*Radio Times* (2016, 19 March) Nowhere for Football Referees to Hide Over Dodgy Decisions if Sports Channels Have Their Way, http://www.radiotimes.com/news/2016-03-19/nowhere-for-football-referees-to-hide-over-dodgy-decisions-if-sports-channels-have-their-way/.

# 2 Media Representations

## What's in this chapter?

- This chapter introduces you to the different ways that the media portray events, issues, individuals and social groups by selecting, constructing and mediating the elements they include. You will see how all types of media consciously or unconsciously reflect the social, cultural, historical and political contexts in which they are produced.
- You will learn how the media re-present the world to create different versions of reality. In particular, you will look at how they re-present gender and stereotypes to convey a particular message.

## The construction of reality

Some people argue that the mass media construct our reality for us. An alternative argument is to say that the media offer us a 'window on the world'. This is the idea that the media extend our senses so that we can see and hear things via our computer screens, televisions or magazines that we could never otherwise experience.

This second argument has a lot going for it. Without BBC1's 2017 series *Blue Planet II* it's very unlikely that you would ever witness the extraordinary sight of a huge fish leaping out of the sea to catch and eat a bird in mid-flight, but we accept, in the context of a documentary, that it is real.

On the other hand, we don't think films such as *Black Widow* (2021) are real. They're a bit of escapism – fun that lets us escape from reality for a couple of hours. It seems that growing up with media products such as these gives us all a good set of skills when it comes to telling the difference between what is real and what is not.

But it's not quite that simple. The version of reality that the media present to us in factual programmes such as *Blue Planet II* could never be the *same* as reality. It is only a *selective* version of reality. Apparently, the seven-episode series took four years to make. Each one of the filming crew worked for nine weeks of real time to create every one minute of screen time. So, the material included in the series was carefully selected from a huge amount of footage (BBC, 2018).

Sir David Attenborough premiered *Blue Planet II* at the Cinema De Lux. We accept that what we see in nature documentaries such as this is real.

How did the programme-makers decide what to include and what to leave out? Certainly, potential audience appeal must have been one factor. Rarely seen events such as the bird-eating fish, and bizarre creatures such as a fish with a transparent skull, feature prominently. The extraordinary beats the ordinary when trying to entertain viewers. This means that certain ideas or 'ways of seeing' nature will be favoured over others.

In an earlier David Attenborough natural history programme, *Frozen Planet* (2011), footage of a polar bear being born caused some controversy. The voice-over and continuity editing strongly suggested that the bear was born in the wild, in the Arctic snow, but the footage was actually shot in a German animal park. Some critics accused the BBC of misleading viewers with fakery. Perhaps, though, they were missing the point that media always distort reality. As soon as any information is encoded for communication by the media, it is no longer 'reality' but 'mediated reality'.

This process, called **mediation**, is an important one to understand. Even when media producers try to portray an accurate view, they must make selections. For example, they may have to condense an hour-long event into two minutes for a news broadcast. This event could have been experienced by hundreds of people, who all saw it from different points of view. Even those who were present will have seen and heard different things. When you think about this, it is obvious that some aspects have to be left out.

Any message communicated by the media is influenced by the codes and conventions of that medium – you learned about these in Chapter 1. For example, television news will signify to viewers how significant and important a story is by using the codes of television news, such as the position of the story in the running order, the length of time given to the story, and the news presenter's facial expression and their tone of voice. If a news story is considered very important, the news presenter will present the whole news programme from the scene of the story rather than the studio. None of this suggests that television news is deliberately trying to mislead or distort facts, but it does show that the process of mediation affects how we understand the media.

So, do the media 'construct reality' or are they a 'window on the world'? Accepting that the media cannot simply present us with reality in the same way as looking through a window is an important part of our understanding of the mass media. Sometimes we can easily recognise the difference between reality and mediated reality; sometimes we have to think harder to see where selections and omissions have been made – this is a key part of media studies.

When we do this, we are looking at representations of the world. Think of this word as '*re*-presentation'. The media are *re*-presenting the world to us. In other words, they are taking what is real and changing it – at least slightly – in order to show it to us more easily. This is the same whether we are looking at factual or fictional media products.

In the wider sense of being a 'window on the world', however, the media bring us a fantastic range of information and entertainment that would never have been available to us without print and electronic media.

Of course, you may disagree. Media studies is not just about learning facts and information, it's also about developing your own ideas and arguments.

### Key term

**Mediation**
The selection and omission of information when creating a media product.

### Activity 2.1

Consider an event that you and at least three other members of your class have all witnessed – it could be as simple as your walk to school or college this morning. Without discussing your memories of the event first, each write an accurate account of what happened. Compare the written accounts. Consider whereabouts in the narrative each person started – did you all choose the same initial event? Which aspects did you each choose to focus on and which did some people leave out?

You have each mediated the event – put it into your own words as a piece of communication.

*A newsreader may present an important story from the scene of the event itself.*

# Who do the media represent?

A lot of media products are focused on people, because we are interested in, and keen to identify with, other people. The media use a combination of different elements – the media language you learned about in the previous chapter – to create a representation. Together, these encourage you to make assumptions about the person being represented. These might include:

- **Appearance**: e.g. ethnicity, dress, age, attractiveness, visible disabilities.
- **Voice**: e.g. accent, choice of words, use of language, volume of speech, speed of dialogue.
- **Behaviour**: e.g. slow, quirky, aggressive, natural, predictable, empathetic – or not.
- **Visual effects**: e.g. camera angles, length of shots, editing, lighting, computer-generated images (CGIs).

Together these aspects help to build up an idea of the person which may, or may not, be positive.

Here are some examples of how the media represent people.

## Individuals (including yourself and celebrities)

Have you ever met Kim Kardashian in real life? It's unlikely, but you have probably formed an opinion about what she's like as a person as a result of seeing her represented in the media – or hearing what other people who have never met her say about her, based on what they have seen in the media. If you have seen her featured in a gossip magazine, you might have a less positive opinion of her than if you've played her Kim Kardashian: Hollywood game, where she is friendly and helpful.

Both representations are just that – representations – and focus on particular elements to create an image.

Often the media actively shape the public perception of individuals, particularly those in the public eye. As we saw in Chapter 1, pages 25–26, the bias of a particular newspaper influences how they represent politicians such as Labour leader Jeremy Corbyn. Whether you gain a positive or negative impression of him depends to some extent on the representations you see (and, of course, how critical you are of those representations).

This idea applies to fictional characters, too. Often, there isn't time in a film or TV show to explain a character's background and motivations in a lot of detail, so certain signs and symbols are given as short-cuts, so that the audience can fill in the gaps. You may also draw from your own experiences of the world to help you do this. Sometimes the representations are so simplistic that they are just **stereotypes**.

> **Key term**
>
> **Stereotyping**
> The reduction of a social group to a limited set of characteristics or preconceived ideas.

> **Link**
>
> Stereotyping will be discussed later in this chapter on pages 58–60.

Take Tyrion Lannister, from *Game of Thrones* (right), for example. Even if you haven't seen the show before, you'll be able to guess just from looking at him that he is rich and high up the social hierarchy (from his often-ornate clothing), has encountered violence (from his scars) and has probably had to overcome certain issues in his life caused by his height. Of course, regular viewers of the show will know that his character is much more complex than that, but this is a good starting point.

And don't forget that you, as an individual, may also be represented in the media, for example, in your social media profile or perhaps in an interview on a vlog.

The visual representation of a character encourages the audience to make assumptions about them.

### Activity 2.2

Think about yours or a friend's social media profile.
- What was the last photograph that was uploaded?
- How did this represent you/your friend? Think about the pose, clothing, hair, etc. and the rest of the mise-en-scène within the image?
- What did you/your friend want people to think when they saw this image?
- Did people react to it the way you/they wanted them to?

Even if you try to shape your own representation by carefully choosing your answers in an interview, or by your choice of photo and bio content in your Instagram profile, you still can't control exactly how you are represented or what the audience will think of you. We all have different experiences in our past, and bring these to bear on what we see and hear when we are decoding representations.

### Activity 2.3

Think about an **avatar** you have made to represent your character on screen. If you haven't got one, create one for Kim Kardashian: Hollywood or a similar mobile game. Then think about how close it looks to the real you.
- What is different?
- What is the same?
- If it is different, was this a conscious choice?
- How was this influenced by the elements (e.g. skin colour, hairstyles, clothes) offered to you by the game?
- Why do you think those particular elements were chosen by the game designer?

### Key terms

**Avatar**
A picture, icon or character that represents a digital media user, e.g. a game-player.

**Social groups**
Two or more people who share a common sense of identity.

## Social groups

All of us belong to several different **social groups**, by sharing a common background or interest with other people. Usually, people within these groups interact. Your family and media studies class are two distinct social groups, as are any clubs or societies you belong to.

There are many different ways of defining social groups. Advertisers are particularly interested in the social groups we belong to, as you will see in Chapter 3 when you look at Media Audiences. However, media producers also need to represent social groups using signifiers, just as they do with individuals.

Here are some ways in which social groups are defined.

## Social class

There are many ways of looking at social class. One way is to find clear distinctions of class based on people's occupations. This method is often used by media industries when they want to target a particular social class with a media product such as an advertisement or newspaper.

### Activity 2.4

Examples of social groups you might see in the media are:
- mothers
- motorcyclists
- pensioners
- pianists
- computer programers.

Choose one of these that you have seen visually represented in the media and list the elements that help you to know what social group they belong to. For example, a computer programer might be represented as a young, bespectacled man.

Of course, some people could belong to more than one of these groups at the same time, for example a mother who is also a computer programer and a biker. How might she be represented in the media?

### Link

We shall discuss some of the ways in which social class is **objectively** measured in Chapter 3 Media Audiences.

How would the media represent a mother who is also a computer programer and a biker?

A second approach to social class is more **subjective**. It's about how you perceive social class. For example, many people feel that they are a member of a different social class to the one suggested by their occupation and income. We also recognise many signs and symbols that we associate with class. It is certainly a subject that can stir up strong emotions. There are many class-related words and phrases that have strong connotations which can be either positive or negative, for example:

- chav
- stuck up
- posh
- common
- toff
- Essex girl
- one of us
- one of them
- airs and graces.

These are just a few; you can probably think of many more.

In this chapter, the second of these two approaches is going to be discussed, as we look at how social class is represented by different media products.

In the UK, people are often described as being working class, middle class or upper class, with some cross-over between the different groups – lower middle class and upper middle class, for example. A person's social class is represented in the media in many ways, for example, via their:

- clothing (scruffy or smart, cheap or expensive)
- accent (people with strong regional accents are often represented as being in a lower social class)
- job (careers that require a lot of study, such as architecture, are often shown as being of a higher social standing than ones that don't take so much time to learn, such as working in a supermarket)

### Key terms

**Objectivity**
Information that is based on facts and analysis or scientific reason. Objectivity is based on observable and measurable evidence. Objective views are often backed up by statistics. Something claimed to be 'objectively true' will be supported by hard evidence.

**Subjectivity**
Information that is based on individual interpretation or opinion. It can be clouded by bias, values or beliefs. Subjective views may not be backed up by scientific proof or hard evidence, but they can still have great value in opening our eyes to a deep understanding of something that is not measurable such as humanity, love or grief.

- choice of leisure time activities (middle-class people are often shown going to yoga lessons or eating in restaurants, while working-class people are often shown watching TV or engaging in unhealthy activities such as drinking alcohol heavily or smoking).

In order to associate characters with a social class, the media often employ stereotypes. Sometimes these can be crude and even offensive but they are generally well recognised by media audiences.

Social class is often said to be a more significant indicator of social status in the UK than in other countries, but, everywhere, the ideas of power and hierarchy are important parts of narrative, and these ideas influence representations. The media often encourage us to aspire to a wealthy, upper- or middle-class lifestyle by representing people within those classes as happy, wealthy and deserving, due to their hard work.

In reality, class is often determined by the family that you happen to belong to (for example, Princes William and Harry were born into the royal family) or by luck (their wives Kate and Meghan were in the right place at the right time to meet to form a relationship with them). This representation of the middle and higher classes as being where we should all aspire to be ignores the barriers of family, poverty, prejudice and inequality that make rising up the social hierarchy impossible for many people.

The producers of advertisements have to create representations that the audience will understand very quickly, as TV and radio ads are typically between only 30 seconds and one minute long, and print adverts use images with only a few words to get their message across.

> **Link**
>
> For more about stereotypes see pages 58–63.

### Activity 2.5

Look at a series of print or TV adverts. Discuss the stereotypes that the media use to define people who are:
- working class
- middle class
- upper class.

Do these reflect your real-life experiences?

Front cover of *Hello!* magazine from 8 January 2018

## Subcultures

A **subculture** is a type of social group that has a particularly strong identity because it has a characteristic or interest that differs from that of most people in mainstream society. It may be a hobby, political belief, fashion choice, musical preference or spiritual view. Examples of people from subcultures include vegans, goths, cosplay fans and nudists.

### Key term

**Subculture**
A group with beliefs or values that differ from most people in the wider culture to which it belongs.

> **Talk about it**
>
> Look at the front cover above, from *Hello!* magazine. Identify the ways in which this magazine cover represents the younger members of the royal family, to show them in a positive light. Consider both the main photograph itself and the other aspects of the front cover.

As with class representations, the media may use signs and symbols as a shorthand for indicating that a person belongs to a certain subculture. Everyone would recognise the unusual hair and clothing of a punk, and make assumptions about their beliefs and behaviour as a result. Often, the mainstream media represent certain subcultures in a negative light, so that the audience believes its members are a threat to the stability of society. If the representation is not quite so negative, then the subculture may be treated as a joke, as they are so different from everyone else. The implication is that we, the audience, are not like them, the subculture.

> **Activity 2.6**
>
> Identify three subcultures that the media often portray negatively. Find a media representation for each, such as from a newspaper. How is media language used to construct a negative view of each subculture?

However, sometimes subcultures are deliberately presented positively to encourage acceptance and inclusiveness. Of course, the viewer's existing prejudices may be a barrier to this understanding. For example, *RuPaul's Drag Race* is a phenomenally successful reality show that positively represents the drag queen subculture (men dressing as glamorous women to entertain an audience). Its viewers are likely to be open to this representation.

## Ethnicity

People's understanding of other ethnicities is often formed by the media, especially if they do not often meet others from that ethnic group. The 2011 UK census showed that there were 56 million people in England and Wales. Of these, 86% identified themselves as white, while 6.9% identified as Asian, 3% identified as black and 2% identified as mixed race. These figures bring together people from a range of different backgrounds, however, as in the same year over 270 nationalities were represented in London alone.

Although overt racism is rare in mainstream media, non-white people remain under-represented – about one in seven of the England and Wales population in 2011 would have been classed as 'non-white' – and stereotypes and negative portrayals are common.

To find out if a social group is under-represented, you can carry out a simple *content analysis* of media output. This involves counting or measuring the number of times the social group appears. For example, select a newspaper, and count the number of images of each social group within that newspaper. Alternatively, select a TV series, and count how many of the characters are from each social group. To refine this further, you could count how long each character is on screen, or note whether the characters are negatively or positively portrayed. Compare the proportion of time the social group is seen in the media product chosen, with the proportion of the overall population.

## Gender

Masculinity and femininity are culturally determined behaviours associated with being male or female. 'Male' characteristics, such as strength and bravery, are often portrayed as better than 'female' ones, such as kindness and empathy. Women are often either sexualised or presented as passive victims, while men are often shown as powerful, violent or authoritarian. However, such representations are increasingly being challenged.

The perceived value of male and female media workers is not helped by the difference in their pay. In 2017, the BBC published the incomes received by its highest-earning presenters. All seven of the top earners were men. Top of the list was Chris Evans, who received over £2 million in 2015/2016; more than four times as much as Claudia Winkleman, the highest-paid woman. The outcry that followed prompted the BBC to commission an inquiry into the gender pay gap.

## Sexuality

Heterosexuality has traditionally been portrayed as the norm across the media. Even now that gay marriage is legal and generally accepted in society, representations of lesbian, gay, bisexual, trans and queer people (the **LGBTQ+** community) are often still problematic. It is not hard to think of examples of LGBTQ+ characters who are represented as deviant, comic or stereotypical. More often, members of the LGBTQ+ community are not represented at all. However, many recent TV series do feature LGBTQ+ characters positively, so that their sexuality is just part of their character and they are not defined by it.

> **Link**
> We will look at the concepts surrounding gender in more detail later in this chapter on pages 72–79.

> **Key term**
> **LGBTQ+**
> Lesbian, gay, bisexual, trans, queer and others.

> **Link**
> We will look at representations of LGBTQ+ characters later in this chapter on pages 76–77.

Pearl Mackie played Bill Potts, Doctor Who's first overtly gay female companion.

### Quick question 2.1
Why has the media often fallen behind social attitudes in terms of representing LGBTQ+ characters?

### Activity 2.7
Two TV formats that have perhaps had positive representations of LGBTQ+ characters for the longest are soap operas and youth TV series. Can you find examples of this? Why do you think these formats have been ahead of the curve?

> **Link**
>
> For more on millennials see page 90.

## Age

The media like to label different age groups as separate social groups, often representing 'millennials' or 'the elderly' as having particular behaviours or preferences. Of course, we may have nothing in common with someone who happens to be the same age as us, but we may be drawn to media representations of those who are close to our own age because we feel we can identify with them. Children love to see other children on TV shows, and the age of models or actors in adverts and music videos reflects that of the target audience.

Original *Strictly Come Dancing* judge Arlene Phillips was said to be a victim of sex and age discrimination when she was replaced with the younger and less experienced Alesha Dixon (Holmwood, 2009).

Often, the representation of age is related to gender – it is often noted that female TV presenters receive less airtime as they become older, because they are perceived as less attractive, while male presenters continue to stay in work because they are perceived as wise and experienced.

From these descriptions of some of the social groups, you can see that you belong to a variety of different groups and can therefore see yourself represented or left out of media products in a variety of ways.

> **Activity 2.8**
>
> Carry out a content analysis across a variety of visual media products (where it is easier to judge age) – newspapers, TV adverts, TV programmes, magazines, etc. Create a simple tally chart of age groups, in ten-year bands.
> - Which age groups are represented the most?
> - Is this the same across each media form?

> **Activity 2.10**
>
> List five social groups and/or subcultures you belong to. You could choose some of those described above, or include others related to your interests and activities. How do the media represent each group?

# What do the media represent?

The media don't only represent people. Remember that they are *re*-presenting reality to us, and that reality is made up of many different aspects.

## Religions and nationalities

Depictions of religion are closely tied to nationality and ethnicity. Just as it is misleading to represent everyone in a particular age group as acting in a certain way, it is equally misleading to represent an entire nation or religion as the same. It is easy to think of examples – crime dramas such as *CSI* frequently represent Muslim women as the victims of male domestic violence (Elghobashy, 2009, cited in Media Smarts, 2018). Positive representations, such as Dust, the Afghan-Muslim girl who fights alongside her fellow mutants in *X-Men*, are less common. Newspapers often use the words Muslim or Islam to describe criminals, even when their faith has nothing to do with the crime, as in *The Times*' front-page headline 'Call for National Debate on Muslim Sex Grooming' (Norfolk, Coates & Datham, 2015).

> **Activity 2.9**
>
> Working in threes, select either a newspaper or a TV news broadcast, and carry out a content analysis. Each member of your group should focus on one of ethnicity, gender or age. Which groups within each category are under-represented?

Hollywood action movies frequently cast Russians such as the character Yuri Kamarov in *A Good Day to Die Hard* (2013), East Europeans, Arabs or Chinese people as villains. The 2012 war movie *Red Dawn* was expensively transformed for release in China by removing all references to the Chinese villains – they became North Koreans instead. The audience is expected to understand such representations as comic-book caricatures, but the frequency of these stereotypes may lead some people to think that everyone from these countries is the same.

John McClane (left) vs Yuri Kamarov (right) in *A Good Day to Die Hard*

## Places

If you were going to make a podcast or radio show about your town, city or region, how would you represent it? Your choice of content depends on your own attitude towards where you live. For example, you might feature a city's fantastic nightlife and shopping, or you might think its poverty makes a more interesting narrative. The countryside might be represented as beautiful or dull – or both. Similarly, residents of Scotland and Wales often note news media's focus on London and the south-east of England. Clearly, how a place is represented is influenced by the media creator's point of view. Unless you actually visit it yourself, you can only build up a picture of it from how it is represented in the media.

## Events and issues

As seen in Chapter 1, the news media in particular are selective about how certain events and issues are presented. Media creators decide whether to, and how to, report politics, conflicts, scandals and even unusual weather. Heavy snow is a good example because it is a relatively unusual event in this country that directly affects the everyday lives of a lot of people, so is often the top news story when it happens.

Issues such as climate change, LGBTQ+ rights and sport may also be represented in certain ways. The chapter began by looking at the concept of mediation. The fact that all events and issues must necessarily be mediated in some way leads to the idea of **bias**. Even when media producers are trying to be honest and truthful, they will be selecting and omitting information to make the media piece fit into existing conventions and perhaps also to fit the space or time available. Bias can be intentional or unintentional, and can be created using vocabulary choices, visual images, spacing, the choice of character portrayal, juxtaposition and other aspects of media language.

### Quick question 2.2

Why might it be a problem if the audience forms opinions on controversial subjects based on a single media channel, for example their Facebook or Instagram feed?

### Activity 2.11

Consider a place you've heard of but never visited. This could be a city, a region or a country. List your expectations of this place. Now consider what these expectations are based on.
- How many have come from representations you have seen in the media?
- Can you remember specific media products that have given you these impressions?

### Talk about it

With a classmate, research and discuss how a significant weather event was reported in the news media. Did different media channels report it in different ways?

### Key term

**Bias**
A prejudice for or against a particular group or individual. Biased reporting in the media may be demonstrated by tone or style but also by selection or omission. A newspaper story may be biased not because of what is included, but by what is left out. Bias can be innocent, for example a bias for tea and against coffee, but in media studies it usually refers to unfair or irrational practices.

### Activity 2.12

Compare how the BBC and other news media represent contrasting sports events, such as the Summer and Winter Olympics. How does their representation of Team GB's role, and the sports events in general, differ between the Summer Olympics, where they are usually expected to win many medals, and the Winter Olympics, where Team GB is traditionally less successful?

Consider at least:
- vocabulary choices
- the use of specific presenters
- length of individual features
- the use of music and/or graphics.

### Link

For more on Propp see pages 30–31.

### Activity 2.13

Write down the first three words that come to mind when describing:
- heavy metal music fans
- librarians
- grandmothers
- fashion models
- footballers.

Compare your list with a friend's.
- Do you have any words or ideas in common?
- Would you be able to say what your versions of these stereotypes are based on?

# Stereotypes

## Functions and uses

As you have already started to discover, stereotyping is a sort of shorthand for constructing representations. Stereotypes are a way of quickly conveying information about a group or person by tapping into assumptions the audience is already likely to have. Human brains are designed to categorise knowledge and make mental shortcuts. Stereotyping is a way of imposing order on diversity by simplifying people's behaviours and traits. This can help to tell a story. Propp's character types could be seen as stereotypes, reducing the characters in a narrative to 'heroes' and 'villains', for example.

Although they can be useful in helping the audience to easily access and understand the message, stereotypes are also problematic. They reduce the complexity and diversity of a group of real people to a few limited characteristics. These may be based on an element of truth, but (as we have seen) it is impossible to represent the whole truth. Exaggerating certain characteristics of one social group over others over-emphasises the differences between people, which can be funny in a comedy show but may also create conflict between groups.

## Constructing stereotypes

Stereotyping is often related to power. Those who create media representations have the power to decide what is included in those representations. This means that stereotypes are often created by **in-groups** (the dominant members of society, such as politicians, business owners or media producers) at the expense of **out-groups** (minorities within a society). For example, a newspaper might stereotype teenagers by portraying them as lazy. Of course, this doesn't mean that out-groups don't create stereotypes too – teenagers might stereotype parents as boring or old-fashioned, for example – but the most influential stereotypes will be those that are most widely circulated in the popular media.

You should not assume that stereotypes are always deliberately constructed – sometimes they are so much part of the culture that they are not questioned.

The media may not invent stereotypes but they do reinforce them by using repeated stereotypical representations. Sometimes, stereotypes just reflect what most people think, but they can also have a more sinister purpose in maintaining the position of those in power by reinforcing what we are expected to believe.

## Positive and negative stereotyping

Clearly, there are many negative (or derogatory) stereotypes. For example, negative age-related stereotypes are common. Older people are often represented as vulnerable, disabled, out-of-touch or confused. By contrast, teenagers are often represented as aggressive, selfish or lazy. Some older people and teenagers do fulfil these stereotypes, but of course the vast majority of older people and teenagers contribute positively to society. There's a danger that unfair or biased media stereotypes are regarded by some audiences as the whole truth – for example, if a TV drama shows a young black man mugging a pensioner in the street, some viewers may start to be wary of all young black men while they are out.

Stereotypical representations categorise groups and place them in a hierarchy, with the most powerful and dominant at the top. We can therefore think of stereotyping as often being at the expense of those represented, often social groups that are seen as being further down the hierarchy, such as women, the LGBTQ+ community or working-class people.

We must be aware, however, that we often also stereotype as 'villains' those we perceive as holding the power – white, middle-class, heterosexual men. Even though this is generally the most powerful group in society, we should not assume that all its members are deliberately oppressing everyone else.

Positive (or laudatory) stereotypes can improve public perceptions of a particular social group. They can also be used to make audiences think positively about related issues or items. For example, advertisers generally use positive stereotypes to endorse products. Look online for the front page of *Men's Fitness* magazine dated March 2018, showing the celebrity fitness trainer Joe Wicks revealing his muscular body. A male 'six-pack' is a symbol of strength, health and sex appeal. The magazine is using the stereotype of what male fitness looks like to sell the magazine – even if you don't know who Joe Wicks is, you can immediately see that he has a physique for other men to aspire to. The magazine doesn't need to spend time and words setting the scene, as the target audience can immediately decode the message as 'if you buy the magazine, you can find out how to look like Joe Wicks'.

## Development and variation

Stereotypes change over time, as messages are passed from one person to another and reinforced.

The royal family were portrayed as remote and inaccessible 100 years ago, but now they are represented as ordinary people who happen to have glamorous lives. This is partly because social attitudes have changed – non-royals such as Kate and Meghan are now permitted to marry princes. What an attractive, and simplified, fairy-tale narrative.

### Activity 2.14

Compare stereotypical representations of your own age group in a variety of media products. Look for products where the young person is only shown for a small proportion of the time, as these will rely most heavily on stereotypes – for example, adverts, sitcoms and dramas where the young characters are not central.
- How are the young people represented?
- How have these representations been constructed?
- What stereotypes do they rely on?

Homeless people are often stereotyped as being weak and a burden to society.

### Link

Consider the image of the young royals presented on page 53.

Fiction media also use stereotypes to establish a narrative, and can be especially useful in turning negative stereotypes into positive ones. *Goodness Gracious Me*, *Citizen Khan* and *Man Like Mobeen* are all comedy series created by British minority groups. Each one has stirred up controversy over its depictions of British Asians or British Muslims, but each one has also paved the way for less stereotypical representations in the future.

### Talk about it

Read online and discuss the article 'Man Like Mobeen: BBC Comedy Defies Muslim Stereotypes' by Dr Sarah Illott (2018), which discusses how the BBC3 comedy *Man Like Mobeen* explores and subverts stereotypes about young Muslim men.

Why do you think comedy is so effective in challenging stereotypes?

### Activity 2.15

The Netflix show *Grace and Frankie* takes on a number of stereotypes, using age as a starting point. The women of the title are in their 70s when their husbands leave them to marry each other. Watch an episode and note how the show both challenges and upholds stereotypes relating to:
- age
- gender
- sexuality
- class
- ethnicity.

When Robert and Sol in *Grace and Frankie* become gay partners in their 70s, they find that domestic life isn't very different from when they were married to women.

## Under-representation and misrepresentation

The idea of bias in representation has already been discussed. This is often created by under-representation of social groups or issues, or by their misrepresentation.

Some biases in the media aren't immediately obvious. It is often a matter of identifying who or what is missing – spotting the gaps in the representations and then thinking about why they occur. We could ask the following questions when we consider representations within the media:

- How is the media product re-presenting the world to us through its codes and conventions?
- What does it suggest is typical and what is not?
- Who is speaking and for whom?
- What is being represented to us? Why?

One of the CSPs for 2023 is used opposite as a case study to provide more ideas about under-representation.

### Quick question 2.3

How are teenagers often misrepresented in the media?

### Link

You can read more about the representation of teenagers on pages 80–84.

**2 Media Representations**

**CASE STUDY:**

# Advertising and marketing – NHS Blood and Transplant online campaign video 'Represent' featuring Lady Leshurr

The 'Represent' video can be found on YouTube. It is one of the targeted CSPs for 2023, for which AQA asks students to focus on:

- Media Language
- Media Representations.

Here, Media Representations will mainly be discussed.

> **Link**
>
> Read more about how media language is used in this product in Chapter 5, pages 191–193.

## Overview

The 'Represent' video was funded and produced as part of an NHS Blood and Transplant marketing campaign. It specifically targets the black and minority ethnic community in order to increase the number of blood donors from that sector of society. In it, Lady Leshurr raps and sings about how ethnic people are represented in many different careers and walks of life, but are not as well represented among blood donors.

The video takes the genre of a music video, intercutting shots of Lady Leshurr performing the song in an urban setting with shots of a succession of black and Asian role models in the contexts of their success. The video stresses the potential of young ethnic people to achieve their ambitions in many types of career.

## Representation of role models

Think about why Lady Leshurr was chosen to head up the campaign. As a successful singer, rapper and producer, nominated for the 2016 MOBO Awards, she is seen as a good role model. Although their names aren't given, other ethnic role models appear in the film – for example, Chuka Umunna MP and the Olympic boxer Nicola Adams. While Lady Leshurr and the other role models are aspirational figures, they are also represented in this campaign as real, relatable people, shown in the environments they work in.

Lady Leshurr in the 'Represent' video

## Range of representations

The video starts by representing the target audience to themselves as people with a capacity to succeed, 'You could be a rapper … you could be a pilot'. The lyrics also incorporate jobs that many ordinary people do, such as nail technician or bar tender, without making any value judgements about how useful or skilled these jobs are. The message seems to be that society's perception of the value of a job isn't relevant; everyone in the target audience can succeed in their field. It follows that everyone in the target audience should consider giving blood.

> **Quick question 2.4**
>
> How might the inclusion of role models in an advertisement such as this help to encourage the audience to take the required action (in this case, to give blood)?

The producers of 'Represent' have chosen an upbeat and positive representation of the ethnic community and linked this to the campaign's inspirational message. The video challenges negative stereotypes of young ethnic people by aligning the 'give blood' message with a sense of pride in the community and the potential of its members.

## What isn't represented?

What would you have expected to feature in a video that encourages people to give blood? Maybe someone in a position of authority, perhaps a doctor, telling the audience why they should be giving blood, or blood donors explaining why they do it, or even people who need blood transfusions playing on our emotions and sense of guilt. This video contains none of those things.

In this chapter so far, we have been looking at how the processes of selection and omission are used to mediate messages. In this video, the producers have selected specific representations to channel the message or 'call to action' – to donate blood.

The target audience is black and ethnic minority people aged 17 to 24. Do you think the video also appeals to a wider audience, for example white or older people? After all, although the visuals show ethnic people, the lyrics address 'you' and 'we', which could be anyone in the audience.

# Representing values and beliefs

Media products reflect the society and times in which they are produced – the social, cultural, historical and political contexts of media production. Different societies often have different **ideologies**, and these are reflected in the media products that are created.

We all have our personal ideology – our own set of rules about what we think is the right or wrong way to behave towards others, and about what is important in life, for example. Each society also has a dominant ideology – the set of ideas and beliefs that is accepted by most people within that society. In 2014, the UK government made it a requirement that schools teach 'British values', for example. These are defined as being democracy, the rule of law, individual liberty, mutual respect and tolerance for others. The dominant ideology offered by British soap operas is that family is all-important (although who is part of your family is a flexible concept) and that bad deeds towards others will always be found out in the end.

Some theories suggest that the dominant ideology is often simply the ideology of the most powerful group in a society, and people are persuaded to conform with the dominant ideology via **cultural hegemony**, often by being indoctrinated (encouraged to uncritically accept a viewpoint) by the media.

---

### Activity 2.16

Compare the representations of young ethnic people in this video with others that you have seen on the news, on TV and in films. How many of these other representations are negative? What effect might these representations have on the ethnic audience and on audiences outside that community?

Consider how the video's different representations are used to appeal to this target audience. Think about how ethnicity, masculinity, femininity, age, class, disability and place are represented. Are they shown as positive stereotypes? How effective is this?

### Quick question 2.5

What else does the video omit that you might have expected to be included? Why do you think the producers chose not to represent these elements in the video?

### Key terms

**Ideology**
A shared sets of beliefs and ideas about what is right and what is wrong.

**Cultural hegemony**
The process of making people see the beliefs and values of the most powerful group as being natural and common sense.

## Dominant representations

Dominant ideologies affect how we live our daily lives, covering such issues as religion, consumerism and gender roles. They are presented as 'common sense' or 'natural', so we may not even notice or question media representations of the dominant ideology. For example, one of the dominant ideas in many societies is that having more money will improve our lives. TV game shows that offer cash prizes reinforce this ideology to a large audience. Anyone who does question these dominant ideas is thought to be radical and different from the rest of society.

As with stereotypes of social groups, adverts are an obvious media form to look at to see examples of assumptions about ideology, beliefs and values in society. Because they have to get their narrative across so quickly, advertisers have to use ideas that most of the audience will accept as being obvious – such as the idea that 'newer' is always 'better'.

'Who wants to be a millionaire?' The expected answer is 'Me!'

### Activity 2.17

You have already been presented with three ideas used in the media, that we don't normally think to question:
- Having more money improves lives.
- Boy-meets-girl romance is always a good thing.
- Newer is better.

Watch a series of TV adverts or look through the adverts in a magazine. Can you spot other examples of values or beliefs that we are all assumed to share?

Dominant representations are those that reflect the dominant values of a society. They are both created and reinforced by the media. Sometimes this is deliberate – as shown in the front-page analysis of the *Daily Mirror* and the *Sun* in Chapter 1, pages 25–26. This is a type of **propaganda**, when the media are used to promote a biased political point of view.

The newspapers are clearly demonstrating partiality – being on one side of the political argument – but the people who buy and read each paper often do so because the way the stories are reported reflects their own ideas. Newspapers are an obvious example of reinforcing a dominant ideology but it may be more subtle in other forms of media.

## Minority representations

The idea of cultural hegemony suggests that if you don't agree with the dominant ideology you may be seen as strange, rebellious or even a threat to society. Media studies allows us to question the media's messages and consider whose views have been represented – and whose have not been represented, for example people from the ethnic community or immigrants.

### Quick question 2.6

What dominant ideologies are often being reinforced in a boy-meets-girl romantic comedy?

### Key term

**Propaganda**
Using the media to promote a biased viewpoint, usually for political purposes.

### Activity 2.18

What elements of this *Shout* magazine cover reinforce accepted ideas about gender?

**AQA GCSE Media Studies**

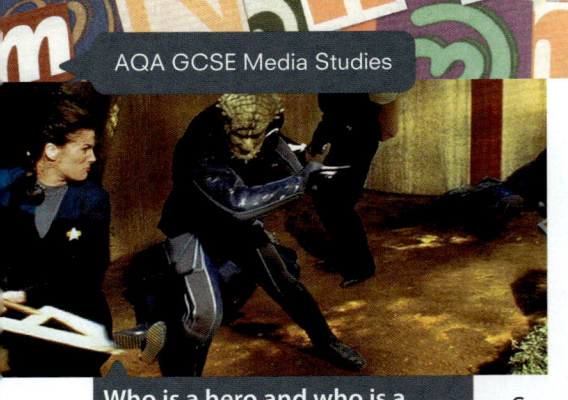

*Who is a hero and who is a villain depends on your point of view.*

Even when some social groups *are* represented, they may be presented simply as opposites to the accepted norm. This applies to fiction as well as to factual media products. For example, in *Star Trek*, Starfleet exemplifies the dominant representation of bravery and heroism, whereas the Klingons' (and some other alien species') different ideas about what is brave and heroic could be seen as the minority representation – they are represented as oppositional to Starfleet and therefore unacceptable.

Some media products deliberately resist the stereotypical representations for a social group or an idea. The TV comedy show *Man Like Mobeen*, mentioned on page 60, is centred on British Muslims, but avoids the usual stereotyped representations, and instead creates new representations with its set of characters.

## Representation of the self

Everyone has a sense of their own identity, formed partly by their background, experiences and social groups, and partly by how they see people like themselves reflected in the media.

Until recently, the mass media (such as TV or newspapers) held most of the power to represent and shape your understanding of different social groups – including your own. Now, though, online participatory media, and social media in particular, make it much easier for anyone to create a representation of themselves. These media have also allowed us to find out about a wider range of identities and representations than we could before the internet, including many that don't conform to traditional mainstream media messages.

It's also easy to create alternative versions of yourself across different media platforms. For example, many video games let you customise the avatar that represents you as you play the game. Naturally, most people create a better or aspirational version of themselves. In an adventure game, or first-person shooter, you might want your avatar to appear strong and intimidating; in a personality-based role-playing game, such as Kim Kardashian: Hollywood, you would probably want to develop a beautiful and glamorous alter ego.

### Activity 2.19

Select a sub-group of society that is not usually regarded as powerful – such as the LGBTQ+ community, Asian women, working-class teenagers or people with disabilities. Look for examples of these people represented in mainstream media. For comparison, find media products that are created by the sub-group themselves. Where are you most likely to find these products? What key similarities and differences do you notice in the representations?

### Link

See Activity 2.3 on page 51 about avatars.

### Talk about it

Discuss with a partner the benefits and pleasures of creating a 'better' version of yourself. Given what has been said about dominant ideology and minority representations, why might some people see the choices offered for creating avatars as problematic?

*Kim Kardashian: Hollywood enables players to customise their avatar according to dominant ideas of physical attractiveness.*

On social media, people represent not a fictional character but their real selves. Or do they? Just like other media producers, they select content and images that construct the particular identity they want to share with others. Whether they select flattering photos or scruffy snapshots, they're still mediating their online image.

### Activity 2.20

**How is your online identity formed?**

Look at how you represent yourself online, for example on your Instagram, Snapchat or TikTok profile, or on YouTube. Also look at what you add to your newsfeed and how you respond to other people's posts, content and comments. Think about not only the words you use online but also photos, images, what you choose to share, and what you like and comment on.

It can be hard to distance yourself from your own representations of yourself but imagine someone you don't know is viewing your online presence and forming opinions about you. You could also ask a friend to honestly tell you whether your online identity reflects your real-life identity. For example, do you seem:

- glamorous
- fun
- thoughtful
- intelligent
- funny
- adventurous
- religious
- opinionated
- rude
- grumpy
- self-obsessed?

How does your online identity give this impression?

Now think about *why* you decided to use that content or those images. How were you influenced by:

- representations of celebrities
- your friends' online identities
- dominant values and beliefs
- your own views, interests and opinions
- your background and culture
- your mood when you posted the content
- the available options on the page
- the target audience?

What do you choose *not* to include in your online profile? Why?

If you have more than one online presence, do you represent yourself the same way in each one?

*What you choose to put online might not be the same as reality.*

Clearly, not only are we all different from each other but we also have several (or fragmented) options for presenting ourselves.

An example of an online celebrity will now be looked at to develop some specific ideas about how an online identity can be formed.

### CASE STUDY:

# Marcus Rashford (2023 CSP)

Marcus Rashford is a British footballer and social action campaigner, awarded an MBE in 2020 in recognition of his services for children during the COVID-19 epidemic. Since starting his Twitter feed in May 2016, Rashford has gained 4.9 million followers (as of 2021), along with 11.6 million Instagram followers and 8.7 million followers on Facebook. His videos on Instagram typically have between 1 and 4 million views and over 200,000 likes each.

### Link

Marcus Rashford's image and vlogs will be looked at in more detail in Chapter 5, pages 168–172.

*Rashford often presents himself in what seems to be an open and honest way. Image from Rashford's official Twitter.*

### Key term

**Brand**
An identity or representation of a product, which distinguishes it from its rivals. These are obviously commercial products. Although an individual person, Marcus Rashford can also be thought of as a commercial product.

*Rashford's brand is reflected in the actions he posts on social media. Image from Rashford's official Twitter.*

His posts are usually either about football or his various campaigns, often showing him alongside the people he is working to support. On Twitter, he will often retweet posts by organisations – particularly those in and around Manchester – who are helping underprivileged children, and enter into social media conversations with them.

Here we will address a question based on representation. This question assumes that Marcus Rashford's media output is one of your CSPs.

> 'Social media allows us to see celebrities as they really are.'
> How far is this true of Marcus Rashford (CSP)?

To answer a question like this, you need to think about ways in which the media re-present the world and construct versions of reality. In particular, if this is one of your CSPs, you will have considered how Marcus Rashford represents himself and his world across the online, social and participatory forms he uses. In doing this, you will have investigated his portrayal of his interests, concerns, relationships with others, his values and beliefs.

## Ways that social media construct identity

As with any media production, posting on social media involves a construction of identity. Consider the ways in which such posts enable the producer to create and control their image. Assuming they are personally responsible for their words, videos and photographs, influencers on social media can choose what content to include and how to create it, and can make editorial choices. Making choices about what to select and omit means they can mediate their life and thoughts, presenting a version of themselves to appeal to a particular audience.

Social media is an unusual format because it enables the creation of shared social networks. Marcus Rashford's social media profile is not limited to Instagram (his most popular platform), and he has a large audience on other online and social participatory formats, such as Facebook and Twitter. He includes the people he is close to, such as his teammates, promoting the image of a shared community of young, outgoing people. He also includes, for example, the children he works with in holiday clubs and food schemes. His followers start to recognise these characters and relationships, and may feel that they are building a relationship with him themselves from repeated viewing.

## Ordinary vs celebrity

Think about how Rashford presents himself as a **brand**. His open and casual, yet determined, approach is extremely likable, and his persona is of a smiling and successful older brother or best friend rather than someone famous and unattainable, such as Kim Kardashian. His focus on helping the underprivileged continues this impression, showing him as caring and willing to stand up for others.

At the same time, he is a celebrity, with an income from football alone of over £10 million a year (Sports Khabri, 2021). You could say that, having gained his celebrity-status through both football and activism for the underprivileged, he is more appealing because he remains 'one of us'.

However, his celebrity status means that he is not only quickly recognisable but also that he is in a position to influence his audience more than someone without such a large following. Having an online presence is a type of self-promotion – much of his success in gathering a large audience that centres on his engaging and honest personality, rather than simply his football skill. Of course, he will not present things that may not appeal to the audience, such as showing when he is grumpy or irritable. However, as a sportsman, he knows that when he fails, he fails in public, and he faces up to this, discussing these failures and how he feels about them. With so many media representations of perfect celebrities, this is refreshing – although this, in itself, could also be a form of managed representation to increase audience empathy and engagement.

Of course, it is nothing new for celebrities to represent themselves as vulnerable or 'normal', but social media offers a particular opportunity to control such representations.

## Gender

As Marcus Rashford is both a footballer and a social activist, it is important to think about how he embodies and reinforces gender stereotyping. Is he reinforcing stereotypes about young men being able to shout louder than others? Or has he shown that he can be successful in promoting the needs of children just by being true to himself, and talking about problems no matter the barriers? Your answer to these questions probably says more about you and your values than it does about his. Remember that, in media studies, you are allowed to voice your opinion, as long as you use evidence from the products you are studying to make your point.

# Representations of reality

At this point, it is useful to look in more detail at what we mean by 'reality'.

We've already seen how difficult it is to represent 'real' life and even our 'real' selves. We have to make decisions about selection and omission. Cultural theorist Stuart Hall reminds us that representation in the media is the production of meaning through media language:

> *Reality exists outside language, but it is constantly mediated by and through language.* (1993, page 95)

As seen in Chapter 1, this language is formed of signs which we share as a culture, and these help us to convey and understand messages.

Objects, characters and events on screen or in print do not have universal, true meanings but are mediated by media producers. They choose what to show us, so their social and personal biases affect the 'facts' through what is shown and how it is shown.

Much of what we believe to be real has been conveyed to us via the media. What do you think is the most realistic form of media that represents the world most accurately? You might say that newspapers report real events, and that TV documentaries can seem like real life. But, as we have seen, all media output is just

### Quick question 2.7
Does the fact that Rashford earns such a high salary influence his representation?

### Activity 2.21
Now that you have read about some of the aspects of representation you can look out for, look at Marcus Rashford's website and one of his social media feeds. Find specific shots, video sequences, images or words that support or contradict the points made in this case study. Think about how the media language used at these points has created specific representations.

Use this research, and the ideas in this case study, to answer the question posed at the start of this section:

'Social media allows us to see celebrities as they really are.' How far is this true of Marcus Rashford (CSP)?

### Quick question 2.8
You have seen that Marcus Rashford presents himself as ordinary, masculine, caring, successful and determined. What other stereotypes do social media influencers often convey?

### Quick question 2.9
Can the media ever truly reflect reality?

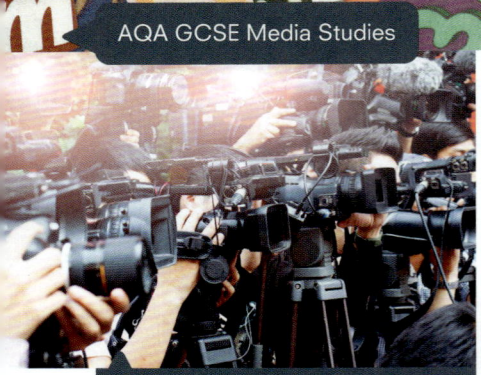

*How real are people's actions when they know they are being filmed?*

a representation of reality because the creators have made choices about what to include and how to present it. Even non-fiction films and TV programmes – such as documentaries, news reports and interviews – are a particular version of the world. Many more hours of footage are filmed than are actually used in the broadcast.

Many media techniques are used to convince audiences that what they are seeing or hearing is real. In film and TV, for example, a sense of reality may be constructed by making decisions about the following essential elements:

- **people**: e.g. stereotyping, gender, class, ethnicity, attractiveness, behaviour, speech, body language
- **places**: e.g. internal/external, locations, positive/negative
- **design**: e.g. mise-en-scène, costume, props, colour
- **ideas**: e.g. reinforcing or questioning dominant ideology
- **script**: e.g. how people interact, what they say
- **sound**: e.g. music, sound effects, dialogue
- **camerawork**: e.g. framing, camera angles, camera movement
- **lighting**: e.g. high/low key, colour filters, direction, shadows
- **editing**: e.g. narrative sequencing, image-editing techniques and transitions, visual effects.

The last of these, editing, can be particularly important. Events can be filmed in one order but shown in another. Actions that were filmed far apart in time or location can be edited together to suggest they flowed into each other. Obviously, this is how fiction-based media are created – watch any 'making of' video as a reminder of how this is done. But this isn't always considered when watching supposedly factual videos. Sound can be used to 'smooth over the joins'. If a TV sequence shows one person asking a question, and then cuts to a second person while the audience is hearing the end of the question, they will obviously assume the second person is reacting to the question. In reality, the second person may not have even been present when the question was asked.

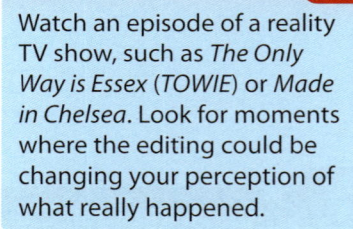

## Constructing 'reality' in the news

As we have seen, 'reality' in the media is difficult to pin down. It's especially problematic in news media, which the audience is supposed to trust to show what is really happening in the world.

This is mediated by news values, that is, the ways in which each news production company will assess the day's news stories and decide on their importance. Each company will have its own news agenda and set of news values. Newspapers and news broadcasters will decide which stories to include or leave out, and how much space or time to give to each story, based on these values. We know, for example, that newspapers may have different political biases, with, for example, the *Daily Mail* reflecting a more right-wing, conservative viewpoint, and the *Guardian* reflecting a more left-wing, liberal viewpoint. This might lead the *Daily Mail* to covering different stories from the *Guardian*, or choosing a different story for its front-page headline. However, you still trust that what is reported is essentially true.

---

**Quick question 2.10**

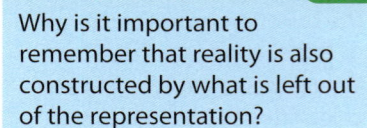

Why is it important to remember that reality is also constructed by what is left out of the representation?

**Activity 2.22**

Watch an episode of a reality TV show, such as *The Only Way is Essex* (*TOWIE*) or *Made in Chelsea*. Look for moments where the editing could be changing your perception of what really happened.

UK-based print and broadcast news providers are very careful to be seen to give factual accounts of events, separating these from opinions. In any individual news item, opinions are apparently only given by the people *within* the news stories, not by the journalists or news presenters. Where possible, images of the events covered are used, as these make the stories more believable – you trust what you see with your own eyes. The people within the stories, whether they were directly involved in the event or are experts or witnesses, are named. Locations and times are also given, which creates a background of facts that we can check. Because of these layers of factual information, and the long history of other truthful stories from the same sources, you believe the stories given to you each day. It is because of this level of belief that newspapers' and news broadcasters' April Fools' Day items can work.

## The impact of fake news

You have probably heard the term **fake news** used more and more in recent years. Different people and organisations use and understand the term in various ways but it is mainly used to mean two things:

- information that has been made up and/or is untrustworthy
- information that is damaging to a person, group or entity, usually but not always in a political context.

In both cases, the intention is to mislead the reader by withholding, misusing or fabricating facts. A moral panic has arisen as it is often seen as a threat to democracy and freedom of speech, because we cannot trust what we see, read and hear. It undermines serious journalism, as people begin to distrust all sources of information.

Most fake news originates online, from providers without a 'long history of other truthful stories'. However, like the April Fools' joke news items, fake news uses the same construction as real news, so it seems believable. Joke items are revealed by the news providers later in the same day or the next day, so we can all enjoy them. The dishonesty of fake news is not revealed by its creators.

While president of the US, Donald Trump frequently used Twitter to denounce 'fake news', by which he meant any report in the news media with which he disagreed. His political opponents and many journalists accused him of being the source of fake news. This long-running dispute shows just how important it is to have a good understanding of media representations and a critical approach to news, especially stories that are circulated on social media.

## The influence of social media

Of course, this is nothing new – people have always made up information and told lies. Propaganda has always been a part of the media. However, in the 21st century, the internet, social media in particular, has made it much easier to spread misinformation because content is easily accessible and can be widely shared. You've probably seen **clickbait** headlines on social media, posted by friends or in the sidebar ads, and probably have been disappointed when the webpages they lead to don't really reflect what you expected.

> **Key term**
>
> **Fake news**
> Information that appears to be genuine but is untrustworthy, misleading, false and/or damaging.

> **Key term**
>
> **Clickbait**
> Eye-catching web content or headlines designed to entice the viewer to click on a link to a webpage with questionable value.

> **Link**
>
> For more on propaganda see page 63.

> **Talk about it**
>
> What are the implications of young people getting most of their news information from social media?

Having people click on these links can be a way of generating advertising revenue, so the creators write and post fake stories that they know people will want to read. However, such stories can be very damaging to the people or groups mentioned in them, especially if the stories are linked to significant events such as elections.

You'll see many of the following words and phrases used online to encourage you to click on the link:

| | |
|---|---|
| Wait till you see | Might look like a |
| Till you see what | Is what happens when |
| That will make you | For the first time |
| Will blow your mind | What he found is |
| It looks like a | This is what happens |
| You need to know | Thing I've ever seen |
| What happened to this | The definitive ranking of |
| The reason why is | Look like a normal |

Source: Adapted from Lee, 2014

> **Activity 2.23**
>
> Find a news story on any subject via social media. Analyse it, using the graphic below to identify whether it could be regarded as fake news. Can you think of any other criteria for deciding the trustworthiness of a news source?

Anyone can upload information to the internet, whether in blogs, vlogs, social media or their own websites. People and organisations can also 'buy' social media comments, posts, tweets and followers. So much information is available that it's very hard to distinguish what is reliable from what is not.

A 2016 study by Ofcom, published in 2017, suggests that the majority of 16 to 24 year olds use the internet as their principal source of news, and rarely read printed newspapers. Contrast this with the over 65s, who are most likely to get their news from the TV, with printed newspapers a close second. Overall, 47% of those who used social media for news said they mostly found news stories through social media, by clicking on a post or tweet about the news, and by reading friends' or contacts' comments.

Researchers at the Massachusetts Institute of Technology (MIT) undertook a massive study of Twitter over a ten-year period. They found that rumours, hoaxes and lies almost always won out over the truth. Fake news spreads faster and deeper than the truth on Twitter. The data scientist who led the research project said in an interview on *The Atlantic* (Meyer, 2018),

*It seems pretty clear that false information outperforms true information.*

## HOW TO SPOT FAKE NEWS

**CONSIDER THE SOURCE**
Click away from the story to investigate the site, its mission and its contact info.

**READ BEYOND**
Headlines can be outrageous in an effort to get clicks. What's the whole story?

**CHECK THE AUTHOR**
Do a quick search on the author. Are they credible? Are they real?

**SUPPORTING SOURCES?**
Click on those links. Determine if the info given actually supports the story.

**CHECK THE DATE**
Reposting old news stories doesn't mean they're relevant to current events.

**IS IT A JOKE?**
If it is too outlandish, it might be satire. Research the site and author to be sure.

**CHECK YOUR BIASES**
Consider if your own beliefs could affect your judgement.

**ASK THE EXPERTS**
Ask a librarian, or consult a fact-checking site.

IFLA — International Federation of Library Associations and Institutions

The International Federation of Library Associations and Institutions produced this infographic to encourage critical thinking.

## Why do producers construct different versions of reality?

All types of media are, by their nature, persuasive communications. Whether it's a radio show or a TV commercial, a media product exists to convey a message. We have seen throughout this chapter that mediation – the process of representing an idea, issue, event, group or person to the audience – changes and influences how we perceive that message.

Patek Philippe watch adverts convey a strong message that a watch is a treasured possession – a good watch is something that is valued emotionally as well as financially, and will be passed on to others.

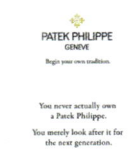

Patek Philippe watch adverts create their version of reality by using the message *'You never actually own a Patek Philippe. You merely look after it for the next generation'*, which it has used for over 20 years.

Sometimes it's hard to identify the message, or no single message is being given, but the producers select content to create their version of reality. They may be asking themselves:

- How can my media product attract the audience?
- How can it engage and immerse the audience?
- How can it nudge the audience to come to certain conclusions or think in a certain way?
- Will it fulfil the audience's expectations or surprise them?
- Will it encourage the audience to part with money?
- Will it encourage the audience to talk about it?
- Does it fulfil the requirements of sponsors or advertisers?
- Will the channel through which the media product is delivered help or hinder the audience to accept its reality?

All these questions will influence how media producers choose to create their products, and therefore how they will represent the people and issues in their products. The final bullet point is particularly interesting now that we have so many ways of receiving media. For example, where you see a film or TV show influences your willingness to accept its reality and your attitude and ability to receive its messages. It could be that, if you have made the effort to go to the cinema, you are more open to accepting the reality of the film being shown. However, if you are watching a YouTube clip on your phone as you eat breakfast at home, you might be more distracted and less able to concentrate.

### Activity 2.24

Imagine you are standing for election – for your school council, perhaps. Write two brief fake news articles: one making yourself more heroic and electable than you really are, and one showing that you can't be trusted. These stories should be written in the same style as real news stories and should be believable – you will need to create imaginary events that seem plausible. If you want to take this idea further, you could also write a truthful but biased article about yourself, and see if others can tell which articles are fake and which one is true. What techniques did you use to make your fake news believable?

### Activity 2.25

What might be the intended message or messages conveyed by:

- an advertisement for nappies?
- a vlog about how to make slime?
- a TV crime drama where the detective catches the murderer?
- a pop video showing women dancing in bikinis beside the male singer?
- a mobile phone slot machine game?

## Why do audiences accept or reject versions of reality?

How you actually understand, or decode, media representations is specific to you as an individual, depending on your experiences and your openness to accepting the reality of the media product at the moment it is received. Whether or not you believe in the particular version of reality presented to us depends on a number of factors, such as:

- the quality of the product: e.g. in the Galaxy 'Audrey Hepburn' commercial, (see Chapter 5) a huge amount of time and money was spent to realistically recreate a young presentation of the actress
- what you are doing at the time of receiving the media product: e.g. if you are trying to watch *Doctor Who* on a crowded bus, you may be distracted or not able to see or hear the show adequately
- why you are engaging with the media product: e.g. Kim Kardashian: Hollywood provides escapism from the stresses of everyday life, so a player is probably happy to accept the unlikely alternative reality of life as an A-lister
- whether you can identify with the characters who are represented: e.g. some teenagers may feel that the young people in the TV drama *His Dark Materials* reflect their own identities.

People may not be consciously influenced by the media, and instead rate their friends, family and own experiences as being more significant to the formation of their opinions and beliefs. If someone belongs to a particular social group, they will use those real-world experiences when they are decoding the media product's message.

Now two different aspects of representation that everyone reading this book has experience of will be looked at – gender and teenagers.

### Link

In Chapter 3, you will look in more detail at how audiences decode the message they receive.

### Activity 2.26

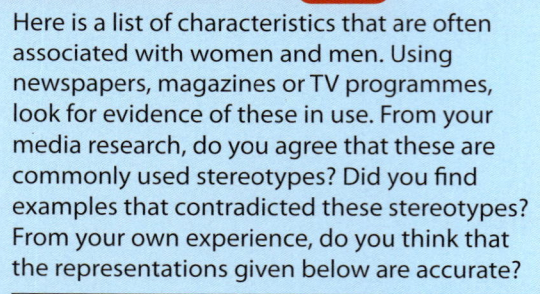

Here is a list of characteristics that are often associated with women and men. Using newspapers, magazines or TV programmes, look for evidence of these in use. From your media research, do you agree that these are commonly used stereotypes? Did you find examples that contradicted these stereotypes? From your own experience, do you think that the representations given below are accurate?

| Women | Men |
|---|---|
| Passive | Active |
| Looked at | Looking |
| In need of protection | Protectors |
| Sexually submissive | Sexually dominant |
| Focus of sexual fantasies | Projectors of sexual fantasies |
| Nurturing | Providing |
| Supporting men | Taking the lead |
| Weak | Strong |
| Emotional | Rational |
| Soft | Rough |
| Dependent | Independent |

## Focus topic: gender

We are identified as being male or female at birth due to our biological differences, but masculinity and femininity are learned as we grow up within our culture. In the media, these are represented as visible traits – including actions – that can be easily understood by audiences. Feminine qualities are often seen as having less value than masculine ones, for example women are often portrayed as either sexual or passive, while men are often shown as powerful and strong. However, such representations are increasingly being challenged in some parts of the media.

If you carried out Activity 2.26, you *may* have found representations of men with some feminine characteristics, and of some women with masculine characteristics. For example, Lord Renly Baratheon in *Game of Thrones*, Joey in *Friends* and Raj in *The Big Bang Theory* all have feminine characteristics. Arya in *Game of Thrones*, Jessica in *Jessica Jones* and Melinda May in *Agents of SHIELD* all have masculine characteristics. However, they stand out against the other characters of their gender because of this.

## Essentialism and social construction

**Essentialism** is the belief that men and women are fundamentally different. According to this theory, biological differences affect and define your skills, preferences and behaviours, and there is nothing you can do to change this. The idea is often used to reinforce gender biases and sexist stereotypes. For example, people who hold this belief may think that women can never excel in maths or physics, and men lack the nurturing skills to bring up children. The idea is not supported by evidence and is mostly discredited. However, some of its influence remains ingrained in society.

By contrast, theories of **social construction** suggest that masculine and feminine behaviours and attributes are constructed by society and not by nature. Babies are labelled and treated as either boys or girls from birth. For example, they are dressed in blue or pink and given different toys to play with – often, boys are given toy tractors and girls are given dolls. The media, of course, have a part to play in reinforcing these stereotypes.

In 2017, the Advertising Standards Authority (ASA, 2017a) published a report called 'Depictions, Perceptions and Harm', which the ASA said presented:

> [A] *case for stronger regulation of ads that feature stereotypical gender roles or characteristics which might be harmful to people, including ads which mock people for not conforming to gender stereotypes.* (ASA, 2017b)

In June 2019, the ASA introduced new rules prohibiting adverts from featuring harmful gender stereotypes, because its members felt that these can limit how people see themselves, how they are seen by others and the choices they might see as being open to them.

### Quick question 2.11

How does having characters who subvert stereotypes help writers to create interesting narratives?

### Key terms

**Essentialism**
The belief that men and women are fundamentally different in terms of their skills, preferences and behaviours.

**Social construction**
The belief that masculine and feminine behaviours are constructed by society and not by nature.

### Activity 2.27

It is obvious that this is a magazine cover aimed at teenage girls. Make a list of the ways it presents 'feminine' characteristics.

## Types of masculinity and femininity

Depictions of masculinity and femininity encompass a range of stereotypes. Think of any teenage high school drama series or movie – typically, characterisations include boys who are jocks (obsessed with sport) and geeks (clever and interested in technology), and girls who are 'princesses' (obsessed with their looks and getting boyfriends) and virgins (quiet and well-behaved, who often 'evolve' into popular and attractive). The only time we see boys as princesses or girls as jocks is when the characters are depicted as LGBTQ+, with the implication that they are different from the norm.

## Gender stereotypes in advertising

Look at this magazine advertisement for fragrance and compare it with the advertisement for 'The Woman Light Your Power' advertisement of Zippo Fragrances (it can be found on the Zippo Fragrance Facebook page): one promoting a product for men and one for women. What do the representations of masculinity and femininity tell us about who the adverts are targeted at?

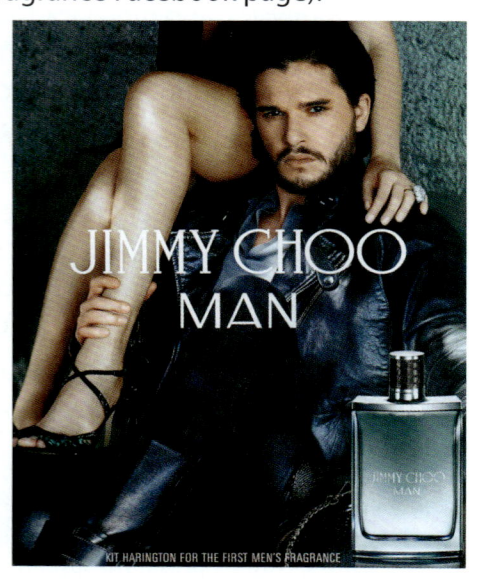

### Activity 2.28

Watch the clip from the sitcom *The Big Bang Theory*, called 'Penny & Leonard's First Kiss'.
- How do the four characters in it fulfil gender stereotypes?
- How do they depart from them?
- To what extent do you think the humour stems from audience assumptions about gender stereotypes?

In the Jimmy Choo Man ad, the man is fulfilling many of the stereotypically 'male' characteristics outlined on page 72. He is staring confidently at the viewer, his body covered in black leathers, which are associated with toughness and independence. The model is the actor Kit Harington, best known as an action hero in the fantasy TV series, *Game of Thrones*. Knowing this context increases the impact of his masculine characteristics.

There is a sense of ownership over the woman in the photo – he grasps her ankle and she rests her hand on him as if for support. She is skimpily dressed, suggesting she is sexually available to him and to those who buy the fragrance. In this representation, fragrance, traditionally seen as a woman's product, has been masculinised.

The second (online) ad shows an interpretation of feminine toughness. The model stares challengingly into the camera in a fighting pose, but this is undermined by the expected boxing gloves (a symbol of masculine power) being replaced with pink ribbons (a symbol of female gentleness). Her confident pose is also undermined by her sexual clothes, which are transparent and expose her shoulders. What message is the female audience of this advert being given?

### Activity 2.29

Choose two similar media products with contrasting representations, such as front covers of two music magazines aimed at opposite genders. Analyse how males and females are represented in each of these, focusing on how media language constructs these representations.

## The influence of feminism on the media

Feminists challenge society's expectations of how women should look and behave. In **feminist theory**, the concept of patriarchy defines a power system in which male privilege is maintained through sexist ideas and attitudes.

Feminist theory tells us that women are often excluded from the media, and when they are present their representation is distorted, because men control media production.

If you look again at the chart on page 72, it's clear how female stereotypes are of a lower status and are seen as less influential than those of men. As already noted, stereotypes are about power, so patriarchy is about how female power is undermined. Look online for examples of how newspapers often focus on the clothing or attractiveness of female leaders such as former British Prime Minister Theresa May or Scottish First Minister Nicola Sturgeon, for example search for the *Daily Mail*, 28 March 2017, on which the front page featured a large photo of the women in short skirts.

Equality for women has been slow; for example, British women were only granted the vote on equal terms with men in 1928, less than 100 years ago. The struggles to win the vote are known as the first wave of feminism. The early to mid-20th century saw progress in terms of women's access to higher education, enabling women to have more influential and prestigious jobs, such as doctors and lawyers. They were granted property rights and divorce became easier and less stigmatised.

The second wave of feminism in the 1960s and 1970s improved rights at work, such as better maternity benefits and the likelihood of equal pay. The wide availability of the contraceptive pill meant that women could choose when – and whether – to have children and therefore be tied down in the domestic space. Unfortunately, men with more traditional outlooks felt threatened by such advancements and a stereotype of feminists as unattractive, crazy lesbians developed which, to some extent, is still used today in some media, such as tabloid newspapers.

The third wave of feminism in the 1990s focused on positive gains, such as celebrating diversity and independence. Girls could drink and party if they wanted to. The girl-group the Spice Girls encapsulated this with their 'girl power' branding. An example of the influence of the media on how they were represented is that *Top of the Pops* magazine assigned them nicknames in 1996 – Sporty, Baby, Scary, Posh and Ginger – which, it could be argued, reduced them to comic stereotypes.

Now we are in an era of so-called post-feminism, in which symbols such as makeup and high heels are re-presented as a more aggressive sexuality. Women are accepted as having a variety of roles, both inside and outside the home, but some media representations still have a long way to go. For example, the Bechdel test is an informal way for audiences to identify whether a film humanises its female characters. The criterion to pass the test is simply that two *named* women have a conversation that is *not* about a man.

> **Key term**
>
> **Feminist theory**
> The belief that women and men should be given equal rights, but that society is currently structured so that women are not equal to men.

The Spice Girls were nicknamed (from left to right) Sporty, Baby, Scary, Posh and Ginger.

Although the test has many flaws, not least of which being that films that pass aren't necessarily feminist, it does encourage audiences to more closely analyse what they're seeing – and what they're not seeing. Unfortunately, the majority of films still fail the test.

> **Activity 2.30**
>
> The video game franchise Tomb Raider has spawned several films. Compare the portrayal of the main character, Lara Croft, in the 2001 film trailer, 'Lara Croft – Tomb Raider – Official Trailer', and the 2018 film trailer, 'Tomb Raider Trailer #2 (2018) Movieclips Trailers', by listing her characteristics in each. What is different? What is the same? On the basis of these representations, would you agree with some critics that the more recent film is 'feminist'?

## Unfixed gender, LGBTQ+ and media representations

Media products often communicate sets of values and beliefs which encourage us to think that certain ideas are 'normal and natural' while other ideas are unacceptable and unthinkable. Essentialism would have us believe that people can (or should) only be heterosexual males or females. Essentialist views are also likely to regard heterosexual relationships as 'the norm' – even assuming that partners in a homosexual relationship must perform a 'male' and 'female' role. Although, increasingly, society is recognising that gender, and gender roles, aren't that simple and are on a spectrum, representations of people who aren't heterosexual still raise a lot of issues.

**Link**

For more on essentialism see page 60.

Historically, media representations of LGBTQ+ people and characters were rare. If they appeared at all, they were normally the target of jokes, such as in the 1960's *Carry On* films, or in TV sitcoms. UK soap operas have included openly gay characters since the late 1980s but it is difficult to find positive – or any – representations of LGBTQ+ characters in other media, such as advertising, before the late 1990s.

Cast of the reality TV show *Queer Eye*, in which gay men offer advice on grooming, fashion, health and décor.

Since the 1990s, however, overall, media representations of LGBTQ+ people, and those of unfixed gender, are becoming more positive as society becomes more inclusive.

Even so, these depictions are still often presented as out of the ordinary – TV programmes such as *RuPaul's Drag Race* and *Queer Eye*, for example, while entertaining, still present gay men as different from the norm, upholding some stereotypes such as their interest in fashion. However, such shows bring LGBTQ+ culture to the mainstream, which could be said to raise awareness of diversity and encourage inclusiveness.

## 2 Media Representations

> **Activity 2.31**
>
> Look at this poster for the 2015 film, *The Danish Girl*. Just from the image shown on the poster, what does the representation of the characters suggest the film is about?
>
> The film is loosely based on the true story of one of the first recipients of gender reassignment surgery, played by male actor Eddie Redmayne (shown on the right). How does this context affect your ideas about the poster's representations? Why do you think there is no reference to this on the poster?

Many recent and contemporary films and TV shows represent LGBTQ+ characters in a generally positive way but often their sexuality is a feature that drives the plot rather than being an integrated part of their character. For example, trans characters are often portrayed as tragic or conflicted, rather than just people living everyday lives. However, more recent positive representations of trans characters, played by trans actors, include Kyle Slater in *EastEnders*, Aaron in *The Fosters* (a family itself led by a lesbian couple) and Nomi in *Sens8* (a series created by Lana and Lily Wachowski, who are both trans).

Generally, advertisements target a heterosexual audience, but increasingly brands are recognising that the LGBTQ+ community also has money and therefore also has 'purchasing power'. For example, adverts such as Tesco's 2016 'Valentine's Day 2016: Introducing Basket Dating - Tesco' and Lloyds Bank's 'This is Real Life' (2016) (both available on YouTube) integrate representations of gay men as the norm, while many companies get on board with the annual Pride campaigns. However, some people identify a bias towards promoting products to and by young, attractive gay men rather than other members of the LGBTQ+ community, such as older trans people. There are also questions over whether they are promoting inclusivity and celebrating diversity or merely targeting lucrative markets.

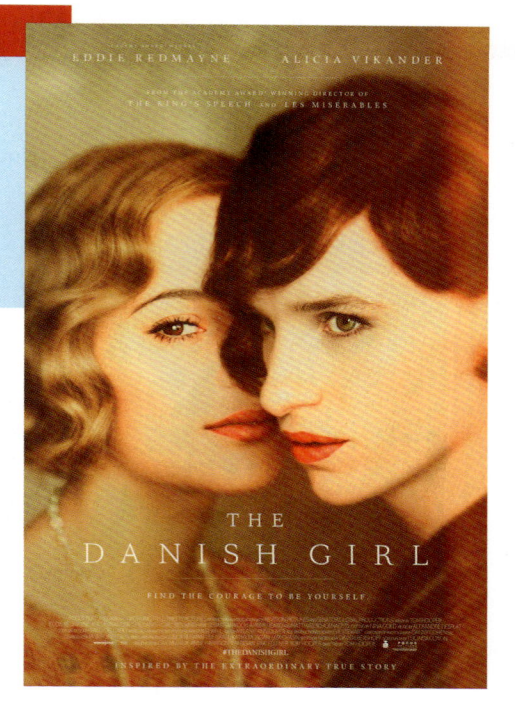

### CASE STUDY:
## Tomb Raider/Lara Croft GO and other video games

Here, you will consider gender in video games, and Tomb Raider/Lara Croft GO in particular.

You looked at the different film portrayals of Lara Croft in Activity 2.30. The character originated from a hugely successful video game franchise, first launched in 1996.

> **Links**
>
> Video games will be looked at in more detail in Chapter 4, pages 145–152 and some of the media contexts for Lara Croft GO in Chapter 5, pages 176–179.

## Representations of Lara Croft

**Activity 2.32**

Compare the 1996 representation of Lara Croft (on the right) with a representation of the characters in another popular 1996 game, Resident Evil, which you can find online.

Lara Croft was the first female protagonist in a major role-playing video game. Even now, protagonists and hero characters are more likely to be male, especially in adventure games. Male game characters are themselves stereotypical, having control over the action, being rational thinkers, being winners, and are skilled in handling cars, weapons and machines. However, Lara Croft adopted many of these attributes to become an independent and assertive action hero. Nevertheless, it was her conical breasts and micro-shorts that attracted the male audience's and wider media's attention.

Some people have commented that this first version of her character would have found the physical challenges of the game impossible because of her bizarre body shape.

## Other female representations in video games

**Activity 2.33**

Research female characters in video games over the last 25 years. In general, are they presented from a feminist or essentialist viewpoint? What aspects of media language are used to construct each representation? What stereotypes can you identify?

In Chapter 5 it will be shown that women are now just as likely to play video games as teenage boys. They are a significant audience and target market for video game and mobile app developers and, while many popular games such as Kim Kardashian: Hollywood are based on 'feminine' interests, many women also like to play adventure, role-playing and first-person shooters. Although representations are improving as a result, it is still difficult to find examples of feminist characters (female or male).

At least Lara Croft is strong and proactive. Over the history of video games, female characters have had much less important roles in the action, often appearing as 'damsels in distress', or 'princesses' made available as the reward for successful male characters. Alternatively, they are sex objects or the victims of male violence.

### Lara Croft GO (2015)

Lara Croft GO (2015) is a turn-based puzzle game in which Lara Croft is essentially the marker or counter. Her actions are dictated by the player, arguably making her a passive pawn whose only relevance is the fact that she has a strong brand to draw in the audience. Although the puzzle solutions often involve killing opponents or monsters, her gender isn't particularly relevant to the gameplay; in fact, she is so small

**Princess Peach from Super Mario**

on a phone or tablet screen that her appearance isn't particularly important. One 'reward', however, is being able to change her outfit, which does not aid gameplay and is not an option usually available for male video game characters, beyond upgrading their armour.

Generally, this game isn't really 'about' the woman Lara Croft, but it is about solving puzzles. Players may be attracted by her name but then become immersed in the detailed graphics and atmosphere. This in itself could be seen as progress in terms of female representation, as the main character's gender is not particularly relevant.

Many of the outfits that can be selected for Lara Croft in the game are practical rather than sexy, such as the one shown above.

Gamers could beome immersed in the graphics and atmosphere.

Gamers could beome immersed in the graphics and atmosphere.

### Activity 2.34

Play the game or watch a gameplay video on YouTube. Note down how the character of Lara Croft influences the gameplay. Is there anything in her responses to events, or in the action choices available to the player, that signifies she is female?

# Putting representation in context

Throughout this chapter you can see that representations reflect (and sometimes influence) historical, social, political and cultural contexts. There is a clear relationship between media representations and the changing values and beliefs of society as a whole. How much one influences the other is a matter of endless debate but as one changes so does the other. It is also the case that some values and beliefs don't change all that much over time.

It is useful to know about the historical contexts that have influenced media production, so you can analyse how changes have come about. This not only means the political and social events of previous years but also the way different media industries worked at the time, and the technologies and media channels that were available. These contexts are looked at throughout this book but here you will examine how representations of teenagers have been presented over the past 70 years.

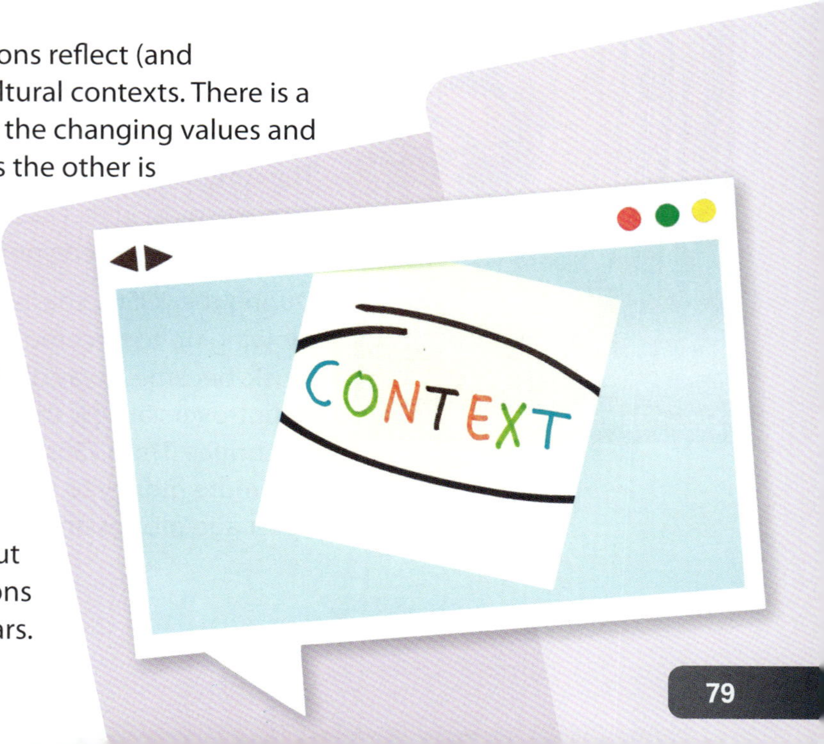

## CASE STUDY:
## The teenager

What is a teenager? Clearly, it is someone in their teens – aged 13 to 19. They are older than children and younger than adults. But how else would you describe a teenager?

Of course, stereotypes are being considered here – for example, a common stereotype is that teenagers are always rebellious, selfish, rude and badly behaved. We know this isn't the case, and that plenty of older and younger people also cause trouble, but teenagers as a demographic group tend to be regarded as a negative influence on society.

Harry Enfield's comic character Kevin the Teenager turned from cute child to rude, lazy and careless overnight on his 13th birthday. You can watch this sketch on YouTube by searching for 'Kevin Becomes a Teenager – BBC Comedy'. Is this representation unfair or is it funny because it is an exaggerated representation of many people's experiences?

## The invention of the teenager

All adults were teenagers once, and the adolescent phase of life has always been seen as a particularly challenging time in terms of the effect of hormonal changes, testing boundaries and learning new behaviours. The word 'teen-age' started being used in the late 19th century when social changes enabled young people to forge their own identities. The notion of what teenagers are like has gradually evolved since then.

It was only about 70 years ago that the media began to identify teenagers as a specific category of people with particular preferences, clothing, music, language and behaviours. It's unclear exactly when 'the teenager' as a media stereotype was invented but it started to appear in American newspapers and magazines at the end of World War II to describe the self-indulgent activities of those who were too young to fight. Free of adult responsibilities, they started to define their own lifestyle and behavioural choices, and businesses realised they could capitalise on this new, emerging market.

The American magazine *Seventeen*, from 1946 (seen left), is clearly targeting teenage girls, in this case with a positive, aspirational representation of a smart, fashionably dressed young woman posing next to a giant book.

During the 1950s, the 'baby boomers' born during or just after the war were growing up to become a larger and more influential population of teenagers. Music became a way of expressing the generation gap, with rock and roll being a controversial new trend that brought with it new styles of dance, dress and celebrities. The 1950s was a period of economic prosperity, so young people had more money to spend and more power to differentiate themselves from other age groups and from each other.

### Activity 2.35

There are many stock photograph sites on the internet. Media producers often use these if they want to find images to illustrate articles in print or other media products. Search one or more of these sites, such as iStockphoto, Shutterstock or Getty Images, using the keyword 'teenagers'.
- Write down words or phrases that the photos make you think of.
- Categorise the results into positive and negative portrayals.
- Do you notice any patterns or themes?

*Seventeen* magazine, 1946

## 2 Media Representations

### Activity 2.36

Watch an extract from the film *Rebel Without a Cause* and consider the representations of teenagers, parents and other authority figures. Contrast this with a non-fictional representation of American teenagers, such as the TV programme *American Bandstand*. You can watch a clip from 1957 on YouTube by searching for 'Rock & Roll Dance 1957 (American Bandstand)'.

- What similarities and differences can you see between the teenagers in these two products?
- How do the nature of the product and the narrative's point of view affect the representations?
- How are the representations influenced by the social and historical context in which the products were made?
- Are you surprised at any representations, for example the portrayal of sexuality?

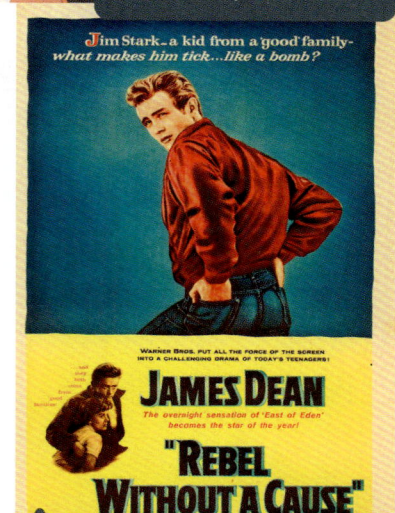

James Dean not only played a glamorously rebellious teen, but also his early death cemented his iconic image still further.

The media helped to create a moral panic at this point over the sexual and social behaviour of teenagers, epitomised by celebrities such as Elvis, who was one of the first overt sex symbols. For GCSE Media Studies, you are not expected to analyse representations in films. However, there were far fewer fictional representations of teenagers on TV in the 1950s than there were in films. The spirit of rebellion seen in music continued in movies, with cool, mean and moody anti-heroes – 'juvenile delinquents' – such as James Dean in *Rebel Without a Cause* and Marlon Brando in *The Wild One* ('What are you rebelling against?' 'Watta ya got?'). There is a tension in these films between teenagers being **demonised** and being glamorised – how the representations were understood depended on the age of the audience.

The 1960s are often thought of as the best time to have been a teenager, as freedom, novelty and entertainment opportunities reached their peak. There was still some expectation of obedience and respecting the authority of parents and other older figures, but at the same time teenagers had an unprecedented opportunity to take advantage of their status as a social group.

The variety of options open to teenagers led to the breakup of the overall social group of 'teenagers' into subcultures. Some remained rebellious, such as mods and rockers in the UK. Other representations of teenagers were more wholesome, such as the singer and actor Cliff Richard. Early music videos and TV shows such as *Top of the Pops* combined music with fashion and behaviour, which teenagers could copy and adapt for themselves.

### Key term

**Demonised**
Making someone or a group of people seem as if they are evil.

### Link

For more about mods and rockers see page 83.

### Activity 2.37

Compare the representations of teenage girls on the two front covers of 1960s magazines, shown here. How do these compare to contemporary representations of the same age group?

Front cover of the American *'Teen* magazine from October 1962

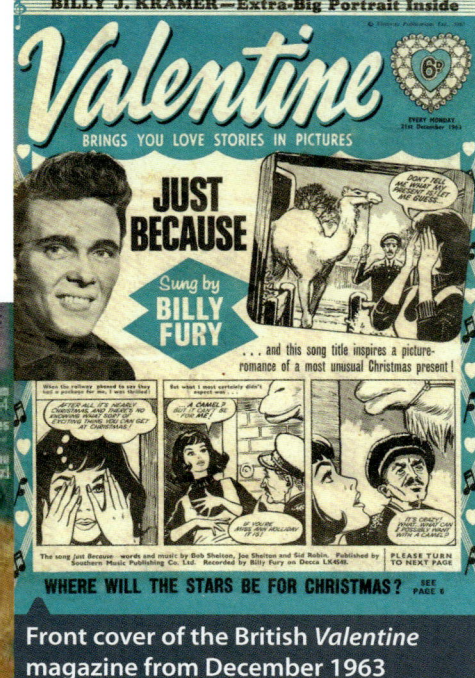

Front cover of the British *Valentine* magazine from December 1963

Pirate radio stations and the eventual launch of BBC Radio 1 influenced musical tastes. The number of music TV programmes for teenagers blossomed, but there was little else on TV directed specifically at this age group. Fiction series featuring teenagers tended to be American, such as the *Brady Bunch* – first aired in 1969 – and didn't reflect life in the UK. Teenage interests were reflected much more widely in films and magazines.

In the 1970s and 1980s, teenage society continued to diversify, mainly as a result of musical influences, from punks and disco queens to New Romantics. UK television developed new drama programmes specifically aimed at, and representing, teenagers. *A Bunch of Fives* and *Grange Hill* were both broadcast at the end of the 1970s and both were set in secondary schools. The music channel MTV was launched as a cable TV station in America in 1981, aimed at young adults and teenagers.

John Hughes' films presented 'ordinary' teenagers forging their identities in everyday communities, epitomised by *The Breakfast Club* (1985):

> *You see us as you want to see us ... in the simplest terms and the most convenient definitions. You see us as a brain, an athlete, a basket case, a princess and a criminal.*

The characters conclude that they all fulfil all these roles.

The rise of satellite and digital TV channels from the late 1990s onwards meant that whole channels, such as E4 and BBC3, could be dedicated to youth programming. Today, the multiplicity of media channels – not only on TV – means we are bombarded with different images of teenagers. In particular, sex is typically represented as a part of teenage life, often without moral judgement, in TV dramas such as *Skins* and *Awkward*, or played for laughs, such as in the sitcom *The Inbetweeners*.

### Activity 2.38

Watch the Season 1 trailer for the TV comedy-drama *Awkward*, created for MTV. How are teenagers portrayed in this series? What is positive? What is negative?

### Activity 2.39

Find out how representations of teenagers and their activities have changed. Interview an adult who was a teenager 50 or more years ago, for example someone from your grandparents' generation. Ask them about:
- what they used to wear
- how they spent their spare time
- what music they listened to
- what films and TV they enjoyed
- which celebrities they admired, and why.

Record or video your interview and note the years they are referring to. You may need to do some research afterwards to find out more about the people, films or TV shows they mentioned.

Now ask a teenager the same questions. You could consider your own experiences too.

Create a presentation outlining the differences between teenagers 50 years ago and now. Remember that everyone's experiences and preferences are different, and that people who grew up in other cultures, with access to other types of media (such as music or TV shows in other languages), will give very different answers. This in itself shows that stereotyping teenagers raises issues.

## How does the media control the construction of teenagers?

We have just seen that the representations of teenagers have changed over the past 50 years. How – and why – did the media help to construct these images of teenagers?

Firstly, it is useful to return to the concept of stereotypes. As we have seen earlier in this chapter, stereotypes exist for a variety of reasons – for example to:

- convey meaning quickly
- impose power over a group
- present or construct shared cultural values
- make a particular point
- increase sales, viewers or users.

All these reasons contribute to why the representation of teenagers involves drawing attention to the similarities and differences of that group, whether from the teenagers' or older people's point of view. Teenagers represent the future, and adults try to project their hopes and fears for the future onto them. Sometimes, however, what we see is the age-old topic of the moral decline of society, a key part of which is both protecting and controlling the young.

It is also useful to remember that youth cultures are constructed around what they choose to use and buy. For example, music and musicians are packaged and presented by the media to manipulate young audiences into parting with their money. Dressing in a particular way – whether in trendy fashion brands or to conform with a particular image, such as goth or punk – also has an economic impact.

## Moral panic and folk devils in news media

Looking at teenagers is a good opportunity to think about **moral panics**. This term comes from a theory developed by Stanley Cohen. He argued that news and other mass media deliberately distort the representation of a group perceived to be negative because their behaviour deviates from what society expects. In this case you are thinking about teenage behaviour, but this theory could also apply to issues such as immigration and terrorism. The group that is represented as deviant is the **folk devil**. Society is placed into a state of moral panic, because the deviant group is seen to be a threat to ordinary day-to-day life for everyone else.

The negative reporting creates public concern, and people want to know more about the threat to themselves and their loved ones. This in turn keeps the issue prominent in media reporting. The more people see the issue in the news, the bigger a threat they perceive it to be, creating a self-reinforcing situation. The negative perception of the issue – such as the behaviour of teenagers – often becomes backed up in 'fact' when, for example, the police are under pressure to tackle the perceived problem and so devote time and resources to identifying and solving the problem. Of course, this means they are more likely to find real-life examples of, for example, teenage knife crime, contributing to and reinforcing the moral panic.

The sensational newspaper reporting of teenage 'deviance' is nothing new. Cohen's theory of folk devils and moral panic emerged from his study of mods and rockers, two 1960s teenage subcultures whose conflicts became a media focus, for example in newspaper front pages of teenagers apparently attacking each other, with headlines such as 'Living for Kicks'.

### Link

Two specific portrayals of teenagers, over 50 years apart, will be compared in more detail in two of the 2019 CSPs on pages 159–165.

### Key terms

**Moral panic**
The impact on society when the mass media play an active role in stereotyping a person, group or issue as a threat to the accepted norms, values and interests of society.

**Folk devil**
The person or group that is the focus of a moral panic.

### Activity 2.40

Are there any social groups that have been demonised by the media in your lifetime? Look up news stories about these groups. How have they been represented to create a moral panic?

### Activity 2.41

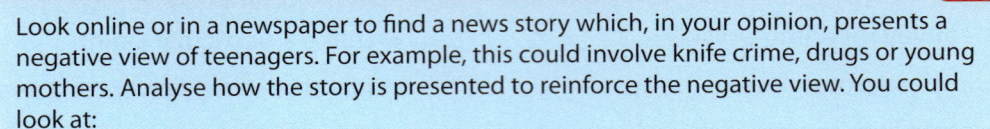

Look online or in a newspaper to find a news story which, in your opinion, presents a negative view of teenagers. For example, this could involve knife crime, drugs or young mothers. Analyse how the story is presented to reinforce the negative view. You could look at:

- the words chosen for the headline
- how the article's focus on alleged deviant acts suggests a threat to social order
- the order in which the content is presented – for example, is the fact that the person in the article is a teenager presented as their most significant characteristic?
- the article's use of exaggeration and subjective language
- how symbols are used as short-hand, such as irrelevant descriptions about the way the person in the article looks (perhaps mention of a hoodie or shaved head)
- the accompanying images and how they are captioned.

Now repeat the activity with a more positive news story about teenagers – perhaps celebrating their exam results, charity work or sports achievements. Were these harder to find? Could they also be regarded as biased?

### CASE STUDY:
## *His Dark Materials* and *Doctor Who*

### Link

In Chapter 5 (pages 159–165), you will be looking at an overview of two of 2023 CSPs, *His Dark Materials* (2020) Series 2, Episode 1: 'The City of Magpies', and *Doctor Who* (1963) Episode 1: 'An Unearthly Child'.

Here you will look at *His Dark Materials* (2020) Series 2, Episode 1: 'The City of Magpies' and *Doctor Who* (1963) Episode 1: 'An Unearthly Child' specifically in terms of what these two products tell you about changing representations of teenagers over the last 60 years. Can social and cultural attitudes, values and beliefs explain the similarities and differences?

## Focus on the main teenage characters

First of all, of course, in the *Doctor Who* episode Susan isn't really a teenager – she is a time-travelling alien who has taken on the persona of a 15 year old in 1963. However, because her teachers believe she is a teenager, she behaves – or tries to behave – as they expect her to. She soon finds that there are fun parts, such as listening to pop music and being part of the school community, and less fun parts, such as having to submit to the authority of her elders. She attracts her teachers' attention because she doesn't fit their stereotypes, to the extent that, when they are following her, they discuss how, if she was meeting a boy, it would be 'so wonderfully normal'.

Susan is accused of being childish but is actually more mature than she appears.

In *His Dark Materials*, Lyra finds herself in a similar situation, initially alone in a strange world, with those who seek her believing her still to be a child they can manipulate (despite everything she has been through in Series 1). She is aware that her knowledge has power over the fates of others. Teenagers are often represented as carrying burdens of stress and anxiety placed on them by the adult world, and both representations being discussed here are sympathetic to this.

## Teenagers and authority

Remember that the dominant representation of teenagers in media products has always been generally negative. Stereotypically they have been represented as a problem to be solved by adults who don't understand them. In these two episodes, Lyra and Susan are both intelligent and articulate girls who at the same time question the knowledge and authority of their elders. The teachers and guardians believe they know best, despite the teenagers having evidence to the contrary. The adults don't really know how to deal with the conflict the teenagers have caused. Even the Doctor isn't entirely in control of the situation Susan has inadvertently created.

Significantly, in both cases their argumentative and rebellious behaviour is caused by outside forces – Susan being an alien, and Lyra seeing her friend being used as a scientific experiment. This could be seen as a sympathetic reading of being a teenager: that there are many reasons, whether social or hormonal, for teenagers to apparently rebel against cultural norms.

Susan's teachers sum up the teenage experience in their comments about her:

- 'I don't know what to make of her.'
- 'I was so irritated with all her excuses …'
- 'Too many questions and not enough answers.'

These types of statements are still made about today's teenagers.

### Activity 2.42

Watch at least part of each of the two episodes, and think about the characters of Susan and Lyra. List what is similar about them and what is different. This could include their:

- appearance
- level of independence
- attitude to teachers and older family members
- bravery in response to threat.

How do you think these similarities and differences are influenced by their social and historical contexts? Consider what you saw in the previous section about how teenagers were represented in the 1950s and 1960s, compared with how teenagers are represented now.

## Teenagers in a changing social context

The first school scene in *Doctor Who* opens with two fashionably dressed girls whispering and rolling their eyes as a boy teases them. The 2020 drama, however, tries to build a more nuanced idea of the diversity of teenage identity, for example with the main characters demonstrating a range of ethnicities and genders. In modern media, teenagers are usually depicted as a group of mixed friends; in this positive case, they are loyal, supportive and thoughtful of each other's needs. When they argue, it is based on their own valid opinions and experiences.

*His Dark Materials* depicts a diverse group of characters.

In *Doctor Who*, Susan is a lone teenager in an adult world; she is less prominent in the story than her teachers and her grandfather, and does not have the power to assert her own will. In *His Dark Materials*, however, Lyra and Will offer a more modern, active representation.

Some of this is to do with the channels through which the dramas were originally broadcast, and the original influences – adult sci-fi programmes on the one hand and Philip Pullman's books on the other. In 1963, there were only two TV channels in the UK, and households were very unlikely to have more than one TV, so *Doctor Who* was designed to appeal to the whole family in the same room. Having a much broader target audience than today's programmes meant that it had to avoid controversy – while the show later developed a reputation for being scary, in this first episode, Susan's status as a teenager is unthreatening and is really only a means to establish the narrative of the human

### Quick question 2.12

How does Lyra reflect modern ideas of feminism?

teachers exploring alien worlds. There is no suggestion of teenage sexuality, for example, which is an underlying but largely unspoken theme in *His Dark Materials*, as Dust and the Spectres are associated with puberty and sexuality.

### Activity 2.43

You could be asked the following question:

To what extent do changing social and cultural attitudes, values and beliefs explain the similarities and differences between the representations of teenagers in *Doctor Who*: Episode 1: 'An Unearthy Child' and *His Dark Materials:* Series 2, Episode 1: 'The City of Magpies'?

Discuss your thoughts on this question with a partner or a wider group. Refer to details from each of the two programmes to support any points you choose to make. Remember that your opinion, supported by such evidence, is important.

At the end of your discussion, you could choose a range of conclusions to your response. For example, you may conclude that:

- any changes in social and cultural contexts have had little influence because representations of teenagers have demonstrated greater continuity than change
- in spite of a certain degree of continuity, the social and cultural context of drama on television today has led to radical changes in the representation of teenagers
- other technical, technological and audience factors have influenced the representations of teenagers in TV drama, but it is hard to separate these from their social and cultural contexts.

Remember to refer to specific moments from the two episodes throughout your answer.

### References

ASA (2017a) Depictions, Perceptions and Harm, https://www.asa.org.uk/asset/2DF6E028-9C47-4944-850D00DAC5ECB45B.C3A4D948-B739-4AE4-9F17CA2110264347/.

ASA (2017b, 18 July) Report Signals Tougher Standards on Harmful Gender Stereotypes in Ads, https://www.asa.org.uk/news/report-signals-tougher-standards-on-harmful-gender-stereotypes-in-ads.html.

BBC (2018a) Dive Deeper to See How *Blue Planet II* Was Made, http://www.bbc.co.uk/programmes/articles/cD5fGcsfj30hhFqJcfPQQR/dive-deeper-to-see-how-blue-planet-ii-was-made.

Elghobashy, S. (2009, 12 January) Muslim Stereotypes in Hollywood: Are they Really Fading?, *elan: The Guide to Global Muslim Culture*, http://www.elanthemag.com/index.php/site/blog_detail/muslim_stereotypes_in_hollywood_are_they_really_fading-nid503043165/.

Hall, S. (1993) Encoding, Decoding, in During, S. (ed.) *The Cultural Studies Reader*.

Holmwood, L. (2009, 9 July) BBC Denies Ageism as Arlene Phillips Shifted Off *Strictly Come Dancing*, *The Guardian*, https://www.theguardian.com/media/2009/jul/09/arlene-phillips-strictly-come-dancing-bbc.

Ilott, S. (2018, 31 January) *Man Like Mobeen*: BBC Comedy Defies Muslim Stereotypes, Manchester Metropolitan University, https://www.mmu.ac.uk/news-and-events/news/story/7103/.

Lee, K. (2014, 19 March) How to Write the Perfect Headline: The Top Words Used in Viral Headlines, https://buffer.com/resources/the-most-popular-words-in-most-viral-headlines/.

Media Smarts (2018) Media Portrayals of Religion: Islam, http://mediasmarts.ca/diversity-media/religion/media-portrayals-religion-islam.

Meyer, R. (2018, 8 March) The Grim Conclusions of the Largest-Ever Study of Fake News, *The Atlantic*, https://www.theatlantic.com/technology/archive/2018/03/largest-study-ever-fake-news-mit-twitter/555104/.

Norfolk, A., Coates, S. & Dathan, M. (2015, 4 March) Call for National Debate on Muslim Sex Grooming, *The Times*, https://www.thetimes.co.uk/.article/call-for-national-debate-on-muslim-sex-grooming-wtqm7lnvv6w.

Ofcom (2017, 29 June) News Consumption in the UK: 2016, https://www.ofcom.org.uk/__data/assets/pdf_file/0016/103570/news-consumption-uk-2016.pdf.

Sports Khabri (2021, 17 May) Marcus Rashford – Sponsors/Endorsements/Salary/Net Worth/Notable Honours/Charity Work, https://sportskhabri.com/player-profile-marcus-rashford/.

# 3 Media Audiences

## What's in this chapter?

- This chapter deals with definitions of the media audience and the effects of the transition to digital technology on the audience.
- The first section looks at how media audiences are categorised and the key terms used to describe different types of audience.
- There is an explanation of how different media industries carry out audience research and the reasons why they do this.
- The next section deals with theories or explanations of the relationships between producers, products and audiences. These include the 'direct effects' idea, the 'active audience' idea and the various ways in which audiences enjoy and interpret media products.
- The final section discusses the ways in which audience members interact with media products as users, creators of our own products and as fans.

## Why study audiences?

You should be interested in media audiences because, after all, you are the people who spend an awful lot of time reading, watching and listening to – as well as sometimes contributing to – the output of the media. You are the consumers of the media and, as such, have a vested interest in how well media products meet your needs.

Media industries, the organisations that create media products, are certainly interested in audiences. For them, audiences are the lifeblood of their industry: without them they would not exist. Media industries are dependent on audiences for at least one of the following reasons:

1 Advertisers pay to reach audiences.
2 Audiences pay directly for the media products themselves.
3 Audiences are needed to justify subsidies or financial support (e.g. the television licence).

Media audiences are also of interest to those politicians, critics and commentators who worry about the influence of the media on society. Usually, they see this influence in fairly negative terms, with arguments beginning with assertions that 'the media are to blame' for any number of society's problems or individual bad behaviour.

On similar lines are the fears expressed by many that the media have become too powerful and are able to manipulate audiences at will.

These are among the many issues that will be addressed in this chapter. You will start by looking at audiences from the viewpoint of industries who need to define, describe and categorise audiences in order to achieve the desired circulation for their products.

# Defining the audience

Although the term audience is used to describe attendance at a theatre or rock concert, the focus here is on the mass media and, therefore, mass audiences. In the case of the traditional media – television, film, radio, magazines and newspapers – the audience are separated from the producers of media products by space and, often, by time as well, in a way they are not at a live event. At a live event the audience and the performer have direct contact and are able to react immediately to each other.

**Media consumption** can be a social occasion, for example, in the case of the cinema audience, shared listening or viewing at home, but the majority of media use is private and individual. Online and social media provide some interesting exceptions, as we can use social media for one-to-one or small group communication.

Facebook, Twitter, Instagram, Snapchat and other social media enable messages, including advertising messages, to be distributed to huge numbers of subscribers or followers. Online video gaming also involves a certain amount of interactivity between players. Increasing opportunities can be seen for audiences to become producers themselves using, for example, YouTube, wikis, tagging and blogs. Most newspapers encourage readers through their websites not only to react to news stories but also to contribute stories of their own.

Another feature of the transition to digital technology is the declining size of audiences for any single media product or event. Following are some examples of massive audiences for traditional media:

- In 1969, 600 million people worldwide watched the Apollo 11 moon landings on TV.
- In 1981, 750 million people watched the wedding of Prince Charles to Lady Diana Spencer.
- In the UK, sitcom *Only Fools and Horses* had record viewing figures of 24 million for its Christmas Special in 1996.

> **Key term**
>
> **Media consumption**
> Audiences and individuals are often described as consumers of media. Media consumption is any engagement with the media by an individual or audience.

> **Talk about it**
>
> How many people in your class have produced and uploaded their own media products?

The 1969 Moon walk

- The 1939 film *Gone With the Wind* made $1.64 billion (adjusted to today's values) and holds the record for box office takings.
- The *Daily Mirror* sold 5 million copies a day at its peak in the mid-1960s.
- Until its closure, the *News of the World* was Britain's best-selling newspaper. At its peak in 1951 it sold 8.4 million copies a week, equal to one issue for every six people in the population.

You must be careful, though, not to overestimate the decline of traditional media. The biggest ever television audience in the USA was as recent as 2015: the 49th Super Bowl final (114 million). The audience for more recent finals has declined only very slightly.

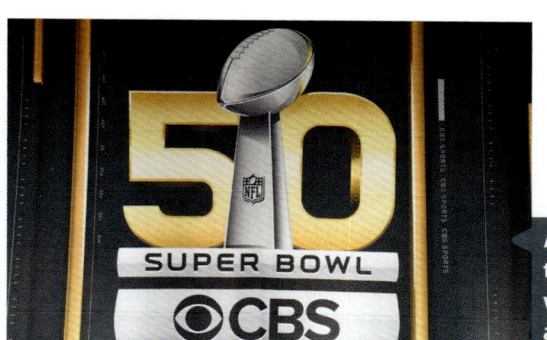

Advertising slots in the live TV transmission of the 2016 Super Bowl were a record $5 million per 30-second advert.

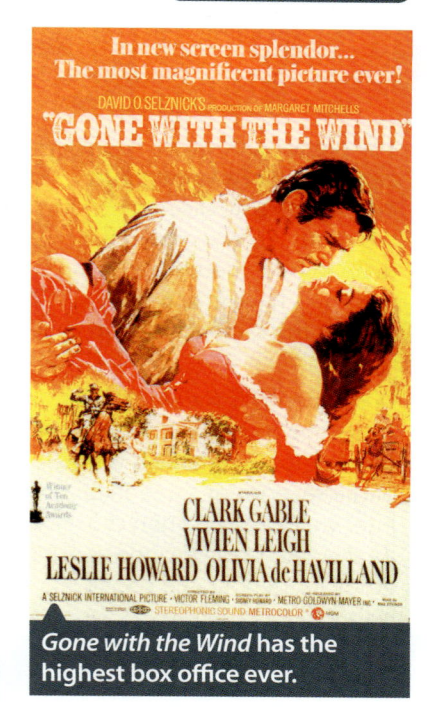

*Gone with the Wind* has the highest box office ever.

# Categorising the audience

Media producers like nothing more than creating really big audiences: the bigger the better. The reasons for this are fairly obvious. The more people who buy a magazine or pay to watch a film, the more money they have coming in. Alternatively, if a really big audience can be created for a product – a show screened on ITV, for example – a very high fee can be charged to advertisers.

However, size isn't everything. As already seen, the really mega audiences for media products are mostly in the past and are unlikely to return. Also, the financial risks to media producers are very high if they gamble a huge investment on a product in the hope of creating a huge audience. Rather than trying to create products that are 'all things to all people', media industries put a lot of time and effort into the careful targeting of specific audiences. A small or **niche audience** can be successfully targeted with the right genre product, as seen in Chapter 1 with the carp fishing magazines.

At the other end of the spectrum, even multimillion dollar blockbuster films are designed to meet the needs of particular sections of the market for films as a whole. Advertisers, too, need to ensure that their marketing messages reach exactly those people who are potential purchasers. There is no point in showing advertisements for £100,000 supercars to those who cannot possibly afford them.

### Link
See the carp fishing magazines on page 38.

### Key term
**Niche audience**
A niche audience is smaller and more specialised than a mass audience. To target a niche audience or market, then, is to attempt to design a product that is perfectly suited to a particular group of people.

### Quick question 3.1
Where would you advertise an expensive supercar?

### Key terms

**Segmentation**
The breaking down or subdivision of a large group into identifiable slices or segments. Each segment is defined by something all members have in common, such as the same age group.

**Demographics**
Demography is the statistical study of populations, so a demographic variable is one of the sections or categories into which a population can be divided. These include age, ethnicity, gender and social class.

**Millennials**
People who reached young adulthood at the start of the 21st century – the turn of the millennium.

### Activity 3.1

Use these categories to create a demographic profile of yourself.

---

All this means that media industries have developed a sophisticated set of tools for analysing and categorising audiences. A key idea is **segmentation**. A mass audience can be broken down into different slices or segments, for example by age or gender. As more media choices become available, the process of segmentation gathers pace. For example, if only two radio stations are available to a population, there will only be limited segmentation. If there are hundreds of radio stations available to the same population there will be much greater segmentation, with each station aiming at a small segment.

But what are these different audience segments? Let's look first at the **demographic** variables: the ways in which the population as a whole can be broken down into categories.

## Demographics

Main categories are:

- gender
- social class
- ethnicity
- education
- place of residence
- religion
- family size
- family lifecycle (full nest, empty nest, double income no kids)
- age
- generation (baby boomers, Generation X, **millennials**, Generation Z).

## Generations

The following categories are often used to describe changing attitudes and preferences, especially by advertisers. The characteristics assigned to each generation are stereotypes based on very broad brush generalisations.

**Baby boomers**
This is the generation born in the post-war period (1945–early 1960s) when there was a bulge in the birth rate in the UK and USA. Stereotypically, this was the generation that rejected the values of their parents, discovered drugs and rock music in their teens, before becoming big spenders of the 'grey pound' in their 50s and 60s.

**Generation X**
These are people born between the early 1960s and the early 1980s. Stereotypically, Generation X are independent, cynical, self-absorbed and like to model themselves on characters from the sitcom *Friends*. Other likes include grunge and Dr Marten boots.

**Millennials (or Generation Y)**
This refers to people born between early 1980 and 2000, the first to grow up with the mass availability of digital technology. Stereotypically, the 'me, me, me' generation are reluctant to grow up. They are confident, high achievers who expect big rewards from work.

### Generation Z

Born in the 21st century, Generation Z are hyper-aware of digital technology and the dangers as well as the opportunities of social media. They are switched on to pop culture and global travel. This generation is growing up in a world marked by global terrorism and recession. They are likely to be realistic rather than idealistic but are more accepting of individual differences and minority rights than previous generations.

## Social class

Social class is particularly difficult to deal with as there is so much debate and disagreement about how to assign people to different classes.

The government's Office for National Statistics (ONS) uses the National Statistics Socio-Economic Classification (NS-SEC):

1. Higher managerial, administrative and professional occupations.
2. Lower managerial, administrative and professional occupations.
3. Intermediate occupations.
4. Small employers and own account workers.
5. Lower supervisory and technical occupations.
6. Semi-routine occupations.
7. Routine occupations.
8. Never worked and long-term unemployed.

However, media advertisers tend to use a simpler classification system when targeting people from different social classes. This is the version used by the Publishers Audience Measurement Company (PAMCo), the company that replaced the National Readership Survey (NRS).

> **Quick question 3.2**
> How do you think advertisers will try to attract Generation Alpha (born from 2010 onwards)?

*A classic 1960s TV sketch representing the British class system (first broadcast on The Frost Report).*

|    |                                                                                    | % of population (PAMCo Jan.–Dec. 2019) |
|----|------------------------------------------------------------------------------------|----------------------------------------|
| A  | Higher managerial, administrative and professional                                 | 4                                      |
| B  | Intermediate managerial, administrative and professional                           | 22                                     |
| C1 | Supervisory, clerical and junior managerial, administrative and professional       | 29                                     |
| C2 | Skilled manual workers                                                             | 21                                     |
| D  | Semi-skilled and unskilled manual workers                                          | 15                                     |
| E  | State pensioners, casual and lowest grade workers, unemployed with state benefits only | 9                                  |

Source: PAMCo, 2020

To see how a media industry makes use of data based on demographic variables such as these, visit Condé Nast's website which includes the **media pack** for *Tatler* magazine: http://digital-assets.condenast.co.uk.s3.amazonaws.com/static/mediapack/ta_media_pack_latest.pdf.

> **Key term**
> **Media pack**
> Contains information for potential advertisers.

### Activity 3.2

Looking at *Tatler*'s readership data from the Condé Nast media pack (see weblink on page 91), draw up a list of ten products likely to use advertising space in *Tatler* and a list of another ten products that would definitely not be advertised in *Tatler*.

### Key term

**Focus group**
A group of people, usually with common characteristics, assembled to discuss a particular product, issue or campaign in order to collect in-depth information. Focus group discussions are often led by a facilitator who guides the discussion or poses questions.

### Activity 3.3

The audiences for most of your CSPs need to be studied in detail. Use the PAMCo website to compile demographic profiles of *The Times* and the *Daily Mirror* (2023 CSPs) readerships in the same way as Condé Nast has presented information on *Tatler*.

# Psychographics

Psychographics is the study of personality, values, opinions, attitudes and lifestyles. Psychographic variables are often used alongside demographic categories to create a more subtle and detailed audience profile. This profile can then be used to target audience segments more effectively or to understand existing audiences more completely. It is an approach that is widely used in advertising and marketing.

Psychographic information is collected by surveys and **focus groups**. Survey questions might include, for example, sections on hobbies and interests, political views and attitudes to change. Psychographics often deals in 'types', for example the VALS (values and lifestyle) categories that can be found here: http://www.strategicbusinessinsights.com/vals/ustypes.shtml.

### Activity 3.4

Choose a print, television or online advertisement for a product aimed at your age group. Devise a set of focus group questions to find out the impression made by the advertisement on its target audience. Your questions should include:
- Open-ended questions such as:
  - What is your response to the advertisement?
  - How does the advertisement make you feel about the product?
- Scaled questions such as:
  - After seeing the advertisement are you more likely, less likely or just as likely as before to buy the product?
- Specific questions such as:
  - Have you seen similar advertisements?
  - How memorable is this advertisement?
  - How would you describe this advertisement to your friends?

Carry out a focus group discussion based on your questions. Give a brief report to the class based on your focus group findings.

Another set of 'types' claims to identify different attitudes among younger audiences:

- **trendies**: crave the attention of their peers
- **egoists**: seek pleasure
- **puritans**: wish to feel virtuous
- **innovators**: wish to make their mark
- **rebels**: wish to remake the world in their image
- **groupies**: want to be accepted

- **drifters**: not sure what they want
- **drop-outs**: shun commitment of any kind
- **traditionalists**: want things to stay the way they are
- **utopians**: want to make the world a better place
- **cynics**: have to have something to complain about
- **cowboys**: want to earn easy money.

Demographic and psychographic information are often combined to create a profile of a typical audience member. This sort of profiling may create stereotypes of certain types of media user such as '*Guardian* reader', '*Sun* reader', '*Doctor Who* fan' or '*Cosmo* woman'.

> **Quick question 3.3**
> Does one of these psychographic variables describe you?

> Media producers recognise the diversity of youth audiences.

# Who does audience research?

Most audience research is undertaken to meet the needs of advertisers. Before buying expensive advertising space in print, television, radio or online media, advertisers will want a good deal of detailed information about the audience they will be reaching. They will need to know more about the audience than just the number of people. For example, information about the sort of people they are, where they live and how much money they have to spend. The media producers could supply this information themselves, but advertisers may be rather suspicious. They certainly prefer audience information from an independent and reliable source. This is why media industries have set up audience research companies that are separate from both advertisers and content providers.

The following websites will be useful in finding audience information about the products you study.

**Audience Measurement for Publishers** (**AMP**): provides a single view of available audiences across all print and digital forms.
pamco.co.uk

> **Activity 3.5**
> Find online the 2013 advertisement for Givenchy's Gentlemen Only, which features actor Simon Baker and model Cameron Russell. How does it address the audience in terms of psychographic variables?

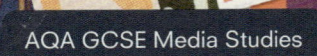

### Audit Bureau of Circulation (ABC)
ABC 'delivers industry agreed standards for media brand measurement across print, digital and events' and is 'run by the industry for the industry'. Most of the information on the website is subscription only but it is widely reprinted in the *Press Gazette*.

abc.org.uk
pressgazette.co.uk

### British Film Institute (BFI)
The BFI produces weekly box office statistics (cinema takings) for the top 15 films on release and all UK films.

bfi.org.uk

### Broadcasters' Audience Research Board (BARB)
BARB measures UK television viewing and collects information about our viewing habits. BARB's figures provide the basis for advertising costs on commercial television. BARB also measures time-shift viewing (for example, BBC iPlayer, the ITV Hub) and non-television viewing on tablets, mobiles and PCs.

barb.co.uk

### Nielsen
A commercial company that provides information on buying trends and media habits in 100 countries.

nielsen.com

### Ofcom (Office of Communications)
The industry regulator for TV, radio, mobiles and video-on-demand, produces useful reports on changing patterns of use in the UK. Ofcom produces an annual report (internet use and attitudes) which includes data on adults' use and attitudes across TV, radio, games, mobiles and the internet, with a particular focus on online use.

ofcom.org.uk

### Radio Joint Audience Research (RAJAR)
Jointly owned by the BBC and the commercial radio sector, RAJAR is the official body for measuring radio audiences.

rajar.co.uk

Broadly, audience researchers collect two types of evidence:

- **Quantitative**: statistical data collected using surveys, polls and sales figures. Quantitative researchers often use sampling techniques. This means gathering information from a small group that is representative of a large group. The small group is carefully selected so that it has the same proportion of people in various categories (by age, ethnicity, social class, etc.) as the large group.

- **Qualitative**: involves observation, discussion and focus groups, for example. It doesn't seek statistical validity but aims instead for more in-depth and personal insights.

---

**Activity 3.6**

Use the websites of the audience research organisations listed above to collect examples of qualitative and quantitative audience research. What are the strengths and weaknesses of these two types of research?

# Audience theories

A theory is an explanation of something. In science, it is usually possible to prove whether a theory is true or not by conducting experiments. In studies of human societies and human behaviour it is not so easy to prove whether theories are true or not, so arguments about theories can go on for years. This doesn't mean to say that theories are useless. They can be very helpful in understanding complex processes and relationships such as the relationship between media producers, media products and media audiences.

A key question for audience theory is:

- How powerful are the media in influencing the ideas and behaviour of the audience?

This question certainly addresses many concerns that have been raised about the role of the media in influencing:

- suicide
- violent behaviour
- promiscuity and teenage pregnancy
- over-eating and obesity
- poor levels of fitness
- poor body image and eating disorders
- bullying, especially cyber bullying
- overspending
- indoctrination and radicalisation
- political apathy
- children growing up 'too quickly'
- immaturity, inability to grow up at all.

News reports about the media's 'blame' for these and other problems appear regularly. Read online Hume (2016) *Munich Gunman Planned Attack for a Year, Officials Say*, CNN, and Bloxham (2010) *Social Networking: Teachers Blame Facebook and Twitter for Pupils' Poor Grades*, *The Daily Telegraph*.

### Talk about it

Do you think the media are responsible for the type of behaviour mentioned in the reports you read online? What is the evidence?

### Quick question 3.4

How convinced are you by the claims about the influence and effects of the media?

## Effects theory

Effects theory claims that the media can have direct influence on the attitudes and behaviour of individuals. However, attempts to prove that exposure to the media has actually caused changes in behaviour have had rather limited success.

In a classic experiment in 1961, Albert Bandura showed children aged three to six years film of an adult hitting a large inflatable doll, a bobo doll. The children were then left alone with various toys, including the doll. This group of children was then compared with groups who watched no film or a film without aggressive behaviour. Observations of different groups' behaviour were then compared. Results showed that the ones who watched aggressive behaviour copied that behaviour; they were more likely to hit the bobo doll.

How much should we read into the bobo doll experiment? One of the problems is the un-naturalness of the laboratory setting. Experiments that tried to test for the same kind of effect in more natural everyday settings were much less conclusive.

Even if we agree that the media may influence some people in some way, this is far from the type of direct cause and effect relationship or 'copycat behaviour' that effects theory suggests.

Two ideas with links to the media effects approach are **cultivation theory** and **desensitisation**.

Cultivation theory is simply effects theory plus time. It's the idea that long-term exposure to the media develops a particular set of attitudes and beliefs in audiences. This often leads to a distorted view of reality. For example, some studies have shown that many of us have a distorted view of crime; we overestimate the threat of violent crime committed by strangers and underestimate the threat of fraud and property crimes committed by people we know.

Desensitisation suggests that constant exposure to natural disasters, war, crime and acts of horror over an extended period of time leaves us less able to react to yet another event.

Desensitisation can be particularly problematic if images of violence are routinely associated with pleasure and relaxation, as they are in many video games. The argument claims that desensitised people find it impossible to respond to appalling acts with sympathy and concern because they have 'seen it all before'. A similar idea is 'compassion fatigue', when continued exposure to droughts, floods and refugee crises leave us indifferent to suffering and decreasingly likely to support charity appeals.

### Talk about it

Think back to your early days at school. Do you recall children being influenced to copy behaviour they had witnessed in the media? Have you ever seen examples of 'copycat' behaviour more recently, for example by younger members of your family?

### Talk about it

Do you recognise the symptoms of desensitisation or compassion fatigue in yourself or others?

### Quick question 3.5

What was the last thing you saw or read or heard that really shocked you?

## The hypodermic syringe theory

Another variant of effects theory suggests that the media's relationship with the audience is very much like the relationship between drugs and drug users. As far back as the 1940s and 1950s, radio and television were referred to as 'plug-in drugs'. Today it is common to hear the language of drug abuse applied to media audiences with expressions such as 'video game junkie' or 'Facebook addict' or 'daily fix of soap opera'.

This idea sets up a number of similarities between the use of media and the misuse of drugs:

- Like certain drugs, including alcohol, the media offer an escape from reality.
- Overuse of the media can result in a dangerous psychological dependency for some people.
- 'Little and often' may be acceptable, but 'binging' on television or video games can be dangerous.
- Like drugs, the media can take away your powers of self-control so that you behave in ways that are out of character.

*Media messages are injected into powerless audiences.*

Overall, then, the idea here is that the media 'injects' dangerous and addictive messages into us in the same way as a hypodermic syringe injects a drug into the bloodstream. Although this idea is commonly used to criticise media users, we should be very suspicious of its claims and implications. Evidence is rarely used to support the idea and simply asserting that the media are like drugs proves nothing. Also, if it was that easy to 'inject' information, attitudes and knowledge into viewers, especially children, the education system would be entirely media based.

## Passive audiences

Effects theory takes the view that the audience's only role in media consumption is as passive consumers, meaning our decisions are limited to turning on, turning off and making selections from the media content made available to us. For effects theory, audiences simply soak up the media: the media does things to them rather than the other way around.

*Are these children powerless to resist the effects of the media? The hypodermic syringe theory would say: 'Yes, they are.'*

## Active audiences

In contrast with the passive audience/effects theory view, many of the recent approaches in media studies have taken a more positive view of the media audience. Rather than having things done to them by the media, active audiences do things with the media.

One sense in which audiences are active is that they make their own meanings from the media products available to them. These meanings are not necessarily the same as the meanings intended by the producers.

**It's my turn to choose!**

**Quick question 3.6**

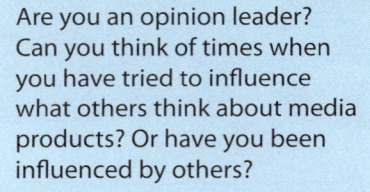

Are you an opinion leader? Can you think of times when you have tried to influence what others think about media products? Or have you been influenced by others?

A second sense of 'active' is that individuals may use the media for their own reasons rather than those of the producers. For example, a *Financial Times* reader may use the printed newspaper to make a barrier to hide behind on a train journey. Perhaps, too, the *Financial Times* can be used to signal to other people that 'I'm a *Financial Times* reader you know'. Television and radio can be used to drown out the din made by noisy children or a DVD could be chosen to make a special 'family time' when everyone gathers together to watch. Alternatively, a television remote control can be used as a weapon in a domestic power struggle between siblings. Giving and taking away access to media is often a form of regulation and control in households.

Effects theory, apart from having a particular concern with children, tends to see audiences as a mass. There is little recognition that individuals within the audience may perceive and react to media products very differently.

The **two-step flow model** of media effects moved away from the idea of a passive audience. This model recognised that when audience members react to the media, they are also influenced by their family, friends, workmates or community. For example, when watching a politician on television you may be influenced by your friends shouting, 'What an idiot!' and throwing cushions at the telly, more than you are influenced by what the politician actually says.

Although the two-step flow model rejects the idea that *everyone* in the audience is passive, it still seems to be saying that some people are especially passive because they are influenced by friends, etc. as well as the media. It's important, though, because it reminds you that the audience is made up of real people in real social situations.

Another approach with a focus on the capacity to be active is Blumler and Katz's (1974) **uses and gratification model**. This idea focuses on the audience members' ability to *select* the media they want to watch, listen to, read or browse and the reasons they may have for making this selection.

Everyone has needs and desires, for example one's needs for entertainment, information and social interaction with other people. It is known that the media can help us fulfil these needs. In other words, active *uses* of the media are made to provide *gratifications* for their needs.

Rather than just passively allowing the media to wash over you, you proactively seek out the media products that meet your needs. But what are your needs? Uses and gratifications theory suggests that they can be grouped as follows:

1 **Entertainment and diversion**: the entertainment provided by the media is used as a means of relaxation and escape from the stresses and demands of everyday life. A fantasy film or computer game diverts attention away from reality.

2 **The need to be informed and educated**: people's desire to know what's going on locally, nationally and internationally and to be stimulated by developing knowledge and understanding of the world. Newspapers, factual television and web surfing are used for this reason.

3 **A need for social interaction**: many conversations are about the media and the media are used as part of our relationships with others. Characters in the media can also become friends. This can be particularly important for media users who have a limited amount of human contact in their everyday lives. Social media also provide the gratification of interacting with others.

4 **Personal identity**: the need to affirm to yourself and others who you are. The media provide many opportunities to measure yourself against role models, heroes and villains. Also, you can find in the media many representations of lifestyles that you may aspire to or you may reject. Social media can fulfil a desire to express yourself to others and confirm your sense of self.

You will find it helpful to talk about your CSPs and other media products in terms of potential uses and gratifications for different people. However, you certainly don't have to confine yourself to this list of needs. Uses and gratifications researchers have developed many lists and examples of audience needs to fit in with different projects.

Uses and gratifications theory does have positive features. It seems to place the power firmly in the hands of consumers rather than producers. Media producers need to recognise the consumers' needs and meet them or else their custom will be taken away.

This all seems very rosy, but there are a few problems with the optimistic view of uses and gratifications. Firstly, we may know what we want, but that doesn't necessarily mean we can afford it. For many people, the subscriptions and up-front costs of the best media packages are just too expensive.

Secondly, not everyone has the same level of 'media literacy' needed to access the sophisticated technology of modern devices. Have you ever had to help someone of your grandparents' generation set up their smartphone?

### Activity 3.7

Choose a media product from each of the following media forms:
- television
- social media
- magazines
- video games
- music video.

Draw a chart for each product based on the four different types of uses and gratifications listed on the left. Remember that different people may have different reasons for liking the same product.

Social integration and escapism

> **Quick question 3.7**
>
> What are your personal motivations for selecting and enjoying a media product? Do these seem to fit in with uses and gratifications theory?

Thirdly, you don't always make active choices about media consumption. A lot of it is 'just there', unasked for, especially advertising.

A final problem for uses and gratifications theory is that it doesn't have any explanations about where these 'needs' come from. How did you know what you wanted in the first place? You couldn't possibly have been influenced by the media. Or could you?

## Audience pleasure

The scope of uses and gratifications theory can be expanded by looking in more depth at the different types of pleasure that are made available to the media audience:

- **Aesthetic pleasure**: the appreciation of experiencing something beautiful. It could be the pleasure of listening to music perfectly matched to visual images in a film or video.
- **Cerebral pleasure**: the intellectual satisfaction that may come, for example, from solving the problems set by a video game or following a perfectly constructed narrative.
- **Visceral pleasure**: in contrast with the above, visceral pleasures are of the body more than mind; the sort of thing that makes the hairs on the back of your neck stand up or makes you want to punch the air. Representations of revenge, triumph, horror, 'come-uppance', violence or sex all provide visceral pleasure.

*Visceral pleasure: Bruce Willis's revenge in* Reprisal *(2018) could be considered a visceral pleasure.*

> **Talk about it**
>
> What is your favourite ever media product? Which of the audience pleasures did you experience?

> **Activity 3.8**
>
> Match each of the following to one or more types of audience pleasure:
> - Watching MMA (mixed martial arts) fight online.
> - Playing a strategy video game such as Civilization 6 or Endless Legend.
> - Watching *A Perfect Planet*.
> - Reading a TV listings magazine such as *Radio Times*.
> - Watching *The Graham Norton Show*.

- **Voyeuristic pleasure**: the satisfaction drawn from spying, prying or knowing something unknown to others. Audiences are often positioned as voyeurs as, for example, when we discover intimate secrets of a character in a drama.
- **Vicarious pleasure**: the pleasure enjoyed second hand through the experiences of others. In sport, you can identify with the skills and triumphs of competitors. Dramas often position the audience to share the experiences and feelings of a character.
- **Catharsis**: not unlike vicarious pleasure, this is the idea that our own pent-up emotions can be relieved by experiences such as witnessing drama or music. Crying at the romantic comedy or enjoying the violent destruction of a villain would be cathartic if it left you feeling emotionally cleansed.

## Active audiences: reception theories

Reception theories see the audience as 'active' because they are able to actively make their own meanings from the messages received from the media.

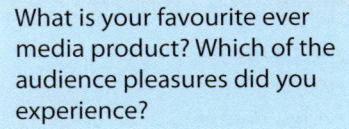

The idea is that members of the audience *perceive* differently for all sorts of reasons. Media codes are discussed in Chapter 1. These codes only work if senders and receivers of messages have a shared understanding of them. Media products are created by **encoding** meanings. Members of the audience **decode** the meanings. Encoding and decoding works very well if the encoder and decoder share the same culture. Often, though, they don't.

An example of this could be when the encoding is done many years before the decoding. Search online for the L&M cigarette advertisement from the 1950s with the actress Barbara Stanwyck on it.

The encoded message is very clear. L&M cigarettes are beneficial for your health ('just what the doctor ordered') and they are endorsed by a film star (Barbara Stanwyck). Celebrity endorsement works because consumers trust famous people and want to be like them.

Seventy years later, nobody would accept these meanings at face value even if it was one of today's film stars instead of Barbara Stanwyck. Cultural values and beliefs about smoking have changed dramatically since the 1950s. Backed up by scientific research, laws about tobacco advertising and bans on smoking in public places, our attitudes towards cigarettes have changed. Very few would accept the advertising claim that 'smoking is good for you'.

All this means that the *decoded* meaning is very different from the *encoded* meaning. Even so, not everyone today will interpret the advertisement in the same way. There may be differences between people of different ages, smokers and non-smokers for example.

The encoding and decoding processes don't have to be separated by decades for audiences to interpret media messages differently.

Some newspapers and television programmes deal extensively with so-called 'benefit scroungers' and 'welfare cheats'. Often, the encoded message is that 'scrounging' is a widespread problem and that the welfare system itself is at fault. Interpretations of these messages are likely to depend on the knowledge, background and experience of individuals as they decode them.

Stuart Hall, who developed the encoding/decoding approach, also suggested three ways in which different audience members may decode media products. Remember that 'reading' here refers to the way in which the media product is interpreted.

| Preferred reading | This is the interpretation that the producers want the audience to have. For example, enjoying *Mrs Brown's Boys*, laughing and recognising the humour |
|---|---|
| Negotiated reading | The audience members accept some of the intended messages but reject others, especially if they conflict with each individual's own experience. For example, enjoying some aspects of *Mrs. Brown's Boys* but rejecting others such as stereotyping |
| Oppositional reading | An interpretation that recognises the preferred reading ('supposed to be funny') by completely rejecting it, perhaps because the language and scenarios cause offence |

### Key term

**Encoding/decoding**
This model of communication claims that media products contain various messages that are encoded using different media codes and conventions. The ways in which audiences decode these messages depend on their social context. The decoded messages may not be the same as the encoded messages.

### Activity 3.9

Find other examples of adverts from the past that would not be acceptable today. What has changed and why?

### Activity 3.10

Identify the potential
- preferred reading
- negotiated reading
- oppositional reading

of the product on the right.

*Healthy* magazine

The encoding/decoding approach is a useful reminder that audience members can't be forced to accept the meaning that the producer wants. This is because products are **polysemic**: they can be interpreted in many different ways. Also, audiences are diverse, made up of individuals with different backgrounds as well as different physical, social and cultural contexts. However, media producers still have power to influence audiences and media products can still be influential. As media students, you have to be careful not to make too many assumptions about this power and influence.

## Audience positioning

If the audience is able to reject or negotiate with the media product, how are media producers able to guide readers towards the *preferred* interpretation? Stuart Hall uses the term **audience positioning** to describe the many techniques used by media producers to steer the audience towards the preferred reading. Using the media codes discussed in Chapter 1, media producers control the reaction or position of the audience or at least try to control the position.

Narrative and genre codes, music, editing, performance and language codes are all included in the ways in which the media product addresses the audience. For example, the **mode of address** of a television news broadcast is formal and authoritative, so the viewer is positioned in the role of a willing learner. This positioning encourages the viewer to accept the values and beliefs that underlie the news. Viewers are not positioned in a way to doubt the content and presentation of the news.

However, television game shows and light entertainment have an informal and 'matey' mode of address, which positions the audience as friends. Presenters may glance directly at the camera and seem to speak personally to the television audience rather than the studio audience so that we feel 'in on the joke'. Viewers are positioned to react as the studio audience does: laughing, cheering, egging on contestants and generally joining in.

In order to reject or negotiate these readings, audience members have to see through the ways in which they are being positioned. This isn't always easy because the media codes used by producers are deeply embedded in your way of seeing the world.

### Key terms

**Polysemic**
A sign or message that can have many different meanings.

**Mode of address**
Involves the style and tone of a media message's presentation; not so much *what* is being said but the *way* in which it is said. Formal/informal, direct/indirect are examples of modes of address.

3 Media Audiences

**CASE STUDY:**

# Newspaper 2023 CSP: the 'Amazon shops' story in *The Times* and the *Daily Mirror*

**Background**: the online retailer, Amazon, had just opened its first UK cashier-free shop: Amazon Fresh, in Ealing Broadway. Having logged in with an app, customers are tracked throughout the store, and are charged afterwards for what they've picked up and taken with them.

*The Times*, Friday 5 March 2021

## My takeaway from Amazon's till-free shop? It's a new era

**Patrick Kidd**

There was a time when if a masked person walked into a supermarket and was seen on camera slipping things into their pockets, a store detective would be sent to the exit faster than you could say "unexpected item in the bagging area". If Amazon's plan for cashier-free shopping catches on, this will be quite normal.

"Just walk out" is the slogan of Amazon Fresh. It is displayed on the signs, the bags and the unmanned exit, an invitation that still makes me feel shifty as I leave the supermarket in west London without reaching for my wallet. I think with guilt about my late grandmother, a former Tesco store detective — 5ft nothing but they say she could tackle like a lock forward — who had collared many a shoplifter who tried to make off with a five-fingered discount.

Walking away from the shop a touch too briskly with a bag of what will not technically be purchases until the money leaves my account three hours later, I half expect a hand to fall on my shoulder and a growl of "you're nicked".

Yet for the previous 18 minutes and 57 seconds, as the app that controls what Amazon calls my "seamless and magical customer experience" reveals, every move I made since entering through an airport-style gate with a flash of a QR code on my phone had been tracked. Every object I picked up was counted, and every one I put back removed, by 100 cameras so that when I left the building, no matter whether the goods were in my bag or under my coat (or even, one assumes, in my stomach), the All-seeing God Amazon would know what I had done.

I have not felt my shopping habits to be so "seen" since the time my wife visited the corner shop near our flat and was asked by the owner if "the gentleman would like his usual" with a gesture at a pile of freshly baked cheese scones.

The technology was developed by Amazon to reduce the time people spend in queues. Their first cashier-free shop, Amazon Go, was opened in Seattle in 2018 and there are now 28 in the US. Amazon Fresh, its UK arm, opened its first in Ealing Broadway yesterday.

Some are concerned about being watched. "It offers a dystopian, total-surveillance experience," Silkie Carlo, from Big Brother Watch, said. "Customers deserve to know how and by whom these analytics could be used." Amazon says it does not use facial recognition software and information about shopping habits will be associated with a customer's account for up to 30 days.

Outside the shop, Maha Salem, who had visited with her baby to buy a coffee and a croissant, admitted unease. "I tried to forget about the cameras and not feel paranoid," she said. However, she felt that with a large pram anything that reduced fuss was very welcome.

Benjamin Rogers had bought ingredients for a cake. "I found it very well stocked and easy to navigate," he said. "Not having to queue sped it up by ten minutes." That said, he then spent 40 minutes waiting outside to receive his receipt by email to check the reckoning. "I want to be sure that they removed things I put back," he said.

He could have been waiting some time. Having left the shop at 10.39am (and 57 seconds), it took until 2.04pm before my bank's app pinged to tell me that £23.95 had been taken from my account and a further two minutes to get the receipt.

However, I could check within an hour on the app what products had been assigned to me. Soup, ham, onions, a disappointingly dry "feta and potato sourdough pocket" (a nod, perhaps, to what Amazon has done for the cardboard industry) and six other items were all correctly registered; a sandwich and radishes that I had put back were not in the final reckoning.

On first impression, it works very well. It may have more of a challenge when the shop is busier: only 20 customers are allowed at a time to maintain distancing. It works so smoothly that the fear is Amazon customers forget that other shops don't let you just walk out. The union of store detectives should not be worried.

*Customers including Patrick Kidd, left, embracing the "seamless and magic" retail experience at Amazon's newly opened Fresh shop in Ealing, west London*

---

Look closely at the language used in the headline and in the article. Think about the running order of the story – remember that the most important information will be at the beginning. What is the significance of the two images used to illustrate in the story? These codes have all been chosen to communicate the meaning of the story. Is *The Times* trying to position the reader?

The choices made suggest that the preferred reading of *The Times* article is that cashier-less stores are easy to use, function well, but that the experience is unfamiliar and at this early stage people have not yet learnt to trust the technology. In fact, four of the paragraphs of the 12-paragraph story are dominated by reference to the way the shop tracks the customer's every move. This is clearly an important aspect for the writer. All three of the interviewees quoted express some reservations about the technology being used. The mode of address is cautious but reassuring to traditional *Times* readers (refer to your audience profile) explaining how the new technology system works, and showing that it can be trusted not to share data or to overcharge. The article concentrates on the personal experience of shopping in such a store.

### Activity 3.11

Compare *The Times* with Graham Hiscott's (2021) coverage of the same story in the *Daily Mirror*. How does the *Mirror* position its readers? What is the preferred reading and why might it be different from *The Times*? You will find it useful to look at the relevant section of Chapter 5 on the two newspapers.

### Key terms

**Diffused audience**
Diffused means to spread over a wide area or between a large number of people. A diffused audience is large but scattered.

**Fragmentation**
The process of breaking something down into smaller parts. A fragmented audience may be very large but the individual members have no connection with each other and use many different devices.

### Talk about it

How do you feel about this 'diffused audience' idea? Does it apply to you?

For example, how would it affect you if you didn't have access to the internet or your phone for, say, a week … or even a day?

Do you agree that many people use technology and media access to 'perform' a version of their identity to others?

The story's point of view is sympathetic to the customer's needs and gives readers an insight into the ways the store operates for them.

*Daily Mirror*, Friday 5 March 2021

**Amazon 'no till' shops will be threat to jobs**

Warning hi-tech store may have knock-on effect

BY GRAHAM HISCOTT
Head of Business

AMAZON'S new hi-tech, till-free supermarkets could cause "considerable" job losses if rivals copy the idea, warns a financial analyst.

The online giant's first Amazon Fresh store outside the US opened yesterday in Ealing, West London.

Customers scan a quick response code as they enter the shop then put items in their bag.

A network of cameras and sensors detect what they have picked. Shoppers simply walk out with their purchases which are then charged to their account.

Amazon's Matt Birch said it offered a "super fast, friction-free way to shop". Rival supermarkets will watch it closely, with some already testing till-less stores.

Clive Black, an analyst at Shore Capital, warned it would have a huge impact on jobs if others follow suit.

He said: "This is a cashless and cardless operation so think of all the people that affects, not just in stores but in banks too.

"It is absolutely going to lead to a considerable reduction in roles for people at head office and in branches."

Mr Black predicted that rather than open hundreds of new Amazon Fresh stores, the huge company may snap up an existing supermarket chain instead.

> Cashless & cardless, think of all those it will affect
> CLIVE BLACK WARNS OF IMPACT ON JOBS

Morrisons and northern chain Booths were among those he mentioned.

Last year Amazon, which already owns the small Whole Food Markets chain, saw its UK sales surge 51% to £19.4billion.

It came as experts at campaigners TaxWatch predicted a measure in the Budget could wipe out Amazon's UK corporation tax bill. Chancellor Rishi Sunak increased the tax to 25% from 2023 but included a "super deduction" for companies when they invest.

Firms can offset the tax break against profits. Amazon has argued that heavy investment since it arrived in the UK two decades ago is one reason it had paid so little corporation tax.

TaxWatch executive director George Turner said: "It is highly questionable whether a tax cut for Amazon today is the best use of public money."

Amazon has not said how many jobs the new stores venture will create in the UK. But it has previously spoken about the large numbers of workers it had taken on in its fulfilment centres, research and development.

The company said it has also launched a By Amazon range of hundreds of own-brand products for the stores.

graham.hiscott@mirror.co.uk
@Grahamhiscott

VOICE OF THE MIRROR: PAGE 8

Mobile phones have become part of the gig experience.

## Interactive audiences

At the beginning of this chapter, the steady swing away from 'traditional' media towards digital media was noted. Audiences for traditional media watched, listened and read. In today's media environment, you also engage in a range of different ways by chatting, voting, surfing, downloading, time-shifting, messaging, playing and so on. The word 'audience' doesn't seem quite right for all this activity. Users of shared internet resources sometimes describe themselves as a community rather than an audience. Perhaps this term would be a better way of reflecting the changed nature of media use.

Another way of looking at these developments was proposed by Abercrombie and Longhurst (1998) who identified three stages in the development of the audience:

- The **simple audience**: the audience for face-to-face contacts such as theatre, sports events or public meetings.

- The **mass audience**: the audience for traditional media – television, radio, print and film.

- The **diffused audience**: the digital technology audience. They are **fragmented** but the media are totally integrated into daily life. These are people who expect 24/7 access to media. For them, media consumption is not a separate activity, it is part of almost everything they do.

Although these are three historical phases of the audience, they don't replace each other. Today, all three co-exist and intermingle. When you watch a scheduled soap opera on television, you are part of a mass audience. If, at the same time, you are following tweets by the soap actors and sharing your thoughts about the programme on Facebook, then you are a member of a diffused audience.

Members of the diffused audience don't just *consume* media, they *perform* with the media. Putting together an identity for yourself on social media is exactly this kind of performance. You may include you own pictures, shared videos, music selections, advertisements you like, selfies and so on to project an image of yourself.

There are many ways in which interactive audience members can use the resources of the internet to perform an identity. These include:

- **Blog** (short for weblog): simply a personal or small group webpage, regularly updated with fresh posts and usually written in an informal or chatty style. Plenty of bloggers are also on Twitter, Google+, Pinterest or Facebook.
- **Vlog**: a video version of a blog (video blog). Many vlogs also have written material and still images as well as video content. YouTube is particularly popular with vloggers. A YouTube channel will also provide followers with an opportunity to post questions, comments or reactions. Successful vloggers can turn vlogging into a lucrative career.
- **Podcasting**: an audio version of a blog. Subscribers to podcasts will often have each episode downloaded automatically to their device.
- **Citizen journalism**: the internet has provided an opportunity for non-professionals to get involved in news gathering (otherwise known as user-generated copy) as well as news photography and comments on news.

  Defenders of citizen journalism claim that it makes the news more democratic and weakens the hold of powerful news corporations. Critics say that it is more likely to be biased and inaccurate without the fact-checking of professional journalism.
- **Crowd sourcing**: a way of collecting ideas, services, funds or signatures for petitions from large numbers of people by using the internet. In the UK, government departments often put proposals online and invite comment. Change.org enables individuals to start petitions or social campaigns and gather supporters.
- **Content sharing**: the distribution of webpage content or links via social media. As noted above, this sharing can be part of the performance of identity, making a statement about who you are, but is also a part of building and keeping relationships with others.

Citizen journalism can offer a different view of events.

'Earthly Messenger', a statue of David Bowie in Aylesbury, Buckinghamshire, was completed thanks to £100,000 raised by a crowd-sourcing appeal on Kickstarter.com.

- **Wiki**: a website on which users can add or edit content. A well-known example is Wikipedia, the online encyclopaedia.
- **Live streaming**: live streamers use apps such as Periscope, LiveMe, Omegle and Houseparty to broadcast the smallest details of their lives to fans and followers. As live streaming has become increasingly popular among teens and pre-teens, concerns have been expressed about the potential dangers. A BBC report in December 2017 (BBC News, 2017) highlighted the steps being taken by the National Crime Agency to alert children and parents to the dangers of live streaming.
- **Video and photograph sharing apps**: TikTok, Flickr, Instagram and many other platform apps – allow users to post videos or photographs that can be seen by their followers and by others who browse for content.

## Advertising, marketing and the interactive audience

> **Talk about it**
>
> Are the dangers of live streaming overestimated or underestimated? How would you advise children and parents about the use of live streaming apps?

The importance of audience research to the traditional media has been discussed above. However, the commercial media (those looking to make a profit) need to create content that will draw in an audience that is attractive to advertisers. This means that the press, magazines, television and radio need to be well-informed about the factors that will make their products successful. Also, they need to provide reliable audience figures to advertisers so that advertising costs can be negotiated.

How have advertisers exploited the potential of digital media, especially the internet with its interactive audience?

We all know that advertising money has rapidly migrated online. Surfing the internet, using social media or search engines and even opening your inbox all involve fighting your way through a forest of promotional messages, pop-ups and advertising links. Advertisers don't necessarily pay for the number of people who may view a website, they pay for:

- **Impressions**: the number of visitors to the page with their ad, usually a cost per 1,000.
- **Clicks**: the number of times an ad is actually clicked on. Price varies enormously and can be as little as a few pence per click to £10 and above per click.
- **Actions**: an action is a click that results in a sale: a sure-fire winner for advertisers.

For advertisers, then, only the first of these – impressions – relies on a passive viewing of the advertisement. Both clicks and actions rely on the user actively doing something.

The active user of the internet and, especially, social media can be helpful to advertisers in other ways too. A great deal of information about social media users is embedded in their accounts, not only demographic and geographic information (age, gender, region, ethnicity) but also psychographic information about hobbies, interests, lifestyle and spending habits.

Specialist analytic companies can data mine this information to provide advertisers with highly tailored targets so that marketing messages only reach exactly the sort of people who are potential customers. The **data mining** of social media also enables companies to evaluate the success of their advertising campaigns.

Advertisers have always known that 'word of mouth' or personal endorsements carry much more weight than a straightforward advertisement. For this reason, a 'shared' or retweeted advert often carries more weight than the original. If you purchase goods or services online you will almost certainly be nudged to provide a review or testimonial, preferably with a photograph. These are valuable resources for sales messages as they come from 'real people'.

The technique used to persuade social media users to pass on advertising messages is called viral marketing. At its most successful, this technique can create an explosion of interest in the product ('going viral'). Dove's Real Beauty Sketches (which can be found online) is a good example of a successful viral social media campaign. If the ad is interesting enough, social media users will distribute it themselves … at no cost to the company!

> **Key term**
>
> **Data mining**
> Turning raw data into useful information.

## Fans and fandom

Most of us are fans of something or someone, whether a sports club, a band or performer, a celebrity, a film franchise or television programme. In some cases, a fan is little more than a member of the 'mass audience' by, for example, simply making sure that they watch every episode of a favourite television programme.

Most fans, though, like to engage more closely than this and, for some, being a fan can be a significant part of life. Being more engaged as a fan may mean purchasing downloads, DVDs or merchandise and watching live performances. Many fans join clubs or online communities. At this stage, fans really are active media consumers: exchanging information, organising conventions, creating networks and (perhaps on Twitter) communicating directly with their heroes.

At another stage, fans contribute their own creative ideas. This may involve dressing up and re-enacting stories, remixing music or video content to create new products or producing original fan material such as fanvids and fanzines. At this level of engagement, fans are genuine 'prosumers', as they combine media production with media consumption.

It was noted on page 105 that social media users can be said to perform their identity. Similarly, performing your identity is certainly part of being a fan. It may involve clothing (wearing replica kits or a band T-shirt, for example), communicating your allegiance with posters and merchandise, choosing other fans as friends and making sure that everyone knows you're a fan. For many, being a fan isn't just something you *do*, it's something you *are* – a key part of your subcultural identity.

All fans have a relationship with the object of their loyalty and affection. For the most part, this is a one-way connection, although some bands, performers and sports clubs go out of their way to

*Fans celebrate Star Wars and other favourite films.*

*Goth weekend in Whitby, Yorkshire*

### Talk about it

Are you a fan? How engaged and active are you? What is your view of fan sites and societies? Does being a fan contribute to your sense of self and help to make you who you are?

forge close relationships with their fans. Sometimes it can be an unhealthy relationship for one or both parties. Celebrities have often felt that fans invade their privacy or try to get 'too close'.

Psychologists use the term 'parasocial relationship' to describe the perception by fans that their relationship with a celebrity is balanced and two-way, perhaps to the extent that the fan feels the star is a 'real friend' or 'the only person who understands me'. For most people though, fandom is a way of sharing their passion and interests, expressing ourselves and developing a sense of self.

### CASE STUDY:
## The Whovians

*Doctor Who* fan societies exist all around the world. In the UK, the Doctor Who Appreciation Society, recognised by the BBC, offers members a fanzine, *Celestial Toyroom*, discounted merchandise, local groups and national events. There are numerous unofficial sites and groups such as Whoviannet. Whoviannet encourages fans to submit pictures of their *Doctor Who* 'stories' and artwork.

### Link

For more on Arctic Monkeys see Chapter 5, pages 212–214.

### CASE STUDY:
## Arctic Monkeys

The rapid rise to fame of Arctic Monkeys in 2005 is an interesting case study of a band who side-stepped the traditional music industry approach.

### Key term

**Spin**
A form of biased communication used by advertisers, marketers or politicians to present someone or something in a very positive or very negative light. Experts in spin are called 'spin doctors'.

Instead of relying on a major record label to **spin** stories to the press, the band relied on their fans and the internet. Their fans uploaded songs to file-sharing sites, gave away free CDs and created a My Space page. Without any of the traditional methods of promotion and musical press coverage, the band created an internet fan base.

Arctic Monkeys' success flew in the face of the music industry's ideas. With downloads overtaking physical sales, the music industry tried to control file sharing to protect copyright interests. Arctic Monkeys gave their music away for free. Far from ruining their career, this move had the opposite effect. When they eventually released their debut single, it went straight to No. 1 and the follow-up album *Whatever People Say I Am, That's What I'm Not* was the fastest selling UK debut album ever.

At the time, the band's novel use of the internet was big news. In a sense, the fans themselves helped to make the band, using the internet to network, share music and create an aura of excitement around them. Fans realised that they no longer needed the music press or the traditional media and the music industry realised that it couldn't survive without the internet.

Alex Turner from Arctic Monkeys

# Reaching the interactive audience

Media users today expect to be able to access media products at a time and in a place of their choosing. This places some heavy demands on the media producers. In order to reach their target audience, media producers need to engage with:

- **Multi-platform approach**: audiences expect the same content to be available on different devices including PCs, televisions and mobile devices.
- **Time-shift viewing or continuous availability**: audiences expect to stream or download video material at times suitable to them. Increasingly, media devices are linked so that; for example, you can resume watching a downloaded film as you move from television to PC to tablet or phone. Devices have multiple functions. Smart televisions can be used for radio listening, internet surfing, music streaming and gaming; another example of technological convergence.
- **Synchronised demand**: when audiences expect access to media products as soon as they are available anywhere in the world. As a consequence, films are much more likely to have simultaneous global release. Television companies often release all episodes of drama series on the same day for online viewers.

Alongside the technological developments, social and cultural changes also have had an impact on the relationship between audiences, producers and media products. Today's audiences are highly **media literate**, with a sophisticated knowledge and understanding of media codes and conventions.

The internet and social media have swung the balance of power between senders and receivers of media messages some way back towards the audience.

However, large global media corporations, politicians, propagandists and advertisers are finding increasingly effective ways of exploiting the potential of social media. Could the pendulum be swinging back the other way?

### Activity 3.12
Investigate the social media presence of your Member of Parliament (MP). How effectively are they using social media to reach out to young people?

### Key term
**Media literacy**
The possession of the range of skills needed to gain access to, critically analyse and create your own examples of media in different forms. GCSE Media Studies is a good way of developing your media literacy.

### References

Abercrombie, N. & Longhurst, B. (1998) *Audiences: A Sociological Theory of Performance and Imagination*.

BBC News (2017, 5 December) Child Exploitation: Live Streaming an 'Urgent' Threat, http://www.bbc.co.uk/news/uk-42224148.

Bloxham, A. (2010, 18 November) Social Networking: Teachers Blame Facebook and Twitter for Pupils' Poor Grades, *The Daily Telegraph*, https://www.telegraph.co.uk/education/educationnews/8142721/Social-networking-teachers-blame-Facebook-and-Twitter-for-pupils-poor-grades.html.

Blumler, J. & Katz, E. (1974) *The Uses of Mass Communications: Current Perspectives on Gratification Research*.

Hume, T. (2016, 24 July) Munich Gunman Planned Attack for a Year, Officials Say, CNN, https://edition.cnn.com/2016/07/24/europe/germany-munich-shooting/index.html.

PAMCo (2020) Social Grade, https://pamco.co.uk/news/newsletter-q1-2020/index.html.

Scutti, S. (2018, 22 February) Do Video Games Lead to Violence?, CNN, https://edition.cnn.com/2016/07/25/health/video-games-and-violence/index.html.

# 4 Media Industries

### What's in this chapter?

- This chapter deals with the industries that create media products. Firstly, we look at some of the background to media industries, including the size of this sector and its importance to the UK economy.

- There is an examination of some trends and processes in the development of large media corporations, followed by a case study of two major technology corporations.

- The remainder of the chapter focuses on case studies of the industries behind the media forms that you will need to study (newspapers, film, radio, television, music video and video games).

## Introduction

Media industries are all of those corporations and companies that make media products for consumption by media audiences. Media industry is big business. The 100 largest media companies in the UK had a combined income of £96 billion in 2017, according to Deloitte (2017). The government includes media within its 'creative industries' category, which is made up of the groups shown on the left.

Some of these sectors aren't really media (for example, architecture and museums) but they are relatively small. Over 2 million people work in the creative industries, about one in 11 of all jobs. The sector contributes more to the UK economy than the automotive, life sciences, aerospace, oil and gas sectors combined. Worldwide, over 29 million people work in the sector.

The media sector is an important and fast-growing sector of the UK economy. MediaCityUK in Salford opened in 2011. It houses BBC and ITV studios, as well as numerous smaller media-related service companies and the University of Salford's media department. A major part of the BBC's operation, including *BBC Breakfast*, *Match of the Day* and Radio 5 Live, moved from London to MediaCityUK. The site is set to double in size by 2026, providing a massive boost to the regional economy.

In GCSE Media Studies, nine different media forms are dealt with:

| *Television | *Newspapers | *Online, social and participatory media (OSP) |
| *Film | Magazines | *Video games |
| *Radio | Advertising and marketing | *Music video |

All of these forms, of course, are produced by media industries, but only those industries marked with an asterisk (*) are studied in detail. This chapter has a case study section for each of these asterisked industries except for OSP, which is dealt with in this introduction. Some of these forms are relatively new (OSP, video games, music video) but the others have longstanding links with their own separate industries. The newspaper industry, for example, once produced a range of print newspapers and was dominated by a small group of publishers specialising in newspaper production. Similarly, a small number of Hollywood studios produced a high number of films. Gradually, this sort of specialisation by companies focusing on the production of a single media form has broken down.

The case studies and examples in this chapter focus on a number of significant aspects of media industries including:

- trends towards bigger, more powerful non-specialist companies
- competition between media companies and corporations
- the effects of the digital revolution, including its impact on the structure and ownership of media industries
- the regulation and control of media industries.

Big multinational companies such as Bauer Media make products in many formats for audiences spread across different countries.

The Bauer Group was a specialist German publisher of youth and listings magazines but it steadily grew by buying other companies. At first, other magazine publishers in Germany were acquired, but the company steadily increased its range by purchasing international publishers and then by branching out into other media, including film, television and radio including the KISS network. This form of expansion, called **horizontal integration**, can be seen in a number of further examples in this chapter. Sometimes, companies only expand within their own sector, as happened with the ITV network. For many years, commercial television in the UK was regional, with each area served by an independent company. Gradually, two major companies, Carlton and Granada, bought out nearly all the others and then merged to form ITV plc in 2004. Since 2016 all of the regional licences in England, Wales and Northern Ireland have been held by one company, ITV. This company also operates ITV2, ITV3, ITV4, CITV, ITVBe and the ITV hub.

The film industry case study shows how studios gained (then lost) control over the distribution and exhibition of films. This process of extending control over other areas of the supply chain is called **vertical integration** and is further explored in relation to the television industry later in this book, where we find distribution companies such as Netflix and Amazon increasingly investing in film and television content.

> **Link**
>
> For more on Bauer Media see pages 133–134.

> **Quick question 4.1**
>
> Which company (or companies) provided the ITV service in your area? Was it well-liked? (You may have to ask someone of your parents' generation.)

> **Key terms**
>
> **Horizontal integration**
> The acquisition of other companies at the same level of the supply chain (for example, making media products) in similar or different sectors of the market.
>
> **Vertical integration**
> A strategy that involves bringing supply, production, distribution and sales together into one unified company.

> **Links**
>
> For more about Netflix and Amazon see pages 138 and 161–162.

### Key terms

**Media synergy**
The co-production and/or co-promotion of a related set of media products or services all developed in-house by a large media corporation.

**Monopoly**
A situation in which one company totally dominates a sector of the market place. There is no competition, leaving customers with no choice to buy elsewhere.

**Oligopoly**
A market that is dominated by a few companies that control the supply of the products or services. There is very little competition within an oligopoly as the companies tend to cooperate with each other by keeping prices high.

### Link

For more on Reach (formerly Trinity Mirror) see page 120.

### Activity 4.1

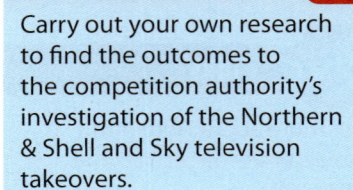

Carry out your own research to find the outcomes to the competition authority's investigation of the Northern & Shell and Sky television takeovers.

A corporation can maximise the benefit of horizontal integration by using the different parts of the organisation. For example, your newspaper could promote your film which happens to have a soundtrack released by your record company and a linked-in video game developed by your game company. You may even have your own theme park to promote and sell these products. This is called **media synergy**.

## Competition and the commercial media industries

With the exception of the BBC – a public service provider – the vast majority of media organisations are commercial operators. This means that they are motivated by the drive for profits.

In order to maximise profits, companies compete with each other for a share of the market place. From the customers' point of view, this competition can be beneficial because it means they have access to a huge range of media products and services. In theory, competition keeps prices low and quality high because any company providing products and services that the customer isn't satisfied with would soon lose out to its competitors. In reality, though, it doesn't always work out like this. Large companies always have an advantage in the market for media products and services. If a small company threatens the profits of a big company, the chances are that it will be swallowed up in a takeover deal. Alternatively, small or medium-sized media companies sometimes merge together to form a new and more powerful mega-company, as was seen in the case of ITV.

The problem with this never-ending process of mergers and takeovers is that it can end up killing off competition altogether. This is called a **monopoly**.

Although out and out monopolies are quite unusual in the media, it is very common for a market sector to be dominated by a small number of very large and powerful corporations: an **oligopoly**. The UK national newspaper industry certainly falls into this category and similar situations can be seen in national commercial radio and social media. Most governments recognise that monopolies and oligopolies are unhealthy because consumers have so little choice and there is a danger that prices may be kept artificially high to protect or increase profits. For this reason, countries such as the UK and USA have laws to protect competition. In 2018, the competition authority in the UK investigated the takeover of Northern & Shell (which owned Express newspapers) by Trinity Mirror because it would concentrate ownership of newspapers in the hands of a very small group of large companies. It decided, though, that the takeover would not substantially reduce competition, and the newly formed group Reach came into existence. Similarly, in March 2020, the government approved the takeover of the *i* newspaper by the Daily Mail General Trust, after a report by Ofcom into the impact on competition suggested this would be minimal. In 2018, regulators cleared 21st Century Fox's plan to win complete control of Sky television (it already owned 39%), but US media company Comcast eventually outbid them for the acquisition, after themselves being cleared to do so by the UK's Culture Secretary.

The processes that lead to monopolies and oligopolies forming are called the **concentration of ownership**. Sometimes, large companies are broken down into smaller parts because government authorities want to ensure greater competition. This is called a **demerger**.

In addition to ownership restrictions, governments also seek to regulate many media industries in the interests of the public. This can also be a problem when very large and powerful companies (e.g. Meta, owners of Facebook) feel that profits could be undermined by regulation. There are well-established systems for content regulation such as age ratings for television, film, video games and other media. These are discussed later in this chapter. In the UK, broadcast media (television and radio) are subject to **statutory regulation**. This means that they are legally required to demonstrate impartiality in news and current affairs reporting. There is no such requirement for newspapers to be impartial; like advertising, the press is **self-regulated**.

### Activity 4.2

Research the ASA website to find out which ads were most complained about last year. How does ASA define 'offensive'? You do not have to study advertising from an industry point of view, but it is useful to bear in mind the industry's codes when looking at representation of issues and groups when you analyse ads.

## Facebook and Alphabet

Many of the trends and issues described above can be explored in relation to two of the media tech giants: Meta (owners of Facebook) and Alphabet (owners of Google). Several of the 2023 CSPs (e.g. the online presence of Marcus Rashford and Kim Kardashian, and the Blackpink music video) have close links to these two corporations. Many music videos are released on YouTube and YouTube is a wholly owned subsidiary of Google.

Firstly, let's look at the development of these two companies before turning to some of the more controversial aspects of the online and social media industry today.

### Key terms

**Concentration of ownership**
The process that results in a small number of corporations or individuals taking an increasing market share, usually by takeovers (buying other companies) or mergers (joining forces with other companies).

**Demerger**
Happens when a large corporation is broken down into smaller independent companies.

**Statutory regulation**
Statutory regulators have legal powers to control the industry for which they are responsible (a statute is a law). For example, Ofcom is the UK regulator for TV, radio, video-on-demand and phones. It sets rules and enforces them in these sectors.

**Self-regulation**
When media industries set up and pay for their own regulatory bodies. Unlike statutory regulators, these do not have legal powers, but they rely on companies within the industry to accept a code of practice. Examples include IPSO (newspapers and magazines) and the Advertising Standards Authority (ASA). The ASA covers press, broadcast, film and internet advertising as well as posters and leaflets. There are various codes for different media produced by the Committee for Advertising Practice. The overall aim is 'to make every UK ad a responsible ad'.

In the world of media industries, the big fish tend to swallow up the little fish.

Alphabet is the parent company of Google. Its first Chief Executive Officer, Larry Page, co-founded Google in 1998 along with Sergey Brin, who became the first President of Alphabet. Google grew rapidly from its search engine base by developing new products and by buying other companies. Google.com is visited more often than any other internet site in the world. Google is the third most valuable brand in the world (after Amazon and Apple).

The list of Google's acquisitions is a long one (see https://en.wikipedia.org/wiki/List_of_mergers_and_acquisitions_by_Alphabet) and provides a very clear illustration of the 'big fish swallowing little fish' trend in media industries. Some of Google's major purchases are:

- YouTube                              $1.7 billion      2006
- DoubleClick (online advertising)     $3.1 billion      2007
- Motorola (partially sold, 2014)      $12.5 billion     2011
- Waze (navigation)                    $1.3 billion      2013
- Nest (home automation)               $3.2 billion      2014
- Fitbit (wearable technologies)       $2.1 billion      2021

In 2015, Google restructured so that all its various components became subsidiaries of a new corporation called Alphabet.

| Rank | Brand | Brand value (billion) | The World's Most Valuable Brands, 2021, according to Statista |
|---|---|---|---|
| #1 | Apple | $263.38 | |
| #2 | Amazon | $254.19 | |
| #3 | Google | $191.22 | |
| #4 | Microsoft | $140.44 | |
| #5 | Samsung | $102.62 | |
| #6 | Walmart | $93.19 | |

Mark Zuckerberg founded Facebook in 2004 and he is still the Chairman and Chief Executive Officer (CEO). He changed the parent company's name to 'Meta' in 2021, to reflect its widening interests. Until this change, the core of Facebook's business had remained its social media service, which grew to 500 million active users by 2010, one billion by 2010, 2 billion by 2017 and 2.89 billion at the start of 2021. Facebook was the seventh most valuable brand in the world (as of January 2021). The company makes money by selling advertising space and, more controversially, by selling data about its users so that advertising can be very accurately targeted. Like Google, Facebook grew by buying other companies, including the following notable examples:

Facebook acquired Oculus for $2.3 billion in 2014.

- Instagram                    $1 billion        2012
- WhatsApp                     $19 billion       2014
- Oculus (virtual reality)     $2.3 billion      2014

Facebook maintained market domination either by buying competitors (the tbh app used by teens to circulate polls about their friends was bought in 2018) or by cloning them. Facebook reacted to the success of Snapchat by developing its own very similar Instagram Stories.

In spite of, or perhaps because of, its enormous success, Meta and Facebook has attracted criticisms on a number of counts. It has such dominance in the market that competition is limited and, as we've seen, competitors are often swallowed up. Privacy issues have also caused concern as, for example, when employers have used the site to spy on workers or interviewees for jobs. Meta has also been accused of failing to monitor and control its content, especially in the case of hate speech, violent extremism, fake news, bullying and trolling.

In 2018, a serious controversy about Facebook's role resulted in Mark Zuckerberg being called to appear before lawmakers in the US senate and Congress. He was tackled about the sale of Facebook users' personal data to another company that used the information to influence the outcome of elections. In other words, millions of people found that their supposedly private information had been made available, without their consent, and used for purposes beyond their control. Numerous apologies were issued, and Zuckerberg admitted that Facebook had not done enough to protect users' data or to prevent other countries from using Facebook to meddle in the US presidential election. There have been many demands for social media to be regulated and supervised more carefully and Mark Zuckerberg has acknowledged that some form of regulation over social media is inevitable.

Alphabet has faced a similar range of criticisms about market domination, privacy, censorship and the integration of advertising into its services. Like Facebook, YouTube has been attacked for failure to exercise sufficient control over content. An issue of particular concern is copyright, as YouTube users persist in uploading (or attempting to upload) material created by someone else. The company has introduced an automated system, Content ID, designed to detect material copied from original sources.

In this chapter you will find many examples of the ways in which the traditional media are regulated either by the government (statutory regulation) or through self-regulatory bodies. At present, no satisfactory model has emerged for the regulation of big tech companies operating on the internet. This is because the platform providers (such as Meta) and the Internet Service Providers (ISPs) such as BT and TalkTalk all claim that they cannot be held fully responsible for the material that is circulated on their systems. The problems are clear enough: abuses of privacy, the use of the internet for extremist propaganda, trolling, bullying and copyright theft, for example, but the solutions are less clear. Big tech companies are gradually tightening their 'rules of use' and are increasingly willing to shut down sites or ban users who upload abusive, dangerous or inappropriate material. Even Donald Trump, the then President of the US, was banned from social media such as Twitter, Facebook, Instagram, YouTube and SnapChat, when his posts were deemed to be too inflammatory. However, the clash between freedom of speech on the one hand and our right to be safe and protected on the other, has not been resolved.

### Talk about it

Should social media providers such as Alphabet and Meta be regulated?

How would you justify the case for or against regulation?

Is there enough competition and choice in the market for social media?

Do you agree with businessman Tim Martin, owner of the J D Wetherspoon pub chain, who announced that his company would close down all its social media accounts, saying: 'It's becoming increasingly obvious that people spend too much time on Twitter, Instagram and Facebook, and struggle to control the compulsion'?

## CASE STUDY:
# The UK newspaper industry

## Print vs electronic media

The UK newspaper industry, in common with most print-based industries around the world, is facing a huge challenge from electronic communications delivered by the internet. Most national and local newspapers now have an online presence as well as physical print editions. Some, such as the *Independent*, have given up print altogether to focus on their websites. The sales of print newspapers have been dropping steadily since the 1990s.

Despite these developments, it would be a mistake to see newspapers as a spent force. The press has a powerful voice in agenda setting. Newspapers don't just report the news, they also express strong opinions and run campaigns.

Broadcast media (radio and television) are generally required to be unbiased and impartial, but newspapers have no such constraints. Newspapers will often praise or attack politicians, urge readers to vote for their favoured political party and report stories in a way that is slanted towards a paper's own political outlook.

**Link**
For more on agenda setting see page 182.

**Link**
For more on impartiality see page 138.

National daily newspapers express strong opinions on referendum day.

## 4 Media Industries

### Activity 4.3

Identify a recent story about a politician, political party or political event.
- Compare the coverage of this story in three different national newspapers either online or in print.
- What prominence is the story given and how is it reported?
- What evidence, if any, is there of bias in the reporting of the story?

### Link

For a definition of bias see the Key term on page 57.

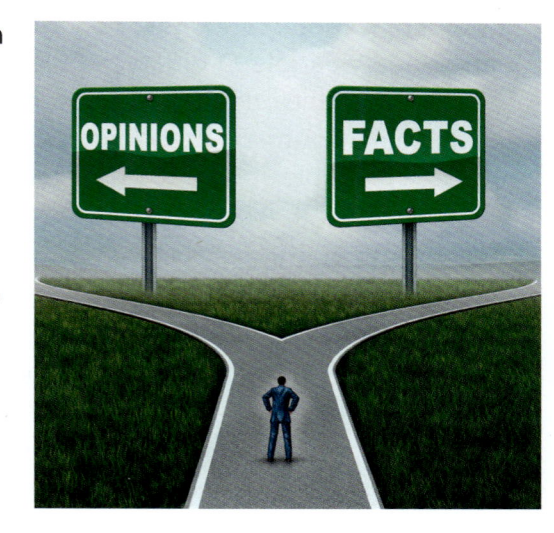

### Key terms

**Op-ed**
Short for 'opposite the editorial page', these are written by named columnists and do not necessarily express the newspaper's official position.

**Editorials**
A statement of the newspaper's position on a topic, often written by the editor. 'Editorial copy' is anything in a newspaper other than advertising.

**Newsworthiness**
Relates to a topical event that is considered sufficiently interesting to the public to be worthy of reporting as news. News media will judge the newsworthiness of an event by applying their own set of news values. These may differ. For example, the *Daily Mirror* sees human interest stories as more newsworthy than *The Times*.

Newspapers often make a distinction between content based on factual news reporting and content that is based on individual points of view such as opinion columns (called **op-ed** pieces) and **editorials**. Readers expect that op-ed pieces and editorials will be biased, but also expect that straightforward news reporting will be unbiased. However, the boundary between these is often very blurry. Part of your job as a media student is to detect the presence and degree of bias in the press and other news media.

## News values

Newspapers can't report everything. They have to filter material and decide which events to ignore and which to give prominence to. Not all newspapers share the same news values. For example, some will favour human interest stories while others will give political or economic stories a higher profile.

However, there is usually a good deal of agreement between newspapers, broadcast and online news services about the major stories of the day. This is because news providers tend to use the same filters to assess the **newsworthiness** of a story.

Newspapers often attack politicians – they can be as biased as they like.

## Key terms

**Running story**
This is a story that appears in two or more consecutive editions of a newspaper or for two or more days in other news media. If a breaking story has this potential, journalists may say, 'this one will run and run'.

**Photo-story**
In newspaper journalism, this is a story that is more newsworthy because of the presence of an interesting photograph. Then Prime Minister Theresa May's meeting with other European leaders (October 2017) would have been newsworthy anyway, but the powerful image below taken from video footage, made it even more so. It was used by almost every UK newspaper and many others around the world.

News values include:

**Timing**: recent news always trumps old news. News providers also like **running stories** so that they can offer day-by-day updates. Diary items also feature strongly on the news agenda. These are events that can be predicted in advance such as royal or presidential visits, sports matches or competitions, political speeches and, of course, GCSE results day.

**Important people**: celebrities, politicians and royalty all get more coverage than 'ordinary people'. Ordinary people are only newsworthy if they meet one or more of the other criteria, but the bar is much lower for celebrities. Wearing a new outfit or attending a party can be enough for a **photo-story**. The same principle applies to powerful institutions such as big companies or the government; their size and importance makes them newsworthy.

**Surprise and significance**: items are more newsworthy if they are out of the ordinary and have an element of surprise. This is often linked to the size of the event or the number of people involved. A demonstration attended by 100,000 people is newsworthy; one attended by 100 is not. This is particularly the case in stories including violence, injury and death; bad news usually carries more weight than good news.

**Closeness to home**: items affecting news consumers directly are more newsworthy. National news is given prominence over international news. Stories from other countries are not ranked by geographical closeness but by other factors such as the country's importance or its cultural links to the UK. For example, stories about China, Australia, New Zealand or the USA will get more attention than stories from physically closer countries such as Bulgaria or Algeria.

**Human interest**: these are stories with emotional impact and/or entertainment value. They may involve unfolding dramas, animals, sex and relationships or quirky good news items. Unusual or interesting photographs, opportunities for humour or witty headlines often help to promote human interest stories above others that may have more obvious newsworthiness in terms of other criteria.

### Activity 4.4

How would you score the following stories for newsworthiness? Give each story a mark out of 10.
- A train crashes in Switzerland – ten people dead.
- A train crashes in Kent – ten people dead.
- Owners announce that their car factory in North-East England will close with the loss of 7,000 jobs.
- A rival newspaper's campaign to strengthen laws on cyber bullying is successful.
- The baby of two well-known celebrities survives a life-saving operation.
- Police charge the boss of Dimco (the UK's biggest online retailer) with murder. (Dimco is a major source of advertising revenue for your newspaper.)
- The Prime Minister trips and falls flat on her face in the mud while on a private visit to a farm. You have exclusive pictures.

Explain the reasons for your decisions.

## Newspaper-owning conglomerates

In the rest of this section, the focus is on two newspaper-owning companies: Reach and News UK. These groups own the two 2023 newspaper CSPs: the *Daily Mirror* and *The Times*. Looking closely at these two examples will bring out some key ideas and terms in the study of Media Industries.

Both Reach and News UK are media **conglomerates**. A conglomerate is a group of many companies drawn together under single ownership. Media conglomerates are comprised of companies in different areas such as newspapers, book publishing, magazines, radio, film, television and internet – all owned by a major corporation.

News UK owns four UK newspapers: *The Times*, the *Sunday Times*, the *Sun* and the *Sun on Sunday*. *The Times* and the *Sun* are both best-sellers in their market sectors. It publishes the *Times Literary Supplement* and also owns radio company The Wireless Group and social media agency Storyful.

The *Sunday Times* is owned by News UK.

News UK itself is part of a bigger group, News Corp, whose interests include:

### News Corp Australia
- 10 Australian newspapers
- Fox Sports (TV)
- Foxtel (subscription TV)
- REA Group (online property sales).

### Dow Jones
- Global provider of news and business information including the *Wall Street Journal*.

### *New York Post*
- The largest daily paper in America by circulation.

### HarperCollins Publishers
- Consumer and trade book publishers.

### Move
- A network of websites for property buyers and sellers in the USA.

In 2013, News Corp split off from an even larger group called News Corporation. The remainder of News Corporation was renamed 21st Century Fox. In 2019, most of the assets of 21st Century Fox – itself a conglomerate – were acquired by the Walt Disney Company. Those that Disney did not buy were renamed as Fox Corp.

21st Century Fox includes:

- 20th Century Fox
- Fox Searchlight Pictures
- Blue Sky Studios
- National Geographic Channels.

---

### Talk about it

National newspapers are sometimes criticised because the selection and style of reporting stories reflects the values of their owners, senior managers and professional journalists who run the newspapers. This group of people does not reflect the composition of the country as a whole.

Others argue that online news sources make much greater use of **user-generated content**. This makes online news more diverse, reflecting a wider range of viewpoints and less likely to be based on London only.

How far do you agree with these different views?

Are newspapers too traditional and old fashioned in the way they deal with news?

Have online news sources provided a breath of fresh air or have they simply lowered the professional standards of journalism practised by newspapers?

### Key terms

**User-generated content (UGC)**
Any form of content (video, blogs, digital images, audio files) created by users of an online system, made accessible to others via social media. Most newspapers have online versions which invite contributions from readers. Unlike the print edition, there is no restriction on the space available. Contributors of user-generated copy are almost always unpaid and sometimes known as **citizen journalists**.

**Conglomerate**
A combination of two or more businesses owned by one parent company.

Rupert Murdoch, whose media empire is worth around $12 billion.

Fox Corp includes:

- Fox News Channel (USA)
- Fox Sports
- Fox Television stations.

Although separate, both News Corp and Fox Corp are both closely associated with Rupert Murdoch. One of his sons, Lachlan, is Co-Chairman of News Corp and Executive Chairman of Fox Corp, while his other son, James, was formerly CEO of 21st Century Fox and Chairman of Sky plc. The Murdoch Family Trust owns both News Corp and Fox Corp and has a net worth of about 18 billion dollars.

You aren't expected to memorise all these company names and the links between them, but it is important to understand the idea of conglomeration in media industries.

News Corp, Fox Corp, Disney and 21st Century Fox also illustrate the globalisation of media industries, as all of these groups have substantial interests in Europe, Asia, Australia, and North and South America.

## News UK and Reach (formerly Trinity Mirror)

News UK's newspapers had leading positions in the market place when comparable figures were last available from PAMCo:

- The *Sun* had the highest circulation of any paid-for UK newspaper.
- *The Times* was the best-selling 'quality' daily paper.
- The *Sunday Times* outsold all other 'quality' papers on a Sunday.
- The *Sun on Sunday* was the best-selling Sunday tabloid.

News UK's four national titles between them claimed about one-third of all paid-for newspapers sold. Reach newspapers – the *Daily Mirror*, *Sunday Mirror*, the *Sunday People*, *Daily Express*, *Daily Star* and *Daily Star Sunday* – had a 20% share. Although Reach could only claim 20% of national newspaper circulation, its ownership of many local and regional newspapers allowed it to make the claim that,

> *We are the largest national and regional newspaper publisher in the UK. In 2016 we sold over 540 million national and regional newspapers.* (Reach, 2018)

In addition to its three national titles and two Scottish titles – the *Daily Record* and the *Sunday Mail* – Reach owns 240+ regional newspapers such as the *Manchester Evening News* and the *Bristol Post*. This is an example of horizontal integration, where a company buys more and more of its competitors' products to give it a dominant position in the market.

In 2015 Trinity Mirror acquired newspaper group Local World with its 100 print titles and 70 websites for £220 million.

In 2018 Trinity Mirror acquired the national newspapers and magazines owned by Northern & Shell: the *Daily Express*, the *Sunday Express*, the *Daily Star* and the *Daily Star Sunday*, in a £200 million deal. The new group rebranded itself as Reach. Following this takeover, three companies almost completely dominate the market: News UK, Reach and DMG (Daily Mail Group). DMG owns the *Daily Mail*, *Mail on Sunday*, the *i* and the *Metro*.

Traditionally, newspaper owners set the political tone for their papers, but the *Daily Express* and *Daily Mirror* are at opposite ends of the political spectrum. So far, the two newspapers have maintained their strong support for Labour (*Daily Mirror*) and the Conservatives (*Daily Express*). Reach has assured readers they will continue to do so.

## Effects of ownership

You have seen that both News UK and Reach have concentrated ownership of many brands and companies in the hands of huge media conglomerates. Does this matter?

The groups themselves can claim advantages from both horizontal and vertical integration, allowing them to:

- run more efficiently
- achieve greater control in their markets
- generate higher profits.

In the newspaper industry, with its steeply declining sales of print editions, the owners would agree that brands can only be saved by mergers and takeovers and by developing the potential of the newspapers' websites.

Critics say that concentration of ownership is destroying competition, with too much power held by a small number of huge conglomerates. Another criticism is that cross-media ownership cuts down on the diversity of different views and opinions expressed in the media. For example, the newspapers and television channels in Rupert Murdoch companies tend to express the fairly right-wing political views of their owner.

A 2015 report by the **pressure group** Media Reform Coalition concluded that concentration of ownership 'creates conditions in which wealthy individuals and organisations can amass huge political and economic power and distort the media landscape to suit their interests and political views'.

## Press regulation

There have always been debates and arguments about the regulation of newspapers because it is so difficult to balance the interests of different groups.

On one hand is the principle of freedom of the press. This means that the right to express views and opinions, including those critical of the government, should be protected.

On the other hand, we value the rights of individual people to have private lives without being subjected to harassment or intrusion by the press.

For many years, the behaviour of certain newspapers in the UK has been criticised. The morality of grabbing long-lens photographs of celebrities, offering financial rewards for information and subjecting members of the public to invasion of their privacy has been criticised.

Newspapers defended themselves by arguing that their activities were in the public interest.

Matters came to a head with the phone hacking scandal, 2005–2011. Phone hacking is a method of spying on people's voicemails or texts to

### Link
For more on the political spectrum see Chapter 5, page 181.

### Activity 4.5
Find the current circulation figures for News UK and Reach group national newspapers.

### Key term
**Pressure group**
An organised group of people that tries to influence government policy in a particular area or in support of a particular cause.

*The final edition of the News of the World, 10 July 2011*

*Phone hacking victims. Former footballer Andy Gray received £20,000 from News Group and actor Sadie Frost was awarded over £250,000 from Trinity Mirror (now Reach).*

### Activity 4.6

Visit the IPSO website at ipso.co.uk.

What are the guidelines for editors on:
- accuracy?
- privacy?
- harassment?
- intrusion?

What does the code say about the responsibility of newspapers to protect children under the age of 16?

---

obtain information. It is illegal. The scandal focused on employees of News International, the predecessor of News UK, publisher of *The Times* and the *Sun*.

At the time, the *News of the World*, a Sunday newspaper, was the group's best-selling title. It emerged that *News of the World* employees had hacked the phones of numerous people, including members of the royal family, to obtain stories.

Several journalists received prison sentences and the *News of the World* paid compensation to victims of phone hacking.

In 2011, it emerged that phones had been hacked to obtain stories about the abduction and murder of children. The scandal escalated to such an extent that Rupert Murdoch announced the closure of the *News of the World*. It printed its final edition on 10 July. In November 2011, a major inquiry into press standards headed by Lord Leveson began.

In 2015, Trinity Mirror (now Reach) also paid compensation to a number of public figures after it emerged that stories in the *Daily Mirror*, *Sunday Mirror* and *People* were all based on information gained by phone hacking. While News International settled claims out of court, Trinity Mirror went to the high court and ended up paying much larger sums in compensation.

The Leveson Inquiry was a public inquiry set up by then Prime Minister David Cameron to examine the culture, practice and ethics of the press. The main focus was allegations of phone hacking at the News of the World newspaper

Following the report of the Leveson Inquiry, a new regulatory body, the Independent Press Standards Organisation (IPSO), was set up by the newspaper industry to replace the Press Complaints Commission (PCC). Leveson found that the PCC was not really independent from the press owners.

IPSO started in 2014 and currently regulates 1,500 print and 1,100 online titles. It seeks to uphold the Editors' Code of Practice on matters such as accuracy, privacy, harassment and intrusion.

IPSO was set up by the newspapers themselves and does not fully comply with the Leveson report because it is not fully independent. The *Guardian* newspaper and the *Financial Times* have their own complaints systems, separate from IPSO.

*Lord Leveson with his report. The Leveson Inquiry was a public inquiry set up by then Prime Minister David Cameron to examine the culture, practice and ethics of the press. The main focus was allegations of phone hacking at the News of the World newspaper.*

An alternative regulatory body called IMPRESS is entirely independent of the major newspaper owners. It is fully compliant with the terms set out by the Leveson Inquiry but currently only a handful of local newspapers have signed

### Activity 4.7

Carry out some internet research to find out why some newspapers have signed up to IPSO, some to IMPRESS and some to neither of these.

up to this body (at time of writing they have 107 members publishing 182 publications).

As it stands (2022), the regulation of the press is still in a state of flux, with a number of unresolved issues.

**CASE STUDY:**
# The film industry

## The American film industry

Have you ever stayed on in the cinema after the closing frames of a film to watch the end credits? If you have, you were probably struck by just how many people and how many companies are involved in the making of a feature film that lasts 100 minutes or so. There are likely to be hundreds of names listed, with a bewildering range of jobs and skills from animal wranglers to key grips (electricians) and helicopter pilots. Many companies will be credited, from the studio to the special effects and post-production companies to location caterers. What all this tells us is that films are expensive or, in the case of major Hollywood releases, *very* expensive, to make. The film industry is big business.

For your GCSE Media Studies course, film only needs to be studied from a media industries point of view. For this reason, you won't need to analyse the media language and representation found in films or to study the audience for films except as a part of understanding the film industry.

Much of the industry information and study material as it relates to your two CSPs can be found in Chapter 5. In this Case Study, some context for these CSPs will be provided by looking in detail at the production of big-budget films by the US film industry (Hollywood) and contrasting this with the production of much smaller budget **UK independent films**.

In both examples, the historical context and cultural significance of the industry and the changing patterns of ownership will be investigated. In conclusion, the regulation of the film industry in the UK and the work of the British Board of Film Classification (BBFC) will be examined.

## Hollywood – the studio system

Hollywood has been closely associated with the American film industry for so long that the word 'Hollywood' no longer stands for only a suburb of Los Angeles but for the industry itself.

Hollywood was the location of the very first movie studios. By the mid-1920s, five studios had become dominant:

- Paramount
- 20th Century Fox
- Warner Bros.
- RKO
- MGM

Each of these powerful studios owned their own production facilities, kept their own 'stable' of stars contracted exclusively to them and owned their own chain of movie theatres (cinemas) that screened only their films.

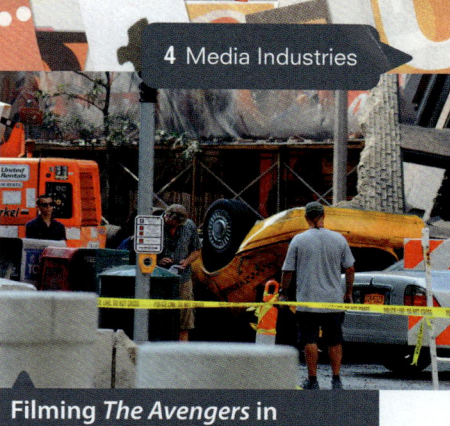

*Filming The Avengers in Cleveland, Ohio.*

**Key term**

**UK independent films**
Films made without any financial or creative input from the big five American studios which also pass the cultural test for 'Britishness'. The individuals and companies producing these films make up the UK independent sector.

**bbfc** View what's right for you

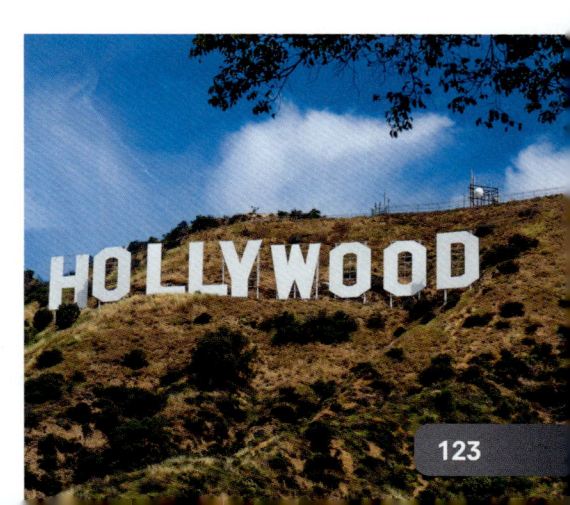

This system, known as the Hollywood Studio System, is a fine example of vertical integration as each studio owned and controlled every aspect of production, distribution and exhibition.

The studios talent-spotted, groomed and developed their own stars, most of whom were tied in to long contracts which sometimes even governed their social lives and relationships. This 'Star System' created many world-famous celebrities such as Bette Davis, Cary Grant, Judy Garland and Clark Gable, who had little or no control over their creative work and their careers were closely controlled and directed by studio bosses.

The studio system blossomed until 1948, forming a period known as the Golden Age of Hollywood. It was brought to an end when the US Supreme Court ruled that the restrictive practices of the studios must end in order to allow more competition and fewer constraints on actors.

## Beyond the studio system

For the next 25 years, Hollywood struggled with censorship and competition from television and from European filmmakers.

In the mid-1970s, though, success came from a new breed of young directors – the so-called 'movie brats' such as Francis Ford Coppola, George Lucas, Martin Scorsese and Stephen Spielberg. Films such as *The Godfather* (1972) and *Taxi Driver* (1976) made the movies seem relevant again, while special-effects-driven blockbusters such as *Jaws* (1975) and *Star Wars* (1977) won huge audiences.

## Contemporary Hollywood

In the 21st century, the American film industry has been increasingly polarised between two sectors. The main focus of the big studios is on ever-more expensive blockbusters designed to provide an unmissable cinema spectacle and experience. The other 'independent' sector comprises the lower-budget productions often made by subsidiaries of the major studios.

The enormous cost of blockbuster films means that studios are very conservative in their approach to risk-taking. Franchises such as *Star Wars*, *Fast and Furious*, *James Bond* and the superhero genre are dominant.

As the studios look to expand their international market, particularly in Asia, the visual spectacle of blockbuster films has become even more important, with less focus on narrative and character development that may seem culturally specific.

Today's big five studios include names familiar from Hollywood's Golden Age. They are:

- Walt Disney
- Warner Bros
- Universal
- Sony (Columbia)
- Paramount.

Although the names may be familiar, all five are part of media conglomerates in which many companies are grouped together under single ownership.

**Hollywood legends (top to bottom) Bette Davis, Judy Garland, Cary Grant and Clark Gable – superstars of the Golden Age**

| Studio | Example film or franchise | Corporate owner | Other subsidiaries (examples) |
|---|---|---|---|
| The Walt Disney Company | *Black Widow* (2021) *Pirates of the Caribbean* (2003–2017) | The Walt Disney Company | Walt Disney Parks and Resorts Pixar Animation Marvel Entertainment Marvel Studios Lucasfilm ABC Television 20th Century Studios |
| Warner Media | *Joker* (2019) *Harry Potter* (2001–2011) | Warner Media | New Line Cinema Castle Rock HBO CNN Cartoon Network |
| Universal | *Jurassic Park/World* (1993–present) *The Fast and the Furious* (2001–present) | Comcast | NBC Television Universal Parks and Resorts Xfinity (internet/cable) Dreamworks animation |
| Columbia | *Spider-man: Far From Home* (2019) *Jumanji* (1995–present) | Sony | Sony Music Screen Gems Sony Interactive (Playstation) Sony Corp (Electronics) |
| Paramount | *Transformers* (2007–present) *Mission Impossible* (1996–present) | Viacom | Viacom Cable MTV Nickelodeon Comedy Central |

# Hollywood films and finance

As you'd expect, the big studios' 'tent poles', the really expensive blockbusters, are complex financial projects. Since 2014, the American film industry has produced over 20 $100 million films a year.

The budget for these blockbusters doesn't tell the whole story. Once the film has gone through the stages of development – pre-production, production and post-production – the production budget has been spent, but the spending doesn't stop.

Film writer Stephen Follows (2016) estimates that a $150 million film adds another $120 million in marketing costs and a further $145 million to make hard copies for exhibition, pay profit shares to actors and creatives, and cover other overheads.

So, the total outlay for a film with a production budget of $150 million is actually over $400 million. That's a lot of money to get back.

Blockbuster films still generate a lot of income from theatrical release. That's why the marketing budget is so important: to fill cinemas in the first few days of the film's release by creating the huge buzz of excitement needed to make the film 'unmissable'.

It is essential that this marketing effort is just as successful internationally, with 60% of box office income for the big five coming from outside North America. The importance of the international market to Hollywood is steadily increasing, especially with the dramatic growth of China as a consumer of American movies.

Box office revenue refers to the money handed over for ticket purchase. Some of this is retained by the cinema. The cinema's share varies from film to film, but for a major blockbuster in its first week of release the cinema would get less than half of ticket receipts but more than half if the film runs for several weeks.

Although box office sales provide the most revenue, the cinema's share and sales taxes must be deducted. Blockbusters make more money from the sale of DVDs, subscription TV and **video-on-demand** (VOD), and sales to free-to-air television channels. For some films, **merchandising** makes a substantial contribution to income.

> **Key terms**
>
> **Video-on-demand**
> VOD is television content that can be watched at any time the viewer chooses. BBC iPlayer is an example.
>
> **Merchandise**
> With regard to films, these spin-off products linked to feature films can include toys, clothing, posters, books, games, food and other items that bear the film's brand.

The top ten merchandising earners (to July 2020) were all franchises:

| Film franchise | Earnings in $ billion |
| --- | --- |
| 1 Star Wars | 42 |
| 2 Cars | 19 |
| 3 Toy Story | 18 |
| 4 Teenage Mutant Ninja Turtles | 13 |
| 5 Transformers | 12 |
| 6 Frozen | 11 |
| 7 Harry Potter | 8 |
| 8 Marvel's Avengers | 7 |
| 9 Minions | 4 |
| 10 The Lion King | 3 |

Source: Adapted from New Free Spins No Deposit, 2020

Stephen Follows estimates that about half of Hollywood blockbusters ($100 million+ production budget) make a profit. Interestingly, the films with really high budgets ($200 million+) are the ones most likely to be profitable.

## The film industry in the UK

In some senses, the UK film industry is a roaring success, but in others it is struggling. Let's look at the more positive side of things first.

British film talent – both on- and off-screen – has a very high international profile and many big budget film projects have been attracted to the UK by a combination of talent, high-quality facilities, attractive locations and government tax breaks. Pinewood Studios, near London, describes itself as 'one of the world's leading destinations for the makers of film, television, commercials and video games'. Recent major productions being shot in full or part at Pinewood or Shepperton (Pinewood's partner in Surrey) include:

- *Black Widow* (2021)
- *Star Wars: The Rise of Skywalker* (2019)
- *Top Gun: Maverick* (2021).

Pinewood Studios has also been closely associated with the *James Bond* franchise. The Roger Moore Stage was opened in October 2017, in commemoration of the former Bond star and the 007 soundstage is one of the biggest in the world. Pinewood is currently undertaking a massive £450 million expansion (phase 3 of an overall expansion that started in 2014), which, it claims, will support a further 3,500 new jobs on top of those already added so far; a good sign of confidence and growth in the UK film industry.

The government has encouraged and supported this growth by providing tax breaks to investors if films qualify as British by passing a cultural test. This test is not particularly difficult to pass. The content of the film is not especially relevant to the test. It is based on the location of the production or filming, whether the cast or crew come from the UK or European Economic Area and whether the film is set in the UK or includes British characters. Numerous Hollywood blockbusters, including *Star Wars: Episode VII – The Force Awakens* (2015), have passed the test and qualified for funds. In the tax year 2018–2019, the government paid out £595 million under this scheme. Despite film industry worries after Brexit, the scheme was confirmed in January 2021 as continuing without change.

Most of the high-end film productions that take advantage of these incentives and the other advantages of working in the UK are made by international companies, principally the big five Hollywood studios. This international backing of films made in the UK is called 'inward investment'. It has contributed substantially to the success of the UK film industry.

However, UK filmmakers seeking to make films with a low or mid-range budget of less than £10 million are not doing quite as well. Small-scale producers have found it hard to make the large investments needed to take advantage of the 'digital revolution' in filmmaking. They have also suffered from a steep decline in the international demand for their work, especially those films made on 'micro budgets' of less than £500,000 without established stars or big-name directors.

As the number of American films released in the UK has increased, small-scale independent producers have found it more and more difficult to obtain distribution deals that will get their work screened. All this has led to a drop in the number of films made by the UK independent sector.

Speaking of the UK independent sector, producer Rebecca O'Brien of Sixteen Films (makers of 2023 CSP *I, Daniel Blake*) said in an interview,

> *Over a number of years we've felt things have become more difficult for us. Our sums haven't added up and our valiant efforts to produce original, indigenous [home-produced] movies have become tougher and tougher.* (Macnab, 2017)

In spite of these problems the independent sector continues to make an important contribution to the UK film industry, and I, Daniel Blake itself was the 11th most successful UK independent film in 2016, with a UK box office gross of £3.2 million. The following chart shows the best-performing UK indie films of 2019, which was the best year for UK independent films for five years.

**Top 20 independent UK films released in the UK and Republic of Ireland, 2019**

| Title | Country of origin | Box office gross (£m) | Distributor |
| --- | --- | --- | --- |
| 1 Downton Abbey | UK/USA# | 28.2 | Universal |
| 2 The Favourite | UK/USA/Ire# | 17.0 | 20th Century Fox |
| 3 Yesterday | UK | 13.8 | Universal |
| 4 Stan and Ollie | UK/USA/Can# | 10.6 | eOne Films |
| 5 Mary, Queen of Scots | UK/USA# | 9.2 | Universal |
| 6 Judy* | UK | 8.1 | Pathé |
| 7 Angel Has Fallen | UK/USA# | 7.5 | Lionsgate |
| 8 Fisherman's Friends | UK | 7.4 | Entertainment Film Distributors |
| 9 Shaun the Sheep Movie: Farmagedon* | UK | 7.0 | StudioCanal |
| 10 Fighting With My Family | UK/USA# | 5.9 | Lionsgate |
| 11 Blue Story | UK | 4.5 | Paramount |
| 12 The Kid Who Would Be King | UK/USA# | 3.7 | 20th Century Fox |
| 13 Blinded By the Light | UK/USA# | 3.2 | eOne Films |
| 14 Wild Rose | UK | 2.9 | eOne Films |
| 15 Horrible Histories: The Movie – Rotten Romans | UK | 2.9 | Altitude Film Distribution |
| 16 Peppa Pig: Festival of Fun | UK | 2.8 | eOne Films |
| 17 Red Joan | UK | 2.8 | Lionsgate |
| 18 Colette | UK/USA | 2.5 | Lionsgate |
| 19 Official Secrets | UK/USA# | 2.4 | eOne Films |
| 20 Cold Pursuit | UK/Can/Fra | 2.0 | StudioCanal |

Notes:
Box office gross = cumulative gross up to 20 February 2020.
* Film still on release 20 February 2020.
# Film made with independent (non-studio) US support or with the independent arm of a US studio.
UK and Republic of Ireland are a single 'territory' for film distribution purposes.
Source: Comscore, BFI RSU analysis

## Regulation

The majority of films and DVDs released in the UK must be rated as suitable for particular audiences by the BBFC. This is nothing new, as the BBFC has been classifying films since 1913 and videos since 1985. It is an independent body which is funded by charges made to anyone submitting work for classification.

The BBFC's guiding principles are:

- *To protect children and vulnerable adults from potentially harmful or otherwise unsuitable media content*
- *To empower consumers, particularly parents and those with responsibility for children, to make informed viewing decisions.*

*(BBFC, 2014)*

**Link**

For more on the audience effects theory see Chapter 3, page 96.

Films are also monitored by the BBFC to ensure that they don't break the law, but most of their decisions are based on judgements of what might be harmful to particular viewers and what the public feel is appropriate to viewers of different ages.

The BBFC works on a system of age classification backed up with information and advice, known as BBFC ratings info, for individual films and DVDs. Age classifications are also supplied for material broadcast on a number of video-on-demand platforms including Netflix, Google Play and Amazon Prime Video.

You will remember from your audience effects theory work that sex, violence and copycat behaviour are always areas of concern and that children are considered to be particularly 'at risk' from the influence of media products.

To help decide the appropriate age classification, BBFC Compliance Officers use the following categories outlined in their Classification Guidelines:

- discrimination
- drugs
- dangerous behaviour
- nudity
- sex
- language
- sexual violence and sexual threat
- violence.
- threat and horror

> **Activity 4.8**
>
> Visit the BBFC website and collect information on the age rating and BBFC insight analysis of the current two film CSPs.

> **Activity 4.9**
>
> Visit the BBFC website for a detailed look at all the criteria used in all the categories for all the age ratings. The latest guidelines were agreed in 2014 to 2019 but are reviewed regularly, as the BBFC pays particular attention to changes in public taste, attitudes and concerns, and changes in the law.

You will probably be familiar with the following age classifications:

|  |  |
|---|---|
| U – Universal | A U film should be suitable for audiences aged four years and over, although it is impossible to predict what might upset any particular child. U films should be set within a positive framework and should offer reassuring counterbalances to any violence, threat or horror. |
| PG – Parental guidance | A PG film should not unsettle a child aged around eight or older. Unaccompanied children of any age may watch, but parents are advised to consider whether the content may upset younger or more sensitive children. |
| 12A/12 | Films classified 12A and video works classified 12 contain material that is not generally suitable for children aged under 12. No one younger than 12 may see a 12A film in a cinema unless accompanied by an adult. Adults planning to take a child under 12 to view a 12A film should consider whether the film is suitable for that child. To help them decide, we recommend that they check the ratings info for that film in advance. No one younger than 12 may rent or buy a 12 rated video work. |
| 15 | No one younger than 15 may see a 15 film in a cinema. No one younger than 15 may rent or buy a 15 rated video work. |
| 18 | No one younger than 18 may see an 18 film in a cinema. No one younger than 18 may rent or buy an 18 rated video work. Adults should be free to choose their own entertainment. |

The history of film censorship is a useful way of understanding the influence of social and cultural contexts. What is deemed 'unacceptable' in one decade may be found perfectly OK in later years. For example, censors in the 1950s were particularly concerned about nudity. Today, the BBFC is more likely to be tough on sexual violence and discrimination. The BBFC website provides some great resources for studying the history of film censorship and regulation. These include a timeline, case studies and detailed explanations of some controversial decisions.

AQA GCSE Media Studies

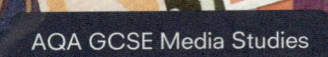

**CASE STUDY:**

# Radio: key events in the development of radio 1967–2021

**Link**

See the Radio section in Chapter 5, pages 196–200.

This case study links the two 2023 radio CSPs, Tony Blackburn's 1967 BBC show and and KISS Breakfast on KISS FM. It explains some of the important developments in radio history. As you work your way through this case study, it will be helpful to refer to the Radio section in Chapter 5.

Over 50 years of radio history cannot be covered in close detail in this book, so the focus here is:

**Radio as a media industry**
- Ownership and control of radio organisations.
- Changes in ownership and how these are linked to the government.
- Changes in ownership and control especially the role of convergence and diversification.
- Different ways of funding the radio industry, public ownership and commercial companies.
- The regulation of radio.

**Radio audiences**
- Changing types of radio audience.
- The role of technology in changing the pattern of radio listening.
- Categorisation of radio audiences and the assumptions radio stations make about their listeners.
- The importance of radio to listeners.

The starting point is 1967. This was an important year in the development of radio in the UK because the BBC made big changes to its radio offering.

At the start of the year the BBC gave radio listeners the following choices:

- **The Home Service**: news, drama, current affairs, discussions and some regional programming.
- **The Light Programme**: middle of the road popular music, light entertainment, sitcoms and soap operas.
- **The Third Programme/Network Three**: classical music, talks on science and culture, some sports commentary.

Although there were some programmes specifically for children, there was little of interest to young adults, especially those with an interest in popular music.

The BBC had a monopoly within the UK – no other broadcasters were allowed to transmit radio.

## Why did BBC radio change in 1967?

Although the BBC had a monopoly within the UK, it was beginning to face serious competition.

Most of this came in the form of so-called 'pirates'. These were broadcasters based just outside territorial waters, where they could safely ignore British laws. Stations such as Radio Caroline and Radio London aimed squarely at youth listeners by supplying nothing but modern pop music, jokey banter from the DJs and, for the first time, jingles.

By early 1967 the pirates were often getting a bigger audience than all the BBC stations put together.

The government wanted to make sure that it could control UK broadcasting and the licence system, so it cracked down on the pirates by making a new law, the Marine Broadcasting Offences Act (1967). This made it illegal for any British person to operate, assist or supply an offshore pirate station. This law ensured a swift end for the pirates.

BBC radio was then revamped with the introduction of Radio 1, Radio 2, Radio 3 and Radio 4 to replace the old Home, Light and Third programmes.

The BBC had to do something to win over the youth audience. It did this by making Radio 1 sound as much like the pirates as possible. Ex-pirate DJs were hired, jingles were bought in from America and the station was closely targeted at its young listeners. Radio 1 was, and still is, the BBC's way of meeting the needs of a youth audience with a taste for popular music.

Radio London started broadcasting in December 1964 from a position three miles off the coast of Frinton-on-Sea, Essex.

## BBC local radio

In the same year, 1967, the government allowed the BBC to set up eight local radio stations. The first three, Radio Leicester, Radio Sheffield and Radio Merseyside, all started in December 1967.

With all these changes, radio had a new image, more choice and a better range of services. However, the BBC still had a monopoly; it was still funded by a licence fee and there were no advertisements. This all began to change in 1970 when the government started to **deregulate** the airwaves. This was the beginning of legal commercial radio in the UK. Only three years after seeing off the pirates, BBC radio found itself with a new set of competitors: the first commercial radio stations.

## Radio funding: public service and commercial radio

The BBC has always acquired the great majority of its income through licence fees, which are set by the government. The radio licence was abolished in 1971, since when radio has been funded by its share of the TV licence (as of 2021, £159 per year for most households with a colour television).

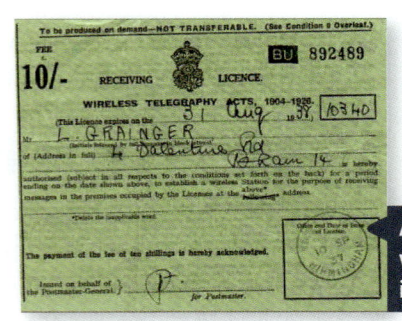

> **Key term**
>
> **Deregulation**
> The reduction or removal of government regulation in a particular industry such as radio or television. Usually, this is done because of a belief that competition will improve quality and choice for consumers.

A ten-shilling (50p, which today would be about £35) radio licence issued in 1937.

This is why the BBC is called a **publicly funded** organisation. The government doesn't control the BBC directly, but it still requires the corporation to provide a public service. For BBC radio this means providing services for the whole population, supplying information and entertainment without the need to make a profit.

Commercial radio, however, is strongly motivated by profit. Commercial radio stations rely on advertisers for their income. The more listeners they have, the more they can charge for every second of advertising.

The Sound Broadcasting Act, 1972, was the first step towards commercial radio in the UK. However, the government had no intention of giving up its control of the airwaves. The companies with plans for commercial radio were disappointed to find that only 19 local stations were allowed and that there were still tight regulations about programming.

In 1973, the first two commercial stations began broadcasting, both in London: Capitol Radio and LBC. Gradually, new independent local radio (ILR) stations appeared around the country, but the government did not allow what many wanted: a national commercial pop music station to compete with Radio 1.

Another wave of development in the early 1980s saw the number of ILR stations double but the next new **national** station was not commercial but BBC: it was Radio 5, specialising in news and sport.

When, finally, the government decided to allow a national commercial music station, it turned out to be Classic FM, only licensed to broadcast non-pop music.

It wasn't until 1993, 26 years after the launch of Radio 1, that an independent national pop music radio station finally broadcast: Richard Branson's Virgin 1215. This station started life as a rock station. It was the first of many to aim for a particular segment of the music audience.

Many new stations targeted listeners with a preference for 'classic hits' pop music, as this proved a reliable way to build the large audiences that advertisers would pay for.

The 1990s and early 2000s saw many of the new commercial stations merging together or being taken over by bigger organisations. This process, known as **conglomeration**, happens in all media industries.

In commercial radio, it is more profitable to group many stations together to form a network so that popular slots such as breakfast, drive time and weekend afternoons can be supplied from a central location. Today's local commercial radio stations tend to have only a few hours a day of 'opt-out' when programming is supplied from local studios rather than the national network.

Examples of commercial networks today include Capital radio (owned by Global Radio) and KISS, Absolute and Magic (all owned by Bauer Media).

## Along came digital

Many of the developments described above came about because the government gradually loosened its grip on the airwaves allowing more stations to compete with the BBC. This process of deregulation was given a powerful boost by a technological innovation: digital audio broadcasting (DAB).

> **Link**
> See Chapter 3, page 90 for an explanation of audience segmentation.

> **Link**
> For more on conglomerates see pages 121 and 124.

DAB is a way of using radio bandwidth more efficiently, so that more stations can be made available with good quality sound. The BBC began DAB transmissions in 1995 and the first five commercial stations, including Planet Rock and Virgin Radio, were launched in 1999. In 2002, the BBC launched BBC1 Xtra and 6 Music among other DAB-only stations.

Although take up was slow at first, it gradually accelerated, so that by 2017 over a third of all radio listening was on DAB radios.

You don't need a DAB radio to listen to digital radio, though. Digital TVs, phones, PCs and tablets all make radio stations available, so that digital makes up just under a half of all radio listening.

The government still has control over DAB, just as it does over traditional analogue radio. The government has given powers to regulate the communication industry to **Ofcom**.

Any person or company wanting to broadcast a radio station in the UK must apply for a licence from Ofcom. They will have to pay the **carriage costs** for transmitting their programmes. For DAB this is likely to be hundreds of thousands of pounds a year.

This is probably why another way of reaching listeners has become so popular: internet radio. An internet radio station only has to worry about paying **royalties** for music and the audience is not restricted by the range of transmitters. Potentially, an internet radio station can be heard by all those billions with online access: 60% of the world's population. The set-up and running costs can be measured in hundreds of pounds.

Established radio stations, including BBC radio, stream over the internet, as do many hundreds of micro-scale internet-only stations. Recently, some rather more powerful media companies have moved into this format. One of those was Apple Beats 1 Radio, in 2015, now called Apple Music 1, broadcasting from the US and the UK to over 100 countries.

## Diversification and radio audiences

As has been seen, most radio stations are part of networks. Within the network, different stations target different audiences. The second radio CSP, KISS Breakfast, is on KISS FM, part of a radio network from Bauer Media.

### Bauer Media's KISS Network

| KISS FM UK | Multimedia brand for 15–34 year olds, plays the freshest new music and biggest tracks. |
|---|---|
| KISSTORY | Non Stop Old-Skool and Anthems with the biggest tunes across hip-hop, R'n'B, Dance and Garage 24/7. |
| KISS FRESH | Exclusive first plays of some of the biggest club tracks right now from the hottest artists and producers in the industry. |
| HEAT Radio | All the brilliant pop songs combined with a warm, fun and relatable mix of music and the latest celebrity news. |
| KERRANG! | The best rock music with attitude, targets 15–34 year old men who want to be in touch with what is happening in the world of rock right now. |

Source: Bauer Media Group, 2020

### Key terms

**Ofcom**
Ofcom regulates TV, radio, video-on-demand, phone and postal services. Ofcom promotes competition, protects the interests of consumers and enforces the rules that apply to different communication sectors.

**Carriage costs**
DAB radio stations do not usually own their own transmitters. They have to pay a monthly sum of money for a DAB transmission service. It can be very expensive.

**Royalties**
Payments paid to performers and songwriters when their music is played on radio (or television or video games).

> **Key term**
>
> **Diversification**
> Occurs when a media company branches out to offer services in more than one media form, for example when a magazine publishing company buys up a radio station.

Many of these are **multimedia brands**. Kerrang!, for example, is a magazine and a television channel as well as a radio station. This is an example of **diversification**, when a media company operates over different media forms. The transition to digital technology means that a brand like Kerrang! can share content between the different forms and all of them can share on online presence. This is an example of **digital convergence**.

KISS is just one of eight Bauer radio networks with a total of well over 150 stations. The style and presentation and the music selection of each station is carefully tailored to meet the needs of a different target audience.

In May 2020, Bauer also acquired First Radio Sales, a company selling radio advertising on behalf of over 100 local radio stations.

Commercial radio stations must persuade advertisers to buy advertising slots or sponsorship on their shows. Advertisers demand a tight audience profile. There is no point, for example, in paying to advertise pensioners' holidays to teenagers.

Also, advertisers want to know how many people will listen to their advertisements. They won't necessarily believe what the stations tell them about audience size. This is where RAJAR (Radio Joint Audience Research) comes in. RAJAR is paid for by the radio industry as a whole to collect audience statistics. Advertisers have confidence that the statistics are reliable and unbiased. RAJAR also produces a report, the MIDAS Survey, which shows the amount of radio listening on different devices and platforms and which also analyses all the different activities undertaken by listeners while they listen to radio.

> **Link**
>
> For more on the uses and gratifications approach see page 99.

Radio can be really important to listeners. Thinking of the uses and gratifications approach in Chapter 3, you can see that radio meets many audience needs including:

- **Information and entertainment**: including news, weather, traffic reports and local announcements.
- **Social needs**: the friendly presenters provide company for the listener. Information about, for example, new music can be an important conversation topic with friends.
- **Diversion**: radio doesn't demand as much attention as television, print or the internet. This means that listeners are able to engage with radio at the same time as driving, looking after children or waking up in the morning, for example.

> **Activity 4.10**
>
> Carry out internet research to find and briefly report on:
> - an internet only station
> - a non-BBC public service radio station
> - an example of digital convergence and multi-media branding that involves a radio station other than KISS
> - a commercial radio network other than Bauer
> - the most recent RAJAR listening figures for Radio 1 and Radio 1 Xtra.

## 4 Media Industries

**CASE STUDY:**

# UK television: today's viewing landscape

This media industries case study will help you put your television CSPs into a wider context by giving an understanding of the UK television industry today. Television remains a popular medium, but the pace of change in the industry has meant big changes in *how* and *what* we watch. The significant change for viewers has been the massive increase in the range of choice available. In a few decades, a choice between a handful of channels has moved to a multi-channel environment in which most of us have access to hundreds of television shows at any time.

## Linear television

'Linear' means 'in a straight line', so linear television is a sequence of television programmes along a timeline. For years of television history, this was the only form of viewing available. Each channel offered a schedule of programmes broadcast at a set time. If you didn't like one channel, you could switch to another but if you missed your programme, hard luck.

Many people still prefer to watch television in this way. Television 'listings' magazines are popular, newspapers and websites carry schedules and 'smart' televisions have built-in guides, enabling people to plan their viewing.

## Catch-up television

From the mid-1970s, video cassette recorders became available to domestic consumers. Owners of these were able to record television programmes for time-shift viewing as well as renting or buying pre-recorded material. Gradually, these were replaced by DVD players/recorders and then by hard disc recorders built-in to set-top boxes or televisions themselves. This ability to record and replay linear television meant schedules no longer had the same grip; viewers could use them to make up their own viewing experience and, if so desired, fast-forward through the advertising breaks on commercial channels.

> **Link**
>
> See Chapter 5, pages 155–165 for more on how to approach television CSPs.

### Today's viewing landscape

| | | |
|---|---|---|
| **Content providers** | Content providers are the companies/brands that provide the programmes/content that you can watch. | E.g. BBC iPlayer, Channel 4, YouTube, Netflix |
| **Mode of viewing** | This is the way in which you can watch programmes and other content. | E.g. <ul><li>'Linear' is viewed when it is broadcast.</li><li>'Catch-up' can be viewed when you choose, but might be available for a limited time, and was previously broadcast.</li><li>'VOD' can be watched at a time you choose and might not have been broadcast before.</li></ul> |
| **TV service providers** | TV service providers are the companies/brands that operate on a particular platform to provide TV, whether free-to-air or subscription. The internet is also a platform. | E.g. Sky, Virgin Media, Freesat, Freeview |
| **Devices** | These are different screens/equipment you can use to watch a programme/content. | E.g. TV set, Smart TV, laptop, tablet, smartphone |
| **Location** | This is where you are when you watch or consume content, on whichever device you're using. | E.g. in home, out of home |

Source: Adapted from Kantar, 2018

> **Talk about it**
>
> Which of the following do you think people would prefer to watch 'live' on linear TV services, and why?
> - Soap opera
> - A ten-part drama series
> - The news
> - A *James Bond* film
> - A competition such as *Strictly Come Dancing*
> - Programmes for the very young
> - The Olympics
> - A quiz show

Another development, the widespread availability of broadband internet, has given television viewers further opportunities to time-shift by using free catch-up services such as the BBC iPlayer, ITV Hub, All4 and My 5. These services don't have quite the same scope of a recorder because most programmes are only available for a limited time, but they do have the advantage of flexible availability, allowing customers to watch on phones, tablets and computers as well as smart television sets.

Look online (www.barb.co.uk) at BARB's (Broadcasters' Audience Research Board) 'The Viewing Report' where the Top Ten Broadcaster Groups chart near the end shows that the majority of UK television viewing is of 'free to air' material. This means that viewers don't have to pay a subscription, whether they watch at time of broadcast or not. Sky is the top-rated subscription service. Its channels had a 9.7% share of all television viewing in 2019 and 2020.

## Television platforms

Most linear television in the UK is transmitted by radio waves from a network of powerful transmitters which cover the whole country. These signals are received by television aerials, connected to television sets by a cable. This system is called terrestrial (meaning earth-based) television to distinguish it from satellite television, in which signals are bounced off orbiting satellites and received by satellite dishes. These are the two main television platforms but there are others:

| TV platform | Example | Note |
|---|---|---|
| Terrestrial | BBC, ITV, Channel 4, Channel 5 | Signal is received through a rooftop aerial |
| Satellite | Freesat (includes BBC, ITV, Channel 4, Channel 5 and all free-to-air broadcasters) Sky (includes the above plus a range of subscription packages: sport, film, entertainment) | Signal received by satellite dish |
| Cable | Paid-for packages similar to Sky. The market is dominated by Virgin Media | Signal is delivered by underground fibre optic cable. About half of UK homes have access |
| Broadband | Paid-for linear services offered by BT, TalkTalk, Sky. Free services provided by the terrestrial broadcaster including catch-up services such as BBC iPlayer, All4. **Subscription video-on-demand** (SVOD). These are non-linear providers that offer paid-for access to a very wide range of material. Customers choose what they want to watch and when. Main providers: Netflix, Amazon Prime, SkyGo, NowTV, Disney + and BritBox | Signal is delivered through internet connection (landline or mobile). Most broadband television providers offer paid-for packages linked to paid-for internet and phone services. Broadband connection needed |

### Activity 4.11

Which of these platforms are used in your home? Survey others in your class to find which are most popular and why?

### Key term

**Subscription video-on-demand**
SVOD is the same as VOD but is only available to paying customers. Amazon Prime Video is an example.

## Who pays for television?

Some platform suppliers such as the BBC and ITV also create television programmes. Organisations that create television programmes are called **content providers**. The production of television programmes can be a very expensive business, so where does the money come from to make these programmes and to invest in the future of television?

The main sources of income for the UK television industry are:

- **Advertising**: the sale of time slots to advertisers who want to reach the audience attracted to the programmes. The amount that advertisers are prepared to pay for these slots will depend on the size and composition of the audience.

- **Subscriptions and TV-on-demand**: many viewers pay for 'premium' television in addition to the free-to-air services provided by, for example, the BBC and ITV. These subscriptions may take the form of the many packages offered by companies such as Sky and BT or they may be 'one-off' payments for specific content such as a film or a sporting event. Some companies, such as Sky, combine advertising and subscription. Others, such as Netflix, are free of advertising.

- **Television licence**: most UK households with equipment to watch or record live TV broadcasts are required to hold a TV licence costing £159 a year (2021). In 2016/2017 the BBC cost about £5 billion to run and 76% of this came from licence fee income. The BBC spends about half its income on its television output.

The television industry as a whole does have other sources of revenue such as sale of programmes to overseas markets. However, the three categories listed above are by far the most important.

## Public service broadcasting

As we have seen, the BBC receives the bulk of its income from the television licence. It is a public corporation whose job is to enrich people's lives by producing programmes and services that inform, educate and entertain. As a non-profit-making organisation, the BBC must serve the public as a whole by reaching all sections of the community whatever their age or wherever they live in the UK. As the corporation itself says, 'The BBC is for everyone and should include everyone whatever their background' (BBC, 2018b).

The BBC is not the only public service broadcaster (PSB) in the UK. All the other terrestrial free-to-air companies, including ITV, Channel 4 and Channel 5, are required to meet certain public service responsibilities such as providing news, arts or cultural programmes as well as provision for children and for people of different religions. Unlike the BBC, these PSBs raise most of their income from advertising.

> **Key term**
>
> **Content provider**
> Any company or organisation that makes material for television viewing on any platform. For example, ITN (Independent Television News) makes news programmes for ITV, Channel 4 and Channel 5.

> **Link**
>
> For more on advertising see Chapter 5, pages 186–196.

> **Key term**
>
> **Watershed**
> The period after 9.00 p.m. and until 5.30 a.m. when television broadcasters may schedule more adult material that could be harmful or unsuitable for viewing by minors (under 16). Premium paid-for services such as Sky Movies do not have to operate a watershed but must be PIN protected with a security code.

## Regulation and competition

The UK television industry is regulated by Ofcom. Ofcom's Broadcasting Code sets out the rules for programme makers on, for example, fairness, impartiality and protection from harmful or offensive material.

The Code also requires that material unsuitable for children must not be broadcast before 9.00 p.m., the so-called **watershed**.

Ofcom also has to ensure that there is plenty of competition within the television industry. For some time, it has been government policy to increase the number of content providers.

In 2016, the BBC's most popular programme, *The Great British Bake Off* (*GBBO*), was poached by Channel 4. *GBBO* is made by an independent company and a bidding war broke out between the BBC, ITV, Channel 4 and Netflix. The BBC offered £15 million, but it wasn't enough to keep *GBBO*, which is now broadcast on Channel 4.

The government has put pressure on the BBC to commission programmes made by independent production companies. The number of programmes made 'in house' by BBC employees has steadily declined.

The BBC will continue to make news, sport and current affairs programmes but an increasing proportion of television output will be sourced from outside the BBC itself. This development encourages independent production but other major platform providers have also jumped into content provision.

These have included SVOD companies such as Netflix and Amazon Video. A recent example is Amazon's *The Grand Tour* made by the producer and three presenters who previously made such a success of *Top Gear* for the BBC. The reported cost of three series of *The Grand Tour* is $250 million. It joins a growing list of 'Amazon originals' only available to Amazon Prime (subscription paying) customers.

## Vertical integration

This is a strategy that involves bringing supply, production, distribution and sales together into one unified company.

A vertically integrated company is less reliant on other businesses and this could give it more power to compete and be more profitable.

An example in the television industry is Netflix. Netflix started in 1997 by specialising in the distribution of DVDs, which they sold or rented by mail. As a sales and rental company, Netflix did not make film or television products and they relied on postal companies to deliver DVDs to their customers.

In 2010, Netflix began a streaming service alongside postal deliveries. By 2017, this streaming service was available in almost every country in the world, far outstripping the DVD service.

Jeremy Clarkson stars in *The Grand Tour*, which is available on demand for Amazon Prime subscribers.

At the same time, Netflix has also invested heavily in film and television content. Some of its successful Netflix Originals television series are:

- *House of Cards*
- *Stranger Things*
- *The Crown.*

Of course, Netflix still relies on many other television and film content producers to provide material for its customers, but the vertical integration strategy alongside global expansion has seen Netflix become a powerful media company with over 200 million subscribers in 2021.

## Debates and issues: is the TV licence fee justified?

Surveys have shown high public confidence in the BBC and other public service broadcasters. However, the rapid growth of internet television has prompted a number of debates about the future of the UK television industry.

In 2017, the BBC's director general, Lord Hall, acknowledged that it may become difficult to justify the licence fee by the mid 2020s. With young people, in particular, preferring social media to television and radio, they 'might not be getting value to justify their licence fee in the future', he said.

Lord Hall's solution is to give the BBC a much higher profile on social media such as Facebook and Twitter and with its own websites and apps such as BBC NewsOnline.

Some people have argued that we should do away with public service broadcasting altogether, allowing viewers to pay for just what they want by subscription or to watch free television paid for by advertising.

On the other side of the argument, defenders of the BBC and the licence fee claim that PSB is essential in a democratic society. Everyone should have open access to impartial news and information so that they can be properly informed when it comes to elections or democratic decision-making, they argue.

The BBC's competitors such as ITV often claim that the BBC has an unfair advantage in the competition for viewers because it has a guaranteed income from the licence fee. Commercial television, however, has to fulfil its public service duties and also has to make sure it can sell advertising slots by building big audiences. This is unfair, they claim.

A recent suggestion by parliament's Media, Culture and Sport Committee admits that the licence fee is based on the outmoded idea that the television set is the main way of viewing. They proposed in 2017 a levy (tax) on every household in the country with any kind of communication equipment. This idea would, in theory, produce more money than the licence fee if charged at the same rate because there are currently 500,000 homes that don't pay a licence fee because the occupiers claim never to watch live TV or BBC iPlayer. At the time of writing (late 2021) the government is negotiating the terms of the TV licence for 2022 onwards..

**Netflix has invested heavily in creating successful series such as *House of Cards* and *The Crown*.**

**How will the BBC be funded in the future?**

### Talk about it

What do you think?
Is public service broadcasting still valuable to us?
Should the BBC be abolished, or forced to make money through advertising or subscription?
Or do you support the idea of a licence fee taken from every home with viewing or recording equipment?

**Link**

For more about how to approach music video CSPs see pages 212–213.

**CASE STUDY:**

# Music videos

This media industries case study will help you to put the music video CSPs into a wider context by giving you an understanding of the music video industry in the past and today.

## A quick history of the music video

When you think about it, it's strange that songs, which you listen to, are usually accompanied by images, which you watch. However, making associations between the two is a good way of engaging audiences and potentially increasing sales of the song or the movie.

So, although music videos really took off in the 1980s, they existed long before that as a promotional tool. Songs accompanied moving pictures as soon as technology allowed it, in the first 'talkies' in the 1920s, and soon musicals and cartoons made certain songs very popular, which of course brought in revenue for both the film companies and the producers of the song.

By the 1960s, bands often performed live (or lip-synched) on TV, with recordings of these performances broadcast again later. Artists with enough financial backing from their record company or label realised that making their own films would increase their audience and popularity. The Beatles appeared in two full-length feature films, released in cinemas, that were really extended advertisements for the accompanying soundtracks – *A Hard Day's Night* in 1964 and *Help!* in 1965. These allowed fans to see the band perform, even if they could not attend concerts.

A significant development in the UK was the long-running BBC music show, *Top of the Pops*, which began in 1964. It featured a number of the best-selling singles – the Top 20 – each week. To begin with, artists and bands appeared in the studio and mimed to their songs, but occasionally artists also made short films to accompany their music.

With typical audiences of 15 million viewers, appearing on the show was an important way to increase a song's sales. Self-contained music videos for specific songs began to become more common, and more sophisticated, as the 1960s went on – for example, the short film for Bob Dylan's 'Subterranean Homesick Blues' (1966) was an early example of today's popular lyric videos, and The Beatles' 'Strawberry Fields Forever' (1967) used unusual editing and camera techniques to catch viewers' attention and reinforce The Beatles' ever-changing brand and image.

*Top of the Pops* is indirectly responsible for the most influential early music video, which remains instantly recognisable today – Queen's 'Bohemian Rhapsody' (1975). The song was number one in the charts – the best-selling single of the week – but the band was touring so couldn't appear live on *Top of the Pops*. Instead, they made a promotional video, packed with special lighting and editing effects, which became an instant classic and ensured that the single continued to sell in huge numbers.

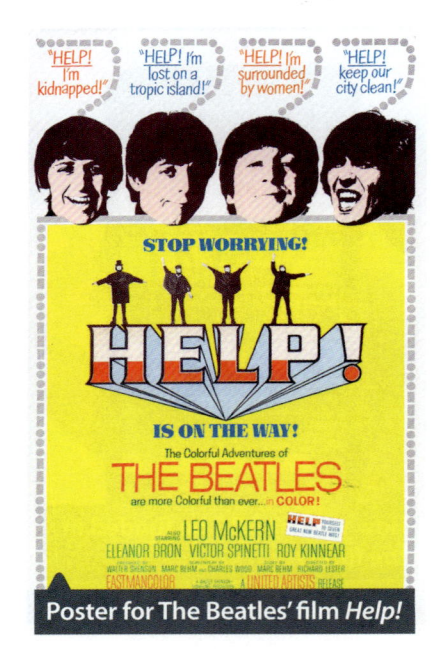

Poster for The Beatles' film *Help!*

Following this success, **record labels/companies** started to offer the BBC free promotional videos for *Top of the Pops*. From the start, the show's producers had imposed limitations on the variety of songs included – for example, no song could be shown on consecutive weeks unless it was number one in the charts or in a different format (e.g. live or recorded over the countdown of the best-selling singles of that week). Trying to get around these limitations encouraged competition between record companies to get their artists featured on primetime TV, leading to both innovative and controversial content.

> **Key term**
>
> **Record labels/companies**
> Businesses in the music industry that fund and coordinate the production, distribution and marketing of music in return for a share of the profits.

The first music TV channel, MTV, was launched in 1981, and initially broadcast music videos 24 hours a day. Its first video was chosen ironically – The Buggles' 'Video Killed the Radio Star' (1980), which is about the impact of visual content on music – and MTV succeeded in bringing the medium of music videos to a wider audience. MTV was a successful concept, bringing in $7 million in advertising revenue in the first 18 months.

Video-recording and editing equipment was becoming cheaper, more portable and easier to use, so that more bands and artists could make videos without needing a lot of money or skill. However, at the same time, big stars appeared in correspondingly big-budget videos, such as David Bowie's 'Ashes to Ashes' (1980) and Michael Jackson's iconic 'Thriller' (1983), which set the standard for high production values and cinematic presentation. Such videos cost more to produce than many feature films. 'Ashes to Ashes' cost $582,000 in 1980, and 'Thriller' cost $1,000,000 in 1983 – both were the most expensive music video made at the time of production. However, both these figures seem quite low compared with Michael and Janet Jackson's later 'Scream' video (1995), which cost $7 million, and Michael Jackson's 'Ghosts' video (1996), which is rumoured to have cost about $15 million. Spurred on by budgets like these, music videos soon became more sophisticated in terms of direction, narrative and genre – some being regarded as short films in their own right, quite apart from the music they promoted. Michael Jackson's 'Thriller' was 14 minutes long, with a 'story within a story' narrative – Michael Jackson and Ola Ray are shown watching a film that also stars them, in a prologue that lasts for over four minutes before any music is heard. This short music movie was directed by John Landis, who had directed the 1981 feature film *An American Werewolf in London*, and the music video used some of the same special effects. The videos for Dire Straights' 'Money for Nothing' (1985) and Peter Gabriel's 'Sledgehammer' (1986) featured stop-motion animation and other special effects.

By the 1990s and 2000s, well-regarded film directors, such as Spike Jonze, Walter Stern and Michel Gondry, were creating memorable videos using novel and striking imagery and techniques.

MTV remains one of the world's most recognisable brands.

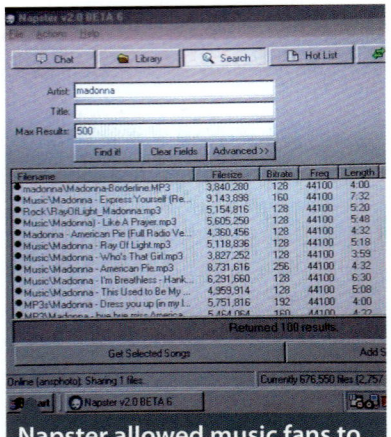

Napster allowed music fans to download and share individual singles rather than having to purchase entire albums.

However, by the late 1990s, the music industry was undergoing significant changes to its business model. Music videos were primarily advertisements for singles and albums but CD sales were declining as music, and eventually music videos, began to be freely available online. Although illegally sharing and copying music was nothing new, the internet made it much easier. For example, a peer-to-peer music-sharing site called Napster was launched in 1999 and soon gained 80 million active users and a lot of lawsuits from record companies and artists who claimed it infringed their copyright. The site was shut down in 2001 but it was too late to prevent free music from being easily available online, and record labels' traditional business model of 'selling' music crumbled.

MTV started to show more lucrative reality shows instead of videos, and, for record labels and artists, live shows began to be as economically important as recorded music.

## Music videos and the internet

The launch of Vimeo in 2004 and YouTube in 2005 revitalised the concept of music videos. At first, music videos were shared without the permission of the artists, but then musicians realised they could use these new internet channels themselves – suddenly, artists could easily make and upload low-budget videos that could go viral. Users could search for their favourite songs and share them on social media. Although this was good news for music fans, it was not at that time a reliable source of revenue for music labels or the bands themselves. Because there were so many illegal uploads, no money was being passed back to the labels and the musicians. YouTube and similar sites argued that the music industry should be pleased to have the free exposure that these videos brought.

After being repeatedly sued for breaching copyright by bands and record labels, YouTube (now owned by Google) identified a way to deliver some money to the music video creators. The website developed an algorithm to detect copyright material – by checking sound profiles against a database of known recordings – and then displayed adverts on this material to raise money to pay the original creator. The system is called ContentID and can recognise known music used within any uploaded videos.

Artists and record companies now receive royalties for each view of recognisable songs, but the intense competition means videos have to work harder than ever to catch viewers' attention. Some say this has resulted in a new golden era for music videos, as artists and bands try harder to make something worth sharing. The band OK Go are renowned for their highly creative videos, which are almost guaranteed to be a viral success. However, this doesn't always make them a financial success. OK Go released 'This Too Shall Pass' in January 2010. Two months later it had been watched 8 million times, but only 25,000 copies of the track had been sold. Even repeated views may not bring in the money. One case study quoted on 'Digital Music News' in 2017, showed that videos using a particular artist's music had been viewed over one million times, and the artist had only received $64.60 in 'partner revenue'.

Although budgets for music videos vary enormously, many are now low budget, as the changes in video production technology have put quality production tools within the reach of many musicians. Unsigned artists – those who don't have a

### Activity 4.12

Choose six artists you like, from at least two different genres, and check how many views their videos have on YouTube or Vimeo. Compare with other students across the class. Which genres tended to have the most views?

### Talk about it

How do you find the videos you want to watch online? How do you find out about new bands and songs?

contract with a record label – can create music videos that look just as good as many of those created by record companies. Some bands and solo artists have used this to gain popularity without being signed to a record label at all.

## Making money from music videos

Viewers are now encouraged to subscribe to an artist's YouTube channel and to share the video on their own social media platforms, so that it reaches a wider audience. The video's success can become self-perpetuating, with more shares generating more views, and therefore more income for the artists and record companies. Psy's 'Gangnam Style' (2013) music video was a notorious YouTube hit, being the first video to exceed a billion views. Its online popularity translated into enough sales to top the charts in more than 30 countries.

There's also a knock-on effect for ticket sales to live shows – for example, Scott Bradlee's Postmodern Jukebox, essentially a collection of musicians (and the odd tap dancer) rather than an actual band, uses low-budget vintage-inspired videos, often starring former *American Idol* contestants, as a springboard to their international stage shows. With 3.2 million YouTube subscribers and more than 400 million total views, that's a lot of potential ticket sales.

Before YouTube launched ContentID, record labels needed to take a new approach to making money via videos. One solution was Vevo – Video EVOlution – a music video streaming service syndicated to YouTube and jointly run by the three biggest record companies – Sony Music Entertainment, Warner Music Group and Universal Music Group. Vevo makes money mainly from advertising at the bottom of each video, as well as from merchandise and links referring viewers to iTunes and Amazon Music to buy downloads. The income is shared between Vevo and Google, the owner of YouTube. The potential number of views (and the resulting revenue) can be enormous. Taylor Swift's 'Look What You Made Me Do', released on 27 August 2017, was viewed 43.2 million times within 24 hours – that's an average 30,000 times per minute and over 3 million views per hour. Luis Fonsi and Daddy Yankee's catchy 'Despacito' clocked up over 4.3 billion views in 2017, no doubt contributing to the 30% increase in Vevo's revenue that year to $450 million.

## Regulation

Being freely available online, it is impossible to control the content of music videos, as anyone can upload content to YouTube and other websites.

Although it is not yet a legal requirement, the BBFC has an agreement with YouTube, Vevo and some key music companies, to age-rate music videos shown or streamed in the UK by artists signed to Sony Music UK, Universal Music UK and Warner Music UK. All UK independent labels have also joined the scheme. The age ratings are similar to those used on DVDs. Music videos that are deemed unsuitable for children younger than 12 years of age, are classified as 12, 15 or 18. The rating symbols are clearly displayed on the website next to the video window.

**Link**

We have already discussed the BBFC in relation to the film industry earlier in this chapter, on pages 128–130.

### Activity 4.13

Research the most expensive music videos ever made. Several are for songs by Madonna and Michael Jackson. Compare them with videos by OK Go and Scott Bradlee's Postmodern Jukebox, which are made for a fraction of the cost.

- What do you notice about when the big-budget videos were made?
- Why do you think record companies were willing to spend so much money on making the videos at that time?
- Do you think record companies are likely to spend so much money on music videos today?

The record labels submit to the BBFC any music videos intended for UK online release for which they expect to receive at least a 12 rating.

The BBFC classifies each video based on content such as:

- drug misuse
- dangerous behaviour presented as safe
- bad language
- sexual behaviour and nudity
- threatening behaviour and violence.

As the scheme is currently limited to the voluntary actions of only a few record labels, the regulation cannot be enforced and, in any case, the ratings don't stop younger audiences watching a particular video online. However, the age ratings do let people know what is and isn't appropriate for each age group.

Music videos are obviously viewed offline too, and artists have every right to be paid for any screening of their work. PPL licenses recorded music and music videos that are played in public or broadcast, for example, in pubs or sports clubs. The venues pay a licence fee, and then PPL distributes the licence fees to performers and record labels.

Michael and Janet Jackson's video for 'Scream' is said to have cost $7 million – equivalent to $11 million today.

**4 Media Industries**

**CASE STUDY:**
# Video games

For your GCSE Media Studies course, video games need to be studied from all four perspectives – Media Language, Media Representations, Media Audiences and Media Industries.

In this case study, some context for the CSPs will be provided by looking in detail at how media industries relate to video games. In Chapter 5 you will find more study material relating to online, social and participatory media and video games, which you can relate to your relevant CSPs.

## The global video games market

Video games – including computer games and apps – are a huge media industry that makes a significant contribution to the global economy. It is estimated that up to 3.24 billion people across the world regularly play video games (Statista, 2021) and that the global games market was worth $162 billion in 2020, and is projected to be worth almost $300 billion in 2026 (Dobrilova, 2021). Gaming is especially popular in the Asia-Pacific market, such as in China, Japan and South Korea – this market makes up over half of global mobile revenue.

There are many reasons for this ongoing, and increasing, popularity:

- Players can choose from a variety of platforms, for example PC, console or mobile, making gaming easily accessible, whether players are at home or not.
- Players can also access new games instantly, using online providers such as Steam or iTunes.
- Games are easier than ever to make and distribute, so players are likely to find a game they enjoy, no matter what their taste. For example, 7,672 games were released on Valve's Steam platform in 2017, and 6.64 billion games apps were downloaded from Google Play in the three months from April 2017 (Sensor Tower, 2017).
- Games often tie in with popular movie franchises or are endorsed by famous brands – or both, as in the case of games such as Lego Harry Potter.
- The availability of broadband and 4G (and beyond) has led to increasingly social benefits, such as communal gaming and the interconnectivity of players of MMORGs (massively multiplayer online role-playing games).

As already seen with other types of media, barriers are breaking down between the media creator and the audience, and between different types of media. Gaming, for example, has a high degree of crossover with the film industry, both in terms of content and technology. The gaming experience can also be enhanced by using **augmented reality** or linking to social media – or both, as in the case of Niantic's Pokémon GO. The combination has proved very popular – Pokémon GO had more than 65 million monthly active users in April 2017, and the total amount spent on the game by players is said to have been more than the global box-office takings of the blockbuster film *Batman vs Superman: Dawn of Justice* (2016) at that time.

> **Key term**
>
> **Augmented reality**
> Technology combining computer-generated images with the user's physical environment.

Pokémon GO successfully combines emerging technology, mobile gaming, social media, real-world experiences and, most importantly, fun.

## Ownership, control and effects of ownership

As with any big business, video games companies are constantly buying and merging with each other.

At time of writing, the biggest gaming company in the world by revenue (financial income) is Tencent Games, part of the Chinese conglomerate Tencent Holdings.

You might not have heard of it but it's also the fourth largest internet company in the world, after Facebook, Alphabet – Google's parent company – and Amazon. Its business model is to either acquire or buy stakes in smaller companies in order to offer a variety of online computer, console and mobile games. While it makes most of its revenue from the Asia-Pacific market, especially China, its reach also means that most gamers are likely to have played a game Tencent has helped to fund. For example, one of its subsidiary companies is Supercell, which makes Clash of Clans, and it owns a stake in Glu Mobile, which produces Kim Kardashian: Hollywood.

Because of the size of the potential income from gaming, Facebook, Amazon and Microsoft have all invested in (and acquired) new streaming and gaming technologies. Buying smaller companies gives these larger organisations access to new opportunities to create and market new games, which will help them to increase their market share and decrease competition.

It's not just games developers and publishers that are commercially successful within the video games industry. Steam is a major digital distribution platform developed by Valve Corporation. Steam offers access to thousands of games to its online community – estimated to be over 120 million players. Although not all the players will be online at once, Steam's own audience counters show that there are usually several million users of the site at any one time. This allows users to play against each other, with each other, chat in-game and form game groups or clans. Valve is estimated to have made $730 million in 2014, and to have earned $4.3 billion in 2017 from Steam alone, in addition to revenue from its own games.

## Funding

Games might be bought by a one-off physical purchase or download, or via a monthly subscription. It is, of course, perfectly possible never to pay directly for any of the games or apps that you play. Many are available to everyone online or can be downloaded onto your phone or tablet for free. But, obviously, games producers have to make money somehow, so need to have a **monetisation strategy** in place. Often, this will be a **freemium** model, where mobile games, in particular, generate income via:

- in-app advertising
- players paying not to have advertisements within their app (premium ad-free services)
- in-app or in-game purchases.

---

**Activity 4.14**

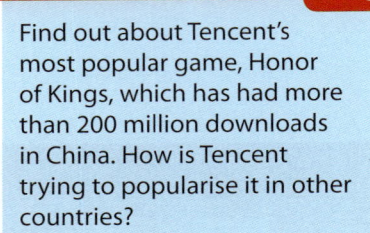

Find out about Tencent's most popular game, Honor of Kings, which has had more than 200 million downloads in China. How is Tencent trying to popularise it in other countries?

**Quick question 4.2**

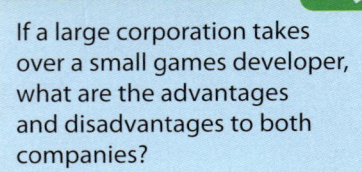

If a large corporation takes over a small games developer, what are the advantages and disadvantages to both companies?

**Key terms**

**Monetisation strategy**
The proposed method for making an income from a product.

**Freemium**
A business model, especially used with internet content and mobile games, that offers basic services, or the basic game, free of charge, but more advanced or special features have to be paid for.

A newer strategy is **paymium (or paidmium)**, where users pay for the game up front but can also choose to pay for in-app purchases. Obviously, this has to be worth their while, so developers are under pressure to keep developing new features that players will be willing to pay for.

Any advertising within the game should be targeted, relevant and (most importantly) not disrupt the gaming experience. Sometimes these ads are linked to cookies already on your phone – for example, you may see Amazon ads for products you were browsing earlier.

Temple Run, released for the iPhone in 2011, became one of the first major freemium games – after a month of being available for 99p, the developers Imangi decided to make it free and offer in-app purchases instead. Revenue for the developers increased tenfold once the game became free to download. Temple Run and Temple Run 2 collectively hit a billion downloads in June 2014.

According to research published in January 2017 (Gartner, 2017), whether or not people are willing to pay for their games depends on their age and gender. It found that people aged 25–34 spend the most on both paid apps and in-app transactions. Women were found to spend less than men on paid downloads and in-app transactions but were more open to a freemium model. One of Imangi's founders, Keith Shepherd, said in 2012 that only 1% of Temple Run's players made in-app purchases, but remember, by 2014 that may have been 1% of over a billion customers.

## Regulation

Pan European Game Information (PEGI) is an age-rating system used across 30 European countries to help consumers, especially parents, make informed decisions on the suitability of computer games. It is supported by publishers and developers of interactive games, as well as by the major console manufacturers, including Sony, Microsoft and Nintendo. The scheme is run in the UK by the Video Standards Council (VSC) Rating Board, which has the power to reject a European rating if it is felt inappropriate for the UK audience.

PEGI labels, as shown on page 148, appear on packaging, or on the online information about a game on sites such as Steam or Google Play, and indicate minimum age levels of either 3, 7, 12, 16 or 18.

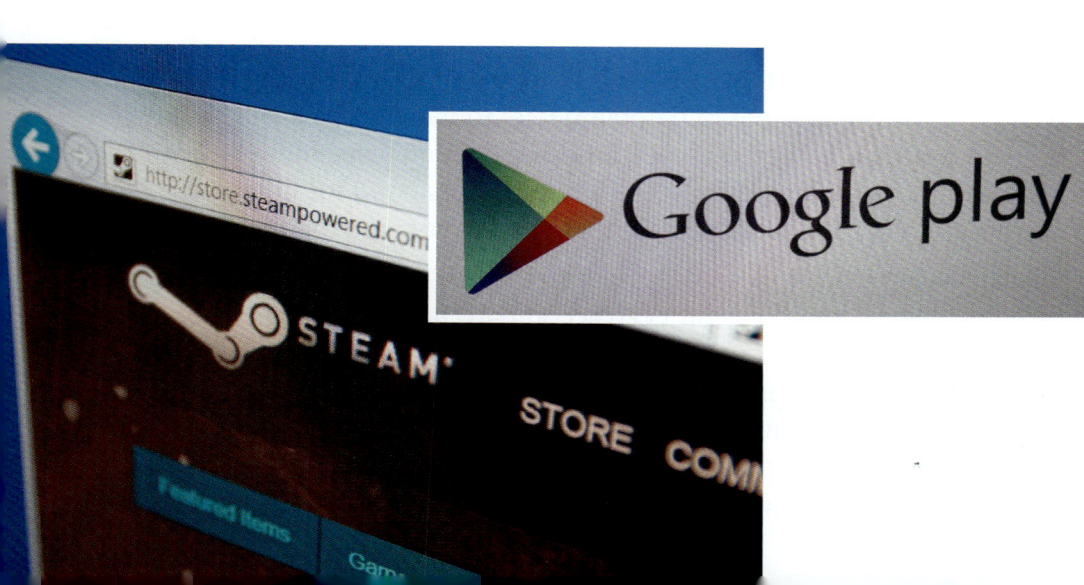

### Key term

**Paymium (or paidmium)**
A business strategy for apps that combines a low initial price with in-app purchases.

### Activity 4.15

Carry out some research into the mobile game, Lara Croft GO. What is its monetisation strategy?

### Activity 4.16

Carry out a survey among your friends, classmates and family to find out their attitudes towards paying for mobile gaming apps. For example, do they prefer to download a free app and then make in-app purchases or to not spend any money at all? If they are prepared to pay for a gaming app, how much will they pay? Make sure you ask a range of demographics, such as different ages and genders.
Make a presentation of your findings. What conclusions can you draw?
How do your findings compare with those of other people in your class?

### Quick question 4.3

Why do you think video games are certified using similar methods to film certification? What impact do you think the age ratings have on players' decisions to purchase or play specific games?

| | |
|---|---|
| **3** | **PEGI 3** The content of games with a PEGI 3 rating is considered suitable for all age groups. The game should not contain any sounds or pictures that are likely to frighten young children. A very mild form of violence (in a comical context or a childlike setting) is acceptable. No bad language should be heard. |
| **7** | **PEGI 7** Game content with scenes or sounds that can possibly frightening to younger children should fall in this category. Very mild forms of violence (implied, non-detailed, or non-realistic violence) are acceptable for a game with a PEGI 7 rating. |
| **12** | **PEGI 12** Video games that show violence of a slightly more graphic nature towards fantasy characters or non-realistic violence towards human-like characters would fall in this age category. Sexual innuendo or sexual posturing can be present, while any bad language in this category must be mild. |
| **16** | **PEGI 16** This rating is applied once the depiction of violence (or sexual activity) reaches a stage that looks the same as would be expected in real life. The use of bad language in games with a PEGI 16 rating can be more extreme, while the use of tobacco, alcohol or illegal drugs can also be present. |
| **18** | **PEGI 18** The adult classification is applied when the level of violence reaches a stage where it becomes a depiction of gross violence, apparently motiveless killing, or violence towards defenceless characters. The glamorisation of the use of illegal drugs and of the simulation of gambling, and explicit sexual activity should also fall into this age category. |

Further descriptors on the packaging or website explain why the game has received this rating:

- The game contains depictions of violence. In games rated PEGI 7 this can only be non-realistic or non-detailed violence. Games rated PEGI 12 can include violence in a fantasy environmentor non-realistic violence towards human-like characters, whereas games rated PEGI 16 or 18 have increasingly more realistic-looking violence.

- The game contains bad language. This descriptor can be found on games with a PEGI 12 (mild swearing), PEGI 16 (e.g. sexual expletives or blasphemy) or PEGI 18 rating (e.g. sexual expletives or blasphemy).

- This descriptor may appear on games with a PEGI 7 if it contains pictures or sounds that may be frightening or scary to young children, or on PEGI 12 games with horrific sounds or horror effects (but without any violent content).

- The game contains elements that encourage or teach gambling. These simulations of gambling refer to games of chance that are normally carried out in casinos or gambling halls. Some older titles can be found with PEGI 12 or PEGI 16, but PEGI changed the criteria for this classification in 2020, which means that new games with this sort of content are always PEGI 18.

- This content descriptor can accompany a PEGI 12 rating if the game includes sexual posturing or innuendo, a PEGI 16 rating if there is erotic nudity or sexual intercourse without visible genitals or a PEGI 18 rating if there is explicit sexual activity in the game. Depictions of nudity in a non-sexual content do not require a specific age rating, and this descriptor would not be necessary.

### Activity 4.17

Why is Lara Croft GO rated as PEGI 7? Look again at the PEGI age descriptors on page 147, and either play the game or watch gameplay videos such as 'Lara Croft GO Android iOS Walkthrough – Gameplay Part 1 – The Entrance, The Maze of Snakes', on YouTube.

-  The game refers to or depicts the use of illegal drugs, alcohol or tobacco. Games with this content descriptor are always PEGI 16 or PEGI 18.
-  The game contains depictions of ethnic, religious, nationalistic or other stereotypes likely to encourage hatred. This content is always restricted to a PEGI 18 rating (and likely to infringe national criminal laws).

(PEGI, 2021)

Small and minor games publishers can self-regulate by using a PEGI OK label to indicate that it is suitable for players of all ages. They just need to submit a declaration that the game contains no unsuitable content.

Digital and online technologies present challenges for media regulation. As with films, there is no way to regulate access to video games once they have been purchased or downloaded.

## Franchising and celebrity promotion

A games franchise is usually a series of games based in the same world or featuring the same characters, for example Tomb Raider and Mario. The company that owns the rights will commission a studio to develop the next game in the series. This may not be the same studio as the previous one, so it might lead to changes in technology, game-playing or graphics.

Some franchised games are a spin-off of a brand, or use **intellectual property** from another form of media, usually films. Examples are FIFA football games or the Lego series of film role-players, such as Lego Star Wars.

Successful franchises can earn billions of dollars for their creators, as audiences become familiar, and engaged, with characters and their gaming world. Nintendo's Mario is the best-selling video game franchise of all time, having sold over 500 million copies and moved into other genres and media, including film. Similarly, Tomb Raider – or specifically its main character Lara Croft – has been part of popular culture for more than 25 years. The key to these and other successful franchises is to continue to appeal to audiences by adapting to gaming trends and technologies.

Celebrities have always appeared in, and endorsed, computer games. As early as 1984, martial arts artist Bruce Lee appeared in his own fighting games. Even if they don't appear in the game itself, celebrities often advertise games – an indicator of the big budgets games studios often have.

## Trends in gaming

### A changing audience

Typical gamers used to be portrayed as teenage boys playing first-person shooter games in their bedrooms. With the increase in social media and mobile gaming, this stereotype is outdated – in fact, the average player is 35 years old, and cooperative play, especially with friends and family, tends to be more popular than competitive play. Women are as likely to play video and mobile games as men (Google Play, 2017; ESA, 2017b).

### Key term

**Intellectual property**
Ideas and designs that are copyright to a company or individual. For example, the characters and narratives in Marvel's Universe are the intellectual property of Marvel and Disney, which owns the Marvel subsidiary.

### Activity 4.18

Watch the advertisement for mobile game Clash of Clans, 'Clash of Clans: Revenge (Official Super Bowl TV Commercial)' on YouTube, starring actor Liam Neeson, which has had 165 million views (July 2018).

Identify reasons for the advert's appeal to its target audience.

*The stereotype of typical gamers has changed.*

*DanTDM has built on his YouTube success by making live appearances.*

Of course, women, in general, may want to play a different type of game from men. Some research reinforces stereotypes of men preferring sports and war games, and women preferring role-playing and puzzle games. In any case, the rise in female players provides a huge opportunity for games companies to develop more games targeted at them.

## Gaming video content (GVC)

One surprising trend is the popularity of 'gaming video content' (GVC). An estimated audience of 1.2 billion people choose to watch videos of other people playing video games on sites such as Twitch and YouTube Gaming. The content can also include trailers, humorous commentaries, reviews and walk-throughs. Advertisers are realising the economic potential of so many people choosing to watch GVC rather than watching standard TV shows.

**Gaming video content**

GVC revenue 2020: $9.3 billion

Global viewers 2020: 1.2 billion

Global viewer annual growth rate 2019–2020: 18%

GVC earned 6.6% of the overall $139.9 billion revenue from games and interactive media in 2020.

| Digital games | | | Interactive media | |
|---|---|---|---|---|
| $73.8B Mobile | $33.1B PC | $19.7B Console | $9.3B GVC | $6.7B XR |

Source: SuperData, 2021

### Key term

**Virtual reality (VR)**
Technology that simulates a three-dimensional world, often enabling users to interact with it.

### Talk about it

VR is a fully immersive experience of presence in an imaginary world. Increasingly, users will be able to manipulate virtual objects with their hands and interact with other players who are physically elsewhere. With a partner, discuss the impact this could have on participants, both while playing the game and when 'back in the real world'.

### Activity 4.19

YouTube GVC star DanTDM was reported to have earned £12.3 million in 2017. Find out more about him and watch some of his videos.
Write down at least five reasons why you think he is so popular with his target audience, and at least five ways in which he has generated income as a result of his YouTube channel. How do you think this is influenced by the demographic of his target audience?

## Increased interactivity

Computer gaming technology is continually developing, especially around the social aspects of gaming and immersion in the gaming world.

**Virtual reality (VR)** and augmented reality (AR) technology is becoming mainstream because it has reached a point at which it is cheap enough for most consumers to afford. The ESA reported in 2017 that 11% of US households owned a virtual reality (VR) headset, and one-third of the most frequent video game players in each household said they would buy a VR headset in the next year (ESA, 2017a). VR is growing significantly in the UK, too. Virtual reality rooms and bars are becoming popular as social spaces where VR headsets can be rented for a timeslot. This represents a great economic opportunity for hardware and software companies, with Sony PlayStation VR and Oculus Rift being the preferred brands at the moment.

# Technological development, from console to PC to mobile device

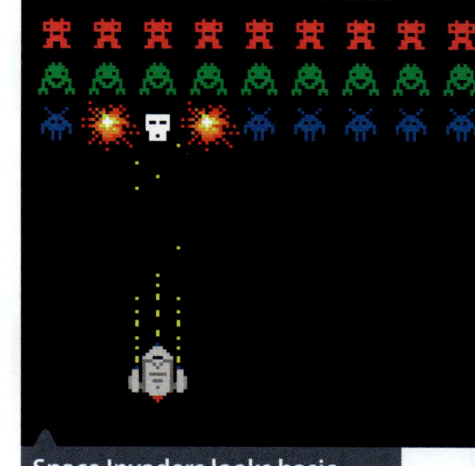

Computer gaming started to take off in the late 1970s, when home ('micro') computers became more affordable to ordinary people. The Commodore PET and the Atari VCS (Video Computer System) were both launched in the US in 1977 – as was the first version of Space Invaders. By the early 1980s, people were using their first PCs to learn programing and play games. These games weren't sophisticated by today's standards but at the time were seen as highly advanced.

Since then, gaming consoles and PCs have constantly vied for prominence, overtaking each other in terms of sophistication and popularity as the technology has advanced. Especially since the early 2000s, computer processor technology and internet capability has improved at such a rate that each new console, new PC, and their games and graphics, quickly make previous versions look old-fashioned.

Space Invaders looks basic today but it is still fun to play.

The following chart shows the devices that have had the most impact on gaming over the last 45 years. Just a handful of brands have dominated the market. Parallel to this, PC capability has improved so that gaming computers now often cost less than the latest console and individual games for PCs are much cheaper, too.

| Year | Device | Type |
|---|---|---|
| 1977 | Atari VCS | Computer video system |
| 1982 | Commodore 64 | Computer |
| 1982 | ZX Spectrum | Computer |
| 1985 | Nintendo Entertainment System (NES) | Computer console |
| 1989 | Nintendo Game Boy | Hand-held console |
| 1989 | Sega Genesis | Computer console |
| 1990 | Nintendo Super NES | Computer console |
| 1994 | Sony Playstation | Computer console |
| 1996 | Nintendo 64 | Computer console |
| 1997 | Nokia 6610 | Mobile phone (supported the first popular mobile game, Snake) |
| 1999 | Sega Dreamcast | Computer console |
| 2000 | Sony Playstation 2 | Computer console |
| 2001 | Nintendo Gamecube | Computer console |
| 2001 | Microsoft Xbox | Computer console |
| 2001 | Nintendo Gameboy Advance | Portable gaming system |
| 2004 | Nintendo DS | Hand-held console |
| 2005 | Microsoft Xbox 360 | Computer console |
| 2006 | Sony Playstation 3 | Computer console |
| 2006 | Nintendo Wii | Computer console |
| 2007 | iPhone | Smartphone (iOS) |
| 2008 | HTC Dream / G1 | Smartphone (Android) |
| 2011 | Nintendo DSI | Computer console |
| 2011 | Nintendo 3DS | Hand-held console |
| 2012 | Sony Playstation Vita | Hand-held console |
| 2013 | Sony Playstation 4 | Computer console |
| 2013 | Microsoft Xbox One | Computer console |
| 2017 | Nintendo NES Classic Edition | Computer console |
| 2017 | Nintendo Switch | Hybrid console and tablet |
| 2018 | C64 Mini | Computer console |
| 2020 | Sony Playstation 5 | Computer console |
| 2020 | Microsoft Xbox Series X | Computer console |

### Quick question 4.4

How is the experience of playing a game on a mobile device different from playing on a console or PC? Which do you prefer and why?

### Activity 4.20

Nostalgic gamers can buy 'retro' consoles such as the NES Classic or C64 Mini, or download Spectrum emulator software, so that they can play the games they (or others) enjoyed 30 years ago. Research these or similar products. What games can be played on them? Why do people want to play games in this way? Create a short presentation outlining why there is a big market for retro gaming hardware and software.

---

Gaming took another step forward when smartphones and tablets brought it into the mainstream and changed the way games are played. Rather than being a niche hobby, everyone can now download a gaming app and play it on the go. People now spend more on mobile gaming than on console and PC-/Mac-based games. Although gameplay is currently restricted by small screens, limited internal memories, short battery life and slow processor speeds, no doubt these problems will be overcome. It is likely that advances in VR and AI will enable the next stage in gaming technology, which could include intelligent computer responses or thought recognition.

#### References

Bauer (2018) KISS, https://www.bauermedia.co.uk/brands-network/kiss.
BBC (2018b) Diversity & Inclusion, http://www.bbc.co.uk/diversity.
BBFC (2014) Age Ratings You Trust, http://www.bbfc.co.uk/what-classification/guidelines.
BFI (2017, 26 January) New BFI Statistics Show Robust Year for Film in the UK in 2016, http://www.bfi.org.uk/news-opinion/news-bfi/announcements/highest-grossing-films-uk-box-office-2016.
Creative Industries Federation (2017) Statistics, https://www.creativeindustriesfederation.com/statistics.
Deloitte (2017) Media Metrics 2017, https://www2.deloitte.com/content/dam/Deloitte/uk/Documents/technology-media-telecommunications/deloitte-uk-media-metrics-2017.pdf.
Dobrilova, T. (2021, 2 October) How Much is the Gaming Industry Worth in 2021?, https://techjury.net/blog/gaming-industry-worth/#gref.
ESA (2017a) Essential Facts About the Competition Industry, http://www.theesa.com/about-esa/essential-facts-computer-video-game-industry/.
Follows, S. (2016, 10 July) How Movies Make Money: $100m+ Hollywood Blockbusters, https://stephenfollows.com/how-movies-make-money-hollywood-blockbusters/.
Gartner (2017, 26 January) Gartner Survey Finds that Most Smartphone Users Spend Nothing on Apps, https://www.gartner.com/newsroom/id/3583817.
Google Play (2017) Change the Game, http://services.google.com/fh/files/misc/changethegame_white_paper.pdf.
Kantar Media (2018) Linear vs Non-linear Viewing, Ofcom, https://www.ofcom.org.uk/__data/assets/pdf_file/0029/68816/km_report.pdf.
Macnab, G. (2017, 2 June) Fixing Britain's 'Broken' Independent Film Sector: Is Tax Relief Enough?, ScreenDaily, https://www.screendaily.com/features/what-can-fix-britains-broken-independent-film-sector/5118700.article.
Media Reform Coalition (2015) Who Owns the UK Media?, http://www.mediareform.org.uk/wp-content/uploads/2015/10/Who_owns_the_UK_media-report_plus_appendix1.pdf.
No Free Spins No Deposit (2020, 30 July) Leading Movies Based on Merchandise Sales, https://newfreespinsnodeposit.com/leading-movies-based-merchandise-sales/.
Ofcom (2016) The Communications Market, https://www.ofcom.org.uk/_data/assets/pdf_file/0026/17495/uk_tv.pdf.
PEGI (2021) What do the Labels Mean?, https://pegi.info/what-do-the-labels-mean.
Reach (2018) Our Newsbrands, https://www.reachplc.com/brands/our-newsbrands.
Sensor Tower (2017) Q2 2017 Report, https://s3.amazonaws.com/sensortower-itunes/Quarterly+Reports/Sensor-Tower-Q2-2017-Data-Digest.pdf.
Statista (2021) Number of Video Gamers Worldwide in 2021, by Region, https://www.statista.com/statistics/293304/number-video-gamers/.
SuperData (2021) 2020 Year in Review, https://www.digitalmusicnews.com/wp-content/uploads/2021/01/SuperData2020YearinReview.pdf.

# 5 Close study products and media forms

## What's in this chapter?

- As you have worked through the four framework chapters, you have already looked at many close study products (CSPs) selected for 2023.

- For example, in the Media Language chapter we looked in detail at the cover of *Tatler* magazine in order to explore the ways in which narrative works in magazine covers.

- This chapter starts by explaining how CSPs and media forms are linked to each other and to the theoretical framework. It shows you how they need to be studied and you will also learn how media forms and CSPs feature in the course.

- The media forms are introduced one by one, each starting with a 'studying' section that helps you to understand historical, social, cultural and political contexts. Following this section, the CSPs linked to the media form are fully discussed with detailed notes on the relevant framework areas.

## Products and forms

A 'product' is something produced by a media industry for a media audience. It could be anything from a television programme to a video game, from a radio advertisement to a daily newspaper. In GCSE Media Studies these products are grouped into various media forms, which are as follows:

- television
- film
- radio
- magazines
- newspapers
- advertising and marketing
- online social and participatory media
- video games
- music video.

### Quick question 5.1

Which is the odd one out? What should it be?

| The media studies framework: | |
|---|---|
| Media Language | Media Resources |
| Media Audiences | Media Industries |

## In-depth study

Some of the forms are studied in depth and these are printed in BLUE in the list above. 'In-depth study' means that the CSPs of these particular media forms are studied in relation to all four areas of the media framework:

- Media Language
- Media Representations
- Media Audiences
- Media Industries.

Some of the example 2023 CSPs link online social and participatory media products with associated video games, for example the Kim Kardashian: Hollywood game and Kim Kardashian's online presence.

153

## Targeted forms and products

The media forms highlighted in GREEN in the list on the previous page must be studied only in relation to one or two of the media framework areas:

Media Language and Media Representations are linked to:
- magazines
- advertising and marketing.

Media Industries and Media Audiences are linked to:
- music video
- radio.

Media Industries are linked to only:
- film.

*Ken Loach's award-winning film*

*Black Widow – superhero*

This means that when you study one of the CSP advertisements such as the OMO advert, for example, you will need to focus on the media language and representation issues rather than industries or audiences. When studying the films, *Black Widow* and *I, Daniel Blake*, you will be focusing on media industries so it will not be necessary to analyse the films in terms of media language, representation or audience.

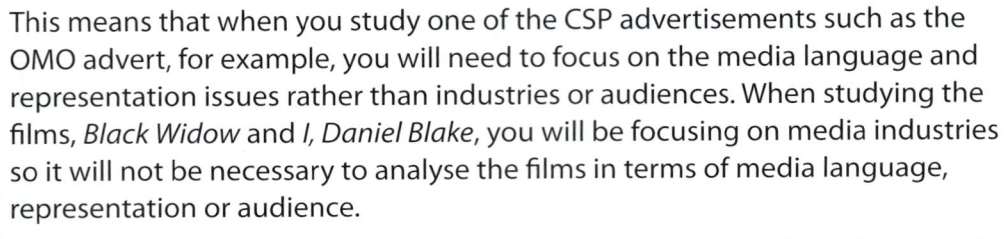

All the CSPs, both in-depth and targeted, need to be explored in relation to the social, cultural and political contexts in which they were produced.

## Making links

This chapter introduces each of the media forms by showing you how to approach the study of television, radio or advertising, for example. These 'Studying the form' sections focus particularly on the historical, social and cultural contexts. This introduction is followed with a much more detailed exploration of the 2023 CSPs. This will help you to understand the links between the form, the CSP, the framework and the contexts.

Case studies throughout the book deal with specific aspects of CSPs and you will find page references in this chapter that link you to relevant material on a particular CSP.

You will need to be familiar with all the current CSPs in order to prepare for the two exams and the production task (NEA). The exam board will change some of the CSPs for new ones, as they will be reviewed annually. Your teacher will be aware of this and will show you how to study any new CSPs in just the same way as the 2023 ones dealt with in this book.

### Quick question 5.2

Which of these are media forms?
- Video games
- Radio
- Books
- Advertising and marketing

### Quick question 5.3

Which media form is studied only in relation to media industries?
- Film
- Music video
- Advertising and marketing

## CSPs and the exam

The first exam paper, **Media One**, has two sections:

- **Section A**: Media Language and Media Representations, including questions on any **two** of magazines, advertising and marketing, newspapers, video games and online social and participatory media.
- **Section B**: Media Audiences and Media Industries, including questions on any **two** of radio, music video, newspapers, video games, online social and participatory media and film.

The questions will be focused on the theoretical framework but you will need to refer to CSPs in your answers.

The second exam paper, **Media Two**, also has two sections:

- **Section A**: Television: including questions on clips from the current television CSPs.
- **Section B**: Newspapers or online social and participatory media and video games, including questions for which you will need to refer to the current CSPs.

## CSPs and the practical production (non-examined assessment)

In this part of the course you will be making an original media product based on a production brief. All the production briefs are linked to the CSPs, so the knowledge and understanding built up by studying CSPs will be very useful in your practical work.

> **Tip**
> Make your own notes on each CSP. Start a CSP folder with sub-folders for each product.

# Studying television

## The popularity of television

You can start by looking at the ways in which television has had enormous cultural and historical significance in the 80-odd years since the first public broadcast in 1936. Measured by audience size, television rapidly became the most popular of the mass media forms. The number of UK homes with a TV set has steadily increased:

- 1956     5.7 million
- 2019     28.5 million

Many homes now have multiple television sets and TV screens are common in shops, stations, pubs and many other sites. People watch TV for an average of (as of 2021):

- Weekdays     3.8 hours
- Weekends     4.8 hours

Although the total number of TV sets has dropped since 2014, the time per day spent watching television continues to rise. This is because so much television viewing today is on devices such as computers, phones or tablets (BBC News, 2014).

Technological developments have seen the number of channels rise from just one in 1936 (BBC) to two in 1955 (ITV plus BBC) to four in 1982, to many hundreds today.

The chart at the top of the following page shows the most popular programmes broadcast in the first 80 years of television. However, these were all outdone by the Euro 2020 final between England and Italy, which peaked at 25 million viewers watching live on BBC, 6 million watching live on ITV and millions more watching on streaming services.

**Here is the full list of the top 20 most-watched TV shows (up to 2016):**

1. *Only Fools and Horses* (BBC1, 29 December 1996): 24.35 million
2. *To the Manor Born* (BBC1, 11 November 1979): 23.95 million
3. The Royal Variety Performance (ITV, 29 November 1967): 22.80 million
4. *Panorama* (BBC1, 20 November 1995): 22.77 million
5. The Royal Variety Performance (ITV, 14 November 1965): 21.70 million
6. *Dallas* (BBC1, 22 November 1980): 21.60 million
7. *To the Manor Born* (BBC1, 9 November 1980): 21.55 million
8. *The Mike Yarwood Christmas Show* (BBC1, 25 December 1977): 21.40 million
9. *Coronation Street* (ITV, 2 January 1985): 21.40 million
10. *Only Fools and Horses* (BBC1, 25 December 2001): 21.35 million
11. *Only Fools and Horses* (BBC1, 27 December 1996): 21.33 million
12. *Only Fools and Horses* (BBC1, 25 December 1996): 21.31 million
13. *The Morecambe and Wise Christmas Show* (BBC1, 25 December 1977): 21.30 million
14. The Royal Variety Performance (ITV, 10 November 1963): 21.20 million
   = The Silver Jubilee Royal Variety Gala (ITV, 4 December 1977): 21.20 million
16. *Bread* (BBC1, 11 December 1988): 20.95 million
17. *The Benny Hill Show* (ITV, 14 March 1979): 20.85 million
18. *Coronation Street* (ITV, 18 December 1980): 20.80 million
19. *Just Good Friends* (BBC1, 21 December 1986): 20.75 million
20. *Sale of the Century* (ITV, 19 November 1977) 20.60 million
   = *Coronation Street* (ITV, 9 January 1985): 20.60 million
   = *Coronation Street* (ITV, 16 January 1985): 20.60 million

(Sky News, 2016)

Note: The figures above exclude all viewing of repeats, **time-shift** or online viewing; they are the total viewers at the time of first **transmission**.

**The most-watched UK TV programmes in 2016 were:**

1. *The Great British Bake Off* (BBC1, 26 October): 15.90 million
2. *The Great British Bake Off* (BBC1, 24 August): 13.58 million
3= *The Great British Bake Off* (BBC1, 5 October): 13.45 million
3= *The Great British Bake Off,* (BBC1, 5 October): 13.45 million
5. *The Great British Bake Off,* (BBC1, 19 October): 13.44 million
6. *The Great British Bake Off,* (BBC1, 14 September): 13.29 million
7. *The Great British Bake Off,* (BBC1, 12 October): 13.26 million
8. *Planet Earth,* (BBC1, 14 September): 13.14 million
9. *The Great British Bake Off,* (BBC1, 28 September): 13.12 million
10. *The Great British Bake Off,* (BBC1, 21 September): 13.12 million
11. *The Great British Bake Off* (BBC1, 7 September): 13.08 million
12. *I'm a Celebrity … Get Me Out of Here!* (ITV, 13 November): 12.66 million
13. *Britain's Got Talent* (ITV, 16 April): 12.46 million
14. *Britain's Got Talent* (ITV, 23 April): 12.32 million
15. *Euro 2016:* Portugal v France (BBC1 19 July): 12.27 million
16. *Planet Earth II* (BBC1, 6 November): 12.26 million
17. *Strictly Come Dancing* (BBC1, 19 November): 11.92 million
18. *I'm a Celebrity … Get Me Out of Here!* (ITV, 4 December): 11.96 million
19. *Strictly Come Dancing* (BBC1, 3 December): 11.92 million
20. *Euro 2016: Wales v Belgium Post-match* (BBC1, 1 July): 11.89 million

Source: Lambert, 2016

### Talk about it

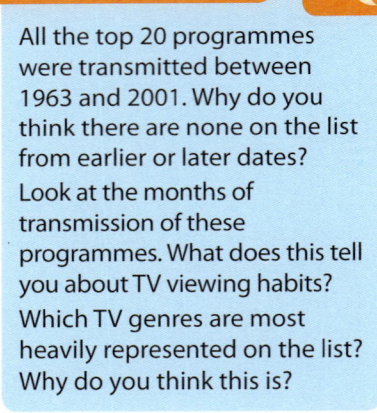

All the top 20 programmes were transmitted between 1963 and 2001. Why do you think there are none on the list from earlier or later dates?

Look at the months of transmission of these programmes. What does this tell you about TV viewing habits?

Which TV genres are most heavily represented on the list? Why do you think this is?

### Key terms

**Time-shifting**
The viewing of a broadcast programme at a time of the viewer's choice rather than at the time of transmission. This may be achieved by home recording, downloading or streaming.

**Transmission**
A broadcast programme on television or radio. A live transmission is broadcast simultaneously with the event actually happening.

## TV genres

You will have noted that all the most viewed programmes of the last 80 plus years come from a narrow range of genres, with sitcoms, light entertainment and soap operas dominating. Looking at the chart for 2016 at the bottom of page 156, once again a small number of genres dominate, but this time it is game shows and talent shows, with a few examples of sport and natural history.

Essentially, television is a genre-driven medium. Television executives commission popular genre programmes because they are easy to market and carry low risks of financial loss. Audiences respond well to the predictability and security of tried and trusted formula television. With game and talent shows (as with sport) we can support our favourites and, in some cases such as *Britain's Got Talent*, participate by voting. This gives a sense of belonging or even ownership because the audience feels a personal investment in the fortunes of the players or competitors. In fictional shows we identify with and invest emotionally in characters.

*Britain's Got Talent*: Alesha Dixon, Simon Cowell and Amanda Holden have all been judges.

## Cultural contexts

Television is a powerful force in communicating and reinforcing **dominant cultural values** but it is equally true that television reflects these values. This can certainly be seen by looking at television products from an earlier era and you will be able to make interesting historical comparisons between the two relevant CSPs.

As already noted, sitcoms and soap operas have been staple TV genres for decades, but watching a sitcom of the 1960s, say, can tell us a great deal about changing cultural attitudes, views and beliefs. For example, the ITV sitcom *Mind Your Language* (1977–1979) was based on the sort of national and ethnic stereotyping that would be rejected by today's audiences. Characters included Danielle, a French woman who flirts constantly, and Anna, a dour German with no sense of humour. Similarly, any early example of *Coronation Street* would be almost certain to include gender role stereotypes that seem strange and unacceptable to today's viewers.

The huge popularity of TV has already been commented on, but this very popularity has been an important factor in contributing to the low value or esteem that is often assigned to television. Television has been criticised as **low brow**, undemanding and trashy, largely because it is enjoyed by a mass audience.

> **Key terms**
>
> **Dominant cultural values**
> The beliefs held by the majority of people in society about, for example, what sort of behaviour is right or wrong, acceptable or unacceptable. These beliefs are so strong that they seem 'just natural', but if they are not constantly reinforced they can break down.
>
> **Low brow**
> Used, often rather insultingly, to describe examples of culture that are simplistic and undemanding. In contrast, anything described as **high brow** is usually an example of culture considered intellectual and demanding.

1970's *Coronation Street* offered familiar gendered stereotypes of the overbearing wife and the lazy husband.

### Activity 5.1

Select an example of a recently made and popular television sitcom. Identify the stereotypes in your chosen programme and compare them with the stereotypes found in 1970's television sitcoms, as described in this chapter.

How has today's cultural context influenced representations of gender, ethnicity, age and social class in your selected programme?

---

Television viewing has even been associated with 'doing nothing' or 'wasting time'. This rather snobbish view of television doesn't really take into account the enormous diversity of modern television programming, with content catering to the needs of very small, specialist audiences as well as to the entertainment needs of mass audiences.

To some extent, television has escaped from the criticism that it is no more than moving wallpaper by production companies investing heavily in complex and gripping dramas. Creative talent has been drawn from film, theatre and literature in order to produce content that has won critical acclaim.

In the same way, factual television, including news and documentary genres, has steadily eroded the cultural dominance of other forms including print newspapers and talk radio.

*The BBC's highly acclaimed literary adaptation of Poldark (2015) starring Aidan Turner.*

## Social contexts of television

In the early days of television, few households could afford more than one television. For those who did have a set it became the focal point of the home. Viewing was a social affair, with family and friends gathered around the television, often accompanied by neighbours who did not have a set of their own.

With few channels available, the emphasis of most programming was on 'family viewing'; the sort of products that would please audiences of all ages. For these reasons, television could be seen as **socially cohesive** because watching it was a shared activity.

Until the 1980s, the small number of channels meant that the most popular programmes drew larger audiences and the content of television therefore became a shared experience for the population. Many daily conversations began with 'Did you see?' and it was essential to keep up with television output in order to participate in these conversations.

Despite the popularity of American imports, home-produced television programmes in family entertainment genres dominated. They often represented a cosy and quaint view of 'middle England' that was increasingly out of date in a diverse and multicultural society. Characters such as Terry and June,

### Talk about it

These are some issues to look at when considering the cultural context of television products:

- What do these products tell us about the cultural values at the time of production?
- Has the critical response to the product been positive or negative?
- Is it seen as 'low brow' or 'high brow'?

Try out this approach on programmes you have seen recently.

### Key term

**Social cohesion**
The tendency for individuals in society to bind together with shared views, beliefs and behaviour.

*Early television viewing was a family affair.*

from the BBC sitcom of that name, seemed increasingly out of touch with the realities of life. Another sitcom, *Til Death Us Do Part*, was based on a character, Alf Garnett, whose bigoted, robust and sexist views were supposed to outrage the audience. Unfortunately, many viewers identified with Garnett rather than laughing at his outspoken prejudices.

It could be argued, then, that television was contributing to **social fragmentation** or division rather than bringing individuals, families and communities together. Combined with technological and social developments in the 21st century, watching television has become a different experience. Multi-channel TV, satellite technology, broadband and time-shift viewing have all contributed to a very different social context for the audience's television experience.

Although television is as popular as ever, few people gather around the home's only set to enjoy a shared experience. They are just as likely to watch television apart from others or on a mobile phone, listening on an earpiece.

These then are questions to ask about television products that you study:

- Do they contribute to social cohesion through a shared identification with the cultural and shared viewing experience?

or

- Does the content and experience of viewing fragment and divide audiences?

> **Key term**
>
> **Social fragmentation**
> The tendency for individuals and groups within society to split apart because they have few values or beliefs or behaviours in common.

# Television: close study products

The 2023 CSPs in this media form are *His Dark Materials*, Series 2, Episode 1: 'The City of Magpies' and *Doctor Who* Episode 1: 'An Unearthly Child'.

## *His Dark Materials* (2020) BBC TV/HBO series
### Episode 1: 'The City of Magpies'

This is an **in-depth CSP**, which will be studied with reference to all four elements of the theoretical framework:

- Media Language
- Media Representations
- Media Audiences
- Media Industries

as well as all relevant contexts.

### Overview

*His Dark Materials* is a series based on the novels of Philip Pullman. The second series was first broadcast on BBC1 in the UK and on HBO in USA in November 2020, and was available at the same time on iPlayer.

The second series consists of seven episodes, with an eighth stand-alone episode about Lord Asriel left unfinished due to the coronavirus pandemic.

The series is centred on Lyra and Will, teenagers from two very different Oxfords, from parallel worlds. They meet in a third parallel world, in the 'city in the sky', called Cittàgazze. The series follows their adventures as they battle against Mrs Coulter and the Magisterium from Lyra's world, and Charles Latrom from Will's.

### AQA GCSE Media Studies

*Lyra and Pan enter Cittàgazze.*

*Witches about to fly to Lyra's aid.*

A plot summary and brief synopsis can be found on the BBC1 website for the series and in Wikipedia.

*His Dark Materials* has received a number of positive reviews (easily found through internet research), especially in comparison with earlier attempts to translate the books to the screen.

Study of the historical, social and cultural contexts of *His Dark Materials* can be sharpened by comparisons with the first-ever episode of *Doctor Who*. There are striking differences in the production values, the technical codes of television, representations of our world and teenagers, and the assumptions made about the respective target audiences.

## Media Language

### 1 Codes and conventions

When studying a television CSP, you will need to concentrate on the **technical codes** of television, for example the type of camera shots and movements that have been used, the lighting, editing and sound.

### 2 Genre and narrative

*His Dark Materials* clearly combines elements of family drama, science fiction and fantasy. It is therefore an example of a hybrid genre, but how are these three genre types demonstrated in 'The City of Magpies'? As an adaptation of a book, *His Dark Materials* obviously has constant references to its 'parent': *The Subtle Knife*. Do you see any other, intertextual, references to other media products?

When you have studied the second television 2023 CSP in this section, the first ever episode of *Doctor Who*, you should be able to make comments about the ways in which television sci-fi/fantasy has developed over the 57 years between the two productions. Can you think of factors that may have influenced the evolution of the genre?

You will need to know something of the story development of the seven-part series as a whole in order to analyse the narrative structure of Episode 1. This doesn't mean that you have to watch all seven parts of *His Dark Materials* but a simple internet search will soon help you to discover the basic elements of the plot.

## Media Representations

There are several interesting areas of focus for your analysis of representation in 'In the City of Magpies'. These include the 21st century, Oxford, age (especially teenage), gender, family relationships and ethnicities.

In addition, several issues are represented, for example the relationships between Will and Lyra, between these two and the children of Cittàgazze, and the changes as teenagers grow up. While Lyra battles with her parents, Will is protective of his mother and searches for his father.

Science fiction is often used to reflect on the moral and ethical issues facing contemporary society. The original author, Philip Pullman, was commenting on the power of organised religion, as well as creating a re-imagining of John Milton's *Paradise Lost* in which original sin is seen as a good thing. Is this evident in the TV series?

---

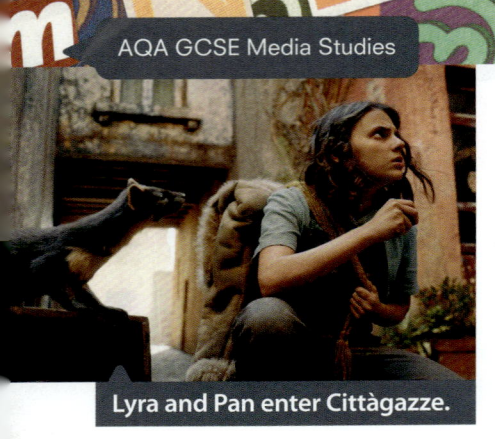

**Activity 5.2**

Analyse the media language codes in a short extract from *His Dark Materials:* 'The City of Magpies' to answer the following questions:

1 What are the connotations of the costumes, props, locations and the performers' voices?
2 How are the fantasy elements of *His Dark Materials* made to seem real to the audience?

---

**Talk about it**

Do you think *His Dark Materials* avoids the use of stereotypes or is stereotyping inevitable in television drama? Are there examples of the audience's expectation of a stereotypical character being used for effect, for example in the character of Lyra's mother?

## Media Audiences

You will need to build up an audience profile for *His Dark Materials* using the information in Chapter 3. BBC1 has a mainstream audience, with Saturday early evening being a traditional 'family' slot, but can you say more about the demographic and psychographic composition of the target audience for this product? Chapter 3 also describes the uses and gratifications approach to the audience. What audience needs are addressed by 'The City of Magpies' and how effectively does this episode meet these needs?

Theories of media effects suggest that audiences are passive and readily influenced by the content of media products. Could any scenes in 'The City of Magpies' have negative effects on a young audience? The series has a BBFC 12 rating. Do you think this age rating is appropriate?

How is the audience **positioned** in relation to the characters and the story presented in 'The City of Magpies'? Are we drawn to sympathise and identify with some characters but not others? Is the audience influenced to interpret the issues raised in a particular way (a preferred reading) or are there possibilities for negotiated or oppositional readings? Could the programme be criticised in any way for prejudicial or biased content? What about your own personal response? Have you been influenced in any way by the **context** of viewing, for example by whether you have watched alone, with a few friends or family members or with your media studies class and teacher?

Other worlds – Cittàgazze

> **Link**
> For more on audience profiling see Chapter 3, page 99–100.

## Media Industries

*His Dark Materials* is a good demonstration of the importance of audience size even to public service broadcasters such as the BBC. The first series was released at a time when Netflix and Amazon Prime were spending lavishly on high-quality drama in order to tempt new subscribers. As a public service broadcaster, the BBC was renowned for quality but could not usually afford the high costs needed to compete outright with these providers. *His Dark Materials* was rumoured to be the BBC's most expensive series to date at the time of launch, with HBO sharing the costs, and guaranteeing an international audience. The first episode of the first series had an audience of 7.2 million in the UK. When broadcast on BBC1 in November 2020, 'The City of Magpies' had an audience of 4.4 million viewers in the UK and 227,000 on HBO.

The third series of *His Dark Materials* was commissioned before the second series was screened, as the young actors couldn't be allowed to age too much between series. The series was created by Bad Wolf, an independent production company founded by two prominent members of the BBC production team involved in the 2005 relaunch of *Doctor Who*. The production company was therefore separate from the BBC but very much known to the organisation.

When the previous CSP, *Class*, was launched online in January 2017, audiences were very willing to use iPlayer, the red button or websites in order to time-shift their viewing of broadcast programmes but they were not yet willing to see the internet as a source for new BBC content.

By the launch of this second series of *His Dark Materials*, in late 2020, viewers were much more familiar with watching wholly new series on Amazon Prime and

Netflix, so the BBC's decision to make the series available on iPlayer at the same time as on broadcast TV was a natural one. The BBC had recognised that it had to respond to shifting patterns and habits of viewing.

By this stage, the BBC had been involved in launching its own (shared) subscription streaming service, BritBox, and was well along the road to 'reinventing' iPlayer to provide a more personalised service.

## *Doctor Who* (1963) BBC TV series

### Episode 1: 'An Unearthly Child'

This is an **in-depth CSP**, which will be studied with reference to all four elements of the theoretical framework:

- Media Language
- Media Representations
- Media Audiences
- Media Industries

as well as all relevant contexts.

### Overview

The first episode of this first four-part serial introduces the four main characters: two teachers at Coal Hill School in East London, a pupil from the same school (the 'unearthly child' of the title) and the Doctor himself. These four became the main cast members for the first year of *Doctor Who*. It is soon revealed that the school pupil, Susan, is strangely different from her peers.

The teachers, Ian and Barbara, investigate Susan's background by visiting her home address, where they meet Susan's grandfather (the Doctor) and discover the secret of the TARDIS. The TARDIS (Time And Relative Dimension In Space), we learn, is a machine for travelling in time and space disguised as a police box. In 1963 the police box was a common sight on British streets. Long after real police boxes disappeared from the streets, the exterior form of Doctor Who's TARDIS has made the blue box famous all over the world, if not the galaxy.

At the end of the first episode the door of the TARDIS opens onto a strange environment. In the second episode we discover that the four travellers have been transported back to Palaeolithic times (the story was originally called '100,000 Years BC'). As a public service broadcaster the BBC has always had a remit to educate and inform as well as to entertain.

The original *Doctor Who* was firmly committed to this ethos, with an emphasis on science and technology in one story, followed by an emphasis on history in the next. *Doctor Who*'s stories also communicated a strong sense of moral order. The Doctor himself always protected human life and safety, particularly when the weak and oppressed were threatened by powerful adversaries.

The first *Doctor Who* serial was only a modest success, although the audience grew steadily from 4.4 million at first to 6.4 million for Episode 4. The second serial saw a huge jump in the size of the audience due to the popularity of a newly introduced race of alien baddies known as Daleks. 'The Dalek Invasion of Earth' (November/December 1964) was viewed by a peak audience of 12.4 million.

A Dalek

## Media Language

### 1 Codes and conventions

Points to consider: what selection of shots is used and how do these create meanings? Describe the camera movements. Are there any zooms, pans, tilts or tracking shots? 'An Unearthly Child' was recorded 'live to video tape'. What does this mean and how does this differ from the techniques to record modern dramas such as *His Dark Materials*? How is the product constrained by the technology of the time – size of cameras, colour, sound recording?

What about performance codes? What can you say about the actors' movements, their non-verbal communication and the sound of their voices? How effective are costumes and props? 'An Unearthly Child' is a studio-based production. Why are outside locations not used? Compare this with the use of locations in *His Dark Materials*.

### 2 Genre and narrative

'An Unearthly Child' is clearly an example of science fiction but this is not immediately obvious in the early scenes. How is the genre established in the minds of the audience? How is this product distinctly different as a 1963 sci-fi drama rather than a modern drama?

As an opening episode for a four-part story and as the first of a brand-new series, 'An Unearthly Child' has to perform particular narrative functions. What are they and how effectively are they accomplished? Can you find examples of equilibrium, disruption, complications or enigmas here?

## Media Representations

As with *His Dark Materials*, your analysis of representations in 'An Unearthly Child' should focus on gender, ethnicities, education, London's East End and age. Don't forget that this analysis should include any significant **absences** from the product as well as what can be seen on the screen. Relationships are not featured to the same extent as they are in 'The City of Magpies' but there are still interesting points to be made about the relationship that Susan has with her peers, her teachers and her grandfather (the Doctor). It is useful to know something of the cultural background of the period in order to understand the representations of science and technology in this first ever episode of *Doctor Who*.

In 1963 both **the Cold War** and the Space Race were tremendously significant. The USA and the Soviet Union built up huge arsenals of nuclear weapons, capable of destroying the world many times over. People were very afraid that 'World War III', a nuclear war to end all wars, could break out at any time.

The two sides in the Cold War also competed to demonstrate the superiority of their science and technology as well as the power of their weapons. The most significant example of this competition was the race to 'conquer space'. The Russians were certainly in the lead in this Space Race in the early 1960s. They were first to launch a satellite, first to send a rocket to the moon and first to orbit the Earth with a manned spacecraft. It wasn't until the mid 1960s that the advantage began to swing towards the Americans, culminating with the first humans to land on the moon (the Apollo 11 mission of July 1969).

> **Key term**
>
> **The Cold War**
> The name for the stand-off between the world's two superpowers, the USA and the Soviet Union, from the end of World War II in 1945 until the collapse of Communism in 1989.

The public were fascinated and obsessed by the Cold War and the Space Race, and it is unsurprising that science fiction films, books, comics and television programmes dealt extensively with both. *Doctor Who* was certainly no exception. The messages and values represented in early *Doctor Who* programmes reflected the public's fears and preoccupations with these events and, perhaps, the relatively insignificant role played by the UK in both.

## Media Audiences

As with *His Dark Materials*, the original *Doctor Who* was targeted at a family audience, although it was (and remains) an audience that includes children rather than the teenage offspring in the target audience of *His Dark Materials*. In order to cater to this family audience, *Doctor Who* is careful to avoid the scary, aggressive or sexual material that can be seen in newer dramas such as *His Dark Materials*.

It is difficult to analyse the needs and pleasures of an audience of a television programme that is over 50 years old, but it is still worth trying to apply uses and gratifications categories to 'An Unearthly Child'. Do you think that audience needs are much different today? Are there any pleasures for you in watching a black and white television programme that is dialogue rather than action driven?

Your analysis of representations in 'An Unearthly Child' should also lead you to think about the ways in which the audience is positioned.

For example, the character of the Doctor is that of a rather eccentric, grumpy but ferociously clever elderly man. He is a patriarchal figure who, despite being an alien with two hearts, embodies many of the values and beliefs that were seen at the time to be the essence of 'Englishness'. What were these patriarchal and English values and beliefs and how does the product position the audience to accept these views? Do you find the programme to be biased or prejudicial in any way?

## Media Industries

In 1963 there were just two TV channels, the BBC and ITV, and, of course, no opportunities for recording or time-shifting or pausing broadcast programmes. The only other place to watch moving images of any sort was the cinema.

The decision to develop a new science fiction series was not taken lightly as there had been very few experiments with the genre prior to 1963. However, the newly appointed head of drama, Sydney Newman, was a sci-fi enthusiast who had enjoyed some success with *Pathfinders in Space* in his former job with Independent Television. The commissioning of a new programme in 1963 was based to a large extent on the enthusiasm and ability of a few individuals to persuade others. Today, commissioning is a much more complex process. See the Commissioning page on bbc.co.uk for some idea of just what is involved and how many people contribute to commissioning decisions.

As a public service broadcaster, the BBC was funded by the television and radio licences and was (and still is) regulated by the state, although not directly government controlled. However, the BBC was very strongly motivated to compete with ITV and this was certainly a factor in launching any new programme.

**5** Close study products and media forms

The impact of technology on the product is very clearly influenced by the context of the time.

Videotape was a recent innovation in 1963 but cameras were still large and unwieldy, and any location shooting was expensive. Very unusually, the BBC decided on making a second attempt at shooting and recording the first episode of *Doctor Who* because of technical problems and mistakes made the first time.

The music is one of the first examples of electronic music used as a TV programme's signature tune. It has remained recognisably the same throughout the many series of *Doctor Who*. Why do you think this music has been such a successful component of the series?

Early TV cameras

# Studying online, social and participatory media and video games

Computer, video game, social and participatory media and apps are different from other types of media because they are interactive and **immersive**. Users interact with the game, or online experience, in a way that traditional media audiences (such as TV viewers or newspaper readers) do not. Social media users can comment on what they see, share media products or chat with other users.

## The media mix

The influence of the media industry on video games was discussed earlier in the book, where it was seen that the games industry is important to the global economy, and its growth shows no sign of stopping as new technologies enable different and exciting ways to play games.

It is important to look into the ways online, social and participatory media and video games converge, for instance looking at the close relationship between video games and social media. Playing games used to be one of the few forms of interactive media, but now everyone can express opinions online and upload their own media products – such as videos, memes, podcasts and indie games. This offers a huge commercial opportunity to companies that can capitalise on this trend.

For example, many mobile games encourage players to share scores and progress with their friends, sometimes allowing them to play against each other. This can make play more immersive because it increases the sense of competition and shared experience. Similarly, games consoles and PCs allow gamers to talk to each other, either through text on screen or by speaking through headsets.

Social media has also brought gaming into the mainstream, offering wider choices, so that it is no longer seen as 'geeky' or 'only for teenage boys'. Women aged 18 and older represent a significantly greater portion (31%) of the game-playing population than boys under 18 (18%) (ESA, 2017b).

> **Key term**
>
> **Immersive**
> An experience that completely draws in the audience or user by enabling them to interact with the product.

> **Link**
>
> For a detailed discussion on the influence of the media industry on video games see Chapter 4, pages 145–152.

## Interaction versus convention

Different examples of the interactive audience were seen earlier in the book, including wikis, live streaming and crowd sourcing. Viewers and users aren't passively receiving the media's message but are helping to shape it. Let's look at some of the ways we can interact with digital media.

By triggering events within the game, players have the illusion of control over the game's world. As you have already seen, social media platforms such as Facebook, Twitter, Instagram and Snapchat enable messages, including advertising messages, to be distributed to subscribers or followers. In the case of adverts, users of the social media channels simply need to click to access the website of the advertiser. Online video gaming also involves some interactivity between players, as well as between a player and the game. Online audiences can become producers themselves using, for example, YouTube, wikis, tagging and blogs.

Digital media is certainly interactive but it still contains some of the codes and conventions you have studied for more traditional media. The same kinds of representations can also be seen. For example, gaming worlds are similar to those in movies and TV shows, using the same mise-en-scène within the same genres. Some games have such high-quality graphics that playing can feel as if you are making, and possibly starring in, your own film.

A standard adventure game fulfils Propp's narrative theory. These types of games involve quests in which a hero sets off on a mission to retrieve something of value or to solve a mystery, overcoming obstacles and difficulties to achieve their ultimate goal. The hero will encounter a variety of character types along the way (such as the dispatcher, false hero, villain, donor and father figure).

A YouTube vlog that is created by a frequent vlogger also has a narrative structure, which regular viewers come to expect.

---

**Quick question 5.4**

What are the benefits to the games developers of linking mobile games to social media?

**Link**

See more about different examples of the interactive audience in Chapter 3, page 109.

**Activity 5.3**

Think of an adventure game you have played, and work out which characters within the game represent the narrative character-types noted by Propp. Even the puzzle game Candy Crush has a narrative. Thinking of this, or another puzzle game that you know, try to work out some of the ways in which it fulfils Propp's narrative theory.

**Link**

For more on Propps' narrative theory see Chapter 1, pages 30–31.

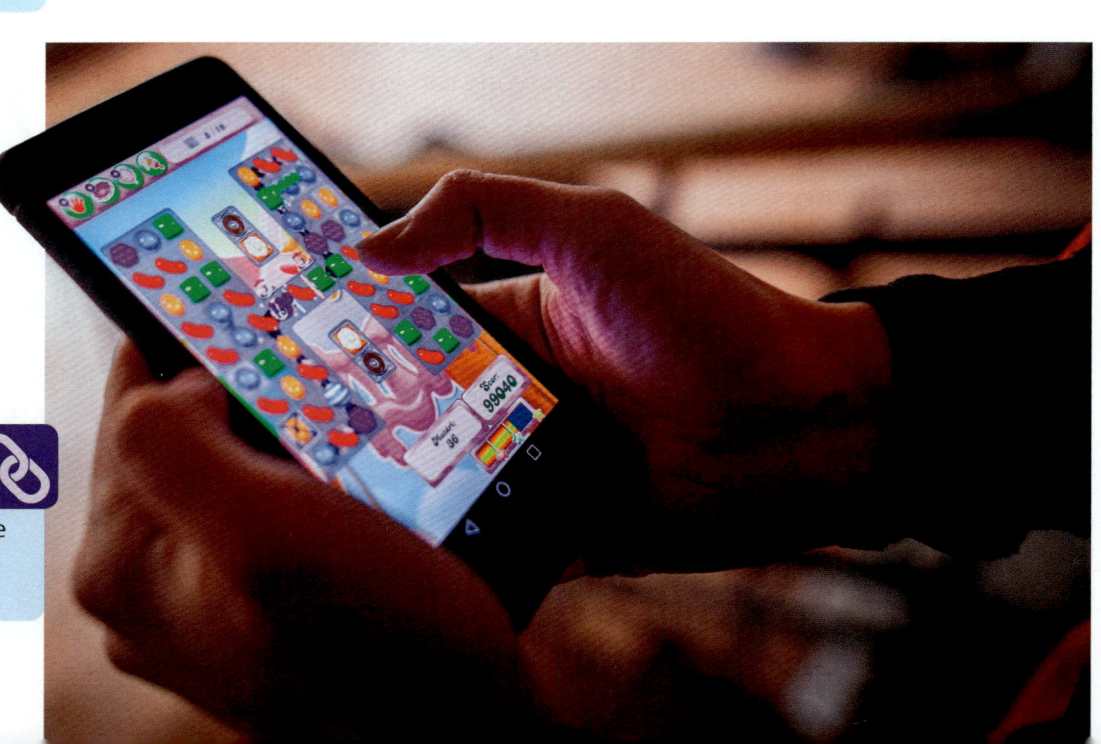

# Key developments

Recent developments in game technologies have had, or could have, an interesting impact on the representations within the games. Following are some examples.

## Augmented and virtual reality

Superimposing computer-generated sound, video, graphics or GPS data onto a real-world environment blurs the boundaries between 'real' and 'game'.

## Social interaction

Some games have in-built social and multiplayer features, making them a shared cultural experience. Players can also discuss and extend their game-playing experience in forums and social media.

## Players as developers

In some games, such as Roblox, players can construct their own games or levels (designing their own representations) and some Kickstarter projects enable players to help create video games, taking control over some of the representations.

## Players as viewers

Game video content (GVC) is incredibly popular as an entertainment genre in its own right and is an example of technological convergence. Gameplaying can now be easily recorded and shared via channels such as Twitch and YouTube Gaming. These videos are watched by others, removing the interactive element and ability to control the game, and putting the active gameplaying participants at the centre of the experience. Vloggers such as DanTDM have harnessed this popularity to gain millions of followers – and millions of pounds.

## Embedded advertising

Mobile apps and franchised games can include advertising content within the world of the game – posters, shop fronts, fliers and so on. This provides more opportunity for audiences to be exposed to representations of big brands, encouraging players to see them as desirable.

## Realistic graphics

Graphics that closely resemble the quality of films add to players' sense of the game's 'reality', increasing their engagement and immersion in the world of the game.

## Changing identities

Players can often choose to create an avatar that looks completely different from their 'real' appearance.

## Issues to consider

Online, social and participatory media and video games offer many benefits to those who use them. Here are some examples:

- They increase the opportunities for social interaction, even when people are on their own.
- They enable people to share interests and experiences with like-minded people.
- They offer information, opinions and opportunities that would not otherwise be available – for example, interaction with people of another culture or religion.
- They are simply fun, offering a satisfying form of entertainment.

However, these media can also raise issues. Here are some examples:

- They can reinforce negative stereotypes, especially those around women and ethnic minorities.
- Children may access inappropriate content.
- People's privacy is eroded, as websites and games collect data about users.
- Making online interaction easier can make it simpler to share damaging views, such as encouraging eating disorders.
- Players can easily become addicted to playing games, which not only erodes their time but can also lead to them spending more money than they can afford, on in-app purchases for example.

## Online, social and participatory media and video games: close study products

The CSPs in these media forms for 2023 are Marcus Rashford, Kim Kardashian: Hollywood and Lara Croft GO. These are in-depth CSPs, which will be studied with reference to all four elements of the theoretical framework:

- Media Language
- Media Representations
- Media Audiences
- Media Industries

as well as all relevant contexts.

## Online, social and participatory media: Marcus Rashford

### Overview

As of August 2021, British footballer and campaigner Marcus Rashford had gained 4.9 million followers on Twitter, 11.6 million on Instagram and 8.7 million on Facebook. He also has his own website, marcusrashfordofficial.com.

The main focus of each of his social media platforms appears to be different although some posts are seen on all three. The Twitter feed tends to concentrate more on his social campaigning, and retweets of those involved in similar activities. His Facebook posts are more likely to be about his life in football, while his Instagram feed focuses more on his lifestyle and emotions. Not surprisingly, his book appeared on all three channels.

## Media Language

The emphasis in most social media influencers' feeds is on sharing something real and authentic from the influencer's life, no matter whether it is something ordinary, adventurous, silly, emotional or useful. Influencers use a range of techniques to achieve this authenticity, starting with the basic notion of talking directly to the camera – and therefore the viewer – in video, and writing directly to the reader in text-based posts. Most people in films and television programmes do not address the camera – those who do include news presenters and gameshow hosts. Similarly, it is 'opinion' writers in newspapers and magazines who are allowed to write in the first person directly to the audience. This direct mode of address suggests they are in control of the programmes and articles they present and are an authoritative source of information.

Think about the codes and conventions that Marcus Rashford uses in each part of his output. For example, you could consider the style and content of the photographs and videos on his website, and the relative lack of text-based information, the vocabulary used in his social media posts, and the images and videos used to illustrate these.

One aspect of editing used in social media videos, such as those on Instagram or TikTok, but rarely seen in fiction-based moving image forms, is the jump-cut. This is an edit between two shots taken from the same or a very similar angle – it could, for example, be created by simply removing a few seconds from the middle of a longer shot. Jump-cuts tend to alert the viewer to the fact that some time has been missed out from a longer action, and therefore point out that this is only a filmed version of an event, not the event itself. Jump-cuts are used within documentaries, as these are often filmed using just one or two cameras.

You also need to think about how social media influencers such as Marcus Rashford construct a narrative. Although he is not creating vlog-style videos, he is nonetheless getting his message across clearly in his social media feed. By talking directly to his followers as if they are friends, he draws in his audience, whether they are new-comers or have been following for a long time. They all feel part of this community.

Each post tells a story of some sort. An example is the 'transformation' of children as they read his book.

## Media Representations

Remind yourself of the discussion of Marcus Rashford's self and think about wider representations beyond Rashford himself, such as the people he can be seen with, the products and campaigns he endorses and the settings he inhabits.

For example, he is (as of 2021) sponsored by Nike and has a commercial deal with Burberry. He is also involved with Macmillan publishers. He has spoken about

### Activity 5.4

By analysing the use of media language, consider how Marcus Rashford achieves a sense of authenticity in his Instagram videos and/or his website videos. Think about:
- probable budget
- probable crew involved
- the use of the camera and editing
- vocabulary and mode of address
- settings
- technology
- props.

### Quick question 5.5

How does a jump-cut add a sense of realism to a vlog?

### Quick question 5.6

How does the narrative contain an enigma? Who or what correspond to Propp's character types here?

### Link

See the discussion of Marcus Rashford's self-representation in Chapter 2, pages 65–67.

how the Burberry and Macmillan deals help to further his campaigns off the pitch, and it is clear that such deals extend the scope of his influence on his audience well beyond football. Contrast his praise of book-reading with Kim Kardashian's endorsement of luxury designer brands. Rashford is aspirational in a different way, showing that it's possible to succeed whatever your background – but sometimes you need help to do that.

In his Twitter feed, Rashford replies to those who tweet him as if he knows them personally, and as if they know him. He also includes his team mates, football friends and his mother in his Facebook posts, as anyone would when talking to their own social circle. This implied accessibility is a similar idea to that of the celebrities created by TV talent shows (One Direction or Little Mix, for example). It is enhanced by the apparent ease of communicating with celebrities such as Marcus Rashford via social media. His Facebook, Twitter and Instagram links are all displayed on his website.

## Media Audiences

If followers and views are a measure of success, Marcus Rashford is certainly popular with his audience. It is difficult to make assumptions about the demographics of his audience – the content of each separate aspect of his online profile is likely to appeal to different groups and, as a star footballer, he has a very wide potential audience. Although his campaigns have caused changes in policy at government level, he often manages to make them seem 'common sense' rather than 'political', so does not push away those who might not agree with him if he campaigned on party political lines. The fact that he has campaigned successfully on issues that many agree with has undoubtedly brought a newer audience to his online products.

It is useful to look at social media in general, and Marcus Rashford's output in particular, in terms of the uses and gratifications theory. As seen in Chapter 3, audiences are drawn to media to fulfil a variety of needs, and social media can fulfil these needs.

- **Information and education**: Rashford provides content that is interesting and helpful to his target audience, for example exercise videos, interviews and information about how to provide food and entertainment for children during the school holidays.

- **Identification with characters and situations**: Rashford is honest and open about personal matters, such as how he feels after public failures, racist abuse, or receiving positive messages of support. He presents himself very much as a 'real' and 'ordinary' person with dignity as well as emotion. His sometimes frank discussions about his feelings and about his background can provide a sense of hope and support for less confident viewers.

- **Relaxation and escapism**: Rashford's posts, particularly those on Instagram, can simply be entertaining and a distraction from the stresses of everyday life. They don't involve a high level of concentration – for example, viewers can just engage with the banter between team mates.

Marcus Rashford selects from a range of representations, as shown on these images from his official Twitter feed.

Marcus Rashford presents aspirations for all.

Rashford's official Twitter feed is both informative and entertaining.

**Link**

See the discussion of Marcus Rashford's self-representation in Chapter 2, pages 65–67.

- **Social interaction**: Rashford is always smiling and relaxed, usually looks straight into the camera, or writes straight to the reader, as if he is talking to the follower personally. He will often comment on a particular subject because a fan has raised this in a tweet. The ability to comment on his posts, and to discuss them both with Rashford and with his other followers, reinforces this sense of relationship.

Think about the audience as an active consumer of social media, rather than a more passive consumer of more traditional media. Interacting can be as important as watching/reading. Followers of all ages can feel as if they are involved and can help shape Rashford's output. Remember, however, that 'by popular demand' is not a new concept – it's just that this demand can now be met more quickly.

## Media Industries

Many influencers on Instagram are paid for posts that endorse specific products, earning approximately $10 per 1,000 followers for each post. Rashford, however, has larger sponsorship contracts and is unlikely to be paid per post.

Advertising his own campaigns and products, however, is an important element of his online profile. Rashford's co-written book, You Are A Champion, topped the children's bestseller charts for four weeks, and was eventually boosted to the top of the overall book sales charts following the racist abuse he received after the Euro 2020 final. Images of children reading the book for inspiration filled his Twitter feed for several days, and he featured the book launch on each of his social media platforms.

When studying your CSPs, research how convergence and synergy between different types of industry and media make being a social media influencer economically worthwhile for some creators.

## Historical, social and cultural contexts

With most people now owning computers, mobile phones and/or tablets connected to WiFi, videos to be posted online are cheaper and easier to make, broadcast and watch than TV shows or movies. This, added to the natural appeal of getting a glimpse into other people's lives, has led to their proliferation over the last ten years.

Because there is a sense that anyone can be a social media influencer even if, in reality, it takes a lot of hard work and technical skill, many young people consider 'influencing' (or being a 'YouTuber') as a viable career. Indeed, a minority of influencers and YouTube stars have made a very successful career from their online presence. Like DanTDM, they tend to be young, attractive and engaging.

It's also worth thinking about whether some of those social media influencers would have become famous in another medium. In the case of the CSP, Marcus Rashford was already famous, but he would not have the time to engage as much with traditional media as he does with online media while being an elite sportsman. How dependent on social media is he for the success of his various campaigns? What might happen to his celebrity status or to his campaigning if his posts were no longer easily accessible?

> **Quick question 5.7**
> How do vlogs and blogs such as Marcus Rashford's reflect the viewpoints and beliefs of the target audience? How does this attract and keep viewers?

Rashford engages directly with his audience, as on his official Facebook page.

> **Link**
> For more on convergence see Chapter 4, page 109, and synergy see Chapter 1, pages 45–46.

> **Quick question 5.8**
> Do you have a favourite vlogger? If you do, why do you return to their channel to watch their new vlogs?

# Video game: Kim Kardashian: Hollywood (2014)

## Overview

The goal of this freemium mobile-platform game is to work your way up through Hollywood society to top the celebrity A-list. You can increase your fame and reputation by hanging out with other celebrities, appearing at the right events, working as a model and actor, getting media and social media coverage, and buying houses, cars and designer accessories. It's all virtual, of course, but contains elements of real celebrity life, including frequent appearances by Hollywood socialite Kim Kardashian herself. Although the game is free to play, players are encouraged to spend real money on in-game currency, and there are in-game adverts for real products.

If you've not already done so, play the game, or watch a gameplay video, such as 'Let's Play Kim Kardashian: Hollywood' on YouTube.

## Media Language

This is an interesting game to analyse using semiotics. Its signs and signifiers are based on a shared understanding of what we consider celebrity culture to be like. The game takes players through specific locations that offer opportunities to become rich and famous. Players earn and find Kash and silver Kstars, which can be exchanged for desirable items that contribute to the avatar's success. Your avatar's measure – or signifier – of success is the number of followers they have on social media.

There's a lot of emphasis on non-verbal codes, such as makeup, clothes and hairstyles. In this game world, keeping up appearances is more important than anything else. It is much easier for players to move up the celebrity ranks when they have more outfits, more homes and more friends. The game itself is intended to be visually engaging, using uncluttered but lovingly detailed, pastel graphics. You can customise your own avatar to suit your preferences, but (of course) all the characters are physically attractive.

The narrative is scripted and controlled – there is little choice in terms of actions, other than selecting the perceived 'correct' response in a conversation, and the order in which tasks are completed. You know that, if you play for long enough and regularly enough, you will progress through the levels of celebrity to reach A-status.

Think about the types of the characters you encounter in the game. What are their jobs? What is their function? Everyone in the game can help – or hinder – your progress to the A-list. It's just as important to think about the types of character you don't meet – your avatar's parents, for example, or, indeed, anyone who is not connected with Hollywood celebrity.

Think about where Kim Kardashian fits into Propp's character types in this game. Is she the hero, helper, donor or dispatcher – or all of them? Who, or what, is the princess?

---

**Talk about it**

Vloggers focus on their own lifestyles and personalities, clearly believing that what they say and do is interesting to others. Consider the social and cultural significance of this attitude. Would it be accurate and fair to say that such self-confidence is a trait of the demographic group millennials? Do you think it's true of your own generation?

**Link**

For more on semiotics see Chapter 1, pages 18–19.

## Media Representations

Kim Kardashian is said to have had a creative input into every part of the game, giving her the opportunity to carefully control her representation.
The game blurs the boundaries between the 'real' Kim Kardashian and her fictional persona. In this game, she casts herself as the ultimate mistress of celebrity – her unique set of skills got her where she is, and now she is kindly sharing tips for the top with others. Whether or not she is such a fairy godmother in real life isn't relevant, but players may believe this is an accurate depiction of her personality. She can reinforce this impression on her (real) social media accounts and in public appearances. She has been quoted as saying that social media is vital for building her brand and that it requires her to 'be authentic' (Fisher, 2017). As a reality TV star who posts photos of her everyday life and family, it can be difficult to define what her interpretation of 'authentic' might be.

This CSP offers ample opportunity to consider stereotypes. Think about its representations of age, celebrities and gender. For example, the vast majority of characters are slim, young, fit and conventionally attractive. The success of either gender depends on how they dress and how positively their photoshoots or public appearances are received.

Also consider how celebrity is represented. There's no question in the game that such a status is the pinnacle of achievement. This could be seen as selfish and materialistic – celebrity is only attained by beating others and going shopping. You are constantly prompted to change your look and buy mansions. Even getting married or visiting the adoption centre becomes an opportunity to gain more followers and money. Your avatar's original job in a clothing store isn't seen as a career – it's just a way to survive until you become famous.

Although the start of your avatar's celebrity career is due to a lucky break (meeting Kim), the game implies that if you work hard enough at appearing in the right places, you'll make it to the top. It's all about who you know and how you can get them to help you. It doesn't take into account the issues you might encounter in real life, such as poverty, prejudice and a lack of opportunity. However, it is a constant grind. Avatars rush across the world from one job to the next, never stopping to rest or sleep (the furniture is just for show). It doesn't seem to be a particularly fulfilling life.

Make sure you think about how audiences may receive this message. How might the game encourage players to aspire to a particular lifestyle or physical appearance? Does it undermine other measures of career and personal success?

### Talk about it

Are there any types of social groups not represented? Why do you think this is?

## Media Audiences

### Gender

In Chapter 4, you saw how the demographics of gameplayers have shifted away from the dominance of male players to a more even split between males and females. One of the reasons for this could be the wider variety of genres now available. The accessibility of games online and the ease of downloading and using games on mobile phones has made them more available to everyone. By 2020, 87% of all adults in the UK, and 100% of 16–24 year olds, owned or had access to a smartphone (Strugar, 2021). This rise in the potential market for mobile games has led to games developers creating games for different target audiences.

Take some time to look at how and where Kim Kardashian: Hollywood is marketed. For example, you could read the description and look at the images of Kim Kardashian: Hollywood on Google Play or iTunes. This might help you to make some assumptions about the intended audience.

### Benefits, uses and gratifications

As with Marcus Rashfod, the uses and gratifications model can help explain the game's appeal. Kim Kardashian herself has testified to its escapist nature:

> *People always want to get their mind off of things and have something fun to do because their lives are so hectic. It's a fun game that you can really get addicted to and just lose yourself in for a couple of hours.* (Weisman, 2015)

There's a vicarious pleasure in creating a beautiful, well-dressed version of yourself, who travels by private jet to mingle with celebrities in various glamorous locations and doesn't have everyday problems such as paying bills or catching a cold.

At first glance, it seems to require very little skill, in contrast to other popular mobile games such as Candy Crush, which at least requires players to solve a puzzle. However, prolonged play and experience reveal some strategies that lead to optimum success, giving players a sense of satisfaction that they are winning the celebrity race.

Another source of pleasure is the self-referential humour of the game. For example, characters often comment on how much time they waste playing 'fashion games' on their phones, which aligns them with the players. Numerous eccentric (and some unpleasant) characters are clearly based on real celebrities, and there is fun to be had in making these links, and wondering what the real people think of these portrayals.

### The interactive audience

The game employs behaviour-shaping strategies to try to persuade players to spend money on the game. Once players have repeatedly experienced the positive reinforcement of being rewarded for completing tasks (by rising through the celebrity ranks in the game), they become more invested in their own success. After all, nobody wants to feel as if the hours they have spent playing (and watching ads) were wasted. Returning day after day soon becomes part of the players' daily habits, increasing the chances of them being willing to pay to progress further. Mobile games are particularly easy to play because they can fill 'dead time', for example while waiting for a friend or travelling on a bus.

> **Link**
> For more about the demographics of gameplayers see Chapter 4, page 149.

The game gives players a certain amount of free playing time and items, but they have to earn – or buy – more if they want to keep on playing. Otherwise players have to wait for their energy to refill.

Chapter 3 looked at reception theory. Kim Kardashian: Hollywood offers many opportunities for oppositional readings. For example, at the start, Kim Kardashian only offers to help you after you give her some free clothes, and it seems that you have to (metaphorically) scrabble on the floor to collect your money and star ratings. How many other oppositional readings can you identify?

## Media Industries

### Kim Kardashian: Hollywood commercial success

Kim Kardashian is an industry all by herself. To many, she is the definition of 'famous for being famous', but this is what her game is all about – becoming rich and famous just by being yourself.

Kim Kardashian: Hollywood has been phenomenally successful by any measure, reportedly earning $1.6 million within five days of release on 27 June 2014. It had been downloaded 45 million times by mid-2016 and has now generated about $200 million of income (as of 2018), despite only about 5% of players actually paying for the premium add-ons, such as extra K-stars or a monthly 'VIP' membership subscription. Other revenue is generated from:

- advertising, such as the 30-second ads, mainly for other apps, that players can watch to gain 'energy' or 'K stars', which are necessary to progress
- sponsorship deals, such as with NARS cosmetics, which includes links to sites where users can buy the real products.

Even four years after its release:

- Its daily revenue was estimated at about $50,000.
- It was downloaded about 12,000 times a day.
- It was still the 60th top-grossing mobile game.

(Think Gaming, 2018)

### Gaming as branding

As already seen in Chapter 2, Kim Kardashian: Hollywood and Kim's online presence converge to create a particular representation – a brand. The game is really an extension of this brand, an advertisement for Kim as a product. Look at Kim Kardashian's Twitter feed and her website: kimkardashianwest.com – think about how she, and other celebrities, use social media and other online technologies to improve and control their public profile. The fact that they often receive sponsorship money for endorsing products on their feeds is also significant.

It has already been discussed how Kim sees social media as an extension of her brand, a clear distinction from her 'real' self. Events on her Twitter and Instagram feeds become news in themselves – who she has followed or unfollowed or argued with on social media is reported daily. Notably, however, she gave up social media for a while after being robbed at knifepoint in a hotel room, her frequent updates being blamed by some for risking her security and flaunting her wealth. On returning to social media, she changed her brand focus from oversharing her flashy lifestyle to family- and friend-orientated content, more filtered and edited than before, putting a greater distance between her and her audience.

### Activity 5.5

Find a definition of 'addictive'. Do you think it is fair to say that games such as Kim Kardashian: Hollywood can be psychologically addictive?

### Link

See pages 100–102 to remind yourself about the reception theory.

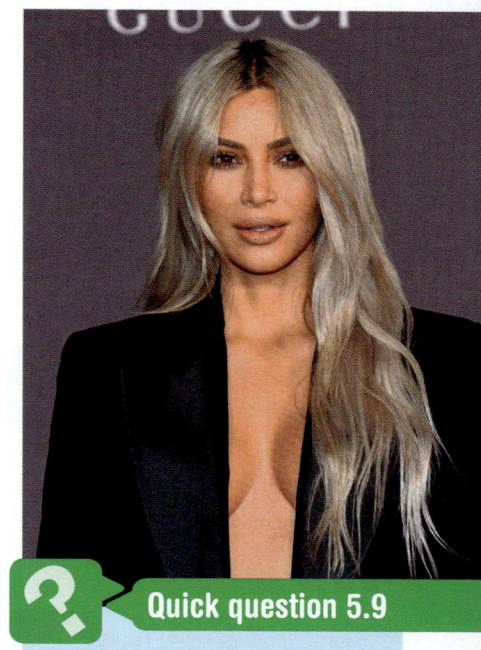

### Quick question 5.9

What does the commercial success of Kim Kardashian: Hollywood tell us about the ways in which the video game industry is changing?

Kim Kardashian's fan base is seen as being upmarket and aspirational, while they – key to developing the game – know about and enjoy using technology. The celebrity promotes the game on her own social media feeds, which has maybe brought in people who wouldn't normally have played video games.

## Historical, social and cultural contexts

Kim Kardashian: Hollywood has cultural significance in this early part of the 21st century, as it epitomises society's current interest in fame and celebrity.

The game's developers, Glu, approached Kim Kardashian with the idea for the role-playing game. Her main involvement has been to approve aspects of her character, the outfits, features, storylines and events.

Compare the emergence of Kim Kardashian as a cultural phenomenon with the impact and influence of Marcus Rashford and Lara Croft. Kim Kardashian first rose to public prominence in 2007, with Marcus Rashfod setting up his Twitter account in 2016. Lara Croft predated both, appearing in her first game in 1996. All three invite comparisons in terms of their cultural influences on gender identity and power. All three are often represented using cultural signifiers of gender and sexuality, whether this is in terms of body shape, makeup and clothing, actions, or all three. Each of the three also has obvious power in some form – physical, business and/or cultural power. Yet they are very different from each other and could therefore attract different audiences.

## Video game: Lara Croft GO (2015)

### Overview

Lara Croft GO is a puzzle-based role-playing game that is part of the Tomb Raider video games franchise. Players control the character Lara Croft as she moves, like a puzzle piece, through the game world. The game is available on a range of platforms, including mobile and console. Either play the game or watch a gameplay video such as 'Lara Croft GO – Gameplay Walkthrough Part 1 – Mobile', on YouTube.

### Media Language

As with Kim Kardashian: Hollywood, you will find it useful to analyse the semiotics of this game. Even though it is basically a puzzle game, there are also elements of narrative. Think about how it uses signs and codes to create a narrative you can understand. Who, and what, are the heroes and villains?

The game crosses several genres – for example, it is a turn-based puzzle game but could also be regarded as a role-playing or action-adventure game. Think about how using and combining these genres draws the player into the immersive gameplay.

Lara Croft GO has been praised for its attractive visual appearance and strong soundtrack. It is also unusual in not employing a tutorial to help players learn how to play. The interface is structured clearly enough for players to learn as they go along, without the storytelling being interrupted. Think about what this attention to detail signifies to the audience.

---

**Quick question 5.10**

How do the three 2023 online, social and participatory media CSPs reflect the nature of participatory audiences and the link between celebrities and their followers?

**Activity 5.6**

Research some other examples of personality-based mobile games. How are the developers using celebrities' social media followers to generate a market? Why do you think such games are popular?

**Quick question 5.11**

Identify the narrative devices used in Lara Croft GO, such as character, setting, conflicts and resolutions.

**Activity 5.7**

Find out about the board game Go. In what ways is it similar to Lara Croft GO? What other elements of intertextuality can you identify in this video game?

## Media Representations

The representation of gender was looked at in detail in Chapter 2. As you saw, gender is a very important issue to consider in relation to this game. Even if you've never played a Tomb Raider game, it's likely you've heard of Lara Croft. She was the first female protagonist in a major role-playing video game, Tomb Raider (1996). Some view her as a strong, proactive female, while others see her as a sexual object, with her skimpy clothes and large breasts, designed to attract the male gaze and therefore male players. Still others argue that Lara Croft has had to adopt elements of stereotypical male identity, such as independence and aggression, in order to take a heroic role. It could be argued that all these representations are valid.

Do the potential negative associations undermine the quality of the game? Observe Lara Croft's appearance and behaviour in the game and decide, in terms of gender representation, whether she is an exception, or an example of a wider problem, in the video game industry.

Moving away from, but still related to, gender, we should consider how the visual representation of Lara Croft has changed over the years. Look at the images on the right. Take into account the wider social and cultural context when considering why these changes were made. Remember that Lara Croft's success goes beyond video games to take on many media forms and platforms, including big budget Hollywood films, comic books and novels. What has stayed constant? Why?

## Media Audiences

### Target audience
As with Kim Kardashian: Hollywood, take some time to look at how and where Lara Croft GO is marketed. For example, you could read the description and reviews of Lara Croft GO on Google Play or iTunes. This might help you to make some assumptions about the intended audience.

### Benefits, uses and gratifications
According to Google Play, 82% of reviews give Lara Croft GO a five-star rating. Reviews describe the game as challenging, addictive, interesting, beautiful, fun and well designed. Players especially like the ability to unlock new levels, bonuses and collectable items.

Players have to solve puzzles to find artefacts and to unlock the route through the world of the game. To do this, in common with other video games, they learn from their failures and can apply the same techniques in a number of situations. Having found a route through, players can then move faster in the next restart to move on quicker.

Applying the uses and gratifications model again, consider how the appeal of Lara Croft GO compares with the appeal of Kim Kardashian: Hollywood. Both games can be played on a mobile in short bursts, while players are waiting or travelling. Like Kim Kardashian: Hollywood, it is escapist and features a strong lead who can defeat obstacles to reach a series of satisfying goals. Unlike Kim Kardashian: Hollywood, it offers players the satisfaction of completing puzzles and defeating enemies.

> **Link**
> For more on gender see Chapter 2, pages 72–79.

> **Talk about it**
> Games developers are often young, white, heterosexual males who create the sort of games they like to play. Discuss the extent to which Lara Croft GO reflects and reinforces the values of white, male-dominated society.

> **Quick question 5.12**
> Identify the positive and negative influences that Lara Croft GO might have on its players.

> **Link**
> The video game industry is discussed in detail in Chapter 4.

> **Activity 5.8**
> Research Core Design, Eidos Interactive and Square Enix Montreal, including their other games and their business strategies – how do they expect to make money from their games. How did these lead to the development of Lara Croft GO?

> **Quick question 5.13**
> How does the availability of the game across a variety of devices contribute to its success?

> **Link**
> You can find out more about gender representation in Chapter 2, pages 77–79.

**The interactive audience**

Like Kim Kardashian: Hollywood, players are encouraged to be immersed inside the narrative or gaming world, so that they feel they are an active part of the story and not just an observer. The players' interaction with the game is driven by the constant feedback between their choice of action, the game's response and their response to that. Touch-based devices – mobile phones and tablets – become an extension of the game's interface, adding to the sense of immersion. While there is in-app advertising, it is not as intrusive as in Kim Kardashian: Hollywood, keeping players involved and playing the game. Again, the gameplay can be so satisfying that it becomes a habit.

## Media Industries

The Tomb Raider franchise was created by British gaming company Core Design. This was originally owned by Eidos Interactive, and more recently by Square Enix. Lara Croft GO was developed by Square Enix Montreal.

Lara Croft GO is available to play on a number of platforms, including mobiles, PCs, Macs, PS4 and PSVita. The Windows and IOS versions of the game have cloud support, so players can pick up where they left off, using any appropriate device.

> **Activity 5.9**
> Investigate the Tomb Raider franchise:
> - How many games are there – so far?
> - What are the key differences between each game?
> - How can you measure the franchise's commercial success?
> - What advantages does a franchise offer to a producer and to the potential audience?
> - How does the success of Tomb Raider compare with other large game franchises?

## Historical, social and cultural contexts

Again, the influence of gender representation must be taken into account.

The emergence of Lara Croft as a commercial brand can be studied and compared with the impact and influence of both Kim Kardashian and Marcus Rashford. On the face of it, they are very different types of people and reflect a diversity of roles and representations.

> Marcus Rashford represents a very different approach to branding gendered celebrity from Kim Karashian, as seen here on his official Instagram.

Also consider what they do have in common, for example:

- being good at what they do
- their focus on reaching a specified goal
- consolidating their popularity by combining a variety of different media, especially social media
- taking on stereotypes and displaying traits that are often regarded as binary opposites, for example assertive behaviour and sex appeal (for Kim and Lara) or glamour and a down-to-earth approach (for Marcus Rashford).

Consider whether they could be regarded as good role models, when they are so closely associated with stereotypically gendered visual elements such as a desirable body shape and involvement in fashion.

### Activity 5.10

At the end of 2017, Google Play produced a **white paper** about diversity in the mobile gaming market (Google Play, 2017). It ended with a checklist for game developers to use to make their games more inclusive for women. It asks developers to:

- know their audience
- build more inclusive games
- use more diverse teams
- maximise the opportunities presented by having more female players.

Find the white paper on the internet and take a look at the details in the checklist, identifying any changes or additions you would make to ensure more gender diversity.

### Activity 5.11

Carry out research among female gameplayers. Find out:
- why they play games
- when and how they play games
- which games they choose to play.

Also find out what they would like to see in a female protagonist in a role-playing video game.

Use your findings to make recommendations for a future female character.

### Key term

**White paper**
A document intended to start a discussion that will lead to change.

# Studying newspapers

## Overview

Newspapers have been around for a very long time in the UK. In fact, the first daily newspaper, the *Daily Courant*, was published in 1702.

It can safely be said that of all the media forms, newspapers were the first to establish themselves as a truly mass medium. Despite warnings and predictions about the decline or even death of the newspaper industry, the press has continued to have a powerful influence on society, culture and politics for over 300 years.

This is not to say that the industry has remained unchanged for all this time, far from it. Individual newspapers – such as the *Daily Courant* – have come and gone, print technology has constantly evolved and fashions have changed. In recent years the development of digital technology and the internet has had a massive impact on the newspaper industry as it has had to face the challenge of the 'online revolution'.

Britain's first daily newspaper consisted of one page of news with advertisements on the back.

Don't worry, you won't need to delve any further into the 300-year history of Britain's press, but it will be useful for you to have a good general understanding of newspapers as a media form in the UK today. Following are some key points that you need to be aware of:

- The range of daily and Sunday newspapers available and the different categories that they fall into.
- The circulation figures (sales and readership) of these newspapers and trends in circulation.
- The target audiences of the main national dailies and Sunday newspapers.
- Who owns the newspapers and how does ownership affect content?
- The political leanings of different newspapers.
- The style of presentation and use of language, layout and images in newspapers.
- The various ways in which newspapers have established an online presence.

Most of these points refer to the national press but you should certainly make a point of looking closely at your local newspaper to see how it compares with the nationals.

Before we move on to a closer study of *The Times* and the *Daily Mirror*, let's see how these titles fit into the overall pattern of our newspapers.

**Newspaper titles**

### Link

See Chapter 3, pages 90–93, for an explanation of these demographic terms.

### Quick question 5.14

Can you name your local newspapers? Are they free or paid for?

## Tabloids and broadsheets

These two categories refer to the physical size of newspapers: the dimensions of the paper they are printed on. Put simply, big ones are broadsheets and small ones are tabloids. Traditionally, broadsheets are aimed at a more upmarket (AB) readership of middle-class professionals and tabloids are aimed at either the midmarket (BC1) or popular (C2DE) sector of the market.

Few broadsheets remain today. The *Guardian*, *The Times* and the *Observer* have all changed to a smaller format but the *Daily* and *Sunday Telegraph* are still broadsheets. Despite this, the terms broadsheet (or 'former broadsheet') and tabloid are still widely used to describe newspapers aimed at different market segments.

## Newspaper circulation

The following chart shows the sales figures of major daily and Sunday newspapers in March 2018 and June 2021, together with the percentage change in sales over the preceding 12 months. The *Metro's* apparent rise in 2021 is due to the lowering of production during the first coronavirus lockdown in the UK the previous year.

| Title | March 2018 | Year on year % | June 2021 (except *) | Year on year % 2021 (except *) |
|---|---|---|---|---|
| Sun | 1,481,876 | −7.52 | 1,210,915* | −11* |
| Metro (free) | 1,473,956 | −0.36 | 1,013,847 | 224 |
| Daily Mail | 1,310,796 | −9.16 | 948,273 | −5 |
| Sun on Sunday | 1,224,261 | −10.08 | 1,013,777* | −11* |
| Mail on Sunday | 1,065,529 | −14.63 | 832,963 | −8 |
| London Evening Standard (free) | 873,982 | −3.04 | 492,406 | 1 |
| Sunday Times | 739,444 | −6.35 | 647,622* | −9* |
| Daily Mirror | 565,074 | −18.38 | 358,178 | −7 |
| Sunday Mirror | 472,291 | −21.79 | 287,740 | −11 |
| The Times | 435,061 | −1.29 | 365,880* | −10* |
| Daily Star | 395,362 | −9.52 | 215,901 | −8 |
| Daily Telegraph | 382,204 | −17.02 | 317,817* | −12* |
| Daily Express | 357,183 | −7.64 | 237,243 | −4 |
| Sunday Express | 307,634 | −7.96 | 208,136 | −7 |
| Sunday Telegraph | 293,360 | −17.63 | 248,288* | −12* |
| i | 252,814 | −4.7 | 143,176 | 2 |
| Daily Star – Sunday | 236,275 | −5.23 | 126,736 | −15 |
| Sunday People | 186,346 | −19.81 | 111,145 | −13 |
| Financial Times | 185,747 | −2.26 | 108,014 | 38 |
| Observer | 175,904 | −1.85 | 139,089 | −3 |
| Guardian | 148,169 | −3.43 | 106,035 | −5 |

Sources: Tobitt, 2020 and Audit Bureau of Circulation 2020–2021

* The *Sun*, *Telegraph* and *The Times* titles have chosen to keep their ABC figures private since early 2020. The figures here are for March 2020 for the *Sun* and *The Times* titles, and for December 2019 for the *Telegraph* titles.

**Key**
- Broadsheet/former broadsheet/'quality press'
- Tabloid, midmarket
- Tabloid, popular press

## Newspapers and politics

Nearly all national newspapers have strong political views, usually reflecting the opinions of the owners. At election times the newspapers campaign forcefully for their chosen political parties and the *Sun* was not afraid to boast that it was responsible for the Conservative Party's victory in the 1992 general election, with its headline 'IT'S THE SUN WOT WON IT'.

Unlike the broadcast media, newspapers can be as biased as they like. There are no restrictions on their freedom to express political opinions and newspapers make no attempt to achieve the sort of balance that we expect in television and radio reporting.

Like political parties, newspapers are often described in terms of the political spectrum. This is a way of describing the various political views from the left wing, through the centre, to the right wing.

### Activity 5.12

Using the chart and your own research, find out:
- Which three newspapers have seen the biggest drop in year-on-year sales.
- Which newspaper has the smallest year-on-year drop in sales?
- Which newspaper has the highest June 2021 sales in the midmarket sector?
- What is the current price of the *Observer*, *Daily Express* and *Sun*? Calculate the sales income for them by multiplying the circulation by the price.
- Two listed newspapers are given away free. How do they still have an income?

**The political spectrum**

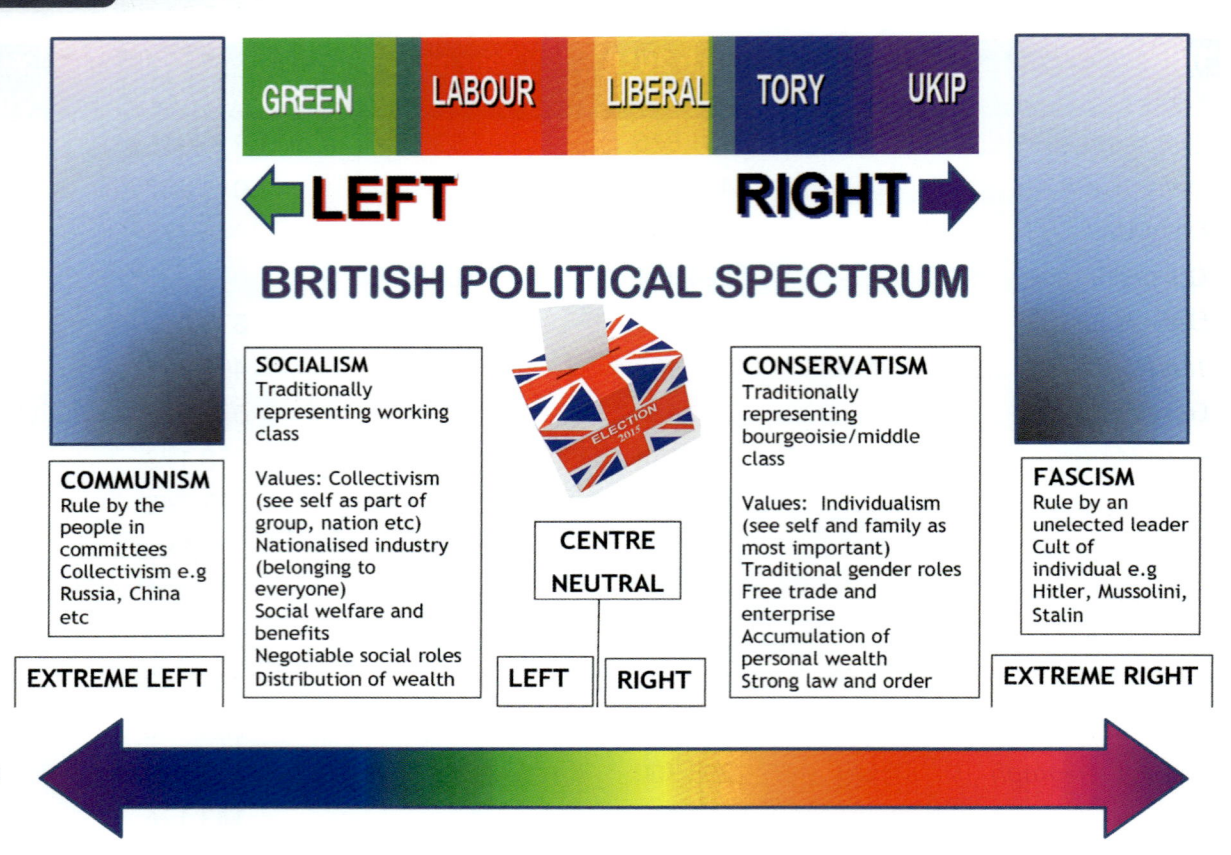

**BRITISH POLITICAL SPECTRUM**

GREEN | LABOUR | LIBERAL | TORY | UKIP

← LEFT    RIGHT →

**COMMUNISM**
Rule by the people in committees
Collectivism e.g Russia, China etc

**EXTREME LEFT**

**SOCIALISM**
Traditionally representing working class

Values: Collectivism (see self as part of group, nation etc)
Nationalised industry (belonging to everyone)
Social welfare and benefits
Negotiable social roles
Distribution of wealth

**CENTRE NEUTRAL**
LEFT | RIGHT

**CONSERVATISM**
Traditionally representing bourgeoisie/middle class

Values: Individualism (see self and family as most important)
Traditional gender roles
Free trade and enterprise
Accumulation of personal wealth
Strong law and order

**FASCISM**
Rule by an unelected leader
Cult of individual e.g Hitler, Mussolini, Stalin

**EXTREME RIGHT**

Source: cbatson1969 in TES, 2018

---

### Key term

**Agenda setting**
The theory that the media have a powerful and influential role in telling politicians and the public what they should be thinking about.

### Activity 5.13

Find out which British newspapers are owned by the following:
- Scott Trust
- News UK
- Reach.

### Talk about it

How does the ownership of Scott Trust, News UK and Reach newspapers influence their political viewpoints?

---

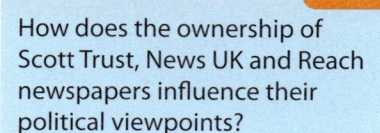

Most national newspapers are right of centre. In the 2017 General Election, the *i*, *Observer*, *Star* and *Sunday People* did not declare support for any political party. The *Guardian*, *Daily Mirror* and *Sunday Mirror* supported Labour, and all the other newspapers supported the Conservative Party. Debates have raged for many years about the 'power of the press' and the ability of newspapers to influence not only voters but also politicians. However, the result of the 2017 election was something of a surprise. The Conservative Party won, but the margin of victory was small. The Labour Party did much better than predicted. Many commentators suggested that this result showed the diminishing power of the press in relation to a new source of power and influence: social media.

Nevertheless, newspapers continue to play an important role in **agenda setting**. Politicians and opinion leaders still react to and care about what the papers say.

## Moving online

The decline in newspaper sales has been very steep in the 21st century. To give some idea of just how serious this fall-off has been, let's compare some of the circulation figures from December 2019 with a time when the internet was only just starting to take off as a mass medium: December 2002 in the following chart.

| Title | December 2002 | December 2019 | % Change |
|---|---|---|---|
| Sun | 3,447,108 | 1,215,852 | −64.7 |
| Daily Mirror | 2,031,596 | 451,386 | −77.8 |
| Daily Star | 819,203 | 282,723 | −65.5 |
| Daily Mail | 2,327,732 | 1,141,178 | −51.0 |
| Daily Express | 916,055 | 295,079 | −67.8 |
| Daily Telegraph | 923,815 | 317,817 | −65.6 |
| The Times | 619,682 | 370,005 | −40.3 |
| Guardian | 378,516 | 133,412 | −64.8 |

Sources: Audit Bureau of Circulation (various)

The declining sales of daily newspapers.

Newspapers always had a strong sense of brand loyalty; many readers felt that their daily newspaper was a statement of identity. Why, despite this, have so many customers deserted newspapers? Here are some of the key reasons:

- **Immediacy**: most people want and expect news to be available 24/7. Radio, television and the internet can supply this.
- **In depth is out of fashion**: the demand for detailed coverage is diminishing. With so much information available many of us prefer lots of brief snippets of information instead of a smaller number of in-depth reports.
- **Cost**: perhaps this is the main reason. It is one of the newspaper industry's biggest complaints that other internet providers lift material from the newspapers without paying for it.
- **Personalisation**: social media, apps and the internet provide tools for any one of us to put together a very specialist menu of news, information and comment that is exactly tailored to our personal tastes and interests.

Smartphones and the internet give people 24-hour access to news, with immediate updates.

**Quick question 5.15**

Do you regularly read a newspaper? If not, have any of the reasons above influenced your choice?

As noted earlier, the newspaper industry has not stood still in the face of declining sales. All the papers have websites, apps and a social media presence. Many have been very successful. Website audiences are measured by PAMCo (Publishers Audience Measurement Company). PAMCo combines audience figures for online (phone, tablet, desktop) with print to give a 'total brand reach' each month for newspaper brands.

**Total brand reach figures (thousands) in 2019 for the top UK newspaper brands were:**

| | | | |
|---|---|---|---|
| Sun/Sun on Sunday | 37,098 | Independent | 24,566 |
| Daily Mirror/Sunday Mirror/Sunday People | 29,365 | Daily Express/Sunday Express | 22,321 |
| Daily Mail/Mail on Sunday | 28,552 | Daily Telegraph/Sunday Telegraph | 21,669 |
| Metro | 27,884 | The Times/Sunday Times | 11,503 |
| Guardian/Observer | 24,273 | i | 7,695 |

Source: PAMCo, 2020

AQA GCSE Media Studies

Some newspapers are making their online content only available to subscribers.

Although these figures dwarf the sales of print editions, the problem for the newspapers is monetisation. Somehow, they need to extract substantial revenue from these websites in order to pay for their very expensive news-gathering operations. The two main sources of income are:

- **Advertising**: digital ad income has grown, but newspapers have found it very tough to match this to the decline in income from printed papers. Another problem is the widespread use of 'adblockers' by people who prefer to use the internet without the distraction of adverts.

- **Subscription**: several newspapers' websites, including *The Times* and the *Daily Telegraph*, operate **paywalls**, so some or all the content has to be paid for.

> **Key term**
>
> **Paywall**
> A website with a paywall is fully or partially restricted to users who pay a subscription.

## Newspapers: close study products

### *The Times* and the *Daily Mirror*

The first CSPs in this media form, for 2023, are *The Times* and the *Daily Mirror*. These are in-depth CSPs, which will be studied with reference to all four elements of the theoretical framework:

- Media Language
- Media Representations
- Media Audiences
- Media Industries

as well as all relevant contexts.

We are going to consider these two CSPs together because you are strongly advised to study them side by side so that you can pick out similarities and differences. Your teacher may be able to provide you with a larger version of the two front pages and the focus story.

Here you are going to look at the front pages and a focus story from the editions of Friday 5 March 2021. If your exam is in summer 2024 or later, you will have a more up-to-date edition of the same newspapers and a different story to study.

*The Times* has three front-page stories and the *Daily Mirror* two. Both front pages carry 'teasers' referring to material inside.

The focus story, which appeared on the inside pages of these papers, is about the first Amazon Fresh store in the UK, which has no cashiers or tills.

184

These stories will be studied in the context of the pages on which they appear.

Remember that you are not only studying a few selected pages from these newspapers, you also need an understanding of:

- who produces the *Daily Mirror* and *The Times*
- each newspaper's readerships
- the context in which the stories are produced
- the context in which the stories are consumed.

## Media Language

You will need to understand the codes and conventions of newspaper design, layout and choice of content material, and use of language. Your starting point is the case study in Chapter 1, which shows you how to use semiotics in the analysis of the two newspaper front pages. The focus is always on **meaning**. For example, two things that strike you straight away about the front pages are:

- the size of the typeface (point size) used – the *Daily Mirror*'s is on the whole much bigger
- the amount of **copy** – *The Times* has much more to read.

The two newspapers use elements of media language to establish the **genre** or category to which they belong. They are clearly designed for different segments of the newspaper market usually classified as:

- broadsheet/former broadsheet
- mid-market
- popular press.

Both of the front pages and the Amazon Fresh stories develop **narratives**. Although the *Mirror*'s version is much the shorter of the two, a clear narrative emerges which strongly contrasts with *The Times*' version.

These will be looked at next as they combine Media Language and Media Representations.

## Media Representations

Across both newspapers, there is clear evidence that they each represent the interests of their target readers. For example, *The Times* chooses to address the Amazon shop story from the point of view of a technology-wary but time-poor customer. The Mirror focuses both its front page story and the Amazon shop story on the impact on ordinary workers. These choices reflect the different social class makeup of the target readerships.

How are other groups and individuals represented? You should also consider:

- **Celebrity**: for example, the reasons for selecting a picture of Meghan, the Duchess of Sussex, on the front page of the *Daily Mirror*.
- **Politics**: is there any evidence of the two papers' different political leanings in the pages being studied?

**Key term**

**Copy**
In the context of newspapers, copy is the written or printed material as distinct from photographs, cartoons, graphics or any other visual material.

**Quick question 5.16**
How do *The Times* and the *Daily Mirror* deal differently with written copy and visual material?

**Activity 5.14**
How do the two headlines emphasise different aspects of the story?

**Link**
Read more about Amazon Fresh in Chapter 3, pages 103–104

**Link**
See Activity 3.11 on page 104.

## Media Audiences

Activity 3.11 (page 104) will guide you through a process of building an audience profile for the two newspapers.

As well as profiling the readerships, you will also need to find out how the papers position their readers. This means the ways in which readers can be gently led towards a particular interpretation (the preferred reading) of a story. For example, the *Daily Mirror* writes that rival supermarkets will watch the new store closely. This invites us to think that till-less shops are likely to be adopted by other major firms if this one succeeds. They also quote Clive Black's remark that cashless and cardless shops will lead to a 'considerable reduction in roles for people'. This reinforces the idea that the shop and others like it are destined to lead to job losses. For *The Times*, on the other hand, this is a cautious good news story for customers as the store 'works very well'.

## Media Industries

A case study in Chapter 4 deals in detail with the owners and implications of ownership of these two newspapers. This will help you to understand the following in relation to the newspaper industry:

- conglomerate ownership
- convergence and divergence
- horizontal and vertical integration
- differing funding models and how newspapers can make money in the digital age.

## Studying advertising and marketing

We are bombarded with advertising all the time, especially now that we use our smartphones so often. Perhaps we rarely notice adverts any more, because we expect them, and, if we do look at them, we often don't remember what product is being advertised. Our attention spans are limited because there are so many distractions, so advertisers need to reach us in new and different ways.

> **Tip**
>
> There are various helpful sources of information for internet-based research into newspaper audiences including:
> - Audit Bureau of Circulation (ABC)
> - National Readership Survey (NRS)
> - *Press Gazette*
> - theguardian.com/media.

> **Link**
>
> See Chapter 3 for an explanation of audience positioning, preferred readings and a more detailed look at the two Amazon store stories.

> **Link**
>
> See the case study in Chapter 4 on pages 116–122.

> **Tip**
>
> Build up a 'fact file' for each newspaper including:
> - readership profile
> - current sales and trends
> - ownership
> - political slant
> - notes about online/social media presence.

> **Link**
>
> Look back at the discussion of the signified and the signifier in the Halfords advert on page 14.

> **Talk about it**
>
> Think about last time you watched a YouTube video that started with an advert. Do you remember what was being advertised? Did you skip it as soon as you could? If you watched it, what caught your eye that encouraged you to watch to the end?

## Activity 5.15

Consider the ways in which this print advert for Kellogg's Special K is intended to catch your attention and encourage you to buy the product. Think about the:
- use of colour
- placement of the elements
- position of the logo
- choice of images
- wording and size of the **strapline**.

## Principles of modern advertising

As we have seen throughout this book, advertisers employ a variety of languages and representations to appeal to their target audience and, of course, to encourage their products to be sold. Some are simply visual, such as using bright colours in images or logos – think of the Coca-Cola logo – or, when advertising cereal, positioning a spoon on the right of the bowl, as most people are right-handed (of course, this may make it less appealing to left-handed members of the target audience!).

However, advertising works on many levels. One of the most effective techniques is to focus on provoking an emotive response in the audience – how it makes you **feel**. For example, this may be based on empathy, when the audience feels close to a brand after seeing its advertising – for example, they might respond positively to representations of people who reflect their own age or race, or to images of babies or kittens.

The idea is that the audience builds a personal connection with the brand, perhaps because its ads make you feel good, or happy, or excited. Related to this, another emotive response is based on creativity, for example being impressed by the imagination or technology a brand uses in its advertising. A good example of this is the CGI company Framestore's recreation of Audrey Hepburn for the Galaxy ad.

The Dove Real Beauty campaign used models who were intentended to look more like everyday women than conventional skincare models. Women are supposed to identify more closely with this type of image.

## Key developments

As with all other media formats, the internet has influenced and changed the way we consume advertising. The younger demographic especially consumes far less print media and live TV than in the past, reducing opportunities for brands to promote their products to young people via these channels.

## Online advertising

Advertising is adapting its business model and media language to the internet. Using data gathered from your use of search engines and social media networks, targeted pop-up adverts can be based on your previous online behaviour. For example, every time you use Facebook or download a new phone app, you see adverts for products you have previously browsed on the internet, or for related products. Advertising messages can be 'personalised' so that consumers get the impression of an individual relationship with advertisers.

**Key term**

**Strapline**
A short headline or description that sums up the message of an ad or news story.

**Link**
The Galaxy ad is discussed on pages 190–191.

App developers have also recognised that many users are willing to pay *not* to be exposed to advertising, by, for example, offering a subscription or one-off payment in return for an ad-free service. This transaction compensates the advertiser for any lost revenue.

## TV advertising

Similarly, TV companies have needed to find ways of overcoming self-selected viewing that means viewers choose what they want to watch and when, which usually doesn't include adverts. Free-to-watch on-demand services, such as All4, include adverts that can't be skipped. But in many cases, the older the programme, the less likely it is to include adverts. Paid-for subscription services have often stopped including ad breaks, as subscribers react negatively to them. Netflix has often been criticised for too obvious product placement in its shows, which sometimes distracts viewers from the narrative.

## Reality advertising

Social media has also seen the convergence of advertising, celebrities and reality television. Among leaders in this field are the Kardashians, whose own celebrity brand is reinforced through the endorsement of other products on Twitter, Instagram and Facebook. Many vloggers will review and recommend products that have been sent to them by manufacturers and marketing companies. In most cases, they will acknowledge that they received these products for free – their audience understand that the commercial organisations are seeking endorsement from the vlogger, but trust their chosen celebrity to be honest in their review.

## Shared experience advertising

Social media has also encouraged the development of 'shared experience' advertising, also made possible by the ability of companies to store and use your data. For example, music streaming site Spotify ran some memorable billboard ads using data it had gleaned from its users. It's interesting to note that a digital service provider chose to use a print channel to make a big impact, showing that, these days, the distinction between advertising channels is becoming blurred. This example also suggests that people now accept that their own habits and ways of consuming media are being used to sell more products.

## Guerrilla advertising

This idea draws its influence from *guerrilla warfare*: a type of resistance based on unconventional tactics such as sabotage, ambush, disguise and surprise attacks.

The focus of guerrilla advertising or marketing is on the creative, the imaginative, the unexpected – something that will generate a social buzz. It is a strategy based on low-cost, unconventional tactics which aim to capture the attention and interest of consumers. Variants include 'stealth marketing' and, more recently, 'experiential marketing'. Advertisers are keen to involve the digital world and all its technological advances to help spread awareness of their campaigns. For example, guerrilla marketeers will place an unusual image or object in a busy urban area hoping that it will be filmed by members of the public and spread across social media. Getting consumers themselves to spread the message has always been a favourite means of product promotion for advertisers.

Spotify used its data to make eye-catching and thought-provoking billboard ads.

A famous example, widely circulated online, was a Canadian security glass manufacturer, 3M, which placed $3 million in banknotes behind a glass case at a city centre bus stop. For one day passers-by were challenged to try and break the glass and win the money.

In 2017, furniture giant IKEA drew attention to the opening of its new store in Sheffield by commissioning a local artist to create a statue of a peregrine falcon made from 17,000 IKEA Allen keys. The statue now has a permanent site at the city's railway station and is a constant reminder of the brand.

## Issues

We have seen throughout this book that internet content is very difficult to regulate. Parental controls over social media sites may not be sufficient. Many of the issues surrounding advertising are related to the more recent key developments. For example:

- lack of parental control over content seen by children – including children being exposed to overtly sexualised ads on YouTube
- children being targeted for adverts while online – there have been instances of young children making in-app purchases amounting to thousands of pounds
- brands needing to make an impression on audiences who are constantly targeted by ads – this could mean using controversial or potentially offensive methods
- user data and behaviours being used to inform advertising – advertisers might argue this helps them to more accurately target consumers but individuals might say it is an invasion of privacy.

There are also the traditional issues that have always surrounded advertising, which we have already discussed, such as stereotyping, gender roles and misrepresentation. While these issues may be problematic on a social level, they often work in the context of advertising, as people still buy the products. Consumers who are offended by the overt sexual nature of American Apparel ads, for example, can boycott the product but sales from the target audience remain high, which suggests that other consumers are entertained enough to buy the brand.

Protein World caused controversy in 2015 with its 'Are You Beach Body Ready?' billboard ad, showing a 'toned and athletic' young woman in a bikini. The advert implied that the 'Weight Loss Collection' products would enable women who are concerned about being overweight to feel more confident about wearing a swimsuit on a beach. Many people felt the message was offensive, sexist and fat-shaming. The ASA – Advertising Standards Authority – investigated the advert after receiving 378 complaints but the accusations of irresponsibility were not upheld (ASA, 2015).

In fact, there was also a male version, also showing a rarely attainable body, but this wasn't the focus of the controversy.

### Talk about it

As a group, discuss the social and cultural issues raised by the Protein World adverts (more can be found online), and consider the role of the ASA in this context. Do you agree with its decision?

# Advertising and marketing: close study products

The CSPs in these media forms, for 2023, are the Galaxy 'Audrey Hepburn' television advert (2013), the NHS Blood and Transplant online campaign video 'Represent' featuring Lady Leshurr, and the OMO print advert from *Woman's Own* magazine (5 May 1955).

These are targeted CSPs, where the focus will be on the following areas of the theoretical framework:

- Media Language
- Media Representations.

## Galaxy 'Audrey Hepburn' TV ad (2013)

### Overview

This 2013 TV and cinema advertisement for a chocolate bar apparently stars iconic actress Audrey Hepburn, who died in 1993 at the age of 63. Set in a 1950s Italian seaside town, a young woman is stuck on a bus which has crashed into a market stall. When a man in an open-top car pulls up beside the bus, she gets out, takes the bus driver's cap, gives it to the car driver and climbs into the back of the car. As they drive along the coastal road, she can finally enjoy her bar of chocolate.

### Conveying a brand image

Audrey Hepburn was an iconic actress who, in the 1950s and 1960s, represented beauty, elegance and quality. The makers of Galaxy chocolate felt that this tied in well with its associations of being 'silk, not cotton' – a cut above other chocolate bars. The connotations of using a representation of Audrey Hepburn could be lost on younger viewers who may not recognise her at all. However, in this ad, we don't need to know who Audrey Hepburn was to understand the symbolism of an attractive young woman 'upgrading' from a crowded, stationary bus to a chauffeur-driven open-topped car.

### Importance of the mise-en-scène

There is no dialogue in the advert at all, so the entire story is told via visual clues, and a musical soundtrack. How do you know when and where it is set? This is conveyed through a shared audience understanding of the cultural references.

### Narrative

Consider the intended meaning of this advert – possibly that Galaxy chocolate is so good, that eating a bar of it merits a glamorous and luxurious setting. Think about how possible oppositional or negotiated readings of the advert could affect the reception of the narrative. After all, the woman steals a hat and effectively hijacks a car. How would our reaction be different if she had been less glamorous, or a man?

### Technical representation

As there wasn't any suitable footage of Audrey Hepburn that could simply be reused, the producers of the advert decided to recreate her using state-of-the-art CGI, with the permission of her sons. They combined body doubles, frame-by-

---

**Activity 5.16**

Find out about the actress Audrey Hepburn and how the film *Roman Holiday* (1953) helped to form her image as a celebrity and style icon.

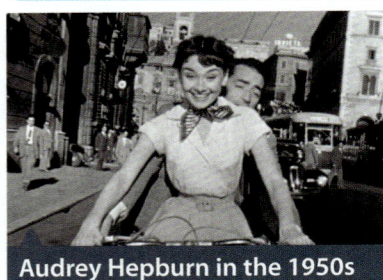

*Audrey Hepburn in the 1950s*

**Quick question 5.17**

What other elements of the ad represent a sense of tradition and quality?

**Activity 5.17**

Consider how the following elements contribute to the narrative and representation of the 'Audrey Hepburn' ad:
- setting
- props
- costumes, hair and makeup
- facial expressions and body language
- lighting and colour
- positioning of objects within the frame.

How would the impact of the ad be different if it was set in the present day?

frame animation and the latest technology to achieve an authentic look, using real film footage and photographs as reference. If you didn't know that the main character had been recreated using CGI, could you guess?

The advert has been both praised and criticised. The technical skill used was cutting edge – the CGI company involved, Framestore, was working on the feature film *Gravity* (2013) at the same time. However, several critics noted that Audrey Hepburn had not starred in commercial adverts while she was alive, so questioned whether it was right that her image should be used in this way after her death – even with the permission of her family.

# NHS Blood and Transplant online campaign video 'Represent' featuring Lady Leshurr

This product was looked at in terms of media representations in Chapter 2, so you will concentrate on media language here.

## Overview

'Represent' is a video, funded and produced by the NHS Blood and Transplant marketing campaign. It specifically targets the ethnic community in order to increase the number of blood donors from that sector of society. Lady Leshurr raps and sings about how ethnic people are represented in many different careers and walks of life, but are not as well represented among blood donors.

The video takes the genre of a music video, interspersing Lady Leshurr performing the song in an urban setting with shots of a succession of black and Asian role models shown in the context of their success. The video stresses the potential of young ethnic people to achieve their ambitions in many types of career.

This is a product that targets a niche audience with a clear persuasive message. The official text under the video on YouTube reads:

> *People of black and Asian heritage are beginning to be represented in all walks of society, from the arts, sport through to politics. However one key place they aren't representing themselves is in blood donation sessions.*

Think about how certain codes and conventions have been chosen to communicate the message and persuade the target audience to perform a particular action – to give blood.

## Non-verbal and production codes

Think about how the non-verbal codes contribute to the persuasive message of the video. These could include:

- facial expression, head movement, gestures
- body movement, body closeness
- **paralanguage** of the rap.

When watching the video to analyse these codes, consider the other people represented, not just Lady Leshurr. It's particularly interesting to look at the mise-en-scène, such as location, lighting, clothing and props. Analyse what the role models are wearing and where they are filmed. What else is in the shot? What do these visual clues suggest in each case?

### Quick question 5.18
Why do you think the producers of the ad thought the time and expense of recreating a real person was worthwhile?

### Quick question 5.19
What are the possible implications, positive and negative, of recreating actors using CGI after their death?

### Link
For more on 'Represent' see Chapter 2, pages 61–62.

### Key term
**Paralanguage**
How we convey meaning through aspects of speech other than the words we use – such as speed, rhythm, tone, volume and hesitation.

### Quick question 5.20
What is the intended message of this product?

### Quick question 5.21
One of the intended representations within the advert is the success of the video's participants. How is this conveyed?

Paralympian and sports presenter Ade Adepitan is shown outside the iconic London Olympic stadium.

**Quick question 5.22**

Can you see other points in the video where the technical and production codes help to convey the overall message?

Also consider how production elements such as camera angles, editing and sound contribute to conveying the message. For example, the video starts with a 16-second opening shot establishing Lady Leshurr as the main personality in the video and London as the main location. Most of the shots in the rest of the video are much shorter, but the shot dollying into the row of empty clinical chairs towards the end of the video lasts for ten seconds. This visually slows the pace at the same time as the music empties out, leaving little else but the vocals. By doing this, the video focuses the audience on Lady Leshurr's words at this point. Juxtaposed with the empty chairs, this emphasises the main point of the campaign.

## Narrative

If the first time you watched this video was for your media studies course, you may have known why it was made before you saw it. However, for most of the original intended audience, its purpose would not have been clear until the end of the video. How is the narrative here created to construct a point of view? In what ways does the narrative structure of the video keep viewers interested?

**Activity 5.18**

Look back at Chapter 1, to remind yourself about intertextuality (page 41) and hybrid genres (page 37). Can you identify any elements of intertextuality or hybridity in this video?

Think too about the hooks that are intended to draw the target audience in. For example, at the start, Lady Leshurr stands on a rooftop with her back to the camera. Who is she? What is she going to do? When she turns around, she's clearly a confident and attractive young woman from the target audience, drawing viewers in because they identify with, or aspire to be, role models such as her.

## Social and cultural contexts

Advertisements normally promote a *product* in order to persuade people to buy it. This video is a marketing campaign persuading people to carry out an action with a positive social impact.

**Quick question 5.23**

Why do think the video does not include information about why it is important to have blood stocks from the ethnic community?

It is particularly important to ensure that enough stocks of blood from the ethnic community are available to the NHS because black and Asian people are more likely to have blood types that are rare in the UK. These blood stocks can help to treat diseases, such as sickle-cell anaemia and thalassaemia, which only affect certain races.

According to the 2011 census, about 13% of people in the UK identify as being in an ethnic group other than white. However, the video states that only 3% of blood donors are from the ethnic community. These facts are a little ambiguous in the video – as comments underneath it point out, this doesn't mean that only 3% of ethnic people donate blood. However, you could argue that the video implies that this is the case, to emphasise the message that not enough ethnic people give blood.

This print ad, also from the NHS, shows an older Asian man about to give blood, suggesting that an older target audience is expected to respond better to a more traditional approach.

The video doesn't suggest the reasons for the low number of donors. Instead, the producers have used an overwhelmingly upbeat and positive representation of the ethnic community, linked to the campaign's inspirational message. Success, in this video, is defined by your contribution to society, and giving blood is part of this contribution.

## Outcome of the video

MediaCom, the agency that made the video, described it as 'an unprecedented success' because it received 15 million impressions across different social media channels and drove 6,665 blood donation registrations within two weeks of the campaign's launch (MediaCom, 2017). Do you agree with this measure of success?

## Representations of women

The three advertising and marketing CSPs all feature representations of female central characters, although each has been chosen for very different reasons. As you will see, it could be argued that the woman in the OMO advert is representing the ordinary woman (the target audience) but that the female character in the Galaxy advert is representing a more aspirational image, one that the target audience might dream of becoming. Where does the central figure in the 'Represent' video fit in?

> **Activity 5.19**
>
> Watch 'The Making of "Represent feat. Lady Leshurr"' on YouTube, which shows behind-the scenes footage and features interviews with some of the participants. How does this add to your understanding of the product's message and outcomes?

# OMO print ad, *Woman's Own* (1955)

This is a targeted CSP where the focus will be on the following areas of the theoretical framework:

- Media Language
- Media Representations.

## Overview

The product is a full-page print advertisement that appeared in the popular women's magazine, *Woman's Own*, in 1955 (your teacher may be able to provide you with a larger version). In the centre of the ad, and taking up about half the available space, is a coloured photo of a middle-aged woman pegging white laundry to what looks like a washing line. She is looking over her shoulder straight at the camera, with a comical expression, her lips pursed as if she is in the middle of speaking. Above her, the strapline reads 'OMO makes whites Bright!' and below her is a panel of two-column text and an image of the product.

The OMO print ad from *Woman's Own* (1955)

## Media Language

### Communicating via signs, codes and conventions

Remember how media products often communicate conventions, sets of values and beliefs that encourage us to think that certain ideas are 'normal and natural' while other ideas are unacceptable and unthinkable. This ad is a good example of how an advertiser exploits such conventions.

What are the connotations and denotations of the various signs that make up this advertisement? Consider the effect of the layout, design, choices of typeface and

> **Quick question 5.24**
>
> How does the combination of elements in the advertisement contribute to a narrative?

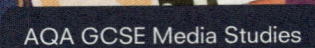

use of colour. The positioning, size and contrast of the large strapline and amusing picture draw our eye first, followed by the image of the washing powder itself.

Think about the colours that have been chosen – what is represented by the different applications of blue, red and white.

### Role of the woman

Now think about the image of the woman. She is doing two things at once, turning from hanging out the washing to talk to you, the viewer. What does this suggest?

The woman is wearing red lipstick, traditionally a symbol of passion and sexuality. However, in this case, the colour serves primarily to emphasise her pursed lips – there is little else in the ad to sexualise it. The model appears to be an ordinary woman, dressed in everyday clothes with her sleeve rolled up to show she is hard at work and is simply keen to recommend a product to people like her.

### Use of language

The text beneath the photo is informal and slangy. It also makes free use of superlatives such as 'wonderful', 'exciting' and 'brilliantly'. There is nothing subtle about the message!

The positioning of the ad as a recommendation of a product is interesting in this age of internet reviews. Modern consumers regard the opinions of other consumers as a vital part of their buying process. However, this 1950s review is (presumably) fictional – there is no suggestion that a real woman has said the words in the copy. This undermines the message for us, as there is little authority in an advertising agency fabricating product recommendations and it is unlikely that such an approach would be permitted today. In 1955 literal word of mouth would have been a prime channel for women to suggest new products to their friends. The informal, friendly and humorous pose of the model sets her up as someone familiar expressing a preference. The audience is positioned as an eager recipient of her advice and wisdom.

'Mother' should not necessarily be taken literally here – in 1950s slang, it was sometimes used to refer to 'a mother', so the speaker is probably not addressing her own mother. However, assuming that she is addressing her own mother opens up some interesting possible readings. For example, the speaker has discovered an exciting new product that makes her life easier, bringing her out of the dark (non-bright) ages of grey laundry that older women had endured in the past. There is also a slightly rebellious subtext – the 'mother' is being ridiculed for 'saying all washing powders were the same'. The speaker is challenging the authority of past beliefs about washing, with OMO representing the 'bright' future. Although the photo is humorous, she is making confident eye-contact with the viewer, indicating she is sure of her point of view.

## Media Representations

Many assumptions are being made in this ad. As well as the obvious stereotype of a woman being the only person in a household who does the laundry, the audience is expected to agree that bright whites represent the ultimate laundry success.

> **Quick question 5.25**
>
> To what extent could the woman be cast as the 'hero' in Propp's narrative character types? What other roles might she fulfil?

## Social, historical and cultural context of gender roles

As we have seen, all adverts reflect the culture and attitudes of the time they were created. Evolving attitudes towards such factors as gender, ethnicity and sexual orientation will result in changes to the images and messages depicted in adverts.

Clearly, this ad was produced at a time when social and gender roles were very different from those we are used to in today's society. In general, husbands and fathers were the breadwinners, who went out to work, while the majority of wives and mothers were expected to stay at home to carry out domestic duties such as cooking, childcare and the laundry. Often, their value and worth to society was measured by neighbours and acquaintances by their domestic successes, such as clean, bright sheets on the washing line. Of course, this wasn't the case for all families, as many women by necessity had to be in paid employment but, even so, they were still more likely to be the ones who did the washing and it was common enough to be the assumption in this ad. It would have been quite natural to address such an ad exclusively towards women, as they were the target market. It simply would not have been of interest to most men.

It could be argued that the ad exploits feelings of the insecurity many women may have experienced when they compared their domestic outcomes with those of other women. The product promises a short cut to this very visual marker of household success.

### Activity 5.20
Research 1950s women's magazines to get an idea of the context for this ad. Make a moodboard showing typical editorial content, types of photos and other ads. How do these aspects combine to emphasise the expected role of women at that time?

## Use of stereotypes

Advertisements often make use of positive stereotypes to endorse and, ultimately, sell products. The image here is immediately recognisable to the target audience as a hardworking and friendly housewife, so the advertisers don't need to spend time establishing the scenario. It assumes that all women in a domestic setting can identify with taking pride in their 'brilliantly bright' laundry and look for ways to make their lives easier. Most advertisements for domestic products in the 1950s were influenced by this assumption.

## The product in context

Often, the job of doing the household washing was assigned to a particular day of the week, the 'washday' referred to in the ad's copy. Washing machines were only just becoming a staple appliance, so it is likely that most housewives would have washed the laundry by hand, a task which would often have taken many hours. The text on the OMO packaging – 'Boil with OMO' – suggests that the product was for boiling on the hob rather than for washing machines. It would have been quite a challenge, at the time, to remove dirt and stains and to ensure that whites retained their whiteness. Perhaps this is why the ad capitalises the word 'Bright' – it was an important and difficult outcome for the person doing the washing.

Think about how you, as a 21st-century person, react to the ad on a personal level. You are likely to interpret the signs and representations differently from a 1950s audience. Are you offended? Do you find it funny? Are you concerned about the claims made about the product? You might even wonder what damage the chemicals or bleach might do, not only to the clothes but also to the

This 1950s ad for another laundry detergent draws attention to the social expectations implicit in the act of washing clothes.

**Quick question 5.26**

What aspects of the 1950s Persil ad were likely to have appealed to the original target audience?

**Talk about it**

The 2024 Galaxy CSP is also a representation of 1950s womanhood, but is quite different. With a partner, compare and contrast the representations of women in the two ads. Consider:
- what they look like
- how they behave
- how their behaviour contributes to persuading the target audiences to buy the products being advertised.

To what extent do you think the representations have been influenced by the different times in which they were made?

**Key term**

**RAJAR**
Radio Joint Audience Research is jointly owned by the BBC and commercial radio. Its job is to measure the number of people listening to radio and the types of radio they listen to. The website www.rajar.co.uk is a great source of information if you are doing any research into radio audiences.

**Activity 5.22**

Download the most recent RAJAR Midas Audio Survey. Survey others in your class to find out if your radio and music listening are typical of the 15–24 age group.

---

person using the product, those who wear the clothes and to the environment. How easy do you find it to put yourself in the place of the target audience? It is important to be aware of how your own experiences and beliefs shape your response, and how difficult it is to separate your response from these influences.

**Activity 5.21**

Find a recent print ad for a laundry detergent. List the ways in which its language and representations are similar to the OMO ad. Think about the signs, codes and conventions, such as the use of colour, layout, positioning of features, the strapline, who or what is shown and the promises it is making to the target audience. You may be surprised at how many similarities there are.

Although the target audience and approach has changed, modern ads for domestic products are not that different in terms of visual elements and intended message.

# Studying radio

## Overview

Although media students sometimes neglect radio as a media form, it is still a powerful and important source of information and entertainment.

The infographic opposite, from **RAJAR** (Radio Joint Industry Research), shows that almost nine out of ten people tuned in to radio every week in early 2020. The figures also show an increase in radio's popularity.

The history of radio as a mass medium in the UK goes back to 1922 and the founding of the British Broadcasting Company, which became the British Broadcasting Corporation in 1926.

Radio listening grew rapidly in the 1930s, along with the sale of radio equipment. By the 1950s, a radio set dominated many living rooms, as the television did by the next decade.

From the early days of radio, the government has regulated both transmission and reception. The first radio licences for listeners were introduced in 1922 and cost 10 shillings (50p); that's around £150 in today's money.

In 1926 the government decided to control **all** broadcasting, giving the BBC a monopoly.

The only realistic alternative for listeners was Radio Luxembourg. The British government did its best to stop people listening to broadcasts from other countries, for example by persuading newspapers never to mention Radio Luxembourg.

## 5 Close study products and media forms

Radio is a very popular medium, as these 2020 figures show.

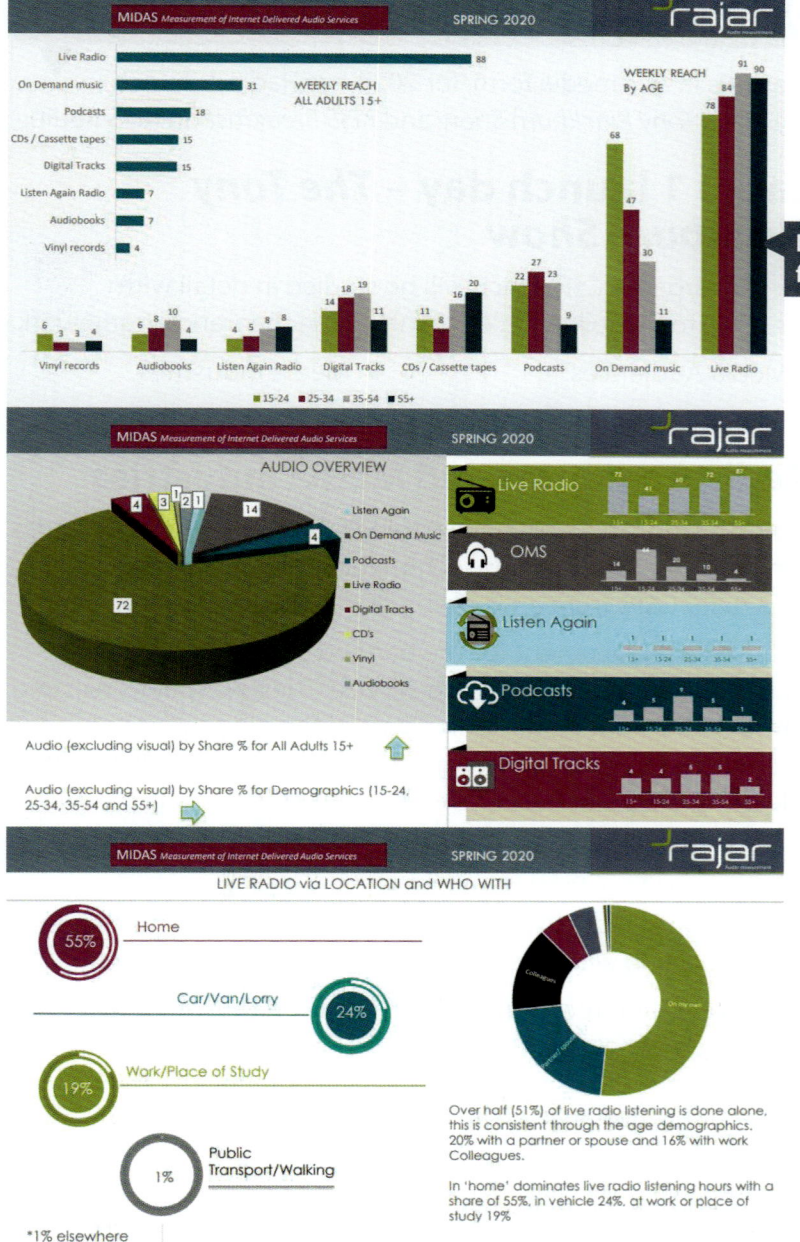

Source: RAJAR, 2020, using data from Ipsos MORI/RSMB

In World War II (1939–1945), radio was extensively used for propaganda, which made the government even more determined to keep a firm control over it in the years after the war.

A big change to listening habits came about in 1956 when the first transistor radio or 'tranny' became available in the UK. Smaller, more mobile and battery-powered, the 'tranny' gave a boost to radio listening, especially among the young. The radio set was no longer a piece of furniture but a portable device. With the arrival of the 'tranny', people stopped giving radio their whole attention; they did other things while listening to it.

The next big challenge to government control and BBC monopoly came in 1964 as the so-called pirate radio stations began to broadcast pop music from ships located just off the coast.

> **Quick question 5.27**
> Is your radio listening above or below the spring 2020 national average of 20.2 hours per week? By how much per week?

> **Link**
> The next stage of the story can be found in the Chapter 4 case study on the history of music radio from 1967 to 2021 (pages 130–134).

> **Quick question 5.28**
> The BBC no longer has a monopoly. List some of the national radio providers that compete with the BBC today.

197

## Radio: close study products

The CSPs in this media form, for 2023, are Radio 1 launch day – *The Tony Blackburn Show* and *KISS Breakfast* on KISS Radio.

### Radio 1 launch day – *The Tony Blackburn Show*

This is a targeted CSP, which will be studied in detail with reference to the following elements of the theoretical framework:

- Media Audiences
- Media Industries

as well as all relevant contexts.

### Media Audiences and Media Industries

The case study in Chapter 4 examines the history of music radio from 1967 to 2021 but this section focuses only on the two 2023 radio CSPs from an industry and audience point of view.

*Radio 1 presenters in 1967. A mixture of former pirate ship DJs and established BBC staff, but not much evidence of diversity.*

The government wanted a replacement for the banned pirate radio stations and asked the BBC to develop a new pop radio service. The BBC split its existing Light Programme into Radio 1 and Radio 2 and started the new service on 30 September 1967. Radio 2 went out on long wave and FM, but Radio 1 had to make do with the lower-quality medium wave. This meant that many parts of the country could not receive Radio 1.

The first show on Radio 1 was Tony Blackburn's two-hour breakfast slot. Like many of the new presenters, Tony Blackburn was a former pirate radio presenter, hired for his experience of connecting with a youth audience.

*Tony Blackburn in 1967*

You should easily be able to find recordings of this show on the internet, although some versions don't have all the music for copyright reasons. That doesn't matter. The important thing is for you to get a flavour of *The Tony Blackburn Show* and to understand what the programme tells us about the BBC, its audience and the social and cultural contexts of production.

*The Tony Blackburn Show* contained many elements that are familiar to radio listeners 50 or more years later. There were jingles, light-hearted banter and studio guests. Traffic news and news bulletins were aired at regular intervals. Tony Blackburn was very keen to involve the listeners and make them feel part of the show rather than just receivers; 'look on the show as your own', he told them.

Today's music radio presenters receive and pass on instant feedback picked up from social media so that their shows feel genuinely interactive. Tony Blackburn had no such resources in 1967, but he still encouraged listeners to send him letters, writing in to PO Box 1A 1AA. It may not have been instant but it was still effective, as record requests and dedications soon flooded in.

### Talk about it

What are your first impressions of *The Tony Blackburn Show*? How does it compare with modern radio breakfast shows?

Although some of the language sounds very dated, there was a strong emphasis on youthfulness, informality and fun. The pop chart was 'the Fun 30' and there were several jokey references to 'your granny'.

These are some of the ways that the BBC tried to position its Radio 1 audience. They were aware that the huge youth audience built up by the pirates generally viewed the BBC as stuffy, stuck-up and boring. Despite the BBC's attempt to escape from this negative image, there are still a few clues in the 1967 broadcast to tell us why many young people were justified in thinking that the BBC was completely out of touch with them.

## *KISS Breakfast* on KISS Radio

This is a targeted CSP, which will be studied in detail with reference to the following elements of the theoretical framework:

- Media Audiences
- Media Industries

as well as all relevant contexts.

### Media Industries and Media Audiences

KISS is a radio service available online, on FM, DAB, Freeview or Sky TV, and via the KISS Kube app. *Kiss Breakfast* with Jordan & Perri is on live every weekday from 6 a.m. to 10 a.m., but it isn't necessary to hear the show live. As with the other 2023 radio CSP, you only need to listen to extracts from the show to get an idea of the content and style of presentation. Recordings are widely available.

Kiss FM began as a London-based pirate radio station in 1985, specialising in black and dance music. With support from media company Emap, the station gained a licence to operate legally across London, broadcasting as Kiss 100 from September 1990. Emap took over fully in 1992, but then sold its radio and consumer magazine divisions to Bauer Media Group at the end of 2007. Other local KISS stations had been developed in other UK cities, joining together to create a national station by 2010. KISS Radio is now part of a group of radio stations and related products under the KISS brand. All of these products are aimed at the 15–34 year old age group.

Bauer Media Group is also the owner of *Heat* magazine, another of the 2023 CSPs. *Heat* was a natural fit for Bauer, as it was originally a German printing company, owned by the Bauer family since 1875, who had gradually expanded to publish magazines in other countries. The acquisition of Emap Consumer Media and Emap Radio by Bauer took the German company into the radio industry. Since then they have acquired well over 150 further radio stations, mostly across northern Europe. They now operate in four different business areas – publishing, audio, online comparison platforms, and services for small businesses – and claim to reach over 200 million people worldwide. KISS is therefore just one small part of a large conglomerate.

Jordan Banjo and Perri Kiely took up the role as breakfast show presenters in August 2020, having co-presented a weekend show on the channel for 18 months prior to this. They were best known for their part in UK dance group Diversity, but they had also presented and appeared on other TV and radio shows, and Perri had a large following on TikTok. The station hoped the duo would bring new listeners to their breakfast show. Their move to the breakfast show was reported with constant references to the Black Lives Matter movement. Many media companies have been keen to expand their diversity in response to the worldwide coverage of this movement.

> **Activity 5.23**
>
> Listen to some extracts from *The Tony Blackburn Show*, including the introduction. Do you think the BBC was successful in reforming its stuck-up and boring reputation with young people?

> **Tip**
>
> Make your own list of the reasons why the BBC set up Radio 1 in 1967.

> **Activity 5.24**
>
> How do Bauer and KISS promote and market the KISS Breakfast show? Who is the target audience?

Jordan & Perri

### Talk about it

At time of writing, RAJAR has not been carrying out audience surveys since early 2020 due to pandemic restrictions. The popularity of the *KISS Breakfast* show with Jordan & Perri is untested. Check the RAJAR website to see if figures are now available, and discuss if KISS's investment in this pair paid off.

### Talk about it

As a group, discuss the strengths and weaknesses of the KISS Breakfast show show compared with other examples of music radio. How successfully is the radio industry meeting the needs of today's audience for popular music?

The *KISS Breakfast* show isn't too different in approach from Tony Blackburn's show back in 1967. Jordan and Perri chat and share banter, while responding to messages from listeners and introducing music aimed at the 15–34 year old target audience. There are special guests, easy-to-enter competitions and regular contributors.

Most music radio stations play a fairly restricted set of songs from a weekly playlist. Often, this playlist is generated by specialist computer software, so presenters have little choice about the tracks played on their shows. KISS play mostly pop, dance and hip-hop music from the charts, and as Perri Kiely put it: 'The entire station is influenced by black culture' (McIntosh, 2020).

Listeners are encouraged to engage with the show via their 'socials', and the use of these social media networks means that interaction can feel very immediate. The presenters will start discussing a topic, and listeners will message in their comments, questions and responses within minutes. Topics are chosen to chime with the target audience, such as the latest blockbuster films, morning coffee and dating. KISS refers to this as its 'youthful, peer-to-peer approach' (Bauer Media Group, 2021).

The KISS Breakfast show is light-hearted and entertaining in the manner of traditional music radio. KISS is, of course, a commercial radio station, so there are advert breaks at various points during the show, which provide the finance to keep the station going. There are also travel and news bulletins, as is normal in many breakfast radio shows.

Unlike in 1967, audio listeners now have a wide choice of types of content – on-demand music streaming, podcasts, catch-up radio listening, audiobooks, downloads and CDs, all in addition to radio. The RAJAR Midas survey of Spring 2020 (see image page 197) shows that live radio remains by far the most popular of all these options. According to this survey, 76% of 'new music discoverers' consider radio to be important for coming across music tracks for the first time. KISS has capitalised on this by teaming up with Apple Music and Shazam to create the 'KISS Hype Chart'. Streaming music services such as Apple Music, Amazon and Spotify make literally millions of tracks available to their customers. The choice is bewildering, especially in comparison with the situation in 1967 when young people struggled to find any outlet for popular music, especially new music. The KISS Hype Chart show makes its playlist available on Apple Music, allowing listeners to find the tracks they want to hear (Bauer Media Group, 2020).

## Studying film as an industry

When studying the film industry, it can be helpful to consider the three key components separately. These are:

- production
- distribution
- exhibition.

### Production

This, of course, involves the actual making of the film, including finding the necessary funding, buying or commissioning the content, filming and post-production work.

When funding and rights permissions are in place, a film is **greenlit** for production. Production costs are high in the film industry but the shift from analogue to digital has helped to offset these costs. Most films are shot, recorded and edited on digital equipment. It saves time, cuts costs and doesn't degrade over time, as celluloid film did.

## Distribution

This involves bringing the completed film to an audience. In smaller-scale film production, a separate distribution company will pay the production company for the right to distribute the film. At the high end of the market, the production and distribution companies tend to have the same owner.

Distributors are also responsible for ensuring that the film complies with regulations concerning age rating in any country in which the film is released. In the UK, the BBFC certificates all films, trailers and videos for public screening.

A substantial proportion of the film's budget is often assigned to marketing. This involves advertising, the circulation of trailers and the promotion of the film through other media.

Distributers make key decisions about the timing of the film's release. Typically, big budget films are initially released in cinemas (known as movie theatres in America) following a spectacular premiere. Other release windows are selected for:

- DVD/BluRay
- video-on-demand/streaming services
- pay TV
- free-to-air TV.

The film's distributors negotiate a price or a percentage of the income with the film's exhibitors.

Films used to be distributed by transporting 35mm prints to cinemas, but today's films are distributed on a Digital Cinema Print – a hard drive containing a massive video file. This form of distribution means that it is much more common for a new film to be released simultaneously in many countries.

## Exhibition

This is the point at which an audience is able to view a film. In the pre-digital age, exhibition was strongly focused in the cinema itself. For most films the cinema remains the most important source of income.

The cinema industry has always been threatened by competition. From the 1950s, television was a key competitor and today's sophisticated home entertainment systems still tempt viewers away from the multiplex.

Exhibitors fought back by making the 'cinema experience' more attractive, with comfortable seats, high-quality sound and vision, special screens and effects such as 3D and IMAX.

Cinema exhibition, too, is almost entirely digital today. Pushed by the distributors, cinema chains rapidly shifted to digital projection between 2009 and 2013. Most large multiplex cinemas are now controlled from a central 'hub' which operates all the projectors for different screens.

> **Key term**
>
> **Greenlight**
> The stage in the process of film development when funding has been agreed and shooting can start.

> **Link**
>
> For more about BBFC certificates see Chapter 4, pages 128–129.

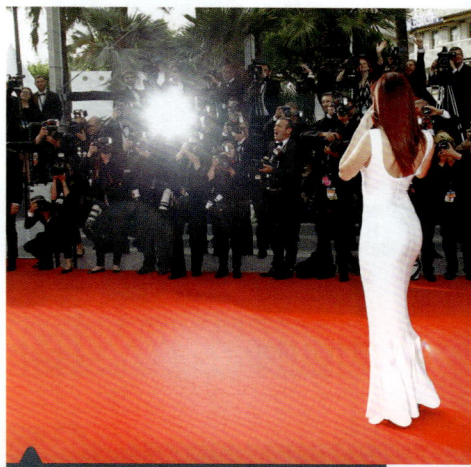

*The glamour of a red carpet premiere*

*The multiplex experience*

> **Quick question 5.29**
>
> How have your local cinemas made themselves attractive destinations?
> What would tempt you to watch a film at the cinema rather than as download?

**Teaser poster for Marvel's *Black Widow***

# Film: close study products

The CSPs in this media form, for 2023, are *Black Widow* and *I, Daniel Blake*.

## Black Widow (Cate Shortland, USA, 2021)

This is a targeted CSP, which will be studied with reference to the following element of the theoretical framework:

- Media Industries

as well as all relevant contexts.

## Overview

This 2021 film is an example of the superhero genre. The character Black Widow, like Iron Man, The Avengers and Captain America, originally appeared in Marvel Comics. The film was produced by Marvel Studios, a subsidiary of Walt Disney. Other production studios had acquired the rights to Marvel Comic superheroes such as Spider-Man (Columbia Pictures, owned by Sony) and the X-Men (20th Century Fox), although Disney has been working to acquire these rights. In buying 21st Century Fox, it gained the X-Men, and they have negotiated with Sony to co-make a number of Spider-Man films and involve Spider-Man in the Marvel Cinematic Universe.

In addition to location shooting in Budapest, Norway, California and Morocco, much of the studio shooting was based in the UK at Pinewood Studios. A British company, Cinesite, also contributed to post-production visual effects.

Florence Pugh, who plays Yelena Belova, is a British actor and there are other UK-based cast members, including O-T Fagbenle (Mason), Ray Winstone (Dreykov) and Rachel Weisz (Melina Vostokoff).

The budget for *Black Widow* was $200 million. It was released simultaneously on Disney+ (Premier Access – an additional charge on top of the monthly subscription) and in cinemas, and it had grossed over $500 million by mid-August 2020. Apart from this financial success, the film also received a good deal of critical acclaim, with 91% positive reviews (Rotten Tomatoes, 2021).

### Quick question 5.30

To what extent would you consider *Black Widow* a British film?

### Activity 5.25

As noted right, *Black Widow* grossed $500 million by mid-August 2021. Obviously, box office receipts are a big component of this gross taking. What other sources of income are available to the producers and distributors of a film such as *Black Widow*?

Do some research of your own to find out which films have been most financially successful in the past year. Who has a claim on the gross revenue of a film once the production costs are taken away?

### Talk about it

*Black Widow* was made by an American production company and distributed by Walt Disney Studios, but what does the making of *Black Widow* tell us about the UK film industry?

- What role does the internet play in marketing a film such as *Black Widow*?
- How else was *Black Widow* promoted to its target audience?
- What factors would make customers want to watch *Black Widow* at a cinema rather than watching at home or on a mobile device?
- 20 years ago, big budget blockbusters such as *Black Widow* would be released in the USA first with a delay of several weeks before UK release. Why is this no longer the case?
- How was the audience for *Black Widow* restricted by its age rating? Who makes decisions about film ratings in the UK and what criteria were used for age rating *Black Widow*?
- Why did Disney decide on a simultaneous streaming and cinema release for the film?

## Media Industries

You will need to know who produced *Black Widow* and why so much money was invested in this particular film. It will help to look at the list of top grossing films 2000–2019.

| Rank | Title | Worldwide gross | Year |
|---|---|---|---|
| 1 | *Avengers: Endgame* (Disney) | $2.798bn | 2019 |
| 2 | *Star Wars: Episode VII – The Force Awakens* (Disney) | $2.071bn | 2015 |
| 3 | *Avengers: Infinity War* (Disney) | $2.048bn | 2018 |
| 4 | *Jurassic World* (Universal) | $1.671bn | 2015 |
| 5 | *The Lion King* (Disney) | $1.663bn | 2019 |
| 6 | *Marvel's The Avengers* (Disney) | $1.519bn | 2012 |
| 7 | *Furious 7* (Universal) | $1.515bn | 2015 |
| 8 | *Frozen II* (Disney) | $1.450bn | 2019 |
| 9 | *Avengers: Age of Ultron* (Disney) | $1.403bn | 2015 |
| 10 | *Black Panther* (Disney) | $1.348bn | 2018 |

Source: IMDb (2019)

### Activity 5.26
Which film genres have been most successful? Is there a formula for making financially successful films? Do the filmstars make any difference to the audience appeal of *Black Widow*?

## Social and cultural contexts

Hollywood is sometimes accused of dominating and even destroying the film industries of other countries because its products are so:

- expensively made
- appealing
- intensively marketed.

How have national film industries outside the USA attempted to resist Hollywood domination?

## *I, Daniel Blake* (Ken Loach, UK, 2016)

This is a **targeted CSP**, which will be studied reference to the following element of the theoretical framework:

- Media Industries

as well as all relevant contexts.

### Overview

This is a **social realism** film directed by left-wing filmmaker Ken Loach and produced by British company Sixteen Films. The production budget is unknown but certainly only a tiny fraction of the $200 million it cost to make *Black Widow*. As a rough guide, the budget for Loach's 2009 film, *Looking for Eric*, was £4 million.

The funding model for *I, Daniel Blake* was completely different from *Black Widow* and relied on a wide range of backers including the BBC, the BFI through the National Lottery and the EU's Creative Europe Fund.

*I, Daniel Blake* is a UK/France/Belgium co-production, as the main funding sources came from these three countries.

*Campaigning filmmaker Ken Loach*

### Key term

**Social realism**
A film genre that deals sympathetically with everyday issues and problems faced by working-class people. Typical themes of social realist films include unemployment, poverty, homelessness, prostitution, drugs and the effects that these have on people's relationships.

**Key term**

**Austerity**
Government policies that reduce spending on public services so that the country does not have to borrow so much money.

**Link**

For more about political spectrum see Chapter 5, pages 181–182.

BAFTA – British Academy of Film and Television Arts

*I, Daniel Blake* won the highest award at the prestigious Cannes Film Festival.

*I, Daniel Blake* won many awards and highly positive critical reviews including a BAFTA (Britain's equivalent of the Oscars) for Best Picture. These, along with the public interest in the film's potential themes, helped to stimulate the film's box office receipts and income from online viewing. Box office receipts for *I, Daniel Blake* are currently (in 2021) $15.8 million, the highest ever for a Ken Loach film.

Although the focus is on industry issues, it is important to be aware of the topic and themes of *I, Daniel Blake*. In portraying the battles fought and indignities suffered by welfare claimants, the film has a clear and strongly expressed left-wing political message.

The government's programme of **austerity**, including the efforts to reduce welfare spending, is shown to have disastrous consequences for the film's main characters. Many reality TV shows represent welfare claimants as 'scroungers' who don't want to work but Loach's film challenges these negative stereotypes.

This is not a film that would have been made at all outside the independent sector.

## Media Industries

What does the promotional material for *I, Daniel Blake* suggest to you about the intended audience for this film?

*I, Daniel Blake* is a very rare example of an independent film whose income is greater than its production costs. Most independent films in the UK rely on subsidies in the form of grants from the BBC, the BFI or Film 4.

**Link**

For more on the independent sector see Chapter 4, pages 127–128.

**Talk about it**

What are the arguments for and against these subsidies?
- How are films such as *I, Daniel Blake* marketed, distributed and exhibited? How is this different from mainstream Hollywood films?
- How important are film festivals and awards in building an audience for films such as *I, Daniel Blake*?
- *I, Daniel Blake* has no established stars. Dave Johns, who plays Daniel, was a comedian with no previous acting experience. Do you think that the role of stars is overrated in making a film attractive to its audience?
- To watch *I, Daniel Blake* you have to be at least 15 years old. What criteria were used to decide this age rating?

## Social and cultural contexts

Can UK films such as *I, Daniel Blake* possibly compete with films such as *Black Widow*? Does it matter? Is it important for UK audiences to see British films dealing with local subjects?

# Studying magazines

## Overview

The focus for this media form is on Media Language and Media Representations but it will still be really useful if you know something about the magazine industry and magazine readers. This will help you to study the two front covers in context.

## Going digital

Magazines face many of the same problems as newspapers. Overall sales of print magazines have dropped steadily. Even when the print version and digital subscriptions are combined, the average drop in sales was 6% in 2020 (Tobitt, 2021).

Magazine publishers have tried hard to:

- replace print advertising income with income from digital advertising
- replace lost sales of print with online subscriptions.

New magazines still keep appearing and some titles have managed to increase sales even in these difficult times.

The most successful magazines are distributed in many different forms:

- print
- apps
- mobile-friendly formats.
- a digital edition
- social media

Despite these tough times, there are still plenty of magazines out there.

## The front cover

The move towards digital doesn't seem to have done anything to undermine the importance of the front cover for magazines. Here's what Terri White, editor-in-chief of *Empire* magazine, has to say:

> *The cover is of course the most important page in a magazine, it's key – it's your shop window.* (The mediabriefing.com, 2017)

Online or print, the front cover is vital.

Whether it's a physical newsstand or an online display, the cover still plays a crucial role in grabbing your attention.

Out shopping, browsing the internet or just walking city streets, it is hard to avoid magazine covers. Even if you don't stop to buy a magazine, just noticing the cover helps the magazine to reinforce its brand.

In a highly competitive marketplace, the front cover of a magazine must have a powerful visual impact. This is usually achieved by an effective combination of the three main elements:

- **The masthead**: the magazine's title, nearly always in a distinctive and easily recognised typographic style. Cover designers usually place the most important parts of the cover, including the masthead, on the left-hand side because it will catch your eye when you glance at a newsstand stacked like the photo below right.

### Activity 5.27

List as many magazine titles as you can. Choose three magazines and describe the brand image of each one.

- **The main image**: usually a photograph. Some magazines have many images on the cover to give the impression that the edition is bursting with exciting contents, but one image always stands out.

- **The main coverline**: the explanation in words of the main image. If there are many cover lines, the main one will be given much more prominence, usually with an extra-large font (point size).

Designers can't start from scratch with each new cover. Their goal is to strike a balance between elements that are already familiar to readers and elements that are stimulating and exciting for both new and existing readers.

### Activity 5.28

Here are some magazine covers for you to evaluate. Remember that the casual shopper will spend less than five seconds on average glancing at magazine covers. Which one do you think stands out and why?

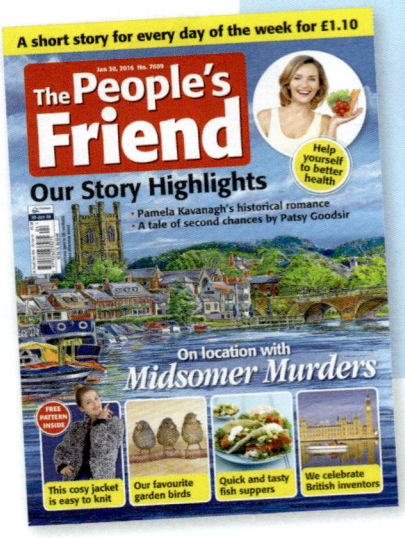

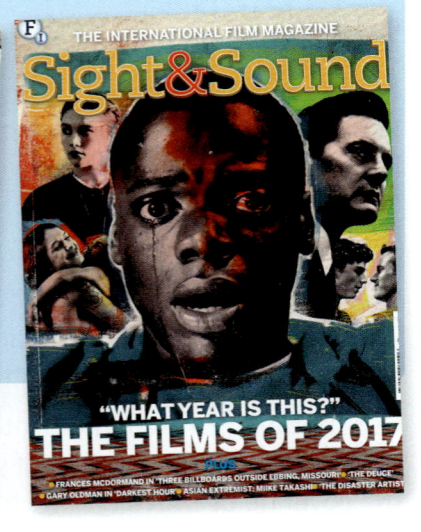

## Readers

You won't need to analyse the audience of the relevant CSPs in much detail, but it is certainly worth knowing:

- how the publisher sees their readership
- how they sell these readers to advertisers
- how the magazines address their readers using media language and representations.

**5** Close study products and media forms

## About this magazine

Heat magazine or also know as heatworld, is the brand that sets popular culture alight and fuels conversation about the celebrity world. Want the real story behind the celebrity news? Our exclusive interviews asks the questions that nobody else dare ask! After a new TV obsession? Then our Unmissables entertainment edit is for you! Led by our hugely credible team of experts - including BAFTA judge Boyd Hilton – we help readers to navigate the tricksy world of TV, film and streaming.

Need to know how to get THAT look? Our style section – Wear It's At – combines an aspirational yet affordable weekly fashion edit. Our all-inclusive approach promises style for everybody, no matter what shape or size, and our team test fashion and beauty products to make sure readers spend their hard-earned pennies wisely. Plus, get down-time inspo by reading our Life Hacks edit delivering the buzziest experiences in travel, food, fitness, wellbeing and homes each week. Your Instagram feed simply won't fill without it!

**Inside each issue of Heat magazine, you will find:**
- The latest celebrity news
- Road tested fashion and beauty
- What to watch (read and download)
- NEW; Lifestyle section for travel, diet, fitness and food

Don't miss the week without Heat!

### 📖 Print

In print – we bring readers a truly unique, quality experience. From clever A-list access shoots no other magazine could pull off to celeb news – *heat* has the celeb contacts to give readers the exclusive every time.

Our Unmissables entertainment edit is led by our hugely credible team of experts – including BAFTA judge Boyd Hilton – helping readers navigate the tricksy world of TV and streaming. Our style section – Wear It's At – combines an aspirational yet affordable weekly fashion edit with the real, trusted voice of the *heat* brand.

Our all-inclusive approach promises style for everybody, no matter what shape or size, and our team test fashion and beauty products to make sure readers spend their hard-earned pennies wisely. And Life Hacks gives readers down-time inspo by curating the buzziest experiences in travel, food, fitness, wellbeing and homes.

> Here, Heatworld give us a very good idea who will be reading *Heat* and their interests.

# Magazines: close study products

The 2023 CSPs in this media form are *Heat* 21–27 November 2020 and *Tatler* January 2021 magazine front covers.

## *Heat* and *Tatler* magazine front covers

These are targeted CSPs, which will be studied in detail with reference to the following elements of the theoretical framework:

- Media Language
- Media Representations

as well as all relevant contexts.

## Media Language

We have already mentioned the masthead, main image and main cover line as three key components of magazine front covers. These are starting points for an analysis of the codes and conventions used in magazine design.

As with other CSPs, you will need to link the design components of magazine covers to the meanings that they make.

Semiotic analysis is a very useful tool in helping to understand how magazine covers create meanings. As you analyse media products you will begin to see more and more. People are used to glancing at something like a magazine cover for only a few seconds, but analysis requires a more intense sort of looking.

Your simple questions are:

- What is there?
- What does it mean?

### 🔗 Link

For more on semiotic analysis see Chapter 1, pages 13–24.

207

### Activity 5.29

Refer to the introduction to semiotics on page 13 and carry out an analysis of *Heat*'s front cover referring to:
- typography
- design elements such as bleeds (anything that touches the edge of the page without a margin), overlays, style lines, diagonals
- use of colour
- photographic images
- language and punctuation.

Your analysis should focus on the **connotations** of the elements you can see on the front cover. For example, there is a relationship between size and importance, so the size of the largest elements, the masthead and the main cover line 'Caught Out', connotes their importance.

Also, the cover uses various techniques to connote excitement. Many of the images burst out of the border that surrounds them, for example Giovanna's picture and its white border line. Parts of the masthead and each of the images are obscured by another overlaying element. The connotations are of a magazine that is bursting with dynamic and exciting content.

That's a start! What other connotations can you find on the cover of *Heat*?

## Genre and audience

Media language also helps you to identify the genre of the magazine and its target readership. Magazine genres include:

- lifestyle
- glamour
- consumer
- specialist interest
- culture and politics
- art
- celebrity

and the UK's bestselling genre:

- TV listings magazines.

Your analysis of *Heat* will also have shown you how the cover design is linked to the target audience's interests: entertainment, fashion, fitness, and celebrity news.

*Tatler*, although it shares some of these interests, is clearly aimed at a more upmarket readership and this is reflected in a different design code for the cover. Everything is arranged on a horizontal and vertical grid with no overlays other than text on the main image. The use of colour and typeface is more restrained and there is much less emphasis on scandal. Most significant of all is that there is only one cover image, a photograph that matches the size of the cover itself.

Hollywood gossip 1950s style and some design ideas similar to *Reveal*.

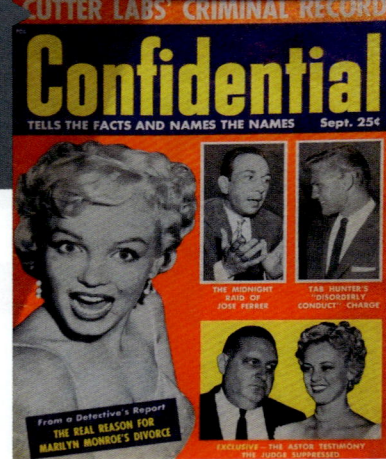

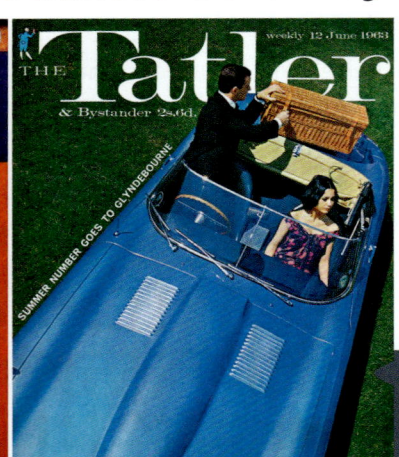

*Tatler*, 1963. No cover lines but otherwise very similar to a modern *Tatler* cover.

These features connote the sort of elegance, taste and timeless class that *Tatler* readers aspire to.

As always, the product designer's job in terms of genre is to strike a balance between the predicted and expected elements and the twists or variations that give each product a sense of being fresh and enticing.

Magazine covers, like all media products, have changed and evolved over the years, partly in response to emerging styles and fashion and partly in response to developments in print technology. However, a glance at these examples from an earlier era shows that many components of the language of magazine cover design remain remarkably unchanged and familiar.

### Narrative

Narrative structures may be more obvious in the case of a television drama or film, but all media products – including magazine covers – have a narrative. Here are some ways of opening up the narrative codes of a magazine cover:

**Time**: narrative puts things in time order so key questions are:

- What happens next?
- What happened before?

Magazine covers often tempt us to find out the answers to these questions by buying the magazine and reading the content. The coverlines of *Heat* suggest that secrets will be told.

**Cause**: narrative also deals with chains of cause and effect. Cover lines will often pose little mysteries or enigmas for the reader such as 'Why did celebrity X end the relationship with celebrity Z?' or 'Which sports car won our best in class showdown?'

If the cover sets you off on a train of thought about 'who did what' and 'what happened when', then you have been drawn into a narrative.

**Heroes, villains and the pot of gold**: as you know, one of the commonest narratives is the **quest**; a type of narrative in which a hero overcomes obstacles to achieve a goal. Often, the hero of the magazine cover is *you*, the reader. You are invited into an imaginary world in which celebrities are your friends, the secrets of health and happiness are yours and wish fulfilment is your reward. It's a fantasy, of course, but a pleasurable and harmless one. Not bad for £1.95!

## Media Representations

The notes on narrative above suggest that magazine covers may draw the reader into an imaginary world. In this sense, the covers are presenting a version of reality that is different from the reality of everyday life. It is probably a version that is preferable to everyday life, at least for the time the reader spends immersed in the magazine.

Part of your job is to describe and explain the 'alternative world' that a magazine presents to its readers. The magazine cover does this by constructing reality, often by telling stories about being a woman or being a man, about class or ethnicity, about fashion, buying and owning things and even about your own identity.

> **Link**
>
> See Chapter 1, pages 33–34 for a detailed analysis of *Tatler* referring to Propp's character types.

> **Talk about it**
>
> Are concerns over body representations on some magazine covers justified?

The reality created by *Tatler* magazine is one in which the purchase and ownership of expensive luxury items and services are absolutely central. It is a version of a reality, a story, in which everybody competes to look good and to feel good by having the most desirable clothes, jewellery and accessories.

Magazines have sometimes been blamed for creating versions of reality that could be damaging for readers. The photoshopping of images and the concentration on 'size zero' models has led some commentators to suggest that these 'ideals' so often presented by magazines can have a damaging effect on the esteem of young readers.

It has also been argued that magazine covers have some responsibility for eating disorders because they include so many unrealistic representations of supposedly perfect bodies. The language of magazine covers has also been blamed for some of these problems, with expressions such as 'bikini body' and 'drop two sizes' held up for criticism.

**Positive representation**

Although there have been criticisms of the magazine industry for its role in reproducing body images that are unrealistic and unattainable, it would be wrong to think that magazines dwell on negative stereotypes. Magazines want to flatter their readers and are more likely to provide strong, positive and independent role models.

Also, it is possible to overemphasise the effect that a media product can have on its audience. As readers, most of us recognise that magazine covers, like so many media products, present us with short-term fantasies that we wouldn't dream of taking seriously.

> **Activity 5.30**
>
> In your classroom are you more likely to be a sender or a receiver?

> **Link**
>
> See Chapter 3, page 96 for more on media effects.

# Studying music videos

Just as music itself has different genres, such as pop, rock and hip-hop, the accompanying music videos reflect the ideologies of the music and the artists' brand.

## Conventions of music videos

Music videos target the artist's existing audience but also attempt to broaden their reach to new audiences. In common with films and TV, music videos use certain conventions to attract and engage different audiences by conveying a message. This message may not directly reflect the lyrics or theme of the song but is likely to signify an essential element of the artist or band's brand. Messages are conveyed via media language such as mise-en-scène, clothing, locations, camera angles, screen time, editing and repetition of visual motifs.

Here are some examples of different music video conventions:

- **Pop**: attractive singers and dancers; colourful, sometimes revealing costumes; set in studio or familiar location; dance routines; eye contact with the camera.

> **Activity 5.31**
>
> Consider the music videos you watch the most. What is the genre? What would you expect to see in these videos? Do you enjoy the visual style of these videos? Why or why not?

Rihanna's videos often fulfil the conventions audiences expect of R&B. Here is Rihanna performing live in Rio de Janeiro.

- **Indie/rock**: live performance, showing the band playing instruments and focusing on the singer; understated or everyday clothing; low-budget feel with few special effects; located outdoors, often in a street, or in a music venue or warehouse.
- **R&B**: often use sexualised images, e.g. scantily clad dancers; colourful outfits; symbols of wealth, e.g. gold jewellery, cars; located at a studio, nightclub or house party.

## Branding and image

Now that less money is made through the sales of music, videos promote the artist's brand as much as the song itself. Fans may strongly identify with certain singers and bands that they feel represent them, or that they want to aspire to be like. Artists' videos allow them to control and project their image, and even to change it. Madonna, in the 1980s and 1990s, and Taylor Swift today, constantly redefine their image to keep the audience intrigued by, and involved in, their brand.

Many popular bands and singers first came to prominence by appearing on a TV talent show, such as *The X Factor* in the UK and *American Idol* in the USA. The heavily edited narratives of this type of show create irresistible 'rags to riches' stories of ordinary people such as Susan Boyle or Alexandra Burke being thrust into the limelight. These singers are portrayed as 'just like you and me', so that the viewer feels empathy and makes an emotional connection.

Rock and indie musicians may also want to present themselves as ordinary people – as authentic musicians who have risen to fame through hard work. Ed Sheeran, for example, is usually to be seen in tartan shirts and hoodies, with his guitar in hand. R&B and rap artists often present themselves as the successful people they have become (or hope to become), surrounded by signifiers of wealth and popularity.

> **Activity 5.32**
>
> Analyse the representations shown in the video for this week's number one single. You can find out which single this is at officialcharts.com. Consider how:
> - the video conforms to the expectations of its genre
> - the artist is being represented
> - other people in the video are represented
> - the song itself is being promoted
> - the audience is expected to feel about what they see and hear.

# Music videos: close study products

The music video CSPs for 2023 are for Arctic Monkeys' 'I Bet You Look Good on the Dancefloor' and Blackpink's 'How You Like That'.

These are targeted CSPs, which will focus on the following areas of the theoretical framework:

- Media Industries
- Media Audiences

as well as all relevant contexts.

## Arctic Monkeys – 'I Bet You Look Good on the Dancefloor' (2005)

### Overview

This music video is a live recording of the band playing in a warehouse-like studio to a small audience. The lead singer, Alex Turner, introduces the band and the song, saying 'don't believe the hype'. The band simply play the song, with cables, speakers and cameramen clearly in shot.

It is a performance-driven video deliberately filmed in the style of the 1970s live-music show *The Old Grey Whistle Test*, even using the same old-fashioned three-tube colour television cameras. The band are dressed in ordinary clothes and shown playing their instruments.

Watching the video is like being at a live performance. It is simple and looks low budget, focusing on the authenticity of the band. Close-ups show the band playing their instruments and none of them look at the camera, making the viewer feel as if they're just another audience member.

## Background

'I Bet You Look Good on the Dancefloor' was Arctic Monkeys' first single, released on 17 October 2005. It sold over 174,000 copies and went straight to number one in the charts. Their first album, *Whatever People Say I Am, That's What I'm Not*, was the fastest-selling British debut album of all time, until the first album by TV talent show star Leona Lewis overtook it the following year.

## Media Audiences

Music videos provide a way for artists to convey an image that they feel will appeal to fans of their music. Arctic Monkeys, in this video, present themselves as authentic, down-to-earth musicians who seem to be playing for their own entertainment rather than to please an audience. This contrasts with slicker, more manufactured bands, such as One Direction.

'I Bet You Look Good on the Dancefloor' represents a change in the way that artists could, potentially, build, and communicate with, an audience. It was Arctic Monkeys' first single but they had already built a word-of-mouth reputation by gigging around Sheffield and handing out free copies of their self-recorded demo CD, which friends and fans copied and left in public places. Fans also took advantage of emerging technology to upload the music to file-sharing sites and MySpace. Although the band did not have an official online presence at the time, fans set up webpages and message boards to stream, share and discuss their music.

By the time the press and record labels became aware of the band's popularity, they were playing sell-out shows in large venues which had mainly been promoted via text and the internet rather than by traditional advertising. They had developed a reputation as a live band worth seeing, which the video for 'I Bet You Look Good on the Dancefloor' reinforces. The video replicates the live feeling of mutual interaction between the artist and the audience.

## Media Industries

Arctic Monkeys came on the scene at a time of major changes within the music industry. Following the issues and instability created by Napster and other free file-sharing sites, labels were identifying new ways of making money. For example, paid downloads were beginning to become popular, following the launch of iTunes in 2004, with 36.6% of singles being bought digitally.

Even so, it still wasn't entirely clear whether it was a smart move to give music away for free. Arctic Monkeys seemed to prove that it was, initially becoming successful without the help or finance of a record label, even turning record company scouts away from their gigs. When they finally signed to an independent record label, Domino, in May 2005, they said they had turned down more lucrative offers and signed to Domino because the label's owner came across as a 'genuine fan' who ran the business from his home rather than corporate offices.

> **Quick question 5.31**
> How would you categorise Arctic Monkeys' original target audience?

> **Quick question 5.32**
>
> How have technological developments made it easier for artists such as Arctic Monkeys to produce and promote their own songs and videos?

> **Talk about it**
>
> What were and are the implications of these changes for mainstream music producers and publishers?

> **Talk about it**
>
> Are you aware of any current new artists who owe their recent success to their own online promotion, rather than to the backing of record labels?

Although 'I Bet You Look Good on the Dancefloor' was produced by Domino, the song and video still have a DIY feel, in line with the band's low-budget, fan-generated success. This was significant for the music industry for two main reasons:

1. From being passive recipients of whatever music they were offered, fans saw that they could now actively shape the careers of artists.
2. The internet, social media and streaming sites, in particular, had made it possible for music to be distributed and promoted at very little cost. The link between sales and online social spaces had not been made effectively before, so labels had to learn how they could use these opportunities to their advantage.

**Social and cultural contexts**

As we have seen, Arctic Monkeys are notable for being among the first bands to owe their success to online social networking.

They emerged towards the end of the post-punk revival of the early 2000s, which had featured gritty independent bands such as The Strokes, The White Stripes and The Libertines. It was seen by some as a backlash against manufactured pop bands, and a return to 'real' musicianship and experience.

There was nothing new about this approach – punk became popular in the mid-1970s partly as a response to the increasingly pompous 'stadium rock' of bands such as Queen and Led Zeppelin.

Robert Plant (left) and Jimmy Page (right) from Led Zeppelin

## Blackpink – 'How You Like That' (2020)

This is a targeted CSP, which will be studied with reference to the following elements of the theoretical framework:

- Media Industries
- Media Audiences

as well as all relevant contexts.

### Overview

In the music video for Blackpink's 'How You Like That', the song is performed within a range of fantastical studio backgrounds, including a jungle, an oil-drilling station in the arctic and a domed hall. Unlike Arctic Monkeys, there is nothing simple about the locations, and Blackpink dance, do not play instruments and all sing directly to the camera, as if to a single viewer. Each different location has a different colour palette and mood, echoing those seen in many films and TV series, but never being fully recognisable as anywhere specific. The members of Blackpink wear different outfits in each location, including a modern version of the traditional Korean costume, hanbok, in the final sequence. The video ends with the band members dancing in the domed hall with 40 to 50 backing dancers, before turning to face the camera as the image fades to black and the name of the song comes up on screen.

A separate video was released two weeks after the first, with the band members performing the dance moves from the first video, in an all-pink studio, wearing black.

### Background

Blackpink were formed by Korean record label and entertainment agency YG Entertainment. Each of the four members was recruited as a trainee for YG Entertainment through hotly contested auditions (including in Thailand and Australia) between 2010 and 2012. The formation of a new girl-group was announced by the company in 2011, but the line-up wasn't finalised until 2016. In the meantime, the then-teenage girls underwent rigorous training, and featured in other artists' music tracks and music videos. Their first recording, the single album featuring 'Boombayah' and 'Whistle', was finally released in August 2016, after a promotional build-up of announcements, teaser images, videos and advertisements. This reached number one in Korea and China, as well as in the Billboard World Digital Song Sales chart. They re-recorded and re-packaged some of their songs for the Japanese market with Japanese lyrics, but, discounting these, 'How You Like That' was their fifth studio release, and was announced as a comeback, as they'd not released any new music for a year, having been on tour. The single was the pre-release track from their first studio album, to be called *The Album*.

### Media Audiences

The band is the brand. In the tradition of girl bands from The Supremes to Little Mix, Blackpink's image was designed to appeal to a young, female audience who are the highest consumers of pop music, while also having enough sex

> **Activity 5.33**
>
> Blackpink said in an interview that the song 'How You Like That' had the message that *'even in the darkest times, we should persevere and fight through'* (Moon, 2020). How does the video reflect this? Choose key moments from the video that make this narrative clear. Compare the moments you have chosen with the choices of other people in your class.

> **Quick question 5.33**
>
> What are the pleasures and rewards for casual music video viewers? What, specifically, are the pleasures for the band's existing audience?

Lisa, like all the Blackpink members, has also been pursuing a solo career.

> **Activity 5.34**
>
> Look again at Chapter 4, page 148, to see how music videos are rated and regulated in the UK. Is there anything in either of the 2023 CSP music videos that would lead to an age rating of 12 or above?

appeal to keep the male audience interested. The video shows off the band member's dance moves and fashion sense, as well as giving a hint of the song's message that people can stay strong no matter what life throws at them. The dance moves and looks to camera were designed to suggest that the band members were strong, powerful and had 'swag'. Each band member is also a brand ambassador for several fashion and makeup brands, and the video and its promotion made fashion a central feature.

Unlike Arctic Monkeys' audience, Blackpink's audience could be seen as passive recipients of a ready-made band that was presented to them. However, they were clearly active in other senses, by buying their music, and attending live concerts and public appearances. As they are most likely to be members of Generation Z, they are also probably highly media literate, aware that their responses are being manipulated and happy to accept this in return for the aesthetic and visceral pleasures offered by Blackpink and their music. Of course, social media has also played an important part in Blackpink's success (see Social and cultural contexts, opposite).

Arctic Monkeys' video was created with a down-to-earth feel that would be recognised by their original fans in Sheffield. The Blackpink video is more international in scope, with dance moves that would be familiar to most pop music fans around the world, and with cultural references from a number of different countries. The lyrics are in both English and Korean, with subtitles in English throughout. The band members perform directly to the camera, in a glossily expensive production with no attempt to represent 'reality'. Instead, there are elements of fantasy and luxury in every sequence. This has obvious features to appeal to K-Pop audiences worldwide.

## Media Industries

YG Entertainment was set up in 1996 by Yang Hyun-suk, a former member of K-Pop group, Seo Taji and Boys. The company is one of three major K-Pop agencies in Korea, each of which has its own roster of trainees and idols. Trainees are taken on between the ages of 10 and 20, and can train for several years before being allowed to debut as an idol – if they make it that far. Traineeship involves dancing, singing, rapping, learning languages, following a strict diet and perhaps learning to inhabit a new personality. As well as holding large-scale auditions, YG Entertainment has taken on some of their trainees from TV talent competition shows produced by themselves or by other companies.

YG Entertainment had a net revenue of £160 million in 2020, although its profit in that year – a difficult one for many companies worldwide – was only £6 million.

Korean entertainment agencies have a greater say over their trainees and idols' careers than would be likely for a UK record company. Contracts tend to last for a decade and dictate behaviour as well as creative production. Trainees are typically not allowed to use social media, but idols have huge social media profiles that are heavily manged to maintain their personal brands. Lisa, the Thai member of Blackpink, had 58.4 million followers on Instagram in August 2021.

The Korean market is not big enough to give the financial return that K-Pop companies are seeking. Japan is the nearest large market, and many K-Pop artists are taught to speak Japanese to help them break into the market there. They also learn English, and most songs include at least some English, to help break other markets around the world. 'How You Like That' is a good example of a product that has exploited the existing cultural imperialism, taking on cultural forms from other countries in order to appeal to the global market.

While Arctic Monkeys retained control of creative outputs and sales (at least in the early days), it is the entertainment agency that decides the K-Pop artists' output and how they are presented. Videos are an official channel for controlling and presenting the artists' brand. Obviously, this is calculated to generate as much income as possible.

Music videos were originally intended to promote awareness of the music artist and sales of the specific music track. With the advent of social media, this promotional relationship changed. Even though the track spent over a year in the Billboard World Digital Song Sales chart, its sales will be in the low millions. As of the end of August 2021, the official 'How You Like That' video had been viewed 951 million times, and the dance performance video had received 828 million views. The Blackpink YouTube channel had almost 65 million subscribers.

YG Entertainment has undoubtedly made a lot of money from Blackpink's success, but the band members have also been richly rewarded. In 2020, it was estimated that Lisa (Lalisa Manoban) had a net worth of over £10 million, after just four years as an idol (Hegde, 2021). The band's songs are written by song-writing teams gathered from the best around the world, who would therefore take most of the music royalties. The band members' income comes instead from deals with fashion and other brands, public appearances and TV work.

### Social and cultural contexts

YouTube and TV talent shows have offered 'ordinary' people a platform to rapidly gain celebrity status. As well as some of YG's artists, international stars who originated from TV talent shows include Will Young, Kelly Clarkson, Jennifer Hudson and Adam Lambert. Despite their success and awards, the origins of their celebrity means that such artists are sometimes not taken seriously by critics and some audiences. Often, their backstory dominated the narrative of the show rather than (some people say) their talent. Others say that these singers did not have to try hard enough for their success – even if they often performed for years before TV gave them their 'big break'.

K-Pop as a genre is often criticised because the idols are quite clearly 'manufactured' by the agencies. Here, though, their long traineeship, with perhaps 12 hours a day of training and then personal practise time beyond that, is no secret but an accepted part of their success story. While undergoing this training, they are already receiving promotion, so that by the time the idols officially debut, some fans will have already invested emotionally in their success.

### Talk about it

Is the Blackpink video promoting sales of the music track, or is it a media product being promoted itself? Explain your answer.

### Activity 5.35

Interestingly, both Arctic Monkeys and Blackpink have performed at the Coachella festival, in 2012 and 2019 respectively. Compare their performances:
- with the videos you've looked at in this section
- with each other.

Think in particular about the social and cultural context of a music festival, and the expectations of a live festival audience. Why do you think each band was chosen? What do you think they added to the marketing or brand of the festival itself?

It is also important to acknowledge the influence of social media on Blackpink's success. YouTube phenomenon Psy, whose 'Gangnam Style' was the first YouTube music video to gain over a billion views, was also signed to YG Entertainment. Such videos enable artists to be seen simultaneously around the world, no matter where they're based, and for online fan communities to grow up around them. The live premiere of 'How You Like That' was watched by a peak of 1.66 million concurrent viewers, gaining it two Guinness World Records. By the end of the first 24 hours, it had received 86.3 million views, gaining it three more world records. Fans can and do share the video with each other, and discuss any and every aspect of it, on social media.

Let's compare the two 2023 CSP music videos. Both reflect the brand of the artists involved. Arctic Monkeys perform a live version of their song – 'keeping it real' – in a low-budget location, with no indication of the record label's financial backing. In contrast, Blackpink mime their performance, acknowledging the camera – and their target audience – throughout, and are also shown in a variety of glamorous fantasy settings and costumes.

### References

ASA (2015, 1 July) ASA Adjudication on Protein World Ltd, https://www.asa.org.uk/rulings/protein-world-ltd-a15-300099.html.

Bauer Media Group (2021) KISS Media Pack, https://www.bauermedia.co.uk/uploads/9a763e0ee49529fcc702f7951bba37ac.pdf.

Bauer Media Group (2020, 1 September) KISS Teams Up with Shazam and Apple Music on New 'Hype Chart' Show, https://www.bauermedia.co.uk/newsroom/press-releases/kiss-teams-up-with-shazam-and-apple-music-on-new-hype-chart-show#:~:text=KISS%20today%20announced%20it%20is,trending%20TV%20and%20film%20soundtracks.

BBC News (2014, 9 December) Number of UK Homes with TVs Falls for First Time, http://www.bbc.co.uk/news/entertainment-arts-30392654.

ESA (2017b) 2017 Sales, Demographic, and Usage Date: Essential Facts About the Computer and Video Game Industry, http://www.theesa.com/wp-content/uploads/2017/09/EF2017_Design_FinalDigital.pdf.

Fisher, K. (2017, 13 June) Kim Kardashian Breaks Down her Social Media Strategy and How it's Helped Expand her Empire, Enews, https://www.eonline.com/uk/news/860845/kim-kardashian-breaks-down-her-social-media-strategy-and-how-it-s-helped-expand-her-empire.

Google Play (2017) Change the Game, http://services.google.com/fh/files/misc/changethegame_white_paper.pdf.

Hegde, V. (2021, 24 July) Blackpink's Net Worth: How Much Does Each Member of the K-Pop Group Earn?, sportskeeda, https://www.sportskeeda.com/pop-culture/blackpink-s-net-worth-how-much-member-k-pop-group-earn.

IMDb (2019) The 50 Highest Grossing Movies of the 2010s (Worldwide), https://www.imdb.com/list/ls026040906/.

Lambert, L. (2016, 21 December) Bake Off Dominates the List of Most Watched TV Shows of 2016 With Nine Episodes in the Top Ten – So How WILL the BBC Replace It?, *Daily Mail*, http://www.dailymail.co.uk/tvshowbiz/article-4053494/The-Great-British-Bake-dominates-list-watched-TV-shows-2016.html.

Mayhew, F. (2020 16 April) National Newspaper ABCs: Print Sales Hold During Coronavirus Outbreak Before UK Lockdown, *PressGazette*, https://www.pressgazette.co.uk/national-newspaper-abcs-print-circulations-held-during-coronavirus-outbreak-before-uk-lockdown.

McIntosh, S. (2020, 30 July) Jordan and Perri: Kiss Breakfast Hosts on 'Stepping into Huge Shoes', https://www.bbc.co.uk/news/entertainment-arts-53361408.

MediaCom (2017, 1 December) #Represent with Lady Leshurr, http://www.mediacomnorth.co.uk/mediacom-news/nhs-blood-transplant-join-forces-mobo-represent-campaign/.

Moon, K. (2020, 26 June) BLACKPINK on the Message of New Single 'How You Like That', *Time*, https://time.com/5859277/blackpink-how-you-like-that/.

PAMCo (2020) Unlocking the Value of Publisher Audiences, https://pamco.co.uk/pamco-data/latest-results.

RAJAR (2020) MIDAS Measurement of Internet Delivered Audio Services, https://www.rajar.co.uk/docs/news/MIDAS_Spring_2020.pdf.

Rotten Tomatoes (2021) *Black Widow*, https://www.rottentomatoes.com/m/black_widow_2021.

Sky News (2016, 31 October) Britain's Most Watched TV Show of Last 80 Years Revealed, http://news.sky.com/story/britains-most-watched-tv-show-of-last-80-years-revealed-10639498.

Strugar, M. (2021, 26 July) 30+ Smartphone Usage Statistics for the UK, cybercrew, https://cybercrew.uk/blog/smartphone-usage-statistics-uk/.

TES (2018) Political Spectrum Diagram, TES, https://www.tes.com/teaching-resource/political-spectrum-diagram-11025057#.

The MediaBriefing.com (2017) Cover Story: Does the Front Page of a Magazine Still Matter?, https://www.themediabriefing.com/analysis/cover-story-does-the-front-page-of-a-magazine-still-matter/.

Think Gaming (2018) https://thinkgaming.com/.

Tobitt, C. (2020, 16 January) National Newspaper ABCs: *Observer* Sees Smallest Paid-for Circulation Drop in December, https://pressgazette.co.uk/national-newspaper-abcs-full-figures-december-2019-observer/.

Tobitt, C. (2021, 11 February) UK Magazine Circulations for 2020: Full Breakdown Shows Average 6% Year-on-year Drop, *PressGazette*, https://www.pressgazette.co.uk/magazine-circulation-uk/.

Weisman, A. (2015, 3 March) Kim Kardashian Reveals the 'Accidental' Reason Why Her Mobile Game is Such a Huge Success, Business Insider, http://uk.businessinsider.com/why-kim-kardashian-hollywood-app-is-successful-2015-3.

# 6 Non-exam assessment

## What's in this chapter?

This chapter looks at the practical work that you have to do as part of your GCSE Media Studies course – the non-exam assessment.

- You will look at what you are expected to submit for assessment, including the Statement of Intent.
- AQA set specific briefs for the NEA each year. This chapter will show you how to read and respond to a brief.
- There is also advice on how to use codes and conventions effectively within each media form, and the types of software and hardware you might need to use.

## What is the NEA?

**Key term**

**Non-exam assessment (NEA)**
Referred to by some people as coursework. You have to carry out this work during the course itself, rather than during an exam at the end of the course. However, the tasks are still set by AQA. Your NEA work is first marked by your teacher and is then sent to AQA who will moderate the marks.

The **non-exam assessment (NEA)** is a crucial part of the GCSE Media Studies course. You have spent a considerable amount of time during the course learning how meaning is communicated in media products – how codes and conventions are used, and how the varieties of codes and signs are put together by media producers to create certain connotations and have particular effects on audiences.

By studying Media Language, Media Representations and Media Audiences, you will have become more confident in analysing media texts and products and you will be able to explain 'how they work'. By studying Media Industries you will have seen how media professionals and others make and market media products.

Now, with the NEA, it is *your* turn to do it yourself. You are all media *consumers* every single day. The NEA is your opportunity to be a part of media *production*.

If we compare the NEA process to the film or TV industries: AQA is the commissioning body, asking for a specific media product; your teacher is the producer who sets the deadlines and makes sure you have the equipment you need; and you are the director who makes all the creative choices to give them the product they want within the timescale they have set.

# What do you have to do for the NEA?

You have to create an **individual** media production using one of the following:

- television
- music video
- radio
- newspapers
- magazines
- advertising/marketing
- online, social and participatory media
- video games.

**Media briefs** are used to communicate to media companies, as in this (fictional) Spotfaze brief.

## Spotfaze

**Media brief: Spotfaze Deeper**

**1. Background**
Spotfaze is a global company, originally based in the UK. It specialises in skin-care products. It is committed to creating products that use natural ingredients to combat skin problems for all skin types.
Spotfaze needs a campaign that targets a new audience, building its brand image with the group. The campaign should have a mix of TV, radio and print.

**2. Product specifics**
Deeper: new facial cream for adults who are suffering from outbreaks of spots.

**3. Campaign objectives**
Create awareness of Spotfaze as a brand with a successful record of previous products, and of Deeper, while removing stigma of older people buying spot creams. USP will be product developed specifically for older skin types, plus defeating outbreaks of spots quickly and with a minimum of fuss.

**4. Target group**
- Men and women
- Aged 30+
- Busy and successful lifestyle
- Meeting people through work everyday
- Don't want to spend time worrying about their skin, when they need to be preparing ideas, presentations, etc. for meetings.

*Example of a media brief issued by the (fictional) company Spotfaze.*

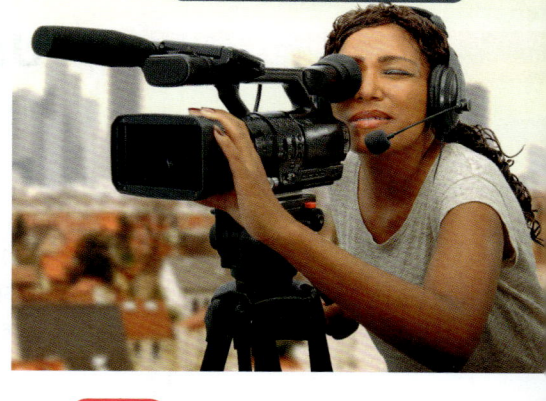

### Key term

**Media brief**
A document setting out what is needed within a media product. It is usually written by a non-media company, such as a manufacturer who wants to advertise their goods, explaining what they want the media products (in the Spotfaze brief, the adverts) to achieve. It is used by their chosen media production company to make sure they get the message and the details right.

### Link

There are sample versions of AQA NEA briefs later in this chapter, pages 224–236.

The media product that you create must be in response to one of the five media briefs released by AQA each year.

Each NEA brief will specify the media form to be used and the intended audience. The media product that you create must communicate meaning to this intended audience. It must also show your understanding of two areas of the GCSE Media Studies theoretical framework: Media Language and Media Representations.

Your teacher will give you a deadline for each stage, e.g. planning, writing your Statement of Intent and carrying out the production work. AQA suggests that no more than 30 hours should be needed for the production part of the process.

*Your media product must appeal to its target audience.*

## Key term

**Unique selling point (USP)**
The factor that makes a specific product or service stand out in comparison to other similar products. The USP of a community radio station could, for example, be that it plays music by local artists or that it features news about the local area.

## Link

For more on carp fishing magazines see page 38.

## Activity 6.1

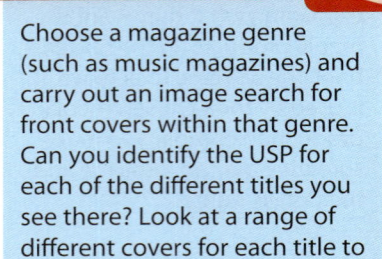

Choose a magazine genre (such as music magazines) and carry out an image search for front covers within that genre. Can you identify the USP for each of the different titles you see there? Look at a range of different covers for each title to help you do this.

# Unique selling point

Many of the briefs will require you to create a new media product that has a **unique selling point** – or USP. In order to appeal to a target audience, your product will need to be similar to existing products in some ways, so that the audience understand the genre and the basic conventions. We all like familiarity to some extent. However, a successful media product also needs to be different in some ways – this is what makes it unique and encourages audience members to engage with this specific product. In Chapter 1 there were examples of three separate magazines about carp fishing. Each one has to compete with the others by providing something slightly different for its readers.

# House style

The briefs for magazines, newspapers and websites will often mention the need to use a house style. This tells you that you need to consider a common look to the pages, so that they clearly belong to the same media product. Look at the pages below from the January 2018 issue of *Q* magazine. Each double page spread is from a different section of the magazine, so there are style changes between the different sections, such as the use of fonts. However, black, red and white are used throughout, along with rectangular boxes and borders; one side of a double page spread is often devoted to graphics – headlines or photographs – while the other side has both graphics and text in columns.

*A selection of pages from Q magazine January 2018*

# The Statement of Intent

You will need to submit a Statement of Intent for your NEA work. This will be discussed in more detail later on in this chapter. It is in your Statement of Intent that you set out what you what you want to achieve and what you intend to do with your media product.

You will need to outline how you will use media language and media representations to create your media product and its meaning. As well as this, you should explain how you intend to meet the requirements of the brief and meet the needs of the intended audience.

## Knowing what to do

It's only natural that you will have plenty of questions about the NEA. For example, if you are creating a music video, how long should it be? If you are creating a magazine, how many – and what – pages do you need to produce? Don't worry, each AQA brief will clearly tell you the length, duration or amount of the media product that you need to create.

In fact, the briefs will give you a lot of helpful information. A section called 'Minimum requirements' lists various things you need to include, such as how many locations you should film in, or which conventions you need to use on a magazine front cover.

If you use the minimum requirements like a checklist, your media product should be well on the way to being a successful piece.

In this chapter, we will look at five sample AQA briefs. These are not 'live' briefs that you can actually work from for your NEA. However, by looking at these exemplar briefs in detail, you will gain a clear understanding of how to approach one. This will be excellent preparation for when you come to create your media product for your own NEA.

## Who can you work with on your NEA?

Your media production needs to be an **individual** piece of work. However, that doesn't mean you have to do everything on your own! Unassessed participants – for example, friends at school – can appear in your media product or operate lighting and camera equipment. This must be under your direction; you have to make all the decisions, and you need to write on your Candidate Record Form what you asked them to do.

## How is the NEA assessed?

There are 60 marks available for the NEA. This is 30% of the overall marks available for GCSE Media Studies. Your work will be marked by your teacher and moderated by AQA.

You need to produce the Statement of Intent and a media product. If you complete a Statement of Intent but do not create the media product, you cannot be awarded any marks at all.

## Using this chapter to help you

You will start your NEA production work with an AQA-set brief. The next section of this chapter gives you five sample briefs. The first thing you will need to do is to plan and design your ideas based on the brief you have been set. Look through the sections on the sample briefs to see how to approach using your brief to help you come up with ideas, to check your ideas against the requirements you have been given and to plan your work.

Your next step after planning will be to write the Statement of Intent, explaining what you intend to create. There is a section designed to help you with this, after the five sample briefs.

Only then will you be ready to start your production work itself. The information about using production resources and techniques is therefore included after the sample briefs and the Statement of Intent. You may want to read about the relevant production techniques before you start your planning, or even before you choose your brief, but if you are already familiar with the basic techniques and resources available to you, you might come to these sections later in the process.

# Product briefs

The sample briefs used in this chapter were all created before the first live Media Studies NEA briefs, to help you and your teachers know what to expect and they have been available on the AQA website since 2017. These are not the actual briefs you will be expected to respond to – they will be given to you by your teacher, as new AQA briefs are issued every year.

## Example Brief One: Television

| Brief One | |
|---|---|
| Brief | Minimum requirements |
| Create a two minute pre-title sequence for a youth-oriented (14-17 year old) television fantasy drama series. This series should be based on life within an educational establishment. | • At least two filming locations<br>• At least two characters including a protagonist<br>• Variety of shot selection, framing of the image and camera movement<br>• Diegetic sound (which could include but is not restricted to dialogue, foley sound and ambience/atmos) and non-diegetic sound (which could include but is not restricted to soundtrack and voiceover) as appropriate to create meanings<br>• Use of narrative codes appropriate to the genre, to introduce a character, further the story **and/or** hook in the target audience<br>• Editing of the footage, soundtrack and dialogue to establish meaning and/or enigma |

**Example Brief One: Pre-title sequence for a TV series**

## Unpicking the brief

In each of the briefs, the left-hand column, 'Brief', sets out what you are expected to create for the NEA – in this example brief, you are expected to create a pre-title sequence for a television drama series.

It also gives you some other bits of key information: the sequence should last for two minutes, it should be aimed at a teenage (14–17 year old) audience, and the genre should be fantasy.

You also see that the series should be based on life within an educational establishment, such as a school or college.

When you think about it, that's a lot of information. This should give you a great starting point to begin your work. You should also be able to see how this links to the 2023 television CSPs, *His Dark Materials* and *Doctor Who*.

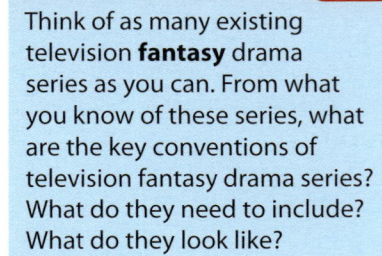

### Link
Look at the TV section in Chapter 5, pages 159–165, for more about the example CSPs.

### Activity 6.2
Think of as many existing television **fantasy** drama series as you can. From what you know of these series, what are the key conventions of television fantasy drama series? What do they need to include? What do they look like?

To create a successful media product, you need to have a good understanding of the form and genre you are working with. Carrying out the activity in this section, you will think about the key conventions of teenage fantasy drama. These conventions are just like the ingredients you might use in a cooking recipe – the things you need to include to make it look and taste how it should. If you use conventions in the right way, your ideas for a fantasy drama series will appeal to a teenage audience.

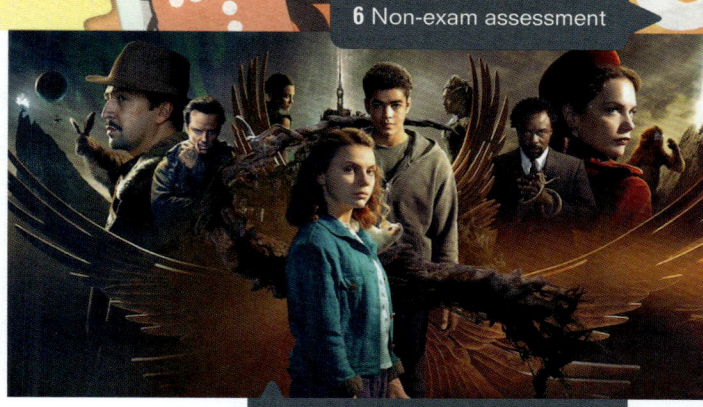

BBC/HBO fantasy drama *His Dark Materials*

## The media form: pre-title TV sequences

Now you need to be clear what you are creating. There is a difference between a **pre-title sequence** and a **title sequence** or an **opening sequence**. You can decide what to include in your pre-title sequence but you need to make sure that you are creating a pre-title sequence and not a title sequence. Getting the details right is part of 'meeting the brief'.

## Planning a pre-title sequence

Once you have established the key conventions of teenage fantasy drama and pre-title sequences you can really begin to plan your own two-minute pre-title sequence.

Of course, you are not creating an entire series (or even a single episode) but it still is a good idea to think of what would happen in your series. Consider who your main characters will be and an outline of how the plot and storylines might develop over the episodes of the series. The brief does not say this is the first episode, so you can choose whether this is the opening to the whole series, or the opening to an episode part-way through the series. Either way, you need to consider what your target audience will think as they watch.

You will need to include actions, characters or situations that make the audience want to see the whole episode. One way to do this is to include an enigma. This will leave the audience guessing what is going to happen and wanting to know more.

### Activity 6.3

Watch the opening few minutes of a variety of television drama series. You should make sure you look at several examples of teenage fantasy, but any genre is fine to look at.

What are the differences between a pre-title, title and opening sequence? What are the key conventions of pre-title sequences? What should be included in a **cold opening** to entice the audience to watch further?

### Key term

**Cold opening**
A short scene that occurs before the opening credits or titles, which hooks the viewer into the characters, the situations and possibly the story.

### Activity 6.4

Prepare a synopsis or treatment for your television fantasy drama series. To do this, you should be able to get your key ideas onto one side of A4, including the characters, the situation and actions, the main visual ideas, and the appeal to the audience. Pitch your proposal to other students and gain feedback to help you improve your ideas.

### Tip

Read the brief carefully to see where you are told what to do, **and** where you can make decisions.

### Link

You might want to look at the section on narrative and enigma in Chapter 1, pages 29–33.

## Using the minimum requirements

Use the minimum requirements set out in the brief as a checklist of things to include in your pre-title sequence:

- ☐ (At least) two locations
- ☐ (At least) two characters – including a protagonist
- ☐ A variety of camera shots and movements
- ☐ Diegetic and non-diegetic sound
- ☐ Narrative codes
- ☐ Appropriate editing

You could also add into your checklist the elements from the left-hand column of the brief:

- ☐ Two minutes long
- ☐ Youth-oriented audience (14–17 year olds)
- ☐ Pre-title sequence
- ☐ Fantasy drama
- ☐ Educational establishment

Planning is vital – you can't rush out and make a television sequence without knowing exactly what everyone is going to do. Before you even think about picking up a camera or arranging to meet your cast and crew, plan and storyboard your pre-title sequence, making sure you include all the minimum requirements. Remember that you are using these aspects of media language to create media representations, and to carry your meaning to the intended audience. You need to make decisions about each part of the mise-en-scène, and be in control of what the audience will see and hear.

## Example Brief Two: Online media

Example Brief Two: Website for a community-based radio station

| Brief | Minimum requirements |
|---|---|
| Create a working homepage and one linked page for a website promoting a new community-based streaming radio service aimed at 16-21 year olds. This will incorporate one minute of audio. | • Original title and logo for the service<br>• Four original images that establish the style of the service and a clear house style for the website.<br>• One linked page introducing one of the presenters on the station, including appropriate imagery and copy.<br>• One minute of audio to establish the style of the service (e.g. an extract from one show or 'snapshots' of multiple shows) including:<br>  • at least 45 seconds of voice<br>  • two different voices<br>  • other sound sources such as music or ambience/atmos.<br>• Use of appropriate language and register for the target audience. |

## Unpicking the brief

The left-hand column of the example brief sets out the expectations of what you should create for your NEA. Notice how this particular brief combines two different forms: websites and audio (streaming radio).

You are asked to produce a homepage and a linked page from the same website. This website is intended to promote a **new** community-based streaming radio service. The radio service (and therefore the website) is aimed at 16–21 year olds.

The linked page introduces one of the presenters and should also feature one minute of audio – taken from the radio station itself.

You should be able to see that this brief relates to your radio CSPs.

## The media form: radio service websites

Having unpicked the brief, you have the outline of what you need to produce, so what next? A good way of starting your response to the brief is to research the two media forms that are required: websites and streaming radio.

Although you are only being asked to create two webpages, it is important to think about how many pages such a website would have, and where the main links would be found on the page. You won't be creating all the other pages, but you should show what those pages would be and how to navigate to them.

For example, your linked page must introduce one of the radio station's presenters. Would this be one of several pages that each introduce a presenter? Or would this be a 'star' presenter who is somehow more important than the others?

The minimum requirements also tell you to create a one-minute audio clip that needs to be embedded into the website. This could be an extract from one particular show or 'snapshots' of multiple shows (think of this as being similar to a trailer or an advert for the station).

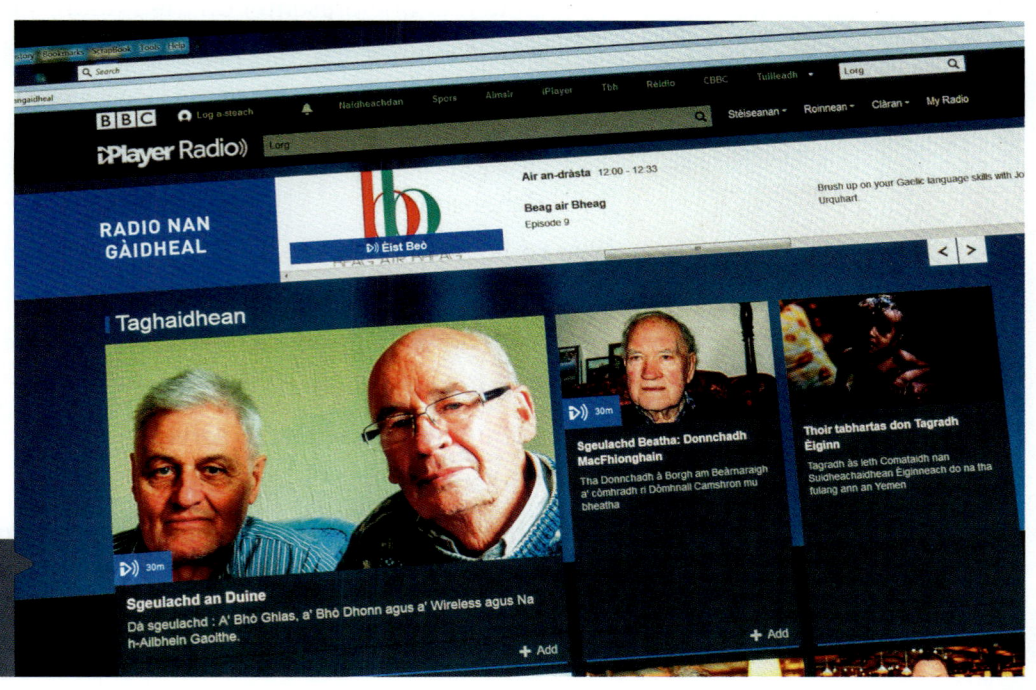

The website of BBC Radio nan Gàidheal, a Scottish local radio station that broadcasts in Scottish Gaelic.

### Activity 6.5

We visit websites every day, but what are the key conventions of a **homepage**? Research a wide range of websites for radio stations. Look at community-based, local and national radio. As well as this, try to include streaming, digital and analogue stations. This will give you a broad understanding of the ways different types of radio stations are promoted through their websites.

### Quick question 6.1

If you check on a radio station's social media platforms, such as Facebook or Twitter, you will often find short excerpts from their shows. Consider why they have chosen these moments to represent the best of their station.

## Planning your website

The website is for a 'community-based' radio service for 16–21 year olds. Before you can design the website for your station, you need to know the service's USP. Who are the 'community' it is serving – are they based in one geographical area, around one location (such as a sports centre or college) or do they share a common interest? What will they get from this service that they won't get elsewhere? Knowing what your radio station is all about will give you some ideas as to how the website should look.

With these ideas, and a good understanding of the conventions of websites and the way existing radio stations use their websites to promote themselves, you can begin to mock-up the visual design for your homepage and linked page.

You only need to create 60 seconds of audio, but it is still worth thinking about what each show would be about, and how it fits within the station's USP: is the personality of the presenter central to the show? What music would be played? What guests will be featured? What will be discussed on the show? How will it appeal to its target audience? From this, you can plan what to include to capture the audience's attention and make them want to listen to the station.

### Activity 6.6
Create a mock-up of the homepage and linked page for your radio station's website.

## Using the minimum requirements

From your research on radio stations you should have plenty of ideas about what to include in your homepage and linked page. Use the minimum requirements of the NEA brief as your checklist to make sure you have everything you need:

- [ ] Title
- [ ] Logo – designed by you
- [ ] Four original images – photographs taken by you
- [ ] House style for the two pages
- [ ] Details of one presenter on the station, including image(s) and words
- [ ] **Plus** 1 minute of audio, including:
- [ ] 45 seconds of voice
- [ ] Two voices
- [ ] Other sounds

You could also add in to your checklist the elements from the left-hand column of the brief:

- [ ] Homepage
- [ ] One linked webpage
- [ ] Community-based radio service
- [ ] Audience of 16–21 year olds

Using the checklist to remind you what you must include, script the talk section of your audio so that it conveys something interesting about the presenter and the style of their show.

### Activity 6.7
Create a profile for one of the presenters for the radio station. Remember the station is youth-oriented (aimed at 16–21 year olds). You will need to photograph someone appropriate to be your presenter.

### Talk about it
As the visual and the audio pieces are separate, and this is also not a real product, you can choose different people to be the 'face' of your presenter for the photograph(s) and the 'voice' of the presenter for the audio. In this way you can choose both the most appropriate look and the most appropriate sound.

# Example Brief Three: Magazines

| Brief | Brief Three |
|---|---|
| Brief | Minimum requirements |
| Create a front page and a double page spread feature for a new magazine that is dedicated, exclusively, to the promotion of the persona, brand and specialist interest area of an online vlogger.<br><br>The target audience is the existing online fans (age 13–16).<br><br>3 pages in total, including at least 5 original images | **Front cover:**<br>• Title for a new magazine and masthead<br>• Selling line<br>• Cover price<br>• Dateline<br>• Main cover image<br>• At least 4 cover lines<br><br>**Double page spread**<br>• Headline, standfirst and subheadings<br>• Original copy for double page feature (approx. 350 words) that links to one of the cover lines on the front cover<br>• Main image plus at least 3 smaller images<br><br>**Both**<br>• Clear brand and house style for the magazine, including use of images, colour palette and fonts. |

Example Brief Three: Magazine promoting an online vlogger

## Unpicking the brief

This example clearly shows how the NEA briefs link with the CSPs. In this brief you are being asked to create a magazine that promotes an online vlogger, their persona, their brand and their area of interest. Your target audience is 13–16 year olds who are already fans of the vlogger.

You need to create the front page and a double page spread for the magazine.

Notice that you are asked to include at least five original images. Theoretically, you could ask somebody you know to pretend to be an existing online vlogger who appeals to 13–16 year olds. However, it is probably a better idea (and certainly more fun) to create the persona of a fictional vlogger instead. This person can then vlog about anything you like, which gives you more scope for interesting pictures. You are only given the *age* of the intended audience, and can choose a smaller group within this, such as skaters or budding computer scientists.

### Activity 6.8

Create a personal profile for your online vlogger. What would their area of special interest be? Explain their personality and think how they would promote their personal brand.

## The media form: magazines

To respond to this brief, you need to combine your knowledge of online vloggers, particularly what makes them appeal to their audiences, with an understanding of magazines as a media form.

You may already have studied the two magazine CSPs, but you should also look at magazine conventions more generally. You will need to look at front covers and double page spreads, and also identify their house style.

It is important to look at magazines that are aimed at the same age group or the same interest group, and consider how these have been constructed to appeal to this audience.

> **Link**
>
> Look at the sections on Print codes in Chapter 1, pages 18–26, and Studying magazines in Chapter 5, pages 205–210.

> **Tip**
>
> If you carry out an online image search for 'magazine front cover' and look at a screen-full of results, you will easily be able to see the main conventions of this form.

> **Activity 6.9**
>
> Analyse the front cover and double page spread of several magazine publications. Identify the key conventions used. Explain how they appeal to the magazine's audience. Explain what the house style of each magazine is.

> **Tip**
>
> You can do an image search for 'magazine double page spread' but be aware that many of these images were posted by media students, and some are their own work, not professional publications.

> **Tip**
>
> Remember that the minimum requirements of the elements to be used within the pages are only the **minimum**, which means if you see other features that you want to use in addition to these, you can do so. However, you will not be rewarded for producing more pages than the number required.

You will see that most front covers carry a number of cover lines, each one indicating a story that readers can find within the magazine. Although you will only be creating one double page feature, you will need to decide on other stories that such a magazine would cover, so that you can write the cover lines. Use your research to help you think about this.

## Planning your magazine

Now that you have looked closely at existing magazine designs, you should be in a position to create a design of your own, that promotes an online vlogger and appeals to a teenage audience.

The key point for planning will obviously be the vlogger themself, along with their special interest. The magazine promotes this person and their 'world'. You can decide whether the vlogger writes all, part or none of the magazine.

Your double page feature will be signposted in one of the cover lines on the front. Sometimes, magazines use different images from the same photoshoot on the front cover and as the main image in the double page spread. This can help readers to recognise the article when they reach it.

> Look for magazines that target 13–16 year olds. *Youth Runner* welcomes interviews, product reviews and blogs for consideration to use in its issues.

Think about *what* you can take photographs of, as well as *who* you can use as your vlogger. You will need to use both the photographs and the words in the article to construct a representation of the vlogger and how they want their interests to be understood by the target audience. The way you phrase the article will convey as much meaning as what you write about.

## Activity 6.10
Produce a mock-up of the front cover and double page spread for your magazine.

## Using the minimum requirements

The minimum requirements section of the brief lists some of the conventions of magazines. Remember that you can add other features if you want.

For the front cover you need to use at least:

- [ ] Title and masthead – designed by you
- [ ] Selling line
- [ ] Cover price
- [ ] Dateline
- [ ] Main cover image
- [ ] Four cover lines, including one that points to your double page spread

For the double page spread you need to use:

- [ ] Headline
- [ ] Standfirst
- [ ] Sub-headings
- [ ] 350 words in the article
- [ ] Main image
- [ ] (At least) three smaller images

This means you need five different photographs in total. Most magazines would not take all of these photographs from the same photoshoot, but all the images used on the double page spread should illustrate something within that spread.

You also need to design your house style, so you need to choose your:

- [ ] Layout style
- [ ] Colour palette
- [ ] Limited range of fonts

and use these across all three pages.

When a viewer looks at the double page spread, it should be obvious that it comes from the same magazine as the front cover.

You could also add in to your checklist the additional elements from the left-hand column of the brief:

- [ ] New magazine
- [ ] Promoting vlogger and specialist area of interest
- [ ] Audience of existing 13–16 year old fans

# Example Brief Four: Music video

| Brief Four | |
|---|---|
| Brief | Minimum requirements |
| Create a two minute music video to be used to support an anti-bullying campaign.<br><br>This music video and message is to be aimed at school students aged 11–15. | • At least two filming locations<br>• At least two 'characters' including a protagonist<br>• Variety of shot selection, framing of the image and camera movement<br>• Diegetic sound (which could include but is not restricted to dialogue, foley sound and ambience/atmos) and non-diegetic sound (which could include but is not restricted to voiceover) as appropriate to create meanings<br>• Use of narrative codes to either introduce a character **or** further the message<br>• Editing of the footage, soundtrack and dialogue for meaning, including continuity and/or visual effect<br>• Use of titles and/or graphics in order to reinforce the message |

**Example Brief Four: Two minute music video supporting an anti-bullying campaign**

## The media form: music video, with a twist

Although this example brief uses the media form of music video, it asks you to do something a little different with it for your NEA. Typically, a music video is created as a promotional tool for a band or artist. For this brief, you need to create a music video that can be used to support an anti-bullying campaign.

This means that although music video is the form you are working with, it would be useful to look at a range of campaign videos and adverts. Key to being successful with this brief is the need to send out a clear message that resonates with the target audience of school students aged 11–15.

### Talk about it

You are not being asked to create the anti-bullying campaign, but a music video that can be used within this campaign. What are the differences between the two?

### Activity 6.11

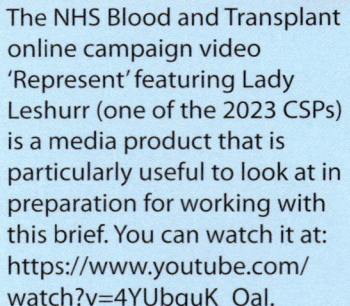

The NHS Blood and Transplant online campaign video 'Represent' featuring Lady Leshurr (one of the 2023 CSPs) is a media product that is particularly useful to look at in preparation for working with this brief. You can watch it at: https://www.youtube.com/watch?v=4YUbquK_Oal.

What conventions of music video can you see in the 'Represent' video? Think about shot sizes and angles, pace of editing, and other editing techniques.

How is the message in the video communicated?

Lady Leshurr in the campaign video 'Represent'

### Link

For more on 'Represent' see pages 61–62 and 191–192.

## Unpicking the brief

As with all the NEA briefs, unpicking it to see what you are being asked to do is important. You already know that the anti-bullying message you give in your video needs to be persuasive and grab the attention of 11–15 year olds, but the information contained in the minimum requirements section teases this out further.

You are told that you should use narrative codes to introduce a key character (a protagonist) or to further get the message across. This tells you that you have two clear options to start from.

Other requirements include the need to use at least two locations and to feature at least two characters. The final video should be two minutes long. You are not expected to create the music itself, so you can use an existing track. Consider carefully which track you will use, so that it will appeal to as wide a segment of the target audience as possible – or at least, not put them off – and will fit thematically with the video you wish to create.

Most music tracks are more than two minutes long, so you will almost certainly need to edit the track itself – the simplest way to do this is to fade it out after two minutes, but you may want to be more selective. Consider when you choose your track whether you might want to cut out a verse (or two) or an instrumental section or start partway into the song. You will be able to use your video-editing software to edit the track as well as the visuals. You now have enough information to begin devising ideas for your video.

## Planning your music video

A good way to begin thinking of ideas for any moving image product is to think of the 'story' that is behind it – what happens, or what's the action? For example, music videos are sometimes inspired by the lyrics of the song, so that the video 'tells the story' of the song. You need to use two locations and at least two people in the video. How will these two people be linked, if at all? How will you include the anti-bullying message? In other words, how will you show that bullying is something the audience should act against? Thinking about where and who you can use might also give you ideas for the look and content of the video.

Remember that you will also need to control the mise-en-scène in order to get your meaning across. What will each character wear? What will their body language be like? Will it be appropriate for them to look directly at the camera? Music video is one of the moving image forms where this is a possible convention.

Answering these questions should help you to come up with ideas for the story of your video. You can then write a short summary of the video style and structure and also explain in a couple of sentences how your ideas will get the anti-bullying message across to your target audience.

> **Quick question 6.2**
>
> How does a music video use media language in a different way to an advert or a TV drama?

**Activity 6.12**

Storyboard your music video, sketching out the camera angles and indicating the camera movements you will use for each shot, to have the most impact and to get the meaning across.

You know that you have two minutes to tell the story, so once you have your overall idea, you could break the two minutes down into segments, and decide how much of the action should happen in each segment. If you break the action down in this way, it will make it much easier to storyboard it accurately.

With any moving image product, having a good story is not enough, the way you tell the story needs to be visually exciting, with a range of camera shots and movement, as well as featuring appropriate sound and editing.

## Using the minimum requirements

As with all the briefs, use the minimum requirements as a checklist to make sure you are creating what has been asked for:

- [ ] (At least) two locations
- [ ] (At least) two characters – including a protagonist
- [ ] A variety of camera shots and movements
- [ ] Diegetic and non-diegetic sound
- [ ] Narrative codes
- [ ] Appropriate editing
- [ ] Titles or graphics

How can you use each of these features to pack your music video with meaning? Consider how you will use the mise-en-scène not only to construct your representations of the characters and the situations but to attract the attention of the audience to your message.

You could also add in to your checklist the elements from the left-hand column of the brief:

- [ ] Two minutes long
- [ ] Anti-bullying theme
- [ ] Audience of school students aged 11–15

## Example Brief Five: Advertising

| Brief Five | |
|---|---|
| Brief | Minimum requirements |
| Create three print advertisements for a new range of watches. The advertisements should emphasise a sense of tradition and history, and will be part of a campaign that will run in upmarket magazines.<br><br>The target audience will be 25–40 year olds. | • Three different advertisements, each emphasising a different aspect of the watches' appeal<br>• A common house style to the overall campaign<br>• Five original images in total, including a different dominant image in each advertisement<br>• A narrative situation represented in the dominant image for each advertisement, featuring at least one 'character'<br>• Pack or product shot in each advert<br>• Logo design (for the campaign or for the watch itself)<br>• Appropriate choice of slogan and call to action<br>• Original copy, within the adverts, to embody the USP of the watch to the target audience (minimum 70 words per advert, each advert having a different emphasis)<br>• Appropriate choices of font, type sizes and colours to create meanings. |

Example Brief Five: Three print advertisements for a new range of watches

## Unpicking the brief

In this example brief, you are expected to create a series of three print advertisements for a new range of watches.

As usual, the brief contains several key bits of information. You are told that the adverts you create should be part of a campaign. This is useful because it indicates that you need to think of the ways that all three advertisements link together visually and thematically, as is usually the case in advertising campaigns.

The brief states that the adverts should emphasise a sense of history and tradition. You will need to consider this important context when you are devising your ideas.

Crucially, you are also told that the target audience is 25–40 year olds and that the campaign will run in upmarket magazines. Again, this is helpful, as it suggests that the product you are marketing should be high-end, designer and exclusive, rather than a budget and affordable-range item.

You should see that this relates to the 2023 CSP *Tatler* magazine and to what you have learned about advertising and marketing.

> **Link**
> For more about *Tatler* see Chapter 5, pages 207–210.

## The media form: advertising campaign

As you know, you need to think of these three advertisements as three linked parts of a campaign. Print advertising campaigns use similar conventions across a series of adverts, so that the audience realise they are linked. 'Repetition builds reputation' is a phrase often used in marketing – repeating a phrase, a visual idea, a colour scheme or an image will add to the impression the viewer has already formed and remind them that they have seen something similar before.

Each advert also needs something unique, while being recognisably part of the campaign. And each advert needs to work on its own, so that the viewer can understand each advertisement individually, and can act on what they see – to buy the watch being advertised.

> **Tip**
>
> Look on adRuby.com for print advertising campaigns.

### Activity 6.13

Look at a range of print advert **campaigns** for different products. At this stage, you don't need to focus on high-end watches or upmarket publications. The adverts can be for any product, the key thing is that they are a series of adverts in a campaign.

How is a sense of campaign created with the adverts you have looked at? What links and similarities can you see? How is each advert different?

## Using the minimum requirements

The analysis activity will have made you think carefully about how advertisers create a campaign, as well as the key conventions of both campaigns and print adverts in general.

Now you need to look at the minimum requirements of the brief to build on the knowledge you have gained. Use these as a checklist to help you design your adverts:

- [ ] Each advert emphasising a different aspect of appeal
- [ ] Five original images
- [ ] Different dominant images for each advert
- [ ] Narrative situation (a 'story') in each advert, with at least one character
- [ ] Product shot
- [ ] Logo – designed by you
- [ ] Slogan
- [ ] Call to action
- [ ] (At least) 70 words per advert
- [ ] Choice of fonts, type sizes and colours
- [ ] Common house style

You could also add in to your checklist the elements from the left-hand column of the brief:

- [ ] Three print advertisements
- [ ] New range of watches
- [ ] Sense of tradition and history
- [ ] To be used in upmarket magazines
- [ ] Audience of 25–40 year olds

## Planning your advertisements

The minimum requirements section also states that there needs to be 'a common house style to the overall campaign'. You will have recognised this too from the previous activity. Consider how you can address each of the minimum requirements above in a way that maintains a suitable house style and a real sense of campaign. Remember, that the campaign should evoke ideas around *history* and *tradition*. Think about what these words might mean to your target audience. How could you signify these concepts within your images and your choice of fonts and vocabulary?

You are asked to use a minimum of five original photos across the three advertisements. Look again at the Nissan Navara campaign on page 236. There are three distinct ideas, but the small image of the product is common to each of the three adverts. Each one also features a different pick-up-shaped landscape and a different jumping vehicle. These could have been created from separate photographs of landscapes and vehicles, manipulated using image software. If so, this campaign would use at least seven photographs across three adverts. As you plan for the overall look of your adverts, consider how you can use at least five images to construct the campaign.

Think about who you can use as the character in each advert, how you can represent three different features of the range of watches, and whether you want the adverts set in specific locations – or against a plain background as in the Rolex watch advert featuring David Beckham, which you can find online.

While you are planning, take care to consider the full mise-en-scène for each advert, including clothes, props, location and lighting. Are your characters going to appeal to the target audience of 25–40 year olds who read upmarket magazines? What would catch their eye as they flick through the magazine? Remember that the mise-en-scène will also be conveying that sense of history and tradition.

You will need to decide on the different aspects of the watch to be emphasised in each of the advertisements, and you will need to design a suitable logo for your product.

Produce mock-up designs for your three print adverts, and use these to plan your photoshoots carefully. When you write the 70 words of copy for each advert, remember that the words you use should also appeal to 25–40 year olds, and should be appropriate within an upmarket magazine.

### Activity 6.14

Create ideas for an appropriate house style for your print advert campaign. What colour palette or fonts would be suitable? You can use a moodboard to convey your ideas at this stage.

# The Statement of Intent

The Statement of Intent is an important part of your NEA. In it you will outline your aims for your media product. It is a compulsory element of the NEA and must be submitted to your teacher. Refer to the specification for the submission deadline.

The Statement of Intent will be assessed by your teacher along with your media product. Both the Statement of Intent and the product itself will then be sent to AQA for moderation.

Of the 60 marks that are available in total for the NEA, just 10 of these are for the Statement of Intent. This might not sound like much, but the Statement of Intent is an extremely important part of the NEA all the same.

Let's look at why this is the case.

## Why is the Statement of Intent so important?

The Statement of Intent is your opportunity to explain how you intend to apply your knowledge and understanding of Media Language and Media Representations to the creation of your media product. As well as this, you need to state how you think the product will appeal to the target audience, as specified in the brief. It will help people to understand your decisions and see what you intended to do.

You need to think carefully about what to include in your Statement of Intent. You can use a maximum of 300 words. If you get it right, it should help you to earn marks in the other sections of the assessment, because it will help the people assessing your product to understand what you were aiming to create.

Of the 60 marks available, 15 marks are for the application of your knowledge of media language. Similarly, 15 marks are for how well you apply your understanding of Media Representations. Last, but definitely not least, up to 20 marks are given for how effective you are at communicating meaning to an audience. You may be designing a product that is quirky or unusual, or where something could look like a 'mistake' to others. In your Statement of Intent, you can explain exactly why you are designing it this way to create a specific meaning or to attract the specified audience's attention. You can direct the people marking your work to look at the areas you are taking most care to include, such as small details in the mise-en-scène, or the use of very specific colours or fonts. You can make sure they don't miss anything important in your decision-making.

Suddenly, you will see just how important the Statement of Intent really is. If you approach it in the right way, you will also give the creation of your media product a clear sense of direction and focus. This can only help you to produce an appealing and successful media product – and gain marks for your NEA at the same time.

### Talk about it

Some of the most interesting TV adverts make no sense to the people who are not in their target audience. Some advertisers say: 'If you don't understand it, it's not meant for you.' Can you think of any adverts like this?

# Writing your Statement of Intent

You should write your Statement of Intent before you *make* your product but after you have finished *planning* it. It is, after all, about what you *intend* to do, not what you have done. There is a little bit of leeway with this timing, because some people make quite major changes after they have started the actual production part of the process – usually because they realise their planning wasn't as good as it should have been. It is possible, therefore, to adapt your Statement of Intent after you start production, but, even so, it should be finished well before your product has to be handed in. Your teacher will set you deadlines for both parts of your NEA.

AQA provides a blank form for the Statement of Intent, with space for your 300 words.

In the Statement of Intent below, the student is working on Example Brief Two – the homepage and linked page for a website promoting a new community-based radio streaming service.

---

Candidate Name          Candidate Number

This form must be completed and given to your teacher before 1 April 20XX

> How will you use Media Language and Media Representations in order to create your product and meet the rquirements of the brief and the needs of the target audience? (Maximum 300 words)
>
> A major aim of my radio station and its website is to represent young people in a positive light and to avoid the negative stereotyping of teenagers that you often see in the media.
>
> One of the programmes that will be mentioned will be about politics, to show that young people are actually interested in current affairs. The presenter will be a local person aged 25. The station will serve North Manchester so it is important that the presenter represents the area. At 25, he will be seen as a role model and someone to aspire to be like.
>
> Both my homepage and linked page will feature lots of interactivity to appeal to the target audience of 16–21 year olds. Social media icons for Twitter, Snapchat and Instagram (and other platforms) will feature at the top of the screen, along with a link to the station's YouTube channel.
>
> The colours and fonts of the homepage design will be bright and funky. There won't be much text on the screen, which would make it look cluttered.
>
> The station will have the Manchester Working Bee as part of its logo. This will feature heavily on the website pages. It has positive connotations of the city and clearly represents the city. This will appeal to the target audience.

**END OF STUDENT BOOKLET**

---

### Talk about it

In pairs, discuss this Statement of Intent. How successful do you think it is? Where and how does it explain how Media Language and Media Representations will be applied? Where and how does it explain how meaning will be communicated to the intended audience?

The writer has used under 220 words so far. Up to 300 words are allowed. What other details would you add if this was yours? You might want to look back at the brief on page 226.

| Level | Marks | Description |
|---|---|---|
| 5 | 9–10 | • An outstanding, detailed statement that refers directly and effectively to the intended uses of media language and representations.<br>• The intentions outlined in the statement are consistently appropriate to the brief and target the intended audience in a clear and direct way.<br>• Excellent evidence of the application of knowledge and understanding of the theoretical framework of media through extensive and sustained use of relevant and accurate subject specific terminology. |

**The highest level of the assessment criteria for the Statement of Intent.**

If you look at the assessment criteria, even at the highest level you will see that there is nothing about *how* the Statement of Intent has to be written or formatted. You can write in continuous prose (as in an essay), in bullet points, or as a list of comments. You can use headings if this helps you. You will, though, get marks for using subject-specific terminology, for referring to your intended use of media language and representations, and for stating how you will target the intended audience.

Look at the two examples below, and see how the same information can be given in different ways:

### Example one: continuous prose

For my anti-bullying music video, I will use 'Judas' by Fozzy, with the lyrics sung by a bully, finally realising that his actions make him a worse person ('the wreckage of my life'). The original song is four minutes long. I will edit it down to two minutes, leaving out the instrumental intro, and ending on 'what have I become?' in the second chorus.

Because the lyrics suggest the POV of the bully, I will show the actions with the bully as my main character (a false hero). I will use a Y7 student as my victim, so they represent innocence, being younger and smaller. I will emphasise this with high-angle shots. I will use a Y11 student as my bully, with low-angle shots to show their power.

The main sequence will involve bullying: taunting, sneering, hitting, in close-ups to show the victim is trapped. There will be a crowd of onlookers around the two characters and the camera, also trapping the victim. I will juxtapose this sequence with shots before the incident in high-key lighting – the victim will look carefree and the bully will look angry. After the incident, the victim will be shown huddled up, crying, in low-key lighting, and then the bully will be shown in the same position in a different, dark location, and the video will end with both characters looking at the camera singing the final line 'what have I become?'

This line will also be shown on-screen, followed by 'bullying destroys lives' to emphasise the effects of bullying on the victim and the bully.

## Example two: sub-headings and bullet points

### Brief Four: Music video for an anti-bullying campaign

**Song chosen**: 'Judas' by Fozzy (from first words to 'what have I become?' in second chorus).

**Reason**: Lyrics could be sung by a bully finally realising what he has become because of his actions.

Characters and representations:

- **Victim**: small year 7 boy, sweet-looking, to signify innocence.
- **Bully**: tall, broad-shouldered year 11 boy, with facial hair, to signify threat and aggression.
- **Crowd**: other students crowding around, to fill up the background and signify being trapped in the situation.

Narrative and media language:

- Victim is seen being carefree with friends, eye-level shots, high-key lighting.
- Bully is seen in MCU and CU walking towards the camera, singing the lyrics, looking aggressive, low-angle shots, high-key lighting.
- Cuts to bullying actions – crowd gathered around, bully taunting, sneering, hitting. Quick cuts between close-ups. Signifies there is no room to move or escape.
- Cuts to victim huddled on his own, high-angle shots, low-key lighting.
- Cuts to bully huddled on his own, possibly by a mirror, signifying he has seen himself for what he really is. Low-key lighting.
- Both sing 'What have I become?'
- Final line also shown on-screen to emphasise the effects of bullying on the victim and the bully.
- Words dissolve into 'bullying destroys lives'.

However you prefer writing, you need to include the same depth of information and cover:

- the uses of Media Language and Media Representations
- how you are meeting the brief
- how you are targeting the intended audience
- the meanings you intend to portray.

You need to use relevant and accurate subject specific terminology.

### Quick question 6.3

How do you prefer to write? Are you most comfortable writing in prose as you would in essays, or using headings and bullet points as you would in factual reports?

### Activity 6.15

Looking at either of the example responses, can you see which of the required aspects they have covered in depth, and which aspects are missing?

How would you complete either Statement of Intent to add in the extra information?

# Production skills and techniques: moving image production

As seen in Chapters 4 and 5, television quickly replaced radio as the most popular media form as soon as television sets became widely available for the home. For over half a century now, television has been a part of the daily fabric of our lives.

However, times change and technology develops at an amazing rate. Now moving image content is watched via the internet on computers, laptops, video games consoles, tablets and smartphones. Some of this content has been created for much larger screens, but much is now created specifically to be circulated via corporate websites, social media and on sites such as YouTube and Vimeo.

For your GCSE Media Studies NEA, you could be given moving image briefs to create work for television, music video, advertising or websites.

## Equipment – filming

Your teacher will tell you what equipment you can use, but moving image equipment no longer has to be expensive. Even some professional films have been shot on mobile phones. As well as these, both compact **cameras** and DSLRs (digital single lens reflexes) allow for good quality video-recording. Video takes up a lot of memory space, however, so make sure you either have plenty of space on the memory cards, or memory space elsewhere to back-up your work frequently.

As you will see in the section on camera movements, a **tripod** with a tilt and swivel head is an important piece of equipment.

Although many students consider their visuals very carefully, many are let down by the quality of the sound. Most professionals don't use the sound recorded on set at all. Instead, they add **foley sounds**, dialogue, ambient sounds, voiceovers and music in the editing suite. This allows them to get rid of the 'wrong' sounds and only include sound that carries meaning. You may not have the time, or the technology, to do this, but should think carefully about how to make your sound as good as it can be. If you can, record sound on a separate **recorder**, rather than on your camera, or use a **microphone**. If you are filming outside, shield your microphone (on- or off-camera) from the wind.

More will be said about lighting when we discuss music videos, but in any moving image form you might need to use **additional lighting**. Many smartphones have great lighting capabilities, but torches, lamps and portable video lights can also be used. Bouncing a light off a wall or ceiling will make it more diffuse, while shining a light straight at something will give a strong shadow. If you want lighting to look natural, hold the lights above the actors. If you want a spooky look, shine the lights up onto the actors' faces from below. To fill in a shadow with a little bit of detail, use a large sheet of white paper as a reflector to direct light into that area.

---

**Key term**

**Foley sounds**
These recreate the diegetic sounds of important actions on screen but are created by foley artists in a studio – named after pioneering Hollywood sound-effects artist Jack Foley. Even footsteps as the actors walk are usually recreated and added afterwards. Foley artists watch an edit of the film as they work to make sure their timing is right.

**Link**

For more on camera movements see pages 26 and 245–246.

Using a tripod and a microphone will improve the quality of your moving image work.

There are no specific marks for the quality of the filming, editing and sound, but the more you can control these, the more you can show that you understand and can use Media Language and Media Representations. Your decisions will be more obvious.

## Planning and filming

Certain media language codes – such as camera shots and movement, diegetic sounds and non-diegetic sounds, and mise-en-scène – will always be required in any response to a moving image NEA brief. These need to be planned for carefully to ensure they carry the meanings you want.

## Camera shot selection

One of the most common mistakes students make with moving image production is with their camera shot selection. Often, students simply don't change their shots frequently enough or get close enough, so shots will last far too long and too much is filmed using long shots. If you watch any television programme of any genre, you will notice how often the camera shot changes. It's rare in a television drama, for example, for any shot to last for more than a few seconds.

The way the shots are selected and framed is also important. So, for every shot you take, you need to consider: the camera distance, the camera angle, the length of time of the shot and what you should include in the frame. All of these carry meaning for the audience.

A mid-shot (or medium shot) is one of the fundamental shots used in professional moving image productions. Typically, the subject is framed from the waist upwards. We cannot see the whole body, but it is clear who the subject is. The way the mid-shot is framed usually allows part of the setting to be shown. This positions the subject in a particular location for the audience.

An example would be a man sitting on a bench reading a newspaper at a railway station. A mid-shot wouldn't enable the audience to see close-up facial details, but they would recognise the man, and understand where he was and what he was doing.

In the high-angle shot above, from the 1996 film *Matilda*, we see Matilda walking up to the librarian for the very first time. From the way that the shot is framed – high from above – Matilda's short height, young age, nervousness and innocence are all emphasised. In contrast, a low-angle shot has the opposite effect. It can make the subject appear to be larger, powerful or confident.

You can see another camera shot, an extreme close-up (ECU), on the right. An ECU is especially useful as a way of highlighting the emotions of a subject. The shot is often used to show the anger, fear or sadness of a character.

### Link

Also look at the sections on Moving image codes in Chapter 1, pages 26–29 and Photographic codes, pages 22–26.

*Mid-shot*

*An extreme close-up (ECU)*

### Activity 6.16

Choose any example of television drama. List and describe the first ten shots. If you can, screengrab them and print them as a storyboard instead.

- What camera angles have been selected?
- How long is each shot?
- Why has each shot been framed in the way it has?
- What is the effect?
- What meaning has been communicated to the audience?
- Could the shots have been framed differently?
- What effect would this have had?

In classical Hollywood-style **continuity editing**, the dominant order for editing within a sequence is to get gradually closer to the action. The chart below shows an example of how a short dialogue could be filmed.

| Shot no. | What | Why | Storyboard frame |
|---|---|---|---|
| 1 | Long-shot or extreme long-shot | Establishing shot – letting the audience know where the action is taking place and who is present | |
| 2 | Medium long-shot, two-shot, including person A and person B | Master shot – showing the two people talking, establishing where they are in relation to each other. In a longer sequence, this shot size will be returned to, to re-establish where the characters are | |
| 3 | Mid-shot, over-the-shoulder shot, from person A to person B | Showing B as they are talking, including facial expressions and any gestures or props | |
| 4 | Mid-shot, over-the-shoulder shot, from person B to person A | Showing A's reaction, including facial expression and gestures. Cutting from one over-the-shoulder shot to the other is called shot-reverse-shot | |
| 5 | Close-up on B's head and shoulders | Showing B's facial expressions more clearly, involving the audience in the emotion | |
| 6 | Close-up on A's head and shoulders | Showing A's facial expressions more clearly, involving the audience in the emotion | |

To make this sequence work, the camera shots need to have been taken following the 180-degree rule. For this, you should imagine a line drawn across the set that goes through both person A and person B. The camera must stay on one side of this line – it can only move within a 180-degree arc.

You will only get such sequences of shots right if you plan them carefully beforehand – storyboarding your sequences is vital to avoid wasting time during the shoot or having to re-film the sequence.

This storyboard for a sci-fi TV sequence clearly shows everyone involved where each shot will be filmed from, to follow the 180-degree rule.

## Key term

**Continuity editing**
Most films and TV dramas are filmed and edited to try to hide the editing, so that the audience doesn't notice the cuts between shots. Actions and visual style need to continue smoothly from one shot to the next. This way the audience can get lost in the narrative and not think about the film-making.

**The 180-degree rule**

### Activity 6.17

Imagine the following scenario: a teenage girl is waiting at a bus stop. She receives a text message. The text clearly upsets her.

Consider the following shots, and either sketch out an image or actually take a photo that has the shot framed in this way. Then explain the effect that you would hope to achieve by framing each shot in such a way:

- over the shoulder
- high angle
- mid-shot
- point of view
- close-up
- long-shot.
- extreme close-up

Now select at least four of these shots to create a sequence that tells the story.

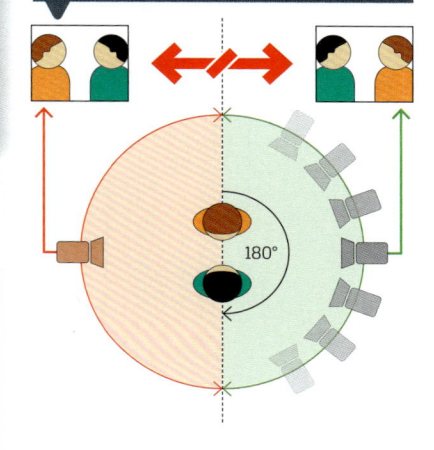

## Link

For more on camera angles and shots see page 22.

## Camera movement

A variety of camera angles/shots are important to make any moving image sequence visually engaging. However, camera movement is also very important.

A **zoom** is one of the most commonly used camera movements by students, by zooming in on the small detail of an object or a physical subject. However, as our eyes cannot zoom, this points out to the audience that they are seeing the action through a camera and detracts from the feeling of being in the world of the film. For this reason, it is rarely used in professional drama on film or TV. It *is* used effectively in music videos and other moving image forms, where getting lost in the narrative is not important.

**Tracking** can be useful for action shots. Here, the camera literally runs as if on a track alongside or towards the subject. For this reason, it is used a lot in the coverage of sports. It can also be used in documentaries and news features, when the presenter is walking forwards and talking straight to the camera.

### Activity 6.18

Watch two-minute extracts from several different television dramas. It would be good to look at a range, so maybe a soap opera, hospital drama, period drama, etc. For each clip, count up how many camera movements are used. Which movements are used? What effects do the movements create? What conclusions can you draw from your viewing research?

245

A **pan** is derived from the word panorama or panoramic. The camera sweeps around a scene horizontally, but it is secured on a tripod. A pan shot is an effective way of establishing the setting and showing who is in the scene. Some dramas use very slow panning or very slow tracking in the majority of shots, which adds dynamics and makes a static scene seem more exciting.

A **tilt** is similar to a pan, but the camera lens moves vertically instead of horizontally, allowing the operator to scan up or down a person, an object or a location. Again, the camera should be secured on a tripod to allow control of the movement.

A **hand-held** camera will move slightly, however careful the operator is, as everyone breathes and constantly shift their weight. When running with a hand-held camera, the shots will move jerkily and look confused. This technique is deliberately used in some moving image products to suggest the viewer is in the thick of the action, but it can be disorienting in others and look like poor camera-work. Always use a tripod or other camera support unless you have a good visual reason for *not* doing so.

Camera movements should be used sparingly. Think carefully about the scenes or particular shots in a moving image production and why particular movements are effective.

You should never just use movements for the sake of it. If, as a general rule, you cannot explain the effect you hope to achieve or the meaning it will communicate to the audience, then don't include the movement.

> **Link**
> For more on mise-en-scène see page 18.

## Mise-en-scène

Often with a moving image production, it's the small things and attention to detail that make all the difference. The best example of this is mise-en-scène. The term literally means everything that is 'put in the scene/shot'.

For moving image products, mise-en-scène involves everything that would be in the shot or the frame. In other words, everything that the viewer can see on the screen.

Mise-en-scène is one of the easiest ways of communicating meaning to an audience. It can be particularly important in period dramas.

## Sound

Sound is just as important as the visuals – a good sound editor will use the sound to direct the viewer's attention to a specific action on the screen. It has been said that a good soundtrack is made up of 'two-and-a half-layers of sound' – for example, if two students were shown walking along a school corridor, you might hear: their conversation, their footsteps and, as the half layer, the distant and muffled sound of classes in progress.

Most moving image dramas are driven by **dialogue** – the words that the characters speak and the conversations they have with each other. What the characters say and how they interact with each other can be the main ways that the audience receives meaning.

Not everyone can act well in front of a camera. Dialogue scenes have to be well rehearsed to make them look good. A lot of the best student work has very little dialogue, so there is less to go wrong during filming.

If you are creating news or documentary work, any **scripted words** can be said straight to camera, and can usually be read from a piece of paper or a screen placed next to or above the camera.

**Voiceover** can be used to add extra meaning for the viewer, especially in documentaries. It can give extra information, add commentary or in a drama it can be used to show the audience what a character is thinking. Voiceovers are best recorded in a quiet space, and scripted after the filming is complete, so that you know how many seconds of footage you have to cover.

**Diegetic sound** is what you would hear in the 'world of the film'. This includes dialogue but also the other sounds that are heard in that setting. For example, a scene in a café might feature dialogue between characters. There might also be the sound of music playing in the background, the sound of glasses or cutlery, or the background sound of other people in the café. There may even be sounds from outside, such as traffic or sirens. All of this is diegetic sound.

**Non-diegetic sound**, however, is sound that is added to a scene to create specific effects. So, a music soundtrack might be added to build tension, or a voiceover to add thoughts or memories.

## Equipment – editing

You may be lucky enough to have access to professional **video-editing software** on your school computers – such as Final Cut Pro, Premiere Pro or Avid's Media Composer. However, there are also many free or cheap video-editing packages available, including Media Composer | First, Windows MovieMaker and iMovie. Most such software allows for a variety of transitions, sound mixing and basic effects.

If you have to upload footage from a phone to a computer, you will either need the correct leads or you can upload via a **web-based cloud service** such as OneDrive or iCloud. Doing this will mean you can access your video footage on any device, wherever you are, and you are less likely to lose your important scenes.

## Editing and transitions

Editing is an aspect of moving image production that can be really important, so you should carry it out very carefully. Even the most basic digital software will allow you to add transitions to your footage.

A **transition** (or **edit**) is the way that two shots are placed together in a film sequence. If one image simply replaces the other on screen then the edits are **cuts** or **straight cuts**. A straight cut is used most of the time as it is the default setting of video editing. The basic edit is called a cut, because it used to be created by cutting film and taping two ends of cut film together. It is by far the most common transition seen in film and television.

However, there are various other transitions that can be used. A **fade** or **dissolve** is often used to show the passage of time, to indicate the end of a scene, or to signify that the location has changed. Dissolves are also often used in music videos, especially in live performance sequences. Unless you're making *Star Wars*, or something tongue-in-cheek, don't use **wipes** at all.

### Activity 6.19

Look at the still from *Downton Abbey at the bottom of the previous page*. The first series of this popular drama was set in 1912 and, as the series continued, it ran through the rest of the 1910s (including World War I) and on into the next decade.
From the still, how can you tell that the drama is set in a different time? Pick out as many details as you can.

### Tip

Many students think that their work is almost done when the filming has finished, but editing can take longer than filming. Schedule your time to allow for planning, filming, editing *and* adding sound. If you set out to give each of these roughly equal time, you'll probably get it about right.

### Tip

If you have been shooting your footage on a phone or tablet, you could edit directly in an **app** on the same device.

A film splicer allowed moving picture editors to cut the film and tape two shots together.

As with camera movements, different transitions can be an excellent way of adding to the overall viewing experience for the audience – but remember that the straight cut should be the default. If you overuse other transitions and camera movements, they will actually hinder the viewers' experience.

## Exporting your video

When you have finished editing you will need to export your production. Each video-editing program creates its own file type while you work on the editing that can only be read within that software. You need to export to a file type that can be read on any computer, or can be uploaded to the internet – MP4, AVI and MOV are the most common video formats. Export to a high quality, so that your audience will be able to see all the detail you have included. For example, along with many other programs, iMovie gives you a choice of output types when you share the video, depending on where the video is going to be seen. The highest quality in this particular case is 'Theatre'. If your software gives you choices based on numerical data, then you could select 1,080p and 30 frames per second for the video and at least 192 kbps for the audio.

## Television for NEA

Television is one of the media forms that can be on the NEA briefs. Obviously, the specific details of the brief, such as the genre, will change with each brief. Television forms include: documentary, news, adverts and drama.

The 2023 television CSPs, *Doctor Who* and *His Dark Materials*, are both in the sci fi/fantasy genre, but the key conventions of **television drama** are largely the same, regardless of the genre or audience. For a TV drama, you should plan your shots so you can use continuity editing. Think about adding meaning with extra shots such as cutaways, or by cross-cutting between two locations to show two events happening at the same time. To create an enigma, leave some things off-screen, in the shadows, or unsaid.

In most TV dramas, no one looks at the camera, but in **news broadcasts** the news presenters look directly out at the viewers. Other people in the programme – such as interviewees – don't do this. Instead, they look at the person interviewing them – if this person isn't shown on screen they will be to the side of the camera, so the interviewee will look slightly off-camera.

In both news and **documentary** interviews, it is normal to have the interviewee positioned to one side of the frame, looking slightly towards the other side. This gives them 'space to speak into'.

Factual programmes can also make use of on-screen graphics, added during editing. In the news, these can appear behind or in front of news presenters in the studio, but only in front of those who are out on location. These are added during editing. News studios usually use of green-screen technology. All or part of the set is literally green. The green areas can be keyed out when editing and replaced with other videos or computer-generated graphics. In this way, visual news material can be shown behind the presenters as if it is being projected in the studio. If you don't have access to green-screen technology, then creating a news feature as an outside broadcast or as a report from a specific location may be easier than trying to create a studio piece.

### Tip
Videos usually take up a lot of memory space, so make sure you have somewhere to store your finished video.

### Link
See Chapter 1 for more on enigma codes, pages 32–33.

### Activity 6.20
Imagine you are producing a television drama based in a school – but imagine the scene is set five years ago. What props and costumes would we see? Think carefully about the mise-en-scène and diegetic/non-diegetic sound that could be used.

You could storyboard a short scene, including camera shots, movements, edits and everything you have covered in this section.

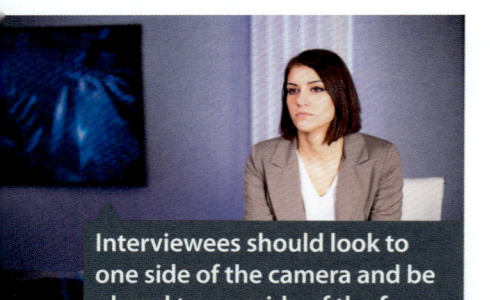

Interviewees should look to one side of the camera and be placed to one side of the frame.

## Music video for NEA

Music video could be one of the options in the AQA-set briefs you can tackle for your NEA. You will need to read carefully who the video is targeting, who or what it is promoting, and any other information you are given.

As music videos are essentially a promotional tool, you will be constructing specific representations of the music act, or of a given theme – such as the anti-bullying theme in the Example Brief Four. These are the representations you want the audience to understand and enjoy, allowing them to buy into the artist and what they stand for – even if this is just entertainment and spreading happiness.

Essentially there are three types of music video:

- performance
- narrative
- abstract or concept.

> **Link**
>
> The Example Brief Four is on page 232.

### Performance

The most obvious type of music video is straightforward performance. After all, the main purpose of music videos is to promote the artists, so videos that features the artists in performance is an obvious choice. The video for Arctic Monkeys' 'I Bet You Look Good on the Dancefloor' features the band performing the song, giving a flavour of what it would be like to see the band live.

### Narrative

The second major type of music video is narrative video. Possibly the most common approach is to combine performance and narrative – elements of performance interspersed with a narrative that is often linked to the lyrics of the song itself. As in the example of One Direction's 'History', we see mimed performance of the song to camera by the band members, and a narrative too – the band's history is revealed through clips of their career to date including their origins on *The X Factor*.

## Abstract or concept

The third main type of music video is abstract or concept video. An abstract video creates emotions or feelings in the audience in an artistic way. Videos can be exclusively abstract, which means they contain no performance or narrative elements. However, abstract music videos can contain or be combined with elements of performance and narrative. Almost anything by Björk or OK Go would fit into this category.

Your choice of style for the music video, and your choice of mise-en-scène (specifically location, costume, props and actions) will be very important.

> **Activity 6.21**
>
> Choose a song that you know well and come up with different ideas for a music video in different types:
>
> - performance
> - narrative
> - abstract/concept.
>
> What are the advantages of each approach? How could each be used to represent a specific 'brand' for this artist?

> **Tip**
>
> If you are choosing the mise-en-scène to create a representation, school uniform is rarely a good idea.

## Editing for music video

One of the main differences between TV drama forms and music videos is the use of editing. Music videos tend to use even shorter shot lengths than other moving image forms. Most music videos are cut on the beat of the song, but not necessarily *every* beat. The pace of the editing tends to speed up when the song gets more lively or frantic – so the cuts are closer together, possibly on every beat or even every half-beat in these sections of the song.

Music videos, even those using narrative, don't necessarily have to follow the rules of continuity editing, so may ignore the 180-degree rule and deliberately show non-continuous action. There is often a dream-like quality where the rules of normal life don't apply, so the main character may change clothes between shots, change locations seemingly at random and even change the people they're with.

Although these differences are being discussed under editing, they need to be planned for before filming begins. Because music video doesn't necessarily need to 'make sense' in terms of narrative, it sometimes seems easier to create than other moving image forms, but the editing can be very complex to make it look right. Be sure to leave plenty of time for this aspect.

*A performance video often looks better with coloured lights and a low camera angle.*

## The music video look

Music videographers are also more likely to play with colour and lighting, both during filming and editing. If you have access to coloured lights, perhaps in a drama studio, hall or theatre, you could use these. Or you can put coloured gels over your smartphone or torch – simple but it works. You can also alter the colours in most editing software – but be careful not to do this too much. There should be a reason for everything you do in order to have a positive impact on the representations you are trying to create.

Music videographers are also likely to experiment with camera distances, angles and movements that would not be used elsewhere, such as using a fish-eye lens to get really close in a distorted view or including shots where the main character is out of focus. Again, be wary of doing this just because you can. Ensure that the visual style you use says something about the music artist or the theme.

### Activity 6.22

Analyse a hybrid music video, containing elements of performance and narrative. Count the number of locations used, the number of costume changes for the main character(s) and notice how these different filming set-ups are intercut throughout the video. If you print out the lyrics to the song, you could mark these up, showing where the narrative and the performance elements are used.

## Planning and filming the music video

As discussed above, make sure you plan your music video. You might not plan every shot, as you would for a TV drama, but you need to plan the visual style, the structure of the video – this is best done in a grid with the lyrics in one column and the actions in another – and you should storyboard any narrative sequences.

It is rare for any editor to use all the footage taken, so make sure you take far more than you think you can use. If you are filming for a performance video, make sure you capture the whole performance from more than one angle – if you don't have the luxury of multiple cameras, the performers will have to go through the song several times. Make sure you get close-ups and mid-shots as well as long-shots.

If shooting a performance video, with real musicians, use a pre-recorded version of the track. You can then edit footage from different shoots together, knowing the music was played at the same speed every time. Play this loud while you film, but ask the 'performers' to sing along out loud – miming always looks like miming, not singing. You will delete the original sound from the video during editing and replace it with the sound from the pre-recorded track.

## Moving image marketing for NEA

Advertising and marketing using moving image includes TV, cinema and online adverts, and trailers for other moving image products. As with all advertising, you need to consider what it is you are trying to sell.

You will need to consider AIDA:

- **A**ttention
- **I**nterest
- **D**esire
- **A**ction

Viewers try to skip adverts if they can, and if they can't they might switch focus to social media. How will your advert grab their attention? Once you have their attention, how do you create an interest in the product or service you are marketing, and how do you make the audience desire that product or service? Finally, how do you guide them to act on what they've seen?

You will need to ensure you clearly indicate the point of the advert or trailer – give all the necessary details about the product or service, such as the title, day, time and channel of an upcoming TV programme, or the brand name and a product shot of a new breakfast cereal. Also use visuals, words and/or graphics to explain its USP – unique selling point. Why should people want to act on this advert? How will they benefit?

Some adverts use intertextuality – such as the Snickers adverts featuring Joan Collins, Mr Bean and Mr T. The original media products, such as *The A Team*, are so iconic that they do not need to be named in the adverts, but most viewers will understand the references being made.

Adverts and trailers often make use of voiceovers or 'talking heads', both of which directly address the audience. This is the case even in adverts with a narrative short scene. A separate actor will explain the benefits of the product, usually towards the end of the advert. This person often sounds authoritative but friendly. Companies spend a long time finding the right voice and tone for these, so think carefully about who should voice your adverts, and how they should read your script. You are the director, after all.

Music is a key feature of the majority of adverts. You are not expected to write your own music, but you should select it carefully – and don't only think about songs with lyrics. Instrumental music is very often used throughout an advert. Most video-editing software will also let you edit sound, so you don't need to use the whole of a music piece. You can loop one section or go straight from the opening section to the ending.

The last thing the audience sees and hears will be the thing they tend to remember, so finish the advert with a final mention of the product or service, or your killer slogan.

> **Link**
>
> For more on intertextuality see Chapter 1, page 41.

> **Activity 6.23**
>
> Watch a series of adverts for the same product, such as the Snickers adverts mentioned in this section, or Hovis adverts from the 1970s and 1980s, and note how the same ideas, themes or slogans are used in different ways.
>
> Plan a new advert to add to the campaign you have chosen to watch, using the shared elements you have identified.

## Web-based video for NEA

Obviously, online videos might use the same conventions as television programmes or adverts, as they may be created within the same form or genre.

Other NEA briefs might, for example, ask you to create a montage of clips, a video that is intended for viral advertising, or a vlog.

Vlogs obviously take many forms, but the key factor is usually the personality and/or expertise of the vlogger. Think of the video as being an extended advert for the vlogger's brand. As with all NEA production, you want to be in control of every part of the video. Successful vloggers choose their locations carefully and leave nothing to chance. Everything within the frame should say something about the vlogger.

With vlogging the sound is very important. Check the quality of the sound by recording a short piece and playing it back before you record the whole thing. Make sure there are no distracting noises in the background. Use an external mic if you can.

Many vloggers are very good at using video-editing software, but even those who are will often have a more informal style of editing than you will see on television. Jump-cuts are used much more often, along with on-screen graphics, titles, out-takes and rewinds. As vlogs use a direct mode of address, they can employ editing techniques that simply would not work in TV drama. This is not the same, though, as bad editing. Editing should help to create meaning, and you should be aware of this every time you add an edit or transition. Ask other people to watch your video when you think it is almost finished, then ask questions to find out if they understood the message you were trying to get across.

### Activity 6.24

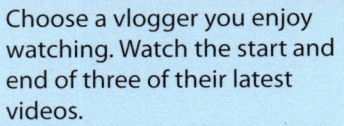

Choose a vlogger you enjoy watching. Watch the start and end of three of their latest videos.
- Where are the videos filmed?
- What can you see in the frame?
- Do the videos always start in the same way?
- Does the vlogger always sign off in the same way?
- How do they attract subscribers?
- What do you think the lifestyle of this vlogger is like?
- What clues are you given to this?

# Production skills and techniques: audio production

Radio was the go-to mass media form that audiences would flock to for news, information and entertainment from the 1920s to the period just after World War II. As televisions became widely available in most homes, the humble radio then dipped in popularity.

However, radio has maintained its important role within the wider media landscape. As with most things to do with the media, the internet has had a considerable impact on the radio industry. Just as YouTube and other video platforms have enabled millions to become video producers and reach a (potentially) massive audience, the prevalence of easy-to-use audio editing software and various radio hosting sites on the internet has opened similar opportunities for radio enthusiasts. In theory, a radio station can now broadcast, cheaply and easily, to a wide audience – all from the comfort of someone's home.

## Audio equipment

If you are creating audio work for your NEA, you will clearly need something to record sound on. This can be done on a mobile phone, if it has a voice recorder app – there are many available and some phones have them built in. Portable MP3 recorders are very effective and even a low-cost version can be surprisingly good quality.

You can also record directly to a laptop or desktop computer. You will need a microphone that plugs into your computer – this could be via a mini-jack or USB port. You will also need some software to record into.

The same software can often be used to record and mix sounds. Macs usually come with Garageband, which can do both jobs well. Audacity is a free, open-source program that works on any computer. Whatever software you use, you will need to be able to export to a file type that most computers can play, such as MP3 or WAV. To create MP3 files from Audacity the free LAME encoder needs to be downloaded from the same site as the original software, in order to export your soundtrack as MP3 files.

> Portable MP3 recorders are useful for both audio production and recording sound for video production.

## Recording audio

Perhaps more important than the type of equipment you record and mix on, is how and where you record. You want your sound to be as 'pure' as possible – with no unintended background noises such as laughter or scraping chairs, and no distortion in the recording. If you can, you should record in a space away from other students.

It is worth taking the time to record each different sound source (such as the different actors and each sound effect) separately. If you do this, you can have full control of the volume of each one throughout the audio piece and you can edit each one separately to remove mistakes, without affecting the others.

**Shot-gun microphone and windshield**

Try to avoid recording background noise, such as the hum of a classroom projector, because this will build up as you layer the sounds. A directional microphone, such as a shot-gun mic designed to fit on a camera or a mic-stand, will only record the sounds directly in front of it.

Another thing to avoid is the sound of turning the pages of the script while someone is speaking. Ensure sounds like this are made when no one is talking, so you can easily cut the noises out afterwards.

Most sound recorders or software allow you to change the input levels, so you are recording the sound as loud as you can without letting it distort. If this is the case, there will be a volume meter, which indicates when the input is too loud – if the needle or light bars go into the red, then distortion could occur. There is an optimum volume level just below this.

You can either adjust the input level on the device or software itself, or you can simply move the microphone closer to or further from the sound source.

You can also move the microphone to get different effects in the recording. Due to something called the proximity effect, a much bassier sound is obtained if you move the microphone closer to the sound source. Speaking quietly into a very close microphone can give your actors a scary-sounding voice. Also, deliberately ask them to shout from the opposite side of the room to give the impression of being at a distance.

Consider as many different sources of sound as you can to give meaning to your production. Background sound is very important in audio work. Outside broadcast interviews, for example, usually feature atmosphere (atmos), also known as 'wild track sound' – this is sound taken from the same environment as the interview, which conveys a specific idea to the audience. Remember, the listeners can't see where the interview is taking place, so they have to be told about the location using sound. If this is mixed in under the interview, it can also cover any gaps and parts where you have edited out mistakes.

**Analogue (above) and digital (below) volume meters**

### Activity 6.25

If you were interviewing each of the following, what background sounds could you add to make the location obvious:
- a doctor in a hospital?
- a musician before a concert?
- a student in a school?
- a mechanic in a garage?

What sounds would signify to the audience that this is a hospital?

Audio-mixing on a computer

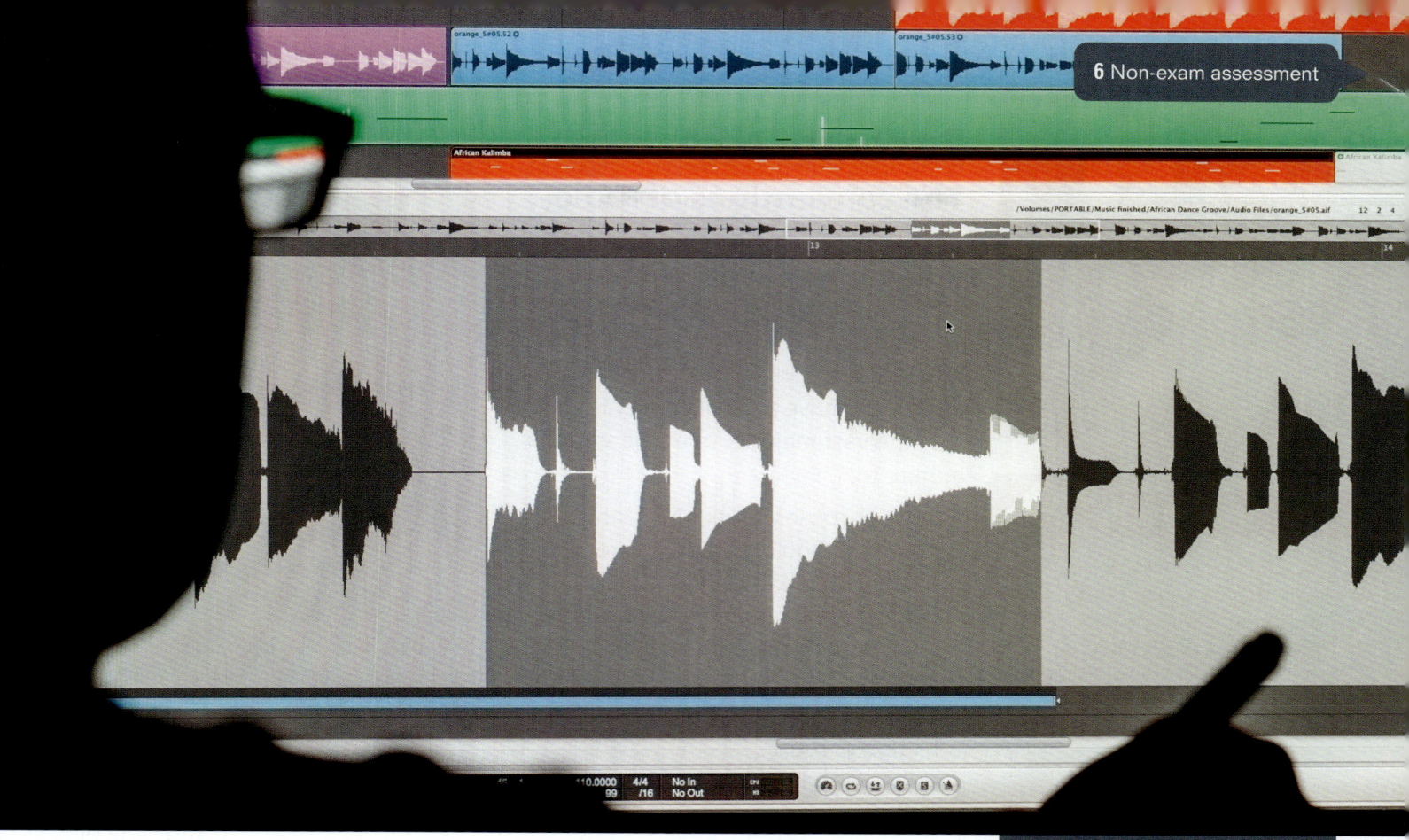

## Editing and mixing audio

Once you have all the sounds you need, you can use your software or app to mix them together. Remember that you are trying to create meaning and you should be in control of everything. If your actors made mistakes, laughed at the wrong moment or took long pauses, cut these out. Otherwise, your audience will think you intended the mistakes to be there.

The sounds can be layered in the software, and then the relative volumes of the sounds changed to mix them together. Make sure that anything that *should* be heard, *can* be heard. Students often make the mistake of having the music too loud when it is supposed to be 'behind' the people speaking. Ask a friend if they can hear and understand what is being said. You will have written the script, and know what is going on, so you'll be able to pick out the words too easily to have an impartial ear.

If you are using sound effects or atmos, make sure they add to the meaning rather than distracting your audience from what they should be listening to.

## Exporting your audio

When you are happy with the edit, and have checked it with an audience, your audio work will need to be exported. The software will create its own file type that can only play in that program or app. You need to export the file to a type that can be read on any computer or mobile device, or can be uploaded to the internet – MP3, AIFF and WAV are the most common audio formats. MP3 works in more situations than other file types, so is the preferred format. Look for 'Export', 'Share' and 'Save As' options in the software. If you have the option to save to different quality levels, choose 'high' or 'highest'. If you are selecting from numerical alternatives, choose 192 kbit/s or higher.

## Radio for NEA

### The conventions of radio

Broadly speaking, the formats of typical radio programmes have changed little over the years. Peak-time radio shows (such as breakfast shows in the morning and 'Drive Time' slots in the late afternoon) have a set of conventions that the vast majority of music stations adhere to.

For the purposes of your NEA, any radio programme you are asked to produce will focus on talk-based sections of radio. Of course, music is vitally important for many radio programmes – but AQA moderators will want to hear evidence of more than just an appropriate selection of music. It is the way the show is scripted and edited together that will display your knowledge of Media Language and Media Representations.

In May 2018, it was announced that Greg James would be taking over as host of Radio 1's 'Breakfast Show' from Nick Grimshaw from September 2018.

Having said that, 'working backwards' from your idea of the station as a whole is a great way of ensuring that the minutes of audio footage you submit for your radio NEA are ideally targeted for your intended audience. So, you should consider the presenter(s), programme scheduling and/or playlists that might be used for the radio station you are creating.

### Radio station identification and branding

An important consideration for all radio stations is the way that idents (identification) and branding are used so audiences can easily identify and relate to the station. This, of course, can be visual – such as logos that will be seen on websites, social media and marketing material. However, as this is radio, audio is crucial too. If you are listening on a radio, you need something to remind you which station you are listening to, as there are no visual clues.

A jingle is the general term that is used for a catchy tune that advertises a radio station, presenter or product – often over a musical background. For radio stations, a jingle will normally include the name and broadcasting frequency – this is known as the station ident.

Commercial stations use station idents, the presenter's speech or sponsor tags – short pre-recorded pieces giving the name of a sponsor – to separate the station's content from the advert breaks. The shortest idents are called stabs. These are only one to three seconds long and mix the name of the station with music or a slogan. They can be dropped in at any point in a show.

Stations that use less music will simply remind listeners of the name of the station from time to time.

### Activity 6.26

Listen to segments of two breakfast shows from a commercial and non-commercial music radio station. Ideally, try and listen to at least half an hour of each. List the features you hear.
- What are the similarities and differences between the two?
- Can you explain why some aspects are very similar and others different?

### Activity 6.27

Check out Radio X, a popular commercial digital radio station, as a case study. By listening to the station and from looking at its website, what information can you find about who the station is aimed at?

From this information, create a listener profile for the station. Devise ideas for a new show that would appeal to this intended audience.

## Voices

If you are making a radio piece, it is just as important as with a visual medium to consider representation. The NEA brief will tell you who the target audience is, the minimum number of people who should speak and some details about the station. With this in mind, you can make some decisions about the people who will be broadcasting and what personality they should put across to appeal to the audience.

Most radio presenters script their words before they speak, even on radio shows that sound 'natural'. The main exceptions are phone-ins and the responses of guests – but the presenters' questions *are* usually scripted beforehand. As the director of the NEA, you will have to script *all* the words, including those that wouldn't normally be pre-planned. Your job is to make them sound as natural as possible, but to use the right level of language and mode of address to convey your chosen representations.

You should choose your presenters and guests carefully – including the people who will play those parts. Their voices will convey their personality. You are making the decisions, so you will need to tell them how to speak – how quickly or slowly, whether to increase or decrease the strength of their accent, whether to smile or stay serious (this affects the voice more than you may think).

## Music

Most stations use **music beds** that run underneath speech, at least for some parts of their output. These can help to signpost to the listener what part of the show they are hearing.

If the station you are creating is a music station, you will also need to choose the music carefully to meet the needs of the target audience. You will only be expected to use a short clip of your chosen music, to set the tone of the programme.

## Planning your radio NEA work

Radio planning can be done using grids, like the one on page 258. Write the timings and character names in the first column, the sections of script in the second column, and you could use a third column for music and other sounds. This way you can keep track of everything you need to produce and tick the items off as you record them. Radio presenters speak at about three words per second, which is useful to remember when you're writing scripts.

> **Key term**
>
> **Music beds**
> Both radio and advertising use music beds in the background, to evoke an atmosphere or mood. The term usually refers to instrumental pieces that are relatively low in volume, allowing other sounds to be heard clearly above them.

### Activity 6.28

When you have edited all your sounds together, ensure you play them back to someone who hasn't read your scripts. Can they work out who everyone is? Can they understand everything that is being said? Are they clear which radio station they are listening to and what the station is about?

**Message from Hero**

Radio Commercial – 60 second ENGLISH

| Description | Audio |
| --- | --- |
| SFX | Park sounds – Dog woofs |
| Announcer Character | We are at a park in Santa Barbara County with a dog named Hero. I will be translating a message that Hero wants to share about dog licensing. |
| Announcer Character | So Hero. What would you like to say to listeners? |
| SFX | Muffled dog woofs and ruffs |
| Announcer translates for Hero | Well, my pals at the shelter call me Hero because I have a dog license. My owner is awesome. He understands that responsible pet owners get their dogs licensed. |
| SFX | Muffled woofs and ruffs |
| Announcer translates for Hero | I want to remind dog owners in Santa Barbara County that they are required by law to license their dogs. Licensing your dog proves that you are a responsible pet owner and helps my pals at the shelters find loving homes. |
| SFX | Woof, woof |
| Announcer translates for Hero | A license is your dog's ticket home. |
| Announcer | Show you care. License your dog. It's the law. To learn more about purchasing a dog license in Santa Barbara County visit **www.ProjectPetSafe.org** |
| SFX | Happy dog sounds |

Note: SFX = sound effects

Radio advert script, created using a simple grid.

Source: Adapted from Santa Barbara County Animal Services, 2018

## Podcasts and online audio for NEA

Podcasts can contain video as well as audio content, but we'll concentrate on the audio side. Some podcasts are created for radio broadcast first and then edited as standalone features to be downloaded from the internet. Others are written and created directly for podcast. Whatever their origin, podcasts are usually free and can be streamed or downloaded from websites and specialist online stores such as iTunes. They can be relatively short – perhaps 15 to 20 minutes – or can be over an hour in length, and often come in series of episodes that the listener can subscribe to, so they will be notified when there is a new episode.

Podcasts use relatively little music, as broadcasters have to pay for a special licence to use most musical content, so it's cheaper to avoid it. Some royalty free or specially created music stabs might be used.

Podcasts can be listened to from any MP3 device and listeners can choose when to hear the latest episode. Because of this there is little or no audience interaction – as the media product is not being broadcast 'live'. This means there can be no phone-ins or presenters responding to live feeds from social media. Although some podcasts are derived from broadcast radio, some are very different to mainstream radio formats. With a podcast, you might be listening to an audio play, an adaptation of a book, a documentary, an expert talking about their chosen subject, a self-help guru, or a 'personality presenter', similar to a vlogger.

You would only have to create a short excerpt or a trailer for your NEA, and it is likely that this would be a sound file to embed in a website. Everything already said about audio production and radio also applies to online sound, but, with the relative lack of music, other sound sources become even more important to signpost what is happening.

There are over 500,000 podcasts on Apple Podcasts alone, so podcasters really need to find a USP and emphasise this in all their content.

## Advertising and marketing for NEA

Your NEA brief could involve radio adverts. These are usually created in multiples of ten seconds, so a 30- or 40-second advert would be quite normal. For an NEA brief, you will need to check how many adverts you are creating, and how long each one should be.

Remember, 'repetition builds reputation', so you need the listeners to recognise each advert as being part of the same campaign. You will need to consider what aspects of sound will be repeated across the different adverts. Most radio campaigns use the same slogan across all the adverts, and the same structure – perhaps a music stab or a sound effect to grab the listeners' attention, followed by two voice actors having a conversation about the product or service over a music bed, followed by a third voice actor who explains the benefits of the product and clearly gives the brand name and a call to action at the end.

Within this overall structure, there will be some elements that are different every time – so, in the example above the conversation would be different each time, emphasising various aspects of the product or service.

As with all audio products, you will need to script your adverts carefully to ensure your message is clear. And you will need to direct and edit the recordings carefully to ensure that all the words can be heard. There is no point to an advert that no one can understand.

> **Activity 6.29**
>
> The average podcast listener is in their 30s or 40s. What factual content might be either useful or entertaining to a teenage listener? In pairs, come up with ideas.
>
> Write a 30-word introduction to your podcast series, summing up its USP.

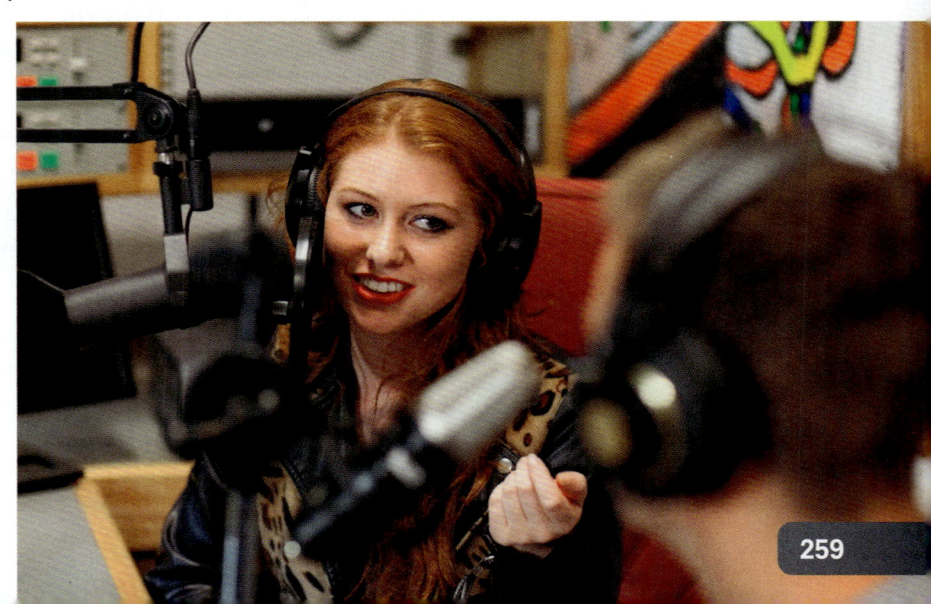

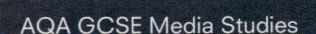

# Production skills and techniques: print production

> **Link**
>
> For more on the first British daily newspaper see Chapter 5, page 179.

Print media products have been around for centuries. In Chapter 5 you learned that the first British national daily newspaper started in 1702. Leaflets and pamphlets were circulated even before this. For an NEA print product, you are likely to be asked to create newspaper or magazine pages, marketing materials such as video game covers, or advertisements.

## Equipment for print production

Most students are more familiar with the equipment for print production than they are for any other media. For this reason, print briefs are often the most popular choices.

For any print brief, you will need to combine words, graphics and photographs. You therefore need to have some way to create these and to combine them.

In the media industry, you would use at least three separate pieces of software to create a print product – a word processor (such as Word) to type the words, or copy, as this will include spell and grammar checking to help writers spot potentional errors (although this is no substitute for proper proofreading); an image-editing program, such as Photoshop; and a DTP/layout program, such as InDesign. Each one is ideally suited to its part of the process. You may not be able to access all three types of software in your school or college, so may need to work out how to use your word-processing software to layout the product, for example.

Make sure that whichever software you use to layout your product you can create text in columns, use different font sizes and styles, move text boxes and images wherever you want them, arrange one item behind or in front of another, and resize the elements of the page.

In addition to the software or apps, you will need a camera to take the photographs. Smartphones often have high-quality cameras; compact cameras and DSLRs could also be used. As you are taking still images, a tripod is not as important as it is with moving images, but it could be useful if you want to set up one viewpoint for a photoshoot and keep returning to it after directing your models.

If you have access to a plain background and some lights, whether this is in a specially equipped studio or just an empty room with a sheet pinned to the wall, you can create more professional-looking shots. A portable light, such as another student's phone or a hand-held video light, can be used wherever you are to fill in harsh shadows.

## Writing copy

Whatever your print product, you will need to write some copy for it. The NEA brief will probably give you an approximate word count. The words are as important as the images in creating a representation. You will need to consider the mode of address and the type of vocabulary you would like to use. Should you use slang or jargon at all? Should you write as if the piece is a formal essay, or as if you are writing some advice or information for a good friend? If you are writing an interview, consider how your main character would speak – this is as much part of their brand as how they dress and how they pose.

There are obviously specific conventions for how various products should be written – some are covered later in this chapter. You should also bear in mind everything you've learned elsewhere about different writing styles, such as persuasive writing or writing a report.

Make sure you use the spellcheck and grammar-check features of your word-processing software before you lay your words out in the product itself – and get someone else to help you proofread, as it is not always easy to spot your own mistakes. After all, you know what you intended to say.

## Taking photographs

You will need to direct any photoshoots for your products, telling people what to wear, where and how to stand, and how to interact with each other or with the camera. You need to look carefully at everything within the frame of the photograph, to make sure there is nothing that detracts from the meaning you want to portray.

The brief will specify a minimum number of photographs, but you should always take more than this, so that you can choose the best ones when you come to laying out your products. Try varying the angle and distance you take the photographs from, so that you have several different versions of the same subject matter.

You will need to plan the whole product before you take the photographs, so you know whether you need some plain areas within the image, where you can overlay text or graphics.

For example, the photograph used on this front cover of *Chess* magazine includes a space to the right of the player's face and another space above his head with little detail. These spaces allow the magazine's designer to add the masthead and cover lines without detracting from the image.

*Chess* magazine

### Activity 6.30

If you were creating adverts for Example Brief Five given earlier in this chapter, what could you include in the mise-en-scène of the photographs? The adverts were for a new range of watches, but were to emphasise a sense of tradition and history. Consider your choices for:

- locations
- the people who would be your models
- the style of clothing you would prefer your models to wear
- any props
- the actions your models would be carrying out.

How would each of these add to the meaning in the image?

## Creating graphics

Your product will need graphics, such as a masthead or a company logo. One of your first considerations for any graphics is colour. You may be able to plan a colour palette for your product before your photoshoot.

*Saga* magazine, however, usually uses a limited colour palette on its front cover, based on an element within the main cover image. Can you see how the background and font colours on these covers relate to an aspect within the photograph of the cover star? Some image-editing programs allow you to use a colour picker to choose a colour from the image that you can then use to fill the background or to colour the fonts.

Another consideration is the style of font you should use within the logo or masthead. This should suggest something about the character of the product itself.

You might also use graphic features – boxes, circles, borders and so on – to break-up your page or to highlight specific information. You should be guiding the audience to read your product in the way you want them to. Signpost clearly where the information begins and ends and where they can find the most important elements. If you are adding captions to a photograph, for example, you will need to separate these visually from any other copy. You can use straplines and **skylines**, which create a coloured strip across a page, to highlight specific text. You can use borders and/or coloured boxes to outline an information box, separating it from the main text or image.

### Talk about it
What does each of these fonts connote?

*a product*

**A PRODUCT**

a product

### Key term
**Skyline**
A line of text, with or without a coloured strip background, that runs across the top edge of a magazine page, poster or other print product. It contains important information to appeal to the audience.

## Laying out the pages

Once you have all the elements of your product, you will need to lay them out.

This will be much easier if you have a sketched plan of the pages, and you have all your image and text files saved to the same folder, in the most accessible file formats. Some image-processing software will automatically save your images in a format that is specific to that program, such as PSD files in Photoshop. You might need to save these as JPEGs, GIFs or PNGs to use them in the software you are using for layout.

We will look at the layout conventions of different print formats in the next sections of this chapter.

## Newspapers for NEA

A newspaper NEA brief will tell you who the paper is aimed at, which pages or features you are creating, and probably something about the articles and photographs you need to create. Start by looking at the conventions of these features, the minimum word count and the number of photographs specified in the brief, so you know exactly what you are expected to do.

If you need to choose if the newspaper is to be a local paper, freesheet, tabloid or broadsheet, this is the first decision to make. This will help you to decide on a mode of address and a conventional layout that you can start from.

Most newspapers, whatever their format, foreground one news story on their front page, giving it the biggest headline and most space. They will also tend to feature one main image on the front, but this may be connected to another story entirely. The broadsheets often also carry other smaller stories on the front page.

Each newspaper has its own house style, which will cover everything from the fonts used, the size of the headlines and the number of columns across the page, to the use of white space and section headings throughout the newspaper. Each newspaper has also adopted its own mode of address, which governs how it 'talks' to its audience – the style of written language used.

> **Link**
>
> Look also at the Print codes section in Chapter 1, pages 18–26.

> **Link**
>
> Look in both Chapter 1 and Chapter 5 for more information on the conventions of newspapers.

### Activity 6.31

Read the main front-page story in three different newspapers, looking for differences in the use of language and the mode of address. Can you sum up each newspaper by describing the type of person who would talk like that?

## Using newspaper conventions

Labelling the parts of newspaper front covers:
- Skyline
- Masthead/flag
- Dateline
- Teaser
- Standalone (image)
- Photograph
- Illustration
- By-line
- Body text/copy
- Headline
- Caption

### Activity 6.32
Look up a breaking news story online, and try to predict the different headlines each newspaper will use for this story tomorrow. Why do you think the different newspapers will word their headlines differently?

Knowing the terminology for the different parts of a newspaper will help you to get the details right and to write your Statement of Intent. For each of these elements, consider how this usually looks in professional newspapers. One common mistake made by students, for example, is to lay-out their copy (the words in the articles) using too large a font and too few columns.

The style of the headlines is determined by the mode of address of the newspaper – would your newspaper use puns, slang or colloquialisms? If so, these would be likely to appear in the headlines. Does your newspaper take a particular point of view or try to remain neutral on specific issues? Headlines normally sum up the newspaper's take on the event.

## Hard news, soft news and feature articles

Read your NEA newspaper brief carefully to make sure you know what type of article(s) you have to create. Hard news refers to events in the world that are reported immediately they happen. These can include political events, financial news, war, crime or disasters. These are up-to-the minute stories telling you what is new in the world. Soft news refers to background information about these events, or to human interest stories. These can include celebrities, the arts, entertainment and lifestyle issues. Although these might give background to the hard news stories of the day, sometimes they could be published at any point within a given week (or longer) and still be regarded as relevant.

Feature articles are usually written by specialists in their area, and often contain no *news* at all. Instead, they are packed full of information that is considered of interest to the newspaper's readers, and/or the opinions of the feature writer. These can include reviews, gardening columns, political commentary and fashion items.

## The five Ws

You will probably have learned about the five Ws in your English lessons. Now is your time to use this format to its full. A newspaper article is usually written using the five Ws – who, what, when, where, why – in the first paragraph, to set the scene for the rest of the story. By giving this information right at the start, journalists are allowing their readers to decide quickly whether to read the whole article and, if they do, to place everything else in context straight away.

Most articles will then add more detail, including quotes from witnesses and experts. News items often end with a pointer towards the future – what do people expect to happen next?

A news article is written so that it can be 'subbed upwards'. This means that if the article is too long for the space available in the newspaper, the sub-editor will start at the bottom of the article and remove sentences or paragraphs until the article is short enough to fit. Check your article after you've written it. Could you remove the ending and still get your main points across?

## Newspaper images

Newspaper images play an important role in communicating the story being told. Depending on their importance, and where they are placed in the paper, some articles carry no photographs at all, while others – especially soft news articles and background features to larger stories – will have several images. Newspapers also use graphs, maps and diagrams to convey factual information. Any images that you use will need to be created by you. Consider what would most help the audience to either understand the story or be attracted to read the story.

Newspaper images have captions to anchor their meanings and relate them to the article. Often these captions use similar words to specific parts of the article, so that readers can easily make the links.

## Newspaper layout

Remember that the front cover of a newspaper acts as an advert for the product. Often, in newsagents and supermarkets, the papers are either folded or placed in racks partly covering each other. The top third of the front page is therefore the most important section to attract potential readers, as it is likely to be on display in every situation. In some shops the whole front cover can be seen, so the main image can be a real attention-grabber.

Inside pages may have several shorter stories. Even where there is only one story, the page often contains several elements. A complete page of text is uninviting to most readers. Ensure that when you are laying out each page you make it visually interesting, to draw readers' attention and make them want to read on. You could address different aspects of the story as if written by different journalists, you could use information boxes, or you could break the page up using graphic features or photographs. Break long columns of copy text up with cross-headings or pull quotes.

> **Talk about it**
>
> Look again at the two front pages on page 264 and discuss with a partner how each element has been designed to grab the attention of a specific audience.

**Quick question 6.4**

Which genres of magazines would more typically include a long-shot of a person on the front cover and why?

## Magazines as NEA

A magazine NEA brief will give you a specific number of pages, a target audience and a guide as to the subject matter – such as the world of the vlogger in the sample brief earlier in this chapter.

You will usually be asked to create the front cover as one of the pages, so it is worth spending some time looking at the key conventions of these, along with the conventions of the other pages of a magazine.

## Using magazine conventions

The front cover of the magazine will need to be designed to catch potential buyers' eyes as it stands on the supermarket's or newsagent's shelf. It will need a clear masthead and an eye-catching image – many magazines feature photographs of people, usually in close-up or mid-shot, and usually looking directly out at the viewer. You are naturally drawn to images of faces, especially when they are looking at you. This direct mode of address pulls you in, and makes you feel that the magazine is talking directly to you.

You can choose to place your image behind your masthead, or have the person overlap the masthead – overlapping is a convention used by well-established magazines, confident that their readers will recognise the magazine despite not being able to read the whole of the magazine's name. *Tatler* magazine sometimes uses this design idea.

The NEA brief will give you a minimum number of cover lines and other conventions to include. You can make decisions about where these are placed, but, as with newspapers, magazine front covers may overlap when displayed in a rack – so the masthead needs to be at the top, and is usually either on the left or spans the full width of the cover. Your splash heads shouldn't cover the face of your model, and you should choose a limited range of colours for the text – three or four colours is usual, including the colours of the masthead.

The pages of a magazine, as with newspapers, are laid out using columns. Where newspapers typically have five columns to a page, magazines usually have three, although designers experiment with different layouts to break up the different sections of a magazine.

**Activity 6.33**

Look at a range of front covers for the same magazine and identify the common elements that make up the magazine's house style. You could write these up as a style guide for designers working for the magazine.

Using this style guide as an example, write one for your own magazine design, explaining its house style.

The brief will specify a minimum number of images. If you are designing a double page spread, spend some time sketching where the images and the text will be placed. Plan the images you are going to take – don't leave them to chance, as they can carry a lot of meaning, and show your understanding of Media Language and Media Representations. If a large image of a person is used, the person will often look straight out at the audience or be turned inwards towards the space on the page. If the person is positioned to look out of the edge of the page, this conveys a feeling that they are distancing themselves from the audience.

Consider carefully whether you want your images to be in colour or in black and white, and how they fit with the colour scheme for your pages. Sometimes images and graphic features are used behind the body copy, with the opacity of the image reduced, so it looks faded. If you do this, ensure that everything is still readable.

## Marketing as NEA

Marketing is one of the eight areas that could be covered by an NEA brief. You looked at TV adverts earlier in the chapter, but marketing covers more than just advertisements. Another marketing possibility for an NEA brief could be to create covers for media products such as DVDs and video games.

As with any brief, begin by looking carefully at the conventions of similar products.

If you are designing a cover, you will need to think about the front, back and spine.

### Activity 6.34

Whatever you are creating a cover for, find five or six examples of professional products and lay them side by side – for this activity, it is best to look at the real things rather than examples online, as the online versions rarely give the whole of the cover. Look for the elements that are included on every cover – these are the conventions that you will need to include. Make a list of these. Look also for logos and fonts that are always used for certain elements, and for the areas where you can make more creative decisions.

### Link

For more about depth of field see Photographic codes in Chapter 1, pages 22–26.

### Tip

Carry out an online image search for covers in the genre you are creating, e.g. 'DVD cover fantasy film'. Look at the range of covers displayed, and notice the similarities in the images, fonts and colours across the genre. If your product is to be recognised by fans of the genre, you will need to use these key conventions.

Sketch your ideas before you start your production.

---

The first thing to notice, when you lay a cover out flat, is that the front is on the right and the back is on the left, with the spine between. There is usually a common colour scheme across the front and back.

Read the NEA brief carefully to see what it tells you about the product you are creating marketing materials for – who is the target audience, what is the USP of the product, or what are the key themes you need to emphasise?

The main cover image will need to tell the audience something about the genre of the game or film. DVD cover images are often collages of different shots from within the film, to show a range of characters, or feature the main characters against a generic landscape background from within the film. Sports game covers often feature one sports player in action, usually moving towards the camera. The background is often a slightly out-of-focus shot of the sportsground or the crowd, suggesting a shallow depth of field.

While the front cover will emphasise the genre, the back is where you can emphasise what is different about this specific product. You will need to write some blurb for the back cover and will probably have been given an approximate word count for this. Make sure you read what is written on professional covers first. Look for the use of persuasive language, rhetorical questions and hyperbole.

Back covers also usually use several images, from the film or gameplay, to emphasise the enjoyment the audience will get from different aspects of the product. You need, therefore, to have decided on some of the key features of the product you are marketing before you can create the cover. Who are the main characters/actors? How will they help to attract the audience to the product? What is the main narrative? How is enigma used? You can refer to this in your blurb, to hook the consumer in, and suggest what they will experience if they buy the product.

## Print advertisements as NEA

An obvious form of marketing is print advertisements, usually for magazines or newspapers, but they could also be for billboards. Use AIDA to help you design your ideas (Attention, Interest, Desire and Action), concentrating on the key points you have been given in the brief. If this is a magazine advert, how will your advert grab the audience's attention as they flick through the magazine? What can your advert promise the audience, to start their interest in the product? How can you make them desire to buy the product? What do you need to let them know, so that they can act on this desire and make a successful purchase?

There are some clear conventions for adverts, but there are also many adverts that seek to attract attention by breaking these conventions.

The Galaxy adverts on this page include a slogan, a main image and a product shot. These are the three basic components of most adverts.

MacDonald's has produced several adverts that could be said to contain the same three elements, but are much less obvious. Red space is used along with the iconic M, which catches the eye of the reader because so much space is very unusual. Try to find some of them online.

Obviously, some adverts carry more features than this, including the use of blocks of copy to communicate more about the product or service.

### Activity 6.35

The way the slogan and the image work together to anchor each other is obviously very important. Some adverts have a very simple mise-en-scène, while others are much more complex. Looking at the two Galaxy adverts below, what do you think the visuals in each one convey about the product? How does the slogan in each one reinforce this meaning?

### Quick question 6.5

What types of products are more likely to have informative text as well as slogans within their adverts?

Notice how both of these Galaxy print adverts include an image of the chocolate bar in its wrapper.

One of a series of three adverts created in response to Example Brief Five.

**Link**

For more information on choosing common elements to create a campaign see page 236.

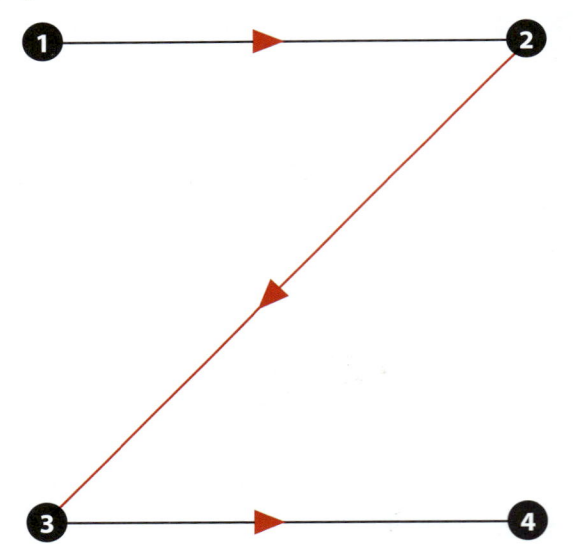

**Activity 6.36**

If you were creating the other two adverts for the Fontaine Royale campaign, what would you include in them? What would be common across the whole campaign?

You will need to plan the photographs for your adverts very carefully, as they carry more of the information than in most print products. Every part of the image must be focused on the media language and media representations that you want to use. Think as carefully about the background as about the people or products. In this partial response to Example Brief Five (advertising watches for an upmarket audience), the background has been added onto the photograph of the man, to convey the sense of tradition and history that was asked for in the brief. The image is directly linked to the product via the slogan.

Some designers refer to Z-pattern reading – this describes the way that many viewers tend to 'read' a cover, advert or poster. You move your eyes across and down the image in the shape of a Z, starting at the top-left corner, and ending up at the bottom right. We tend to remember the last thing we see, so the information you most want viewers to remember should be placed in the bottom right-hand corner, as shown in the diagram below. In an advert this could be a pack shot or product shot, so that the audience know what to look for when they hit the shops or the online store. You could bear this in mind when you design your advert.

The fonts and colours of the text are also involved in the representation of the product. In the Fontaine Royale advert, for example, for Example Brief Five, the designer has chosen a gold-coloured, traditional-looking, serif font, while in the McDonald's advert the designer has chosen a more modern, white, sans-serif font. Whatever software you use to design your adverts, you will have a choice of fonts and colours, and need to make a deliberate choice that reflects the nature of the product being advertised.

If you are responding to a print advertising brief, you will have been asked to create more than one advert.

# Production skills and techniques: e-media production

E-media is a term used to describe media forms that are accessed via electronic devices. As far as NEA briefs are concerned, e-media are online, social and participatory media, including video games.

Video games have been popular since the 1970s, with growing complexity to the gameplay, the narratives and the graphics. Video games started as a discrete medium, played on arcade machines, standalone computers and games consoles, but have increasingly moved online. Even when games are bought on disc for a console there is often additional online content to access.

The internet has been used by the public and commercial organisations since the early 1990s. As seen when examining the other media forms, the internet has changed the way all media industries work, opening up new ways for audiences to access familiar products.

Although social media networks existed on the internet before the turn of the century, they really took off in the early 2000s. Instagram arrived in 2011, Snapchat in 2011 and TikTok in 2016. Wikipedia listed over 215 social media sites in March 2018, and such sites count their users in the millions or billions.

An NEA brief could ask you to create online content, social media content or products related to video games.

## Equipment for e-media production

To create a website, you can use an online website builder such as Weebly, WordPress or GoDaddy, or an offline app such as Mobirise. These services enable you to build a functioning website without having to use complex coding. There are many similar services available, often offering a free version. These free services often insert their own logo at the bottom of each page you create, whether you want to include this or not, but this will not count against you in your NEA. Whichever service you choose, you will need to be able to use your own photographs and graphics – you cannot gain marks for using the ones built into the templates, as these do not show how *you* have designed and used media language to create media representations. You will obviously need internet access while using the online services, and will need to be able to upload your own material to the site you are creating. Using an offline app may be easier.

One of the options when submitting your website NEA to AQA is to export your complete website into an offline version that will function from a memory stick or data DVD. You need to check before you start that you can do this, as not all online website builders offer this function. At the time of writing this book, Weebly does this very well, but others don't. However, offline apps such as Mobirise do this easily.

You will need to take your own photographs, create your own graphics and write your own copy for any online content you create. This means you will need a camera, image-editing software and word-processing software. All of these have already been discussed in the section on print production (pages 260–264).

For any online form, be it websites or social media, you could be asked to create audio or video content – these have also already been covered in the relevant sections in this chapter.

For video game production, as with website production, the ability to code is not required. This means you can use existing online game-making software, such as the game engines provided by GameMaker, Atmosphere, GamesFactory, GameSalad and Unity. Even MIT's Scratch can be surprisingly good. Many of the paid-for programs have free versions available – while RPG Maker VX Ace costs money, for example, RPG Maker VX Ace Lite is free. Most of these programs have active online communities and tutorials to help you as you create your game.

Your focus will be on the playability and engagement with the game for the targeted audience – and how these are constructed by the representations and media language used within the game. As with websites, if you use game engine software that relies on templates, you will need to create the design aspects – assets such as props, backgrounds and characters – yourself and embed these in the templates provided. If the software doesn't enable you to import assets you have created from scratch, you must be able to customise the look of the assets provided within the program. Many apps will allow you to switch the hair colour, hair length, face shape and eye colour of the characters, for example. Check what choices are available before deciding on your game engine.

## Online products as NEA

As with all the other products discussed so far, you will need to begin with the NEA brief. Read it carefully so that you understand exactly what you are asked to create. Are you creating the webpages themselves and, if so, how many? Are you being asked for audio or video content, photographs or interactive elements? What is the purpose of the website or social media feed, and the purpose of each of the elements you need to create?

## Designing a website

You may be asked to create a homepage and at least one linked page, or other pages from a website. More and more websites are designed with mobile phone use in mind. In October 2016, for the first time, the number of webpages accessed from mobile devices surpassed those accessed from computers. The vast majority of these were accessed from smartphones rather than tablets. Because people are viewing websites on much smaller screens, the design of the sites has had to change.

## 6 Non-exam assessment

### Activity 6.37

Compare these two pages from different linked websites for Wild Bunch – a film production and distribution company involved with the film *I, Daniel Blake*.

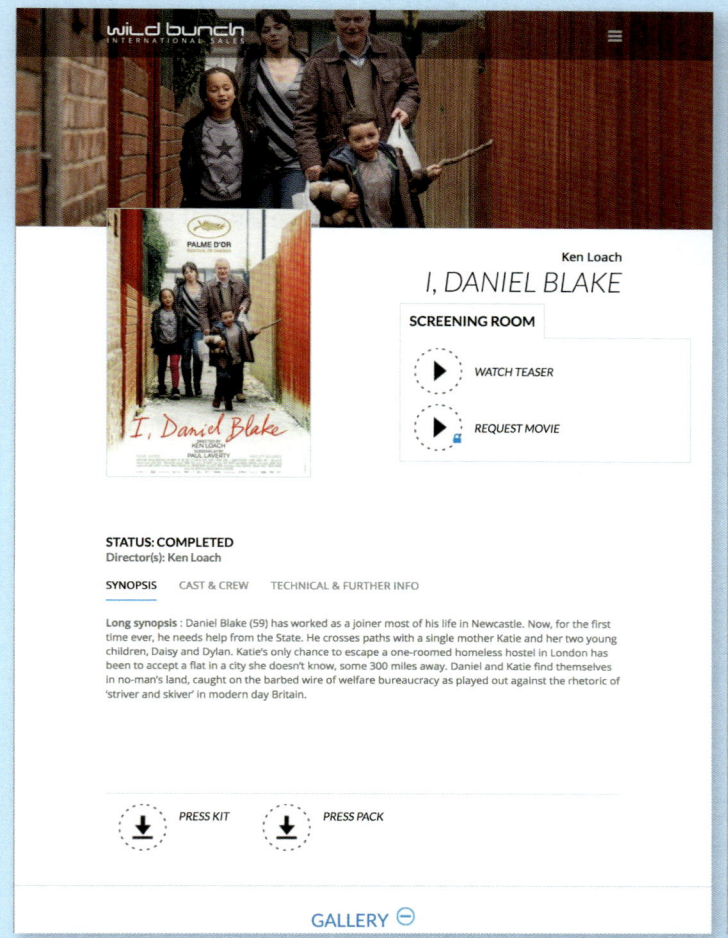

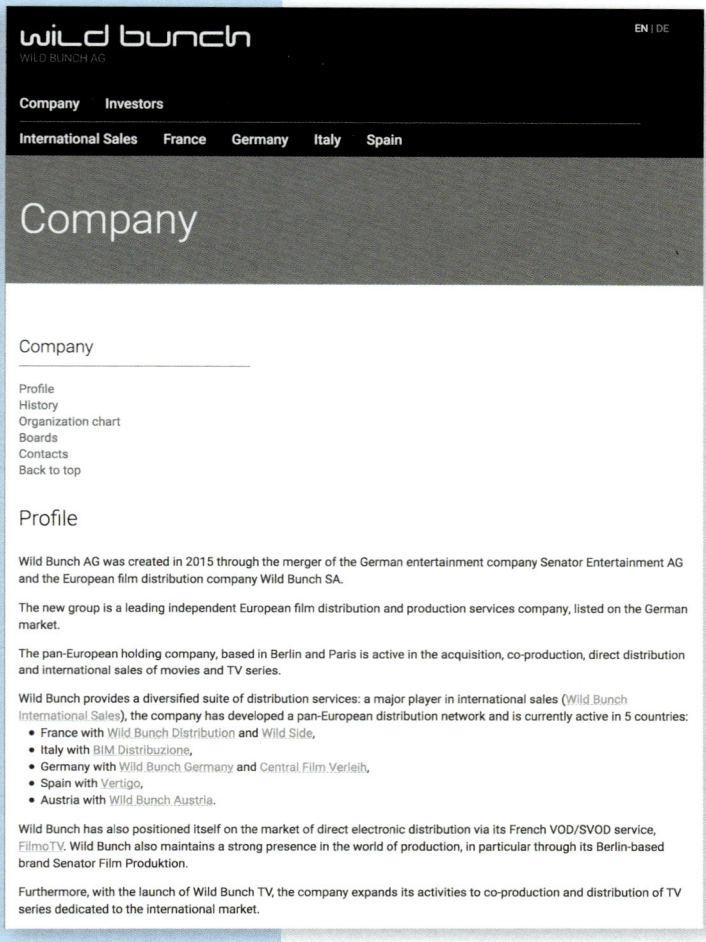

**Page 1 (Wild Bunch International Sales – I, Daniel Blake):**

wild bunch
INTERNATIONAL SALES

PALME D'OR
I, Daniel Blake

Ken Loach
**I, DANIEL BLAKE**

SCREENING ROOM
▶ WATCH TEASER
▶ REQUEST MOVIE

**STATUS: COMPLETED**
Director(s): Ken Loach

SYNOPSIS | CAST & CREW | TECHNICAL & FURTHER INFO

Long synopsis : Daniel Blake (59) has worked as a joiner most of his life in Newcastle. Now, for the first time ever, he needs help from the State. He crosses paths with a single mother Katie and her two young children, Daisy and Dylan. Katie's only chance to escape a one-roomed homeless hostel in London has been to accept a flat in a city she doesn't know, some 300 miles away. Daniel and Katie find themselves in no-man's land, caught on the barbed wire of welfare bureaucracy as played out against the rhetoric of 'striver and skiver' in modern day Britain.

⬇ PRESS KIT    ⬇ PRESS PACK

GALLERY ⊖

**Page 2 (Wild Bunch AG – Company):**

wild bunch
WILD BUNCH AG                                                  EN | DE

Company    Investors
International Sales    France    Germany    Italy    Spain

# Company

Company
Profile
History
Organization chart
Boards
Contacts
Back to top

## Profile

Wild Bunch AG was created in 2015 through the merger of the German entertainment company Senator Entertainment AG and the European film distribution company Wild Bunch SA.

The new group is a leading independent European film distribution and production services company, listed on the German market.

The pan-European holding company, based in Berlin and Paris is active in the acquisition, co-production, direct distribution and international sales of movies and TV series.

Wild Bunch provides a diversified suite of distribution services: a major player in international sales (Wild Bunch International Sales), the company has developed a pan-European distribution network and is currently active in 5 countries:
- France with Wild Bunch Distribution and Wild Side,
- Italy with BIM Distribuzione,
- Germany with Wild Bunch Germany and Central Film Verleih,
- Spain with Vertigo,
- Austria with Wild Bunch Austria.

Wild Bunch has also positioned itself on the market of direct electronic distribution via its French VOD/SVOD service, FilmoTV. Wild Bunch also maintains a strong presence in the world of production, in particular through its Berlin-based brand Senator Film Produktion.

Furthermore, with the launch of Wild Bunch TV, the company expands its activities to co-production and distribution of TV series dedicated to the international market.

---

Both pages have been designed in very different ways, with mobile access in mind. Why do you think the two pages look so different? Think about the intended audience and the purpose of the pages.

Note the key features of each of these pages. What would make each one easy to understand on a smartphone screen? What similarities are there? How do they differ?

---

Before designing your pages, look at websites for similar products or services. Website styles change very quickly and are designed so that the 'look' can be updated even if the words, images and embedded content stay much the same. Look at several sites before deciding what conventions and design ideas you need to use.

You will need to decide on a house style that covers all of your pages. This will include colours, fonts, image styles and layout ideas. You will also need to include some form of navigation. Although you may only be creating one or two pages, you should consider what other pages your site would contain, so that you can show how your page would link to these, and how you would tempt your audience to visit those pages.

You can use a navbar across the top and very bottom of a desktop computer homepage which becomes a navburger or hamburger drop-down menu on a mobile screen, or some web-builder services will allow you to create a 'sticky navbar' that stays at the top of a mobile window. You need to consider your target audience when choosing – the hamburger icon is also known as a hidden menu, because it doesn't reveal what it is, or what the website contains, until you click on it.

However you create the navigation, you should only include the main pages of your site – four is a good number for a navbar, and four to eight for a hamburger icon. If you were creating a fully-fledged professional site, any sub-pages could be linked to from these main ones.

## Writing copy

Both websites and social media will require some form of copy-writing. If your homepage is going to carry text, then this is particularly crucial. Visitors to websites need to know that they have come to the right place, so you need to tell them – quickly and clearly. You should outline the key reasons why they should stay on your site.

Not all homepages carry much text, of course. For some, this is on the linked pages. Is your website a blogging site, conveying a sense of one individual's personality? It could be a corporate website, giving information about a company, or it could be a marketing website, trying to engage visitors with a product such as a film or a video game. Each of these would need a different mode of address and would position the audience differently. You need to understand the purpose of the site before you can start to write your copy. Then you need to understand the purpose of the page you are creating. Only once you know the point of the text can you start to write the copy itself.

### Quick question 6.6

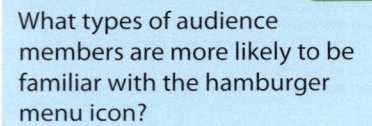

What types of audience members are more likely to be familiar with the hamburger menu icon?

### Activity 6.38

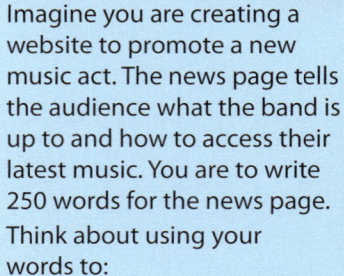

Imagine you are creating a website to promote a new music act. The news page tells the audience what the band is up to and how to access their latest music. You are to write 250 words for the news page.

Think about using your words to:
- Give an idea of what the band is like.
- Explain what the band has been doing recently.
- Tell the audience where to buy or listen to their latest music now, and make them want to do so.

You will probably have been given an approximate word count. Think about your purpose and try to divide the words up to ensure you cover everything you need to.

If you are writing for social media, some social media platforms have a limit to the length of each post, while others will only initially show a limited part of a longer post. In circumstances such as these, it is important to consider how to get the main message across as succinctly and efficiently as possible. This is similar to writing copy for a newspaper article – summing up the main thrust of the article in the first sentence or two – but here the style is usually much less formal, and probably needs to catch the eye of the reader within a longer flow of posts, stories or threads. The opening words are key to this.

Large organisations will usually employ someone to create their social media profile. They may post on social media several times a day. The best such feeds will not only talk about the organisation itself but will post other items of interest to the audience it serves, while trying not to put anyone off. If you are writing social media posts for an NEA product, bear this in mind, and write a series of posts rather than a one-off. When read together these should convey the representation you have designed.

> **Tip**
>
> Next time you check your social media feed, notice what catches your eye, making you want to stop scrolling and pay attention.

## Taking photographs and creating graphics

Of course, social media uses images and videos as well as words. As already suggested, and seen in the screengrabs, some websites and webpages are dominated by images rather than text. This makes images very important for conveying meaning online. Where images are usually illustrating an article in magazines and newspapers, they can be the main form of communication in a social media post, a blog item or a homepage. Therefore, you need to think very carefully about the visual aspects of your NEA product.

Think about the purpose of your site and what is relevant to include in the images. Try to tie in each photograph clearly with the heading superimposed on it. This makes the site easy to understand, so the visitor knows what to expect from each section.

When you take photographs, remember to look at everything within the frame – why is it there? What meaning does it convey? If something is not adding to the meaning, can you take it out? This can be done while you are taking photographs – remove unwanted objects from the scene before you press the shutter, or change the angle and position you are shooting from so you can only see what is relevant. Getting closer often removes unnecessary clutter from the background. You can also remove problems while you are editing the photographs, by cropping closer to the main subject or using more sophisticated software to re-touch the image. Make sure you understand how to use the image-editing software available to you, before you take your photographs. Otherwise you may be relying on it to do something that it can't do.

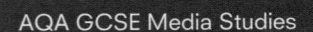

You will be creating all the graphics for the website as well, including logos, headings and possibly backgrounds. Your house style will cover the colours and major font styles to be used for these. Remember that they need to make sense on a small screen as well as a computer screen – so if you are creating graphics elements on a large screen, try resizing the view by zooming out from time to time, to make sure they will work within the site as a whole.

Look at the logo below for Wild Bunch AG and see how readable it is even when it is small in size.

**wild bunch**

Logos need to be readable and visually interesting at all sizes.

Finally, remember that on websites and in social media, visitors can rarely see a whole page or a whole profile at a time. They will be scrolling through your content. Plan your content so that as they scroll they have a visually interesting and varied experience. Give them reasons to keep scrolling, using enigma within your body text and your headings to make them want to see more.

## Video games as NEA

If you are creating a video game for your Media Studies GCSE, as with all products you will need to begin with the NEA brief. Read it carefully to work out what you need to create. You may, for example, have been asked to create the opening level of a game with enough content to give one to two minutes of gameplay, or perhaps you have been asked for two or three scenes or levels. There may be a limit on the length of any cut-scenes or intro movie. Is the genre of game specified? Who is the target audience and what would they expect from such a game?

Work out what the minimum requirements are, make yourself a checklist then see what decisions are left up to you. Can you choose whether the game is an arcade game, an RPG (role-playing game), a shooter, etc.? Can you choose where the game is set and who your main characters are? Can you choose the obstacles to be overcome in the game?

## Designing a video game

Once you know the genre, and what choices are available to you, you can start to design your game. Although you may have only been asked to create one to two minutes of gameplay, you should have a clear idea for the overall game and its final objective. As with all media products, you will need a USP that makes your game stand out from the rest. This USP will probably then give you ideas for the objectives, locations and obstacles as well as the main characters.

You will need to ensure the goals of the game are obvious and are appropriate to the genre you are creating. The narrative of the game must be simple enough for players to understand with limited explanation, but complex enough to keep them interested. Your characters will need to react in predictable ways, so that their role within the game is understood, but not so predictable that playing is boring. You will therefore be using stereotypes that others can understand, but should also include random events to keep your players interested.

Also ensure that the gameplay uses the conventions of the genre you are trying to replicate, so that players are using familiar controls and ideas within your unique creation. You will need to signify the interactive parts of your environment clearly enough so that users know they need to try to reach, hit, shoot, collect or save them. Plan for this from the outset.

If you are creating two or three levels, make sure the first level is the easiest and introduces players to how the game works, ramping up the difficulty as you move up through the levels.

Don't be over-ambitious and design too much. As with all of the NEA briefs, this is a product that is limited in size. It will not be a full-blown game that will enable players to while away several hours. Even an indie game will usually have a team of five to ten people. You are creating this game on your own, so a mobile game with simple visuals and programing is more appropriate. Make sure the narrative covered within this glimpse of the game is easy-to-follow – you may have thought of several clever twists, but you won't have time for them all in this product.

## Creating graphic elements

In many games, you will need to create a protagonist that your game-playing audience wants to invest time and effort in. If you can import graphics into your chosen game-making app, then you can control every aspect of your character – but first check carefully what size (e.g. in pixels) any assets need to be. If you can't import graphics, you will need to choose the aspects of your character's look carefully from those offered within the game-making software. Remember that you are being marked on your use of media language and representations, so you must make the key decisions about these aspects.

You will need to make the same decisions for each of the important assets of your game – the locations and backgrounds, the obstacles to be overcome and any other characters to be used. As in all media products, the mise-en-scène is an important aspect in conveying meaning to the audience.

## Sound in video games

Sound in video games can be used both to enhance the atmosphere of the game and to give users feedback on how they are doing – whether this is the sound effects created by the characters' interaction with the environment, dialogue, or signifiers such as fanfares. There is not always such a strong distinction between diegetic and non-diegetic sound as in other media formats.

Again, your ability to import sounds will be dictated by the software you use, but it is important that *you* choose the sounds used in *your* game. These convey meaning just as much as the visuals, and need to do so in ways that your audience readily understand.

### Activity 6.39

Either start a new game you've not played before or go back to the beginning of a game you know well. You can do this by playing the game itself or by watching gameplay videos.
- How does the game teach its users what to do?
- How many different methods of instruction are used?
- Which ones rely on the player having played similar games before?
- How does a game-player coming to this genre for the first time know what to do?

AQA GCSE Media Studies

### Activity 6.40

Imagine your gameplayer has to make their character jump and hit the same target three times in order to gain life points. What sounds will you use throughout the sequence to let the player know they are getting nearer to success?

## Exporting your game

Some games engines have limited export options. GameMaker's free engine, for example, will only let you export PC Windows versions of games. Unity, on the other hand, will let you export to a wide variety of platforms. Your game needs to be playable by your teacher and the AQA moderator – if you can export an online version that would be preferable, as this can be accessed from any browser. If not, .EXE or .DMG files are probably the next most usable alternatives.

Before you decide that your game is finished and ready to be marked, ask someone else to play it. This should be someone (or several people) who you trust to be honest. As well as talking to them, watch them play and see how they interact with your game. If they are not acting as you expected, consider how you can adapt your game to either force them to play in a specific way, or to make the most of the way they are naturally playing.

Before you export the final version of your game, ensure it is bug-free and therefore fully playable – otherwise the people marking the game may not be able to experience all the features you have chosen to include.

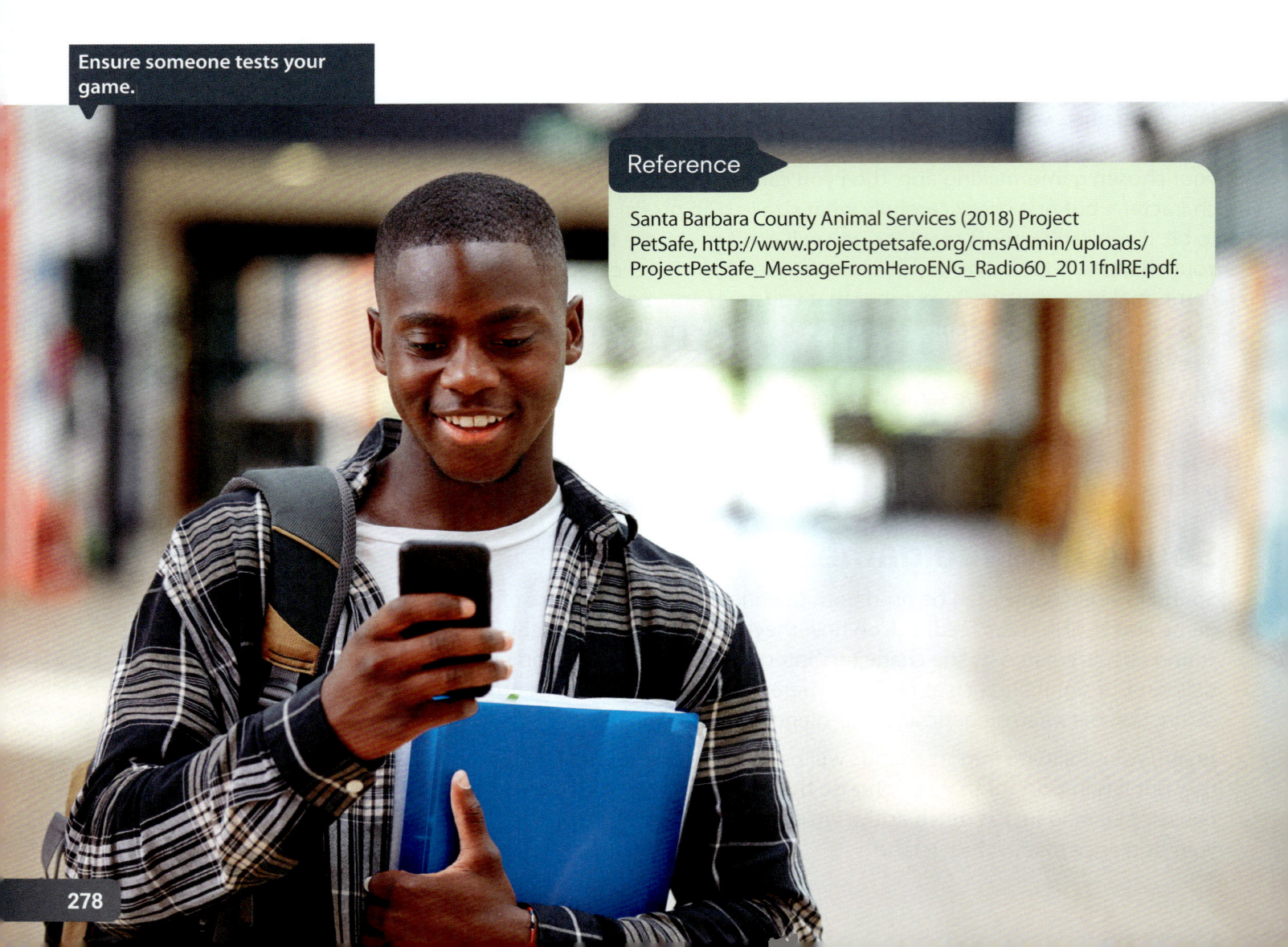

Ensure someone tests your game.

### Reference

Santa Barbara County Animal Services (2018) Project PetSafe, http://www.projectpetsafe.org/cmsAdmin/uploads/ProjectPetSafe_MessageFromHeroENG_Radio60_2011fnlRE.pdf.

# Glossary of key terms

**Agenda setting**  The theory that the media have a powerful and influential role in telling politicians and the public what they should be thinking about.

**Ambiguous/Ambiguity**  A sign with several possible meanings which could be confused.

**Augmented reality**  Technology combining computer-generated images with the user's physical environment.

**Austerity**  Government policies that reduce spending on public services so that the country does not have to borrow so much money.

**Avatar**  A picture, icon or character that represents a digital media user, e.g. a game-player.

**Bias**  A prejudice for or against a particular group or individual. Biased reporting in the media may be demonstrated by tone or style but also by selection or omission. A newspaper story may be biased not because of what is included, but by what is left out. Bias can be innocent, for example a bias for tea and against coffee, but in media studies it usually refers to unfair or irrational practices.

**Brand**  An identity or representation of a product, which distinguishes it from its rivals. These are obviously commercial products. Although an individual person can also be thought of as a commercial product.

**Carriage costs**  DAB radio stations do not usually own their own transmitters. They have to pay a monthly sum of money for a DAB transmission service. It can be very expensive.

**Cerebral pleasure**  Pleasure of the mind rather than the body.

**Clickbait**  Eye-catching web content or headlines designed to entice the viewer to click on a link to a web page with questionable value.

**Cold opening**  A short scene that occurs before the opening credits or titles, which hooks the viewer into the characters, the situations and possibly the story.

**The Cold War**  The name for the stand-off between the world's two superpowers, the USA and the Soviet Union, from the end of World War II in 1945 until the collapse of Communism in 1989.

**Computer-generated imagery (CGI)**  The use of graphics software to generate still or moving images. CGI is often associated with animation and special effects in blockbuster film but is increasingly being used to enhance conventionally shot sequences in advertising and television.

**Concentration of ownership**  The process that results in a small number of corporations or individuals taking an increasing market share, usually by takeovers (buying other companies) or mergers (joining forces with other companies).

**Conglomerate**  A combination of two or more businesses owned by one parent company.

**Connotation**  Meaning by association. As you grow up, in your culture you learn that many signs have meanings that are not obvious or direct. For example, the word pig can connote greed or dirtiness or arrogance, among many other connotations. Signs often have different connotations for different groups of people.

**Content provider**  Any company or organisation that makes material for television viewing on any platform. For example, ITN (Independent Television News) makes news programmes for ITV, Channel 4 and Channel 5.

**Context**  Used in two ways in media studies:
1  The immediate surroundings of something, like the other words in a sentence providing a context for each individual word.
2  The wider social, cultural, political or historical circumstances of a media product or process.

**Continuity editing**  Most films and TV dramas are filmed and edited to try to hide the editing, so that the audience doesn't notice the cuts between shots. Actions and visual style need to continue smoothly from one shot to the next. This way the audience can get lost in the narrative and not think about the film-making.

**Conventions**  Established rules or shared understandings are used in media products as 'the way we do things'. Conventions are more likely to be taken for granted than formally stated.

**Convergence**  There are two ways in which we use the term convergence in media studies.

Firstly, it refers to the ways in which media industries converge through takeovers and mergers.

Secondly, it refers to media forms merging together as a consequence of digital technology.

**Copy**  In the context of newspapers, copy is the written or printed material as distinct from photographs, cartoons, graphics or any other visual material.

**Cultural hegemony**  The process of making people see the beliefs and values of the most powerful group as being natural and common sense.

**Data mining**  Turning raw data into useful information.

**Demerger**  Happens when a large corporation is broken down into smaller independent companies.

**Demographics**  Demography is the statistical study of populations, so a demographic variable is one of the sections or categories into which a population can be divided. These include age, ethnicity, gender and social class.

**Demonised**  Making someone or a group of people seem as if they are evil.

**Denotation**  The straightforward, obvious or literal meaning of a sign. For a word it would be a dictionary definition of that word. A photo of you simply denotes you. A denotation has no hidden, subtle or underlying meanings.

**Depth of field**  In photographic or video terms this is the distance between the nearest and furthest points from the camera that are in focus.

**Deregulation**  The reduction or removal of government regulation in a particular industry such as radio or television. Usually, this is done because of a belief that competition will improve quality and choice for consumers.

**Diegesis** The world of the characters in the story. Information available to any of these characters is diegetic, information only known to the audience is non-diegetic.

**Diffused audience** Diffused means to spread over a wide area or between a large number of people. A diffused audience is large but scattered.

**Diversification** Occurs when a media company branches out to offer services in more than one media form, for example when a magazine publishing company buys up a radio station.

**Docudrama** A genre that combines fiction with real events. Real people and actual events are recreated in a docudrama.

**Dominant cultural values** The beliefs held by the majority of people in society about, for example, what sort of behaviour is right or wrong, acceptable or unacceptable. These beliefs are so strong that they seem 'just natural', but if they are not constantly reinforced they can break down.

**Dominant signifier** On a page or a poster or in a photo containing a number of signifiers grouped together, the dominant signifier is simply the most important (usually the largest) of these signifiers.

**Editorials** A statement of the newspaper's position on a topic, often written by the editor. 'Editorial copy' is anything in a newspaper other than advertising.

**Ellipsis** In film and video editing, ellipsis is the omission of a period of time. The audience is expected to work out what has happened from the context.

**Encoding/decoding** This model of communication claims that media products contain various messages that are encoded using different media codes and conventions. The ways in which audiences decode these messages depend on their social context. The decoded messages may not be the same as the encoded messages.

**Essentialism** The belief that men and women are fundamentally different in terms of their skills, preferences and behaviours.

**Establishing shot** A type of shot that fulfils the narrative function of locating the action in space. For example, a television news report about UK politics may begin with an establishing shot of the Houses of Parliament.

**Fake news** Information that appears to be genuine but is untrustworthy, misleading, false and/or damaging.

**Feminist theory** The belief that women and men should be given equal rights, but that society is currently structured so that women are not equal to men.

**Focus group** A group of people, usually with common characteristics, assembled to discuss a particular product, issue or campaign in order to collect in-depth information. Focus group discussions are often led by a facilitator who guides the discussion or poses questions.

**Foley sounds** These recreate the diegetic sounds of important actions on screen but are created by foley artists in a studio – named after pioneering Hollywood sound-effects artist Jack Foley. Even footsteps as the actors walk are usually recreated and added afterwards. Foley artists watch an edit of the film as they work to make sure their timing is right.

**Folk devil** The person or group that is the focus of a moral panic.

**Fragmentation** The process of breaking something down into smaller parts. A fragmented audience may be very large but the individual members have no connection with each other and use many different devices.

**Freemium** A business model, especially used with internet content and mobile games, that offers basic services, or the basic game, free of charge, but more advanced or special features have to be paid for.

**Greenlight** The stage in the process of film development when funding has been agreed and shooting can start.

**Hierarchy** A system with different levels based on rank, size or importance.

**High definition (HD) and ultra-high definition (UHD) TV** Standard definition (SD) television is gradually being replaced by HD television (at four times the resolution) and the next generation of UHD and 4K (eight times SD resolution) television sets are available. UHD and 4K TV adds other technologies that increase the clarity, definition and colour range of images. Making programmes in UHD has many implications for media language. The quality of the image is so high that viewers are able to interact with their television sets, for example in sports coverage, by panning and zooming within the images to pick out a particular piece of action. UHD television is much more expensive to produce, so it is likely to be used to create material that can be used many times, for example natural history and science programmes.

**Horizontal integration** The acquisition of other companies at the same level of the supply chain (for example, making media products) in similar or different sectors of the market.

**Hybrid** A genre that combines two or more pre-existing genres to create a new category.

**Ideology** A shared sets of beliefs and ideas about what is right and what is wrong.

**Immersive** An experience that completely draws in the audience or user by enabling them to interact with the product.

**Intellectual property** Ideas and designs that are copyright to a company or individual. For example, the characters and narratives in Marvel's Universe are the intellectual property of Marvel and Disney, which owns the Marvel subsidiary.

**Interactivity** Two-way communication in which the participants both actively engage in the process.

**Intertextuality** A feature of texts (media products) that borrow or quote from other texts.

**LGBTQ+** Lesbian, gay, bisexual, trans, queer and others.

**Low brow** Used, often rather insultingly, to describe examples of culture that are simplistic and undemanding. In contrast, anything described as **high brow** is usually an example of culture considered intellectual and demanding.

**Masthead** A publication's name or title in a distinctive form, usually placed at the top of the front or cover page.

**Media brief** A document setting out what is needed within a media product. It is usually written by a non-media company, such as a manufacturer who wants to advertise their goods, explaining what they want the media products (in the Spotfaze brief on page 221, the adverts) to achieve. It is used by their chosen media production company to make sure they get the message and the details right.

**Media consumption** Audiences and individuals are often described as consumers of media. Media consumption is any engagement with the media by an individual or audience.

**Media literacy** The possession of the range of skills needed to gain access to, critically analyse and create your own examples of media in different forms. GCSE Media Studies is a good way of developing your media literacy.

## Glossary of key terms

**Media pack**  Contains information for potential advertisers.

**Media synergy**  The co-production and/or co-promotion of a related set of media products or services all developed in-house by a large media corporation.

**Mediation**  The selection and omission of information when creating a media product.

**Merchandise**  With regard to films, these spin-off products linked to feature films can include toys, clothing, posters, books, games, food and other items that bear the film's brand.

**Millennials**  People who reached young adulthood at the start of the 21st century – the turn of the millennium.

**Mise-en-scène**  All the elements chosen by producers to make up the content of images, including codes such as location, lighting, non-verbal communication (NVC), props, accessories, etc. are often referred to as the mise-en-scène. It is a French term meaning 'put in the scene', which emphasises the idea that elements are included deliberately to communicate specific meanings.

**Mode of address**  Involves the style and tone of a media message's presentation; not so much *what* is being said but the *way* in which it is said. Formal/informal, direct/indirect are examples of modes of address.

**Model**  A model seeks to capture an idea or concept in a simplified form, often as a graphic or diagram.

**Monetisation strategy**  The proposed method for making an income from a product.

**Monopoly**  A situation in which one company totally dominates a sector of the market place. There is no competition, leaving customers with no choice to buy elsewhere.

**Montages**  A technique of putting together fragments of still or moving images and/or sounds from different sources to create a meaningful sequence. Often used to compress time.

**Moral panic**  The impact on society when the mass media play an active role in stereotyping a person, group or issue as a threat to the accepted norms, values and interests of society.

**Music beds**  Both radio and advertising use music beds in the background, to evoke an atmosphere or mood. The term usually refers to instrumental pieces that are relatively low in volume, allowing other sounds to be heard clearly above them.

**Newsworthiness**  Relates to a topical event that is considered sufficiently interesting to the public to be worthy of reporting as news. News media will judge the newsworthiness of an event by applying their own set of news values. These may differ. For example, the *Daily Mirror* sees human interest stories as more newsworthy than *The Times*.

**Niche audience**  A niche audience is smaller and more specialised than a mass audience. To target a niche audience or market, then, is to attempt to design a product that is perfectly suited to a particular group of people.

**Non-exam assessment (NEA)**  Referred to by some people as coursework. You have to carry out this work during the course itself, rather than during an exam at the end of the course. However, the tasks are still set by AQA. Your NEA work is first marked by your teacher and is then sent to AQA who will moderate the marks.

**Objectivity**  Information that is based on facts and analysis or scientific reason. Objectivity is based on observable and measurable evidence. Objective views are often backed up by statistics. Something claimed to be 'objectively true' will be supported by hard evidence.

**Ofcom**  Ofcom regulates TV, radio, video-on-demand, phone and postal services. Ofcom promotes competition, protects the interests of consumers and enforces the rules that apply to different communication sectors.

**Oligopoly**  A market that is dominated by a few companies that control the supply of the products or services. There is very little competition within an oligopoly as the companies tend to cooperate with each other by keeping prices high.

**Op-ed**  Short for 'opposite the editorial page', these are written by named columnists and do not necessarily express the newspaper's official position.

**Paralanguage**  How we convey meaning through aspects of speech other than the words we use – such as speed, rhythm, tone, volume and hesitation.

**Patriarchy**  A system or society in which men are all-powerful and women are excluded from positions of influence or responsibility. Patriarchal attitudes are the views and beliefs that justify this inequality.

**Paymium (or paidmium)**  A business strategy for apps that combines a low initial price with in-app purchases.

**Paywall**  A website with a paywall is fully or partially restricted to users who pay a subscription.

**Photo-story**  In newspaper journalism, this is a story that is more newsworthy because of the presence of an interesting photograph. Then Prime Minister Theresa May's meeting with other European leaders (October 2017) would have been newsworthy anyway, but the powerful image on the right, taken from video footage, made it even more so. It was used by almost every UK newspaper and many others around the world.

**Polysemic**  A sign or message that can have many different meanings.

**Pressure group**  An organised group of people which tries to influence government policy in a particular area or in support of a particular cause.

**Propaganda**  Using the media to promote a biased viewpoint, usually for political purposes.

**Protagonist**  The main character in a story. The protagonist is actively opposed by another character: the antagonist.

**RAJAR**  Radio Joint Audience Research is jointly owned by the BBC and commercial radio. Its job is to measure the number of people listening to radio and the types of radio they listen to. The website www.rajar.co.uk is a great source of information if you are doing any research into radio audiences.

**Record labels/companies**  Businesses in the music industry that fund and coordinate the production, distribution and marketing of music in return for a share of the profits.

**Royalties**  Payments paid to performers and songwriters when their music is played on radio (or television or video games).

**Running story**  This is a story that appears in two or more consecutive editions of a newspaper or for two or more days in other news media. If a breaking story has this potential, journalists may say, 'this one will run and run'.

**Segmentation**  The breaking down or subdivision of a large group into identifiable slices or segments. Each segment is defined by something all members have in common, such as the same age group.

**Self-regulation** When media industries set up and pay for their own regulatory bodies. Unlike statutory regulators, these do not have legal powers, but they rely on companies within the industry to accept a code of practice. Examples include IPSO (newspapers and magazines) and the Advertising Standards Authority (ASA). The ASA covers press, broadcast, film and internet advertising as well as posters and leaflets. There are various codes for different media produced by the Committee for Advertising Practice. The overall aim is 'to make every UK ad a responsible ad'.

**Semiotics** The use and study of signs, sign systems and their meanings. Also known as semiology.

**Serif and sans serif** A serif is a small decorative line added to the letters of certain typefaces, as shown below left. Sans means without, so sans-serif typefaces, as shown below right, don't have these features.

E E
Serif  Sans serif

**Skyline** A line of text, with or without a coloured strip background, that runs across the top edge of a magazine page, poster or other print product. It contains important information to appeal to the audience.

**Social cohesion** The tendency for individuals in society to bind together with shared views, beliefs and behaviour.

**Social construction** The belief that masculine and feminine behaviours are constructed by society and not by nature.

**Social fragmentation** The tendency for individuals and groups within society to split apart because they have few values or beliefs or behaviours in common.

**Social groups** Two or more people who share a common sense of identity.

**Social realism** A film genre that deals sympathetically with everyday issues and problems faced by working-class people. Typical themes of social realist films include unemployment, poverty, homelessness, prostitution, drugs and the effects that these have on people's relationships.

**Spin** A form of biased communication used by advertisers, marketers or politicians to present someone or something in a very positive or very negative light. Experts in spin are called 'spin doctors'.

**Statutory regulation** Statutory regulators have legal powers to control the industry for which they are responsible (a statute is a law). For example, Ofcom is the UK regulator for TV, radio, video-on-demand and phones. It sets rules and enforces them in these sectors.

**Stereotyping** The reduction of a social group to a limited set of characteristics or preconceived ideas.

**Strapline** A short headline or description that sums up the message of an ad or news story.

**Subculture** A group with beliefs or values that differ from most people in the wider culture to which it belongs.

**Subjectivity** Information that is based on individual interpretation or opinion. It can be clouded by bias, values or beliefs. Subjective views may not be backed up by scientific proof or hard evidence, but they can still have great value in opening our eyes to a deep understanding of something that is not measurable such as humanity, love or grief.

**Subscription video-on-demand** SVOD is the same as VOD but is only available to paying customers. Amazon Prime Video is an example.

**Target audience** Producers of media products always have in mind an intended audience, often defined by age, gender or social class. The product is fashioned to appeal to the specific wants and needs of this group, a process called targeting the audience.

**Time-shifting** The viewing of a broadcast programme at a time of the viewer's choice rather than at the time of transmission. This may be achieved by home recording, downloading or steaming.

**Transition (editing)** The joining together of two shots. The most common type of transition is the **cut**: an instant shot change between the two shots. Others are **crossfade** (or **mix** or **dissolve**), in which one shot gradually merges into the next. Digital editing can also achieve many special effect transitions. A **fade in** is a transition between a blank screen (usually black) and a shot. **Fade out** is the same in reverse.

**Transmission** A broadcast programme on television or radio. A live transmission is broadcast simultaneously with the event actually happening.

**UK independent films** Films made without any financial or creative input from the big five American studios which also pass the cultural test for 'Britishness'. The individuals and companies producing these films make up the UK independent sector.

**Unique selling point (USP)** The factor that makes a specific product or service stand out in comparison to other similar products. The USP of a community radio station could, for example, be that it plays music by local artists or that it features news about the local area.

**User-generated content (UGC)** Any form of content (video, blogs, digital images, audio files) created by users of an online system, made accessible to others via social media. Most newspapers have online versions which invite contributions from readers. Unlike the print edition, there is no restriction on the space available for this material. Contributors of user-generated copy are almost always unpaid and are sometimes known as **citizen journalists**.

**Vertical integration** A strategy that involves bringing supply, production, distribution and sales together into one unified company.

**Video-on-demand** VOD is television content that can be watched at any time the viewer chooses. BBC iPlayer is an example.

**Virtual reality (VR)** Technology that simulates a three-dimensional world, often enabling users to interact with it.

**Visceral pleasure** A type of audience pleasure that is like a physical experience.

**Watershed** The period after 9.00 p.m. and until 5.30 a.m. when television broadcasters may schedule more adult material that could be harmful or unsuitable for viewing by minors (under 16). Premium paid-for services such as Sky Movies do not have to operate a watershed but must be PIN protected with a security code.

**White paper** A document intended to start a discussion that will lead to change.

# References

Abercrombie, N. & Longhurst, B. (1998) *Audiences: A Sociological Theory of Performance and Imagination*.

ASA (2017a) Depictions, Perceptions and Harm, https://www.asa.org.uk/asset/2DF6E028-9C47-4944-850D00DAC5ECB45B.C3A4D948-B739-4AE4-9F17CA2110264347/.

ASA (2015, 1 July) ASA Adjudication on Protein World Ltd, https://www.asa.org.uk/rulings/protein-world-ltd-a15-300099.html.

ASA (2017b, 18 July) Report Signals Tougher Standards on Harmful Gender Stereotypes in Ads, https://www.asa.org.uk/news/report-signals-tougher-standards-on-harmfulgender-stereotypes-in-ads.html.

BARB (2018) The Viewing Report, http://www.barb.co.uk/viewing-report/updated-insight/.

Bauer (2018) KISS, https://www.bauermedia.co.uk/brands-network/kiss.

Bauer Media Group (2020, 1 September) KISS Teams Up with Shazam and Apple Music on New 'Hype Chart' Show, https://www.bauermedia.co.uk/newsroom/press-releases/kiss-teams-up-with-shazam-and-apple-music-on-new-hype-chart-show#:~:text=KISS%20today%20announced%20it%20is,trending%20TV%20and%20film%20soundtracks.

Bauer Media Group (2021) KISS Media Pack, https://www.bauermedia.co.uk/uploads/9a763e0ee49529fcc702f7951bba37ac.pdf.

BBC (2018a) Dive Deeper to See How *Blue Planet II* Was Made, http://www.bbc.co.uk/programmes/articles/cD5fGcsfj30hhFqJcfPQQR/dive-deeper-to-see-how-blue-planet-iiwas-made.

BBC (2018b) Diversity & Inclusion, http://www.bbc.co.uk/diversity.

BBC News (2017, 5 December) Child Exploitation: Live Streaming an 'Urgent' Threat, http://www.bbc.co.uk/news/uk-42224148.

BBC News (2014, 9 December) Number of UK Homes with TVs Falls for First Time, http://www.bbc.co.uk/news/entertainment-arts-30392654.

BBFC (2014) Age Ratings You Trust, http://www.bbfc.co.uk/what-classification/guidelines.

BFI (2017, 26 January) New BFI Statistics Show Robust Year for Film in the UK in 2016, http://www.bfi.org.uk/news-opinion/news-bfi/announcements/highest-grossing-films-uk-box-office-2016 statistics.

Bloxham, A. (2010, 18 November) Social Networking: Teachers Blame Facebook and Twitter for Pupils' Poor Grades, *The Daily Telegraph*, https://www.telegraph.co.uk/education/educationnews/8142721/Social-networking-teachers-blame-Facebook-and-Twitter-for-pupilspoor-grades.html.

Blumler, J. & Katz, E. (1974) *The Uses of Mass Communications: Current Perspectives on Gratification Research*.

Chie, M. (2015, 11 November) How Autobiographical is One Direction's New Album?, *People*, http://people.com/celebrity/how-autobiographical-is-one-directions-newalbum/.

Creative Industries Federation (2017) Statistics, https://www.creativeindustriesfederation.com//statistics.

*Daily Mail* (2016, 21 December) Bake Off Dominates the List of Most Watched TV Shows of 2016 With Nine Episodes in the Top Ten – So How WILL the BBC Replace It?, http://www.dailymail.co.uk/tvshowbiz/article-4053494/The-Great-British-Bakedominates-list-watched-TV-shows-2016.html.

Dainty, S. & Kilkelly, D. (2016, 18 February) *EastEnders* Cliffhangers Ranked: The 13 All-time Greatest Duff-Duff Moments, http://www.digitalspy.com/soaps/eastenders/feature/a783903/eastenders-cliffhangers-ranked-the-13-all-time-greatest-duff-duff-moments/.

Deloitte (2017) Media Metrics 2017, https://www2.deloitte.com/content/dam/Deloitte/uk/Documents/technology-media-telecommunications/deloitte-uk-media-metrics-2017.pdf.

Dobrilova, T. (2021, 2 October) How Much is the Gaming Industry Worth in 2021?, https://techjury.net/blog/gaming-industry-worth/#gref.

Elghobashy, S. (2009, 12 January) Muslim Stereotypes in Hollywood: Are they Really Fading?, *elan: The Guide to Global Muslim Culture*. http://www.elanthemag.com/index.php/site/blog_detail/muslim_stereotypes_in_hollywood_are_they_really_fadingnid503043165/.

ESA (2017a) Essential Facts About the Competition Industry, http://www.theesa.com/about-esa/essential-facts-computer-video-game-industry/.

ESA (2017b) 2017 Sales, Demographic, and Usage Date: Essential Facts About the Computer and Video Game Industry, http://www.theesa.com/wp-content/uploads/2017/09/EF2017_Design_FinalDigital.pdf.

Fisher, K. (2017, 13 June) Kim Kardashian Breaks Down her Social Media Strategy and How it's Helped Expand her Empire, *Enews*, https://www.eonline.com/uk/news/860845/kim-kardashian-breaks-down-her-social-media-strategy-and-how-it-s-helped-expandher-empire.

Follows, S. (2016, 10 July) How Movies Make Money: $100m+ Hollywood Blockbusters, https://stephenfollows.com/how-movies-make-money-hollywood-blockbusters/.

Gartner (2017, 26 January) Gartner Survey Finds that Most Smartphone Users Spend Nothing on Apps, https://www.gartner.com/newsroom/id/3583817.

Google Play (2017) Change the Game, http://services.google.com/fh/files/misc/changethegame_white_paper.pdf.

Hall, S. (1993) Encoding, Decoding, in During, S. (ed.) *The Cultural Studies Reader*.

Hegde, V. (2021, 24 July) Blackpink's Net Worth: How Much Does Each Member of the K-Pop Group Earn?, sportskeeda, https://www.sportskeeda.com/pop-culture/blackpink-s-net-worth-how-much-member-k-pop-group-earn.

Holmwood, L. (2009, 9 July) BBC Denies Ageism as Arlene Phillips Shifted Off *Strictly Come Dancing*, *The Guardian*, https://www.theguardian.com/media/2009/jul/09/arlenephillips-strictly-come-dancing-bbc.

Hume, T. (2016, 24 July) Munich Gunman Planned Attack for a Year, Officials Say, CNN, https://edition.cnn.com/2016/07/24/europe/germany-munich-shooting/index.html.

Ilott, S. (2018, 31 January) *Man Like Mobeen*: BBC Comedy Defies Muslim Stereotypes, Manchester Metropolitan University, https://www.mmu.ac.uk/news-and-events/news/story/7103/.

IMDb (2019) The 50 Highest Grossing Movies of the 2010s (Worldwide), https://www.imdb.com/list/ls026040906/.

Kantar Media (2018) Linear vs Non-linear Viewing, Ofcom, https://www.ofcom.org.uk/__data/assets/pdf_file/0029/68816/km_report.pdf.

Kirst, (2015, 17 December) The Kardashian's Social Media Influence, Forbes.com, https://www.forbes.com/sites/seamuskirst/2015/12/17/the-kardashians-social-media-influence/?sh=1513797b1f03.

Lee, K. (2014, 19 March) How to Write the Perfect Headline: The Top Words Used in Viral Headlines, https://buffer.com/resources/the-most-popular-words-in-most-viral-headlines/.

Lambert, L. (2016, 21 December) Bake Off Dominates the List of Most Watched TV Shows of 2016 With Nine Episodes in the Top Ten – So How WILL the BBC Replace It?, Daily Mail, http://www.dailymail.co.uk/tvshowbiz/article-4053494/The-Great-British-Bake-dominates-list-watched-TV-hows-2016.html.

Macnab, G. (2017, 2 June) Fixing Britain's 'Broken' Independent Film Sector: Is Tax Relief Enough?, ScreenDaily, https://www.screendaily.com/features/what-can-fix-britains-broken-independentfilm-sector/5118700.article.

Mayhew, F. (2020, 16 April) National Newspaper ABCs: Print Sales Hold During Coronavirus Outbreak Before UK Lockdown, PressGazette, https://www.pressgazette.co.uk/national-newspaper-abcs-print-circulations-held-during-coronavirus-outbreak-before-uk-lockdown.

Moon, K. (2020, 26 June) BLACKPINK on the Message of New Single 'How You Like That', Time, https://time.com/5859277/blackpink-how-you-like-that/.

McIntosh, S. (2020, 30 July) Jordan and Perri: Kiss Breakfast Hosts on 'Stepping into Huge Shoes', https://www.bbc.co.uk/news/entertainment-arts-53361408.

Media Reform Coalition (2015) Who Owns the UK Media?, http://www.mediareform.org.uk/wp-content/uploads/2015/10/Who_owns_the_UK_media-report_plus_appendix1.pdf.

Media Smarts (2018) Media Portrayals of Religion: Islam, http://mediasmarts.ca/diversity-media/religion/media-portrayals-religion-islam.

MediaCom (2017, 1 December) #Represent with Lady Leshurr, http://www.mediacomnorth.co.uk/mediacom-news/nhs-blood-transplant-join-forces-moborepresent-campaign/.

Meyer, R. (2018, 8 March) The Grim Conclusions of the Largest-Ever Study of Fake News, *The Atlantic*, https://www.theatlantic.com/technology/archive/2018/03/largest-studyever-fake-news-mit-twitter/555104/.

Norfolk, A., Coates, S. & Dathan, M. (2015, 4 March) Call for National Debate on Muslim Sex Grooming, The Times, https://www.thetimes.co.uk/.article/call-for-national-debate-on-muslimsex-grooming-wtqm7lnvv6w.

No Free Spins No Deposit (2020, 30 July) Leading Movies Based on Merchandise Sales, https://newfreespinsnodeposit.com/leading-movies-based-merchandise-sales/.

Ofcom (2016) The Communications Market, https://www.ofcom.org.uk/__data/assets/pdf_file/0026/17495/uk_tv.pdf.

Ofcom (2017, 29 June) News Consumption in the UK: 2016, https://www.ofcom.org.uk/__data/assets/pdf_file/0016/103570/news-consumption-uk-2016.pdf.

PAMCo (2020) Social Grade, https://pamco.co.uk/news/newsletter-q1-2020/index.html.

PAMCo (2020) Unlocking the Value of Publisher Audiences, https://pamco.co.uk/pamco-data/latest-results.

PEGI (2021) What do the Labels Mean?, https://pegi.info/what-do-the-labels-mean.

*Radio Times* (2016, 19 March) Nowhere for Football Referees to Hide Over Dodgy Decisions if Sports Channels Have Their Way, http://www.radiotimes.com/news/2016-03-19/nowhere-for-football-referees-to-hide-over-dodgy-decisions-if-sportschannels-have-their-way/.

RAJAR (2020) MIDAS Measurement of Internet Delivered Audio Services, https://www.rajar.co.uk/docs/news/MIDAS_Spring_2020.pdf.

Reach (2018) Our Newsbrands, https://www.reachplc.com/brands/our-newsbrands.

Rotten Tomatoes (2021) *Black Widow*, https://www.rottentomatoes.com/m/black_widow_2021.

Santa Barbara County Animal Services (2018) Project PetSafe, http://www.projectpetsafe.org/cmsAdmin/uploads/ProjectPetSafe_MessageFromHeroENG_Radio60_2011fnlRE.pdf.

Sensor Tower (2017) Q2 2017 Report, https://s3.amazonaws.com/sensortower-itunes/Quarterly+Reports/Sensor-Tower-Q2-2017-Data-Digest.pdf.

Sky News (2016, 31 October) Britain's Most Watched TV Show of Last 80 Years Revealed, http://news.sky.com/story/britains-most-watched-tv-show-of-last-80-years-revealed-10639498.

Sports Khabri (2021, 17 May) Marcus Rashford – Sponsors/Endorsements/Salary/Net Worth/Notable Honours/Charity Work, https://sportskhabri.com/player-profile-marcus-rashford/.

Statista (2021) Number of Video Gamers Worldwide in 2021, by Region, https://www.statista.com/statistics/293304/number-video-gamers/.

Strugar, M. (2021, 26 July) 30+ Smartphone Usage Statistics for the UK, cybercrew, https://cybercrew.uk/blog/smartphone-usage-statistics-uk/.

SuperData (2021) 2020 Year in Review, https://www.digitalmusicnews.com/wp-content/uploads/2021/01/SuperData2020YearinReview.pdf.

*The MediaBriefing* (2017) Cover Story: Does the Front Page of a Magazine Still Matter?, https://www.themediabriefing.com/analysis/cover-story-does-the-front-page-of-amagazine-still-matter/.

Think Gaming (2018) https://thinkgaming.com/.

Tobitt, C. (2020, 16 January) National Newspaper ABCs: *Observer* Sees Smallest Paid-for Circulation Drop in December, https://pressgazette.co.uk/national-newspaper-abcs-full-figures-december-2019-observer/.

Tobitt, C. (2021, 11 February) UK Magazine Circulations for 2020: Full Breakdown Shows Average 6% Year-on-year Drop, *PressGazette*, https://www.pressgazette.co.uk/magazine-circulation-uk/.

Weisman, A. (2015, 3 March) Kim Kardashian Reveals the 'Accidental' Reason Why Her Mobile Game is Such a Huge Success, Business Insider, http://uk.businessinsider.com/whykim-kardashian-hollywood-app-is-successful-2015-3.

White, S. (2017, 15 March) At Last.. Muirfield Men Let Women Join Their Golf Club', *Daily Mirror*.

# Index

action codes 32–33, 35
advertising 12, 14, 18, 20, 29, 45, 47, 51–53, 56, 59, 63, 70–71, 73–74, 76–77, 87–93, 100–101, 105–107, 111, 113–114, 115, 117, 131–132, 134–135, 137, 139–143, 146–150, 153–154, 166–167, 171–172, 175, 178–179, 184, 186–196, 200, 205–206, 213, 221, 227, 232, 235–237, 242, 248, 251–252, 256–260, 265, 269–270
    developments in 187–188
age
    classification/rating 113, 129, 143–144, 147–148, 160, 200
    representation 17, 50, 56, 59, 160, 163, 173, 187
Alphabet 113–115, 146
'Amazon shops' story 103–104, 184–186
anchorage 15, 25
Arctic Monkeys 107–108, 212–218
    Media Audiences 213
    Media Industries 213–214
audience
    active 97–99, 100–101
    age 34, 62, 81–82, 90, 229–230
    categorisation 89–91
    diffused 104–105
    interactive 104–106, 109, 166, 174–175, 178
        niche 89, 191
        passive 97–98
        research 93–94
    target 34–35, 37, 56, 59, 61–62, 67, 85, 92, 109, 134, 160–161, 164, 170, 174, 177, 180, 187, 189, 191–193, 195–196, 208, 216–217, 221–222, 224–226, 228–229, 231–233, 235, 237–239, 257, 266, 268, 274, 276
    theories 95–102
audio production 253–259
'Audrey Hepburn' Galaxy TV ad 190–191
augmented reality 145, 150, 167
avatar 51, 64, 167, 172–174

Bauer Media 111, 132–134, 199–200
BBC 32, 37–40, 48–49, 55, 80, 82, 94, 106, 108, 110, 112, 130–133, 136–141, 155–156, 158–162, 164–165, 167, 196–199, 203–204, 225
bias 50, 52, 57, 60, 77, 117
big close-up (BCU) 22–23, 26
binary opposites 32, 35, 179
*Black Widow* 48, 125, 127, 154, 202–204
    contexts 203
    Media Industries 203
Blackpink 113, 212, 215–218
    Media Audiences 215–216
    Media Industries 216–218
blog 40, 46, 65, 67, 70, 88, 105, 119, 166, 169, 274–275
body movement 18, 191
brand/branding 21, 25, 45, 66, 75, 77, 79, 83, 94, 114, 120–121, 126, 133–134, 140–141, 145, 149–150, 167, 169–173, 175, 178, 183, 187–190, 205, 210–211, 215–216, 229, 251–252, 256, 259, 261
broadsheet 37, 180–181, 185, 263

camera shots/movement 26–27, 243–246
carriage costs 133
cerebral pleasure 35, 100
character types (Propp) 30–31, 33–35, 58, 166, 173
citizen journalism 105, 119
'City of Magpies, The' (*His Dark Materials*) 33–35, 47, 72, 84, 159–164, 224–225, 248
    Media Audiences 161
    Media Industries 161–162
    Media Language 160
    Media Representations 160
clickbait 69
close-up 22–23, 26, 212, 240, 241, 243–244, 250
clothing 18, 39, 51–52, 54, 74–75, 80, 107, 126, 172, 176–177, 194–196, 209–210, 212, 237, 250
codes
    definition of 10
    digital 27–28
    English language as 11–12
    moving image 26–27
    non-verbal 17–18, 26, 163, 172, 191
        photographic 22–26
        post-production 27–28
        print 18–21, 24, 26
composition
    audience/population 119, 137, 161
    shot 22–23
computer-generated imagery (CGI) 47, 50, 145
concentration of ownership 113, 121
confrontation 31–32
conglomerate 119–121, 124, 132, 146, 186
connotation 14, 17, 19, 20, 25–26, 34, 52, 190, 193, 208, 220, 239
construction of reality 48–49
context 12, 14–15, 17–18, 28, 31, 41, 48, 61–62, 69, 74, 79, 85–86, 101–102, 123, 129, 135, 140, 145, 154, 157–162, 165, 169, 171, 176–179, 184–185, 189, 191–192, 195, 198–199, 201, 203–204, 207, 212, 214–215, 217, 235, 265
cultural 31, 41, 62, 79, 102, 129, 154, 157–158, 160, 171, 176–179, 192, 195, 198, 203–204, 214, 217
    historical 62, 79, 123, 160, 171, 176–179, 195
    political 41, 62, 69, 79, 154
social 41, 62, 79, 85–86, 101–102, 129, 154, 158–160, 171, 176–179, 192, 195, 198, 203–204, 214, 217
continuity editing 27–28, 49, 244–245, 248, 250
conventions 10, 26–28, 30, 35, 38, 40, 44–45, 49, 57, 60, 101, 107, 109, 160, 163, 166, 169, 185, 191, 193, 207, 210–211, 222–223, 225, 228, 230–231, 233, 235–236, 248, 252, 256, 261–262, 264, 266–269, 273, 277
convergence 44, 109, 130, 134, 165, 167, 171, 175, 186, 188
crowd sourcing 105, 166
cultivation theory 96
cultural hegemony 62–63

*Daily Mirror* 20–21, 25–26, 36, 40, 63, 89, 103–104, 117, 119–122, 180–186, 263
    Media Audiences 186
    Media Industries 186
    Media Language 185
    Media Representations 185
data mining 107
decoding 47, 51, 59, 72, 101–102
demerger 113
demographics 34, 80, 90–93, 106, 161, 170, 174, 187
denotation 14, 26, 193
depth of field 24, 268
desensitisation 96
diagonals 23
diegesis 29, 35, 224, 226, 232, 234, 242–243, 247–248, 277
diversification 130, 133–134
*Doctor Who* 41–44, 47, 55, 84–86, 108, 159–165, 224, 248
    Media Audiences 164
    Media Industries 164–165
    Media Language 163
    Media Representations 163–164
dominant
    cultural values 157
    representation 63–64, 85
    signifier 25

editorials 117
effects theory 96–98, 129
ellipsis 28
encoding 49, 101–102
enigma 32–33, 35, 163, 209, 224–225, 248, 268, 276
equipment for production 242–243, 247, 253, 260, 271–272
essentialism 73, 76
establishing shot 34–35, 244
ethnicity 17, 50, 54–56, 68, 90, 94, 106, 195, 209, 279
extreme close-up (ECU) 22, 243

Facebook 45, 65–66, 88, 95, 97, 105, 113–115, 139, 146, 166, 168–170, 187–188
facial expression 9, 12–13, 17, 25, 39, 49, 191, 244
fake news 69–70, 115
fandom 107–108
femininity 32, 55, 72, 74
feminism 75–76, 78
feminist theory 75
films 26, 36–37, 94, 111, 120, 123–129, 143, 200–201, 203–204
    distribution 201
    industry (case study) 123–129
    production 200–201
    regulation 128–129
five Ws 265
focus (in shots) 24, 268
focus group 92, 94
foley sounds 224, 232, 242
folk devil 83
font 20–21, 26, 205, 222, 229, 231, 235–236, 238–239, 260, 262–264, 270, 273–274, 276
fragmentation 65, 104, 159
franchising 77, 107, 124–127, 145, 149, 167, 176, 178, 216
freemium 146–147, 172

*Game of Thrones* 51, 73–74
gaming video content (GVC) 150
gender representation/roles 17, 34, 44, 55–56, 63, 67–68, 72–79, 85, 90, 103, 106, 147, 157, 160, 163, 173, 176–178, 189, 195
genre 31, 36–42, 61, 89, 102, 124, 141, 149, 156, 158, 160, 163–164, 166–167, 174, 176, 185, 191, 199, 201, 203, 208, 210, 216, 222, 224–225, 243, 248, 252, 268, 276–277
    appeal of 39
    pros and cons 40–41
    recognising 38–39
    types of 36–37
gesture 9–10, 17, 25, 191, 244
graphics creation 262, 275–277

hair 17, 34, 44, 54, 172, 272
Halfords advert 14, 18
*Heat* 207–210
    Media Language 207–209
    Media Representations 209–210
hierarchy 38, 51, 53, 59
Hollywood 27, 57, 111, 123–127, 177, 203, 208, 242, 244
horizontal integration 111–112, 120

house style 222, 226, 228–231, 235–237, 263, 273, 276
hybrid genre 37, 180
hypodermic syringe theory 97

*I, Daniel Blake* 127–128, 154, 203–204
    contexts 204
    Media Industries 204
iconic 16, 81, 140–141, 190, 251, 269
icons 16, 26, 51, 190, 239, 274
ideology 62–63, 68, 210
Instagram 45, 51, 65–66, 88, 106, 114–115, 166, 168–171, 175, 188, 216, 239, 271
intellectual property 149
interactive 9, 45, 104–109, 147, 165–166, 174, 178, 198, 272, 277
internet 8, 27, 45–46, 64, 69–70, 94, 104–106, 108–109, 113–116, 119, 125, 133–134, 136, 139, 142, 146, 151, 160–162, 179, 182–184, 187, 189, 194, 198–199, 205, 213–214, 242, 248, 253, 255, 258, 271
    advertising 184, 187, 189
    news 183
    radio 133, 253
    regulation 189
    television 139, 161–162
intertextuality 41, 160, 251

juxtaposition 19, 57, 192, 240

Kardashian, Kim 45, 50, 64, 66, 72, 113, 146, 153, 167–170, 172–178
*Kim Kardashian: Hollywood* 50, 64, 78, 146, 167–168, 172–178
    contexts 176
    Media Audiences 174–175
    Media Industries 175–176
    Media Language 172–173
    Media Representations 173
*KISS Breakfast* 130, 133, 199–200
    Media Audiences 199–200
    Media Industries 199–200

Lara Croft/Tomb Raider 76–79, 149, 166, 168, 176–178
    contexts 178–179
    Media Audiences 177–178
    Media Industries 178
    Media Language 176
    Media Representations 177
left wing 68, 181, 203
licence fee 131, 137, 139, 144
LGBTQ+ 55, 57, 59, 74, 76–77, 86
lighting 18, 22, 24, 50, 68, 140, 160, 190, 223, 237, 240–242, 250
linear model of communication 8–10
live streaming 106, 166

magazines 13, 18–20, 25, 33–34, 36, 38, 48, 50, 53, 59, 73–75, 80–82, 89, 91, 102, 106, 111, 113, 119, 121, 134–135, 153, 190, 193, 195, 200, 205–210, 221–223, 229–231, 235, 237, 260–262, 269, 275
    conventions 266–267
front cover 19–20, 33–34, 53, 59, 73, 80–81, 91, 102, 205–210, 222–223, 229–231, 261–262
readers 206
masculinity 32, 55, 72, 74
mass media 8–10, 12, 17, 48–49, 64, 83, 88, 155, 253
masthead 20–21, 25–26, 34, 205, 207, 229, 231, 261–262, 264
media
    brief 221
    consumption 88, 97, 100, 104, 107
    industries 39, 46, 52, 79, 87, 89–91, 93, 110–154, 159, 161–162, 164–165, 168, 171, 175–176, 178, 184, 186, 198–199, 201–204, 212–216, 220, 260, 271
    language 8–47, 50, 57, 61, 67, 123, 145, 153–154, 159–160, 162–163, 168, 172, 176, 184–185, 187, 190–191, 193, 204, 206–208, 210, 220–222, 225, 238–241, 243, 256, 270–272, 277
    literacy 99, 109, 216
    mix 165
    pack 91
representations 14, 16, 26, 37, 48–86, 99–100, 123, 129, 145, 153–154, 159–164, 166–167–168, 170, 173, 175, 177–178, 184–187, 189–196, 204, 206–207, 209–210, 215, 220–223, 226, 231, 234, 238–241, 243, 249–250, 256–257, 261, 270, 272, 275, 277
synergy 112
mediation 49, 57, 71
minority representation 63–64
mise-en-scène 18–19, 68, 166, 190, 210, 226, 233–234, 237–238, 243, 246, 249, 277
misrepresentation 60, 189
mode of address 102–103, 169, 252, 257, 261, 263–264, 274
monetisation strategy 146
monopoly 112, 130–131, 196–197
montage 28, 34–35, 252
moral panic 69, 81, 83
moving image marketing 251
music beds 257, 259
music videos 28, 36–37, 56, 61, 81, 111, 113, 140–144, 153–154, 191, 210–218, 221, 223, 232–234, 240–242, 245, 247, 249–251
    abstract 249
    branding and image 211–212
    case study 140–144
    concept 249
    conventions 210–211
    editing 250

    and internet 142–143
    making money from 143
    planning and filming 250–251
    regulation 143–144

narrative 29–35, 40, 45, 53, 57–60, 63, 68, 85, 100, 102, 124, 141, 149, 160, 163, 166, 169, 172, 176, 178, 185, 188, 190–192, 209, 211, 217, 224, 226, 232–236, 241, 245, 249–251, 268, 271, 276–277
    structure 29–31, 33, 160, 166, 192, 209
    theory (Propp) 30–31, 33–35, 58, 166, 173
news 27, 33–34, 37, 38–40, 43, 47, 49, 57, 68–70, 83, 88–89, 95, 102, 105–106, 112–113, 115–118, 130, 132–133, 137–139, 155–156, 158, 162, 169, 175, 179, 183–184, 186–187, 198, 222, 245, 247–248, 253, 263–265
    values 68, 117–118
News UK 119–122
newspapers 18, 20–21, 25–26, 29, 36–37, 45, 50, 54–57, 63–64, 67–70, 75, 80, 83, 88–89, 98–99, 101, 103–104, 111–113, 116–123, 135, 153–154, 158, 165, 179–186, 196–197, 204, 221–222, 260, 263–266, 269, 275
    circulation 180–184
    front page 20, 25–26, 184, 186, 263–266
    industry (case study) 116–122
    and politics 25–26, 181–182
newsworthiness 117–118
non-exam assessment (NEA) 220–278
non-verbal communication (NVC)/codes 17–18, 26, 163, 172, 191

objectivity 52
Ofcom 70, 94, 133, 138
oligopoly 112
OMO print ad 193–196
One Direction 'History' 215–217
online, social and participatory media 66, 111, 145, 165–179, 221, 271
op-ed 117

paralanguage 18, 191
patriarchy 44, 75, 164
paywall 184
photo-story 118
pirate radio 82, 197–198
podcast 57, 105, 165, 258–259
polysemic 102
press regulation 121–123
pressure group 121
pre-title sequence 34–35, 224–226
product brief 224–237
production

    of audio 253–259
    of e-media 271–279
    of moving image 242–252
    of print 259–270
propaganda 63, 69, 115, 197
Propp, Vladimir 30–31, 33–35, 58, 166, 173
protagonist 31, 78, 177, 224, 226, 232–234, 277
psychographics 92–93, 106, 161
public service broadcasting 112, 131–132, 137–139, 161–162, 164

radio 8, 36–37, 39, 45, 53, 57, 71, 82, 88, 90, 93–94, 97–98, 105–106, 109–113, 116, 119, 130–134, 136, 139, 153–154, 156, 158, 164, 181, 183, 196–200, 221–222, 226–228, 239, 242, 253, 256–259
    audiences 130, 133–134
    development (case study) 130–134
    digital 132–133
    funding 131–132
    regulation 94, 113, 133
    voices 257
Radio 1 launch day (*The Tony Blackburn Show*) 198–200
    Media Audiences 198–199
    Media Industry 198–199
Rashford, Marcus 65–67, 113, 166, 168–171, 176, 178–179
    contexts 171
    Media Audiences 170–171
    Media Industries 171
    Media Language 169
    Media Representations 169–170
reception theory 100–102, 175
record labels/companies 108, 141–144, 213–214, 216–217
regulation 94, 113, 115, 121–122, 128–129, 133, 138, 143–144, 147–148, 189
'Represent' video 61–62, 190–191, 193, 232
representation
    of age 17, 50, 56, 59, 160, 163, 173, 187
    of events/issues 57
    of gender 17, 34, 44, 55–56, 63, 67–68, 72–79, 90, 103, 106, 147, 157, 160, 163, 173, 176–178, 189, 195
    of places 57
    of reality 67–72
    of religion/nationality 56–57
    of the self 64–65
    of sexuality 55, 75, 77, 86, 176, 194
    of values/beliefs 62–67
right wing 43, 181
role models 61, 99, 179, 191–192, 210, 239
royalties 133, 142, 146

rule of thirds 23
running story 118

sans serif 20–21, 26, 270, 274
secret code 10
segmentation 90
self-regulated 113, 115, 148
semiotics 10, 13–14, 16–17, 172, 176, 185
serif 20–21, 26, 270
sexuality representation 55, 75, 77, 86, 176, 194
shot types 22
signifier 13–14, 25, 39, 51, 172, 176, 212, 277
skyline 262, 264
social
    class 17, 34, 52–53, 90–91, 94, 185
        cohesion 158–159
        construction 73
        fragmentation 159
        groups 50–53, 56, 58–60, 63–64, 72, 81
    media 10, 24, 36–37, 45, 51, 64–67, 69–70, 88, 91, 99, 105, 106–107, 109, 112–115, 119, 139, 142–143, 145, 149, 165–167, 169–173, 175–176, 179, 182–183, 186–189, 193, 198, 205, 214–217, 242, 251, 256, 259, 271–272, 274–276
    realism 203
sound 28–29, 246–247, 277–278
Statement of Intent 221–224, 238–241, 264
statutory regulation 113, 115
stereotypes 50, 53–54, 57–60, 63–64, 67–68, 73–76, 78, 80, 83–85, 90, 93, 101, 149–150, 157, 168, 173, 177, 179, 189, 194–195, 204, 210, 239, 277

constructing 58–59
development and variation 59–60
positive and negative 59
subculture 53–54, 81, 83, 160
subgenre 37–39
subjectivity 52
subscription video-on-demand (SVOD) 136
subverting genre conventions/stereotypes 40–41, 58
*Sun* 25–26, 36, 63, 119–120, 122, 181, 183
superimposition 19, 26, 34
symbols/symbolism 16, 25, 42, 50, 52, 54, 59, 74–75, 81, 190, 194, 211

tabloid 36–37, 75, 120, 180–181, 263
*Tatler* 33–34, 91, 207–209, 235, 266
    Media Language 207–209
    Media Representations 209–210
teaser 33, 184, 201, 264
technological convergence 45, 109, 167
teenager (case study) 80–84
television 8–10, 27–30, 32, 34–41, 45, 47–49, 82, 87–89, 93–94, 97–99, 101–102, 104–107, 109, 111–113, 116, 119–121, 124–127, 131, 133–139, 153–160, 164, 169, 181, 183, 188, 190, 196–197, 201, 209, 212, 221, 224–226, 242–243, 247–248, 252–253
    catch-up 135–136
    genres 157
    linear 135–136
    payment 137

platforms 136
popularity of 155–156
regulation 94, 113, 138
sequence 224–226
social contexts of 158–159
viewing landscape (case study) 135–139
*The Times* 20, 56, 103–104, 117, 119–120, 122, 180–181, 183–186, 263
    Media Audiences 186
    Media Industries 186
    Media Language 185
    Media Representations 185
TikTok 106, 169, 199, 271
time-shift 94, 104, 109, 135–136, 156, 159, 161, 164
Tomb Raider *see* Lara Croft/Tomb Raider
transition
    to digital 88, 134, 205
    in editing/shots 27–28, 35, 68, 247–248, 252
transmission 27, 43, 89, 133, 135, 156, 196
Twitter 45, 65–66, 69–70, 88, 95, 105, 107, 115, 139, 166, 168–171, 175–176, 188, 217, 271

UK independent film 123, 127–128
under-representation 54–55, 60
unique selling point (USP) 222, 251
uses and gratification model/theory 98–100, 134, 161, 164, 170, 174, 177

vertical integration 111, 121, 124, 138–139, 186
video exporting 248–249
video games 30, 36–37, 50, 64, 77–79, 95–97, 100, 105, 111–113, 127, 133, 145–155, 165, 167–168, 172–179, 221, 242, 260, 271–272, 274, 276–278
    audience, changing 149–150
    case study 145–152
    designing 276–277
    developments in 167
    exporting 278
    funding 146–147
    global market 145–146
    issues 168
    regulation 147–148
    sound 277–278
video-on-demand 94, 113, 126, 129, 133, 136, 201
Vimeo 142, 242
virtual reality (VR) 114, 150, 167
visceral pleasure 35, 100, 216
vlog 36, 51, 70, 105, 166–167, 169, 188, 229–231, 252, 259
voiceover 28, 34, 49, 224, 232, 242, 247, 251

watershed 138
web-based video, producing 252
website design 272–274
Wiki 88, 106–114, 160, 166, 271
writing copy 261, 274–275

YouTube 36, 46, 61, 71, 77, 80, 88, 105, 113–115, 135, 142–143, 150, 166–167, 171–172, 176, 189, 191, 217–218, 239, 242, 253

Zuckerberg, Mark 114–115

# Acknowledgements

p1 Dinga / Shutterstock; p5 TORWAISTUDIO / Shutterstock; p6 Everett Historical / Shutterstock.com; p7 (top) Kosoff / Shutterstock; p7 (bottom) Poznyakov / Shutterstock; p9 (top) Dooder / Shutterstock; p9 (bottom) Daniel M Ernst / Shutterstock; p10 (top) madpixblue / Shutterstock; p10 (bottom) United Kingdom Government / Public domain; p11 (top) kentoh / Shutterstock; p11 (bottom) Oleksandr Molokovych / Shutterstock; p12 (top) Filip Warulik / Shutterstock; p12 (bottom) Kuliperko / Shutterstock; p13 Nikitina Olga / Shutterstock; p14 Credit: Chapter Agency Ltd; p15 (top to bottom) oksana2010 / Shutterstock, Vladislav T. Jirousek / Shutterstock, Kiattiscotk / Shutterstock, Rtimages / Shutterstock, 123dartist / Shutterstock, Montu Sutariya / Shutterstock, nd3000 / Shutterstock; p16 (top to bottom) sharpner / Shutterstock, vieira72 / Shutterstock, Bildagentur Zoonar GmbH / Shutterstock, Jstone / Shutterstock.com, Nemanja Cosovic / Shutterstock, oksana2010 / Shutterstock; p17 (top) Roger Hutchings / Alamy Stock Photo; p17 (bottom) Pictorial Press Ltd / Alamy Stock Photo; p18 (top) Andrey_Popov / Shutterstock; p18 (middle) Courtesy of Galaxy; p18 (bottom) Courtesy of Halfords; p19 (top) Inside Soap / Courtesy of Hearst Magazines UK; p19 (bottom) Pictorial Press Ltd / Alamy Stock Photo; p20 David Kleyn / Alamy Stock Photo; p21 (top) Claudio Divizia / Shutterstock.com; p21 (bottom) Niloo / Shutterstock.com; pp22–23 Pixels; p23 (bottom) Dennis Jarvis / Shutterstock; p24 (top left) Eugene Onischenko / Shutterstock; p24 (top right) Maxisport / Shutterstock.com; p24 (bottom) NIKITA TV / Shutterstock; p25 (left) Mirrorpix / Reach Licensing; p25 (right) News UK / News Licensing; p26 Stuart Elflett / Shutterstock; p27 Jacob Lund / Shutterstock; p29 Syda Productions / Shutterstock; p30 Bad Wolf / BBC / HBO; p31 (all) Bad Wolf / BBC / HBO; p32 Mark Bourdillon / Alamy Stock Photo; p33 Tatler © The Conde Naste Publications Ltd; p34 Bad Wolf / BBC / HBO; p35 (all) Bad Wolf / BBC / HBO; p37 Stephen Coburn / Shutterstock; p38 (left) Courtesy of Free Line; p38 (middle) Courtesy of Big Carp Magazine; p38 (bottom) Courtesy of Total Carp; p39 (top) Alamy Stock Photo; p39 (bottom) Everett Collection Inc / Alamy Stock Photo; p40 Steve ilston / Alamy Stock Photo; p42 (top) M&N / Alamy Stock Photo; p42 (middle) SPUTNIK / Alamy Stock Photo; p42 (bottom) chrisdorney / Shutterstock.com; p43 (top) neftali / Shutterstock.com; p43 (bottom) Uncle Leo / Shutterstock.com; p44 Allstar Picture Library Ltd. / Alamy Stock Photo; p46 (top) Ekaterina Kondratova / Shutterstock; p46 (bottom) Atlaspix / Alamy Stock Photo; p47 Ron Dale / Shutterstock; p48 Alistair Heap / Alamy Stock

Photo; p49 2p2play / Shutterstock; p51 (top) Allstar Picture Library Ltd / Alamy Stock Photo; p51 (bottom) LH Images / Alamy Stock Photo; p52 Halfpoint / Shutterstock; p53 Courtesy of Hello!; p54 (top) Gina Smith / Shutterstock; p54 (bottom) Everett Collection Inc / Alamy Stock Photo; p55 Everett Collection Inc / Alamy Stock Photo; p56 Featureflash Photo Agency / Shutterstock.com; p57 Entertainment Pictures / Alamy Stock Photo; p59 BravoKiloVideo / Shutterstock; p60 Album / Alamy Stock Photo; p61 Courtesy of NHS Blood and Transplant; p63 (top) Allstar Picture Library Ltd / Alamy Stock Photo; p63 (bottom) Reproduced with kind permission of D C Thomson Media; p64 (top) AF Archive / Alamy Stock Photo; p64 (bottom) OpturaDesign / Shutterstock; p65 coka / Shutterstock; p66 (both) Courtesy of Marcus Rashford; p68 stockphoto mania / Shutterstock; p70 International Federation of Library Associations and Institutions; p71 Retro AdArchives / Alamy Stock Photo; p72 Courtesy of Galaxy; p73 Reproduced with kind permission of D C Thomson Media; p74 (left) Retro AdArchives / Alamy Stock Photo; p75 Featureflash Photo Agency / Shutterstock.com; p76 ZUMA Press, Inc. / Alamy Stock Photo; p77 Everett Collection Inc / Alamy Stock Photo; p78 (top) Moviestore Collection Ltd / Alamy Stock Photo; p78 (bottom) carlos andre photography / Shutterstock.com; p79 (top) Lauren Elisabeth / Shutterstock.com; p79 (middle) aslysun / Shutterstock; p79 (bottom) Gonzalo Aragon / Shutterstock; p80 Seventeen; p81 (top) Everett Collection, Inc. / Alamy Stock Photo; p81 (bottom left) Teen; p81 (bottom right) Valentine; p85 Bad Wolf / BBC / HBO; p87 Audrey_Popov / Shutterstock; p88 NASA; p89 (top) AF Archive / Alamy Stock Photo; p89 (bottom) Cal Sport Media / Alamy Stock Photo; p90 astel designs / Shutterstock; p91 ITV / REX / Shutterstock; p93 rob zs / Shutterstock; p97 (top) koya979 / Shutterstock; p97 (bottom) stockfour / Shutterstock; p98 Pixel-Shot / Shutterstock; p99 Ollyy / Shutterstock; p100 Everett Collection Inc / Alamy Stock Photo; p102 Africa Studio / Shutterstock; p103 News UK / News Licensing; p104 (top) Mirrorpix / Reach Licensing; p104 (bottom) Jstone / Shutterstock.com; p105 (top) 1000 Words / Shutterstock.com; p105 (bottom) Peter Manning / Alamy Stock Photo; p107 (top) Phillip Maguire / Shutterstock.com; p107 (bottom) SteveSimonsPhotography / Shutterstock.com; p108 Christian Bertrand / Shutterstock.com; p110 Debu55y / Shutterstock.com; p113 Bobb Klissourski / Shutterstock; p114 (bottom) BigTunaOnline / Shutterstock; p114 (top) Steve Heap / Shutterstock.com; p115 ALEX_UGALEK / Shutterstock; p116 (top) chrisdorney / Shutterstock; p116 (bottom) Lenscap Photography / Shutterstock; p117 (top) Lightspring / Shutterstock; p117 (bottom) Hadrian / Shutterstock; p119 Michael715 / Shutterstock.com; p110 Debu55y / Shutterstock.com; p120 Featureflash Photo Agency / Shutterstock.com; p122 (top) Jeffrey Blackler / Alamy Stock Photos; p122 (middle) David Edsam / Alamy Stock Photo; p122 (bottom) TC / Alamy Stock Photo; p123 (top) David Walter / Alamy Stock Photo; p123 (middle) Courtesy bbfc; p123 (bottom) Kirk Wester / Shutterstock; p124 (top to bottom) Public domain / Photoplay Publishing Company, Warner Bros., Public domain / RKO publicity still from Suspicion (1941), Public domain / Eric Carpenter (1909–1976) for Metro-Goldwyn-Mayer, Public domain / Publicity photo; p129 (all) Courtesy BBFC; p131 (top) Gray Pierson and Radio Longon Ltd; p131 (bottom) Public domain; p133 Georgejmclittle / Shutterstock; p138 landmarkmediai / Shutterstock.com; p139 (top left) jvphoto / Alamy Stock Photo; p139 (middle) Mr Pics / Alamy Stock Photo; p139 (bottom) MyAgency / Shutterstock.com; p140 BFA / Alamy Stock Photo; p141 Public domain; p142 Northfoto / Shutterstock.com; p144 Vicki L. Miller / Shutterstock.com; p145 (top) sezer66 / Shutterstpcl; p145 (bottom) Randy Miramontez / Shutterstock.com; p147 (top) dennizn / Shutterstock.com; p147 (bottom left) g0d4ather; p147 (bottom right) 360b / Shutterstock.com; pp148–149 Public domain; p149 (bottom) Pe3k / Shutterstock.com; p150 (top) Robert Kneschke; p150 (middle) GingeSwagTia / Shutterstock.com; p150 (bottom) DFIO CRACHO / Shutterstock; p151 StockSmartStart / Shutterstock; p154 (top) Album / Alamy Stock Photo; p154 (bottom) Pictorial Press Ltd / Alamy Stock Photo; p155 Tero Vesalainen / Shutterstock; p157 (top) Featureflash Photo Agency / Shutterstock.com; p157 (bottom) Allstar Picture Library Ltd. / Alamy Stock Photo; p158 (top) Album / Alamy Stock Photo; p158 (bottom) Everett Collection Inc / Alamy Stock Photo; p160 (both) Bad Wolf / BBC / HBO; p161 Bad Wolf / BBC / HBO; p162 (top) Tero Vesalainen / Shutterstock; p162 (bottom) Andy Pearson / Stockimo / Alamy Stock Photo; p165 (top) Imago History Collection / Alamy Stock Photo; p165 (bottom) focal point / Shutterstock; p166 Alexandru Nika/ Shutterstock.com; p168 (left) sezer66 / Shutterstock p168 (right) Anikei / Shutterstock; p170 (all) Courtesy Marcus Rashford; p171 Courtesy Marcus Rashford; p175 Dfree / Shutterstock.com; p178 Courtesy Marcus Rashford; p179 Public domain; p180 Lenscap Photography; p182 TES; p183 Jane Kelly / Shutterstock; p184 (top) IanDagnall Computing / Alamy Stock Photo; p184 (middle) News UK / News Licensing; p184 (bottom) Mirrorpix / Reach Licensing; p187 Retro AdArchives / Alamy Stock Photo; p188 ThomasAFink / Shutterstock.com; p189 (top) Richard Levine / Alamy Stock Photo; p190 Public domain; p191 NHS Blood and Transplant; p192 NHS Blood and Transplant; p193 Retro AdArchives / Alamy Stock Photo; p195 Neil Baylis / Alamy Stock Photo; p196 Courtesy of The Advertising Archives; p198 (top) Chris Barham / Daily Mail / REX / Shuterstock; p198 (bottom) Trinity Mirror / Mirrorpix / Alamy Stock Photo; p200 PA Images / Alamy Stock Photo; p201 (top) Andrea Raffin / Shutterstock.com; p201 (bottom) DR -images; p202 Entertainment Pictures / Alamy Stock Photo; p203 (top) Alexey V Smirnov; p203 (bottom) Denis Makarenko / Shutterstock.com; p204 (top) chrisdorney / Shutterstock.com; p204 (bottom) LongJohn / Shutterstock.com; p205 (top) 3dmask / Shutterstock; p205 (bottom) Kaspars Grinvalds / Shutterstock; p206 (top) Niloo / Shutterstock.com; p206 (bottom left) Courtesy of People's Friend; p206 (bottom middle); p206 (bottom right) Courtesy of Sight & Sound; p207 (top) Courtesy of Heatworld; p207 (bottom) Courtesy of Heat; p208 (left) Peter Horree / Alamy Stock Photo; p208 (bottom) Neil Baylis / Alamy Stock Photo; p211 (top) Andre Paes / Alamy Stock Photo; p211 (bottom) Kathy Hutchins / Shutterstock.com; p212 Tom Rose / Shutterstock.com; p214 Pictorial Press Ltd / Alamy Stock Photo; p215 Sipa US / Alamy Stock Photo; p216 Everett Collection Inc / Alamy Stock Photo; p221 (top) PHILIPIMAGE / Shutterstock; p221 (bottom) Vasyl Shuga / Shutterstock; p222 All rights in any translated text shall belong to H BAUER and the Client hereby assigns to H BAUER all its rights, title and interest worldwide in and to any translated version of the Material for the full period of copyright and any extensions and renewal thereof; p225 Bad Wolf / BBC / HBO; p227 sjscreens / Alamy Stock Photo; p229 Atstock Productions / Shutterstock; p230 Reproduced with kind permission of Gosportz Media LLC; p232 NHS Blood and Transplant; p233 279photo Studio / Shutterstock; p234 Pavel L Photo and Video / Shutterstock; p236 Anil Ghawana / Alamy Stock Photo; p238 A. and I. Kruk / Shutterstock; p242 patat / Shutterstock; p242 (bottom) Sergey Edentod / Shutterstock; p243 (top) Sigur / Shutterstock; p243 (bottom) ALEX_UGALEK / Shutterstock; p247 Steve Collerider / Shutterstock; p248 (top) StockLite; p248 (bottom) Yodchompoo / Shutterstock; ; p250 vectorfusionart / Shutterstock; p251 Retro AdArchives / Alamy Stock Photo; p252 Dean Drobot / Shuttersatock; p253 Vitally Karimov / Shutterstock; p254 (top) David J. Green / Alamy Stock Photo; p254 (2nd) Smileus / Shutterstock; p254 (3rd) brem stocker / Shutterstock; p254 (bottom) sfam_photo / Shutterstock; p255 antb / Shutterstock; p256 (top) Dmitri Ma / Shutterstock; p256 (bottom) Independent / Alamy Stock Photo; p258 Rawpixel.com / Shutterstock; p259 ESB Professional / Shutterstock; p257 (top) Kzenon/ Shutterstock; p257 (bottom) Kzenon / Shutterstock; p261 (bottom) Courtesy of Chess; p262 (top 2) Courtesy of Saga; p263 Lasse Ansaharju / Shutterstock; p264 (top left) Mirrorpix / Reach Licensing; p264 (right) i; p267 Mickis-Fotowelt / Shutterstock.com; p268 Pattama Chalapinyo / Shutterstock; p269 (left & middle) Galaxy; p271 (top) CandyBox Images / Shutterstock; p271 (bottom) APA PROD / Shutterstock; p272 Slaven / Shutterstock; p273 (left) I, Daniel Blake, courtesy of Wild Bunch; p273 (right) Courtesy of Wild Bunch; p274 Monkey Business Images / Shutterstock; p275 Monkey Business Images / Shutterstock; p276 Courtesy of Wild Bunch; p278 Mongkol Foto / Shutterstock;